OXFORD WORLD'S CLASSICS

THOMAS MANN

Mario and the Magician

and Other Late Stories

Translated by

IAIN GALBRAITH

Edited with an Introduction and Notes by

RITCHIE ROBERTSON

OXFORD
UNIVERSITY PRESS

OXFORD
UNIVERSITY PRESS

Great Clarendon Street, Oxford, OX2 6DP,
United Kingdom

Oxford University Press is a department of the University of Oxford.
It furthers the University's objective of excellence in research, scholarship,
and education by publishing worldwide. Oxford is a registered trade mark of
Oxford University Press in the UK and in certain other countries.

The translation of this work was supported by the German Translators' Fund.

Published in the United States of America by Oxford University Press
546 Fifth Avenue, New York, NY 10036, United States of America

British Library Cataloguing in Publication Data
Data available

Library of Congress Control Number: 2026933301

ISBN 9780198852223

Printed and bound in the UK by
Clays Ltd, Elcograf S.p.A.

The manufacturer's authorized representative in the EU for product safety is
Oxford University Press España S.A. of Parque Empresarial San Fernando de Henares,
Avenida de Castilla, 2 – 28830 Madrid (www.oup.es/en or product.safety@oup.com).
OUP España S.A. also acts as importer into Spain of products made by the manufacturer.

CONTENTS

INTRODUCTION

Of the stories collected here, published between 1925 and 1953, the first two are clearly rooted in Mann's own life.[1] Similarly, his early stories are set in his native Lübeck and *Death in Venice* is based on a Mediterranean holiday. Mann declared in 1926: 'I can or must say that I have never invented anything.'[2] So *Disorder and Early Sorrow* is recognizably though loosely based on the Mann household in the early 1920s, and *Mario and the Magician* draws on another Italian holiday. Yet of the others, the longest is set in ancient India; another in the world of the Old Testament; and a third in Düsseldorf, admittedly an accessible location, but not one where Mann himself had ever spent much time. Taken together, the stories move from everyday realism to an increasing fascination with myth and the further layers of meaning it makes possible. In the background stands the huge tetralogy of novels about the biblical Joseph, which Mann began writing in November 1926, beginning with *The Tales of Jacob* (published in 1933) and culminating in *Joseph the Provider* (1942). For this massive work, Mann immersed himself not only in biblical studies but also in theories of myth, especially those of the nineteenth-century Swiss classical scholar Johann Jakob Bachofen, whose influence is first discernible in *Mario and the Magician* and is most powerful in the Indian legend *The Transposed Heads*.

*

Disorder and Early Sorrow (1925) is one of three short works based in the Manns' domestic life in the Munich of the early Weimar Republic. *Herr und Hund* (*Master and Dog*, 1919) concerns Mann and his dog Bauschan; *Gesang vom Kindchen* (*Song of the Little Child*, 1919) centres on the christening of the Manns' youngest daughter, Elisabeth (1918–2002), who reappears in *Disorder* as 'Lorchen'. The third story

[1] This introduction is heavily indebted to the edition of Mann's late stories by Hans Rudolf Vaget, *Große Kommentierte Frankfurter Ausgabe* (hereafter *GKFA*), 6/2 (Frankfurt a.M.: Fischer, 2021).

[2] Extract from a letter to an unnamed correspondent, *Gesammelte Werke*, 13 vols (Frankfurt a.M.: Fischer, 1974), xiii. 55. This edition, needed for texts not yet included in *GKFA*, is henceforth cited as *GW*.

is a somewhat skewed portrayal of the Mann family. Katia Mann is marginalized as a weary and worn-out figure, though she effectively ran the household. There are only four children, though the Manns by then had six: Erika (1905–69) appears as Ingrid, her brother Klaus (1906–49) as Bert; the youngest, Michael (1919–77) appears as a disturbed toddler with the ominous nickname Biter, while Gottfried ('Golo', 1909–94) and Monika (1910–92) are completely screened out. Klaus was so offended by his portrayal as a harum-scarum teenager that he retaliated with a short story, *Kindernovelle* (*Children's Novella*), in which the father is already dead and the mother marries again.[3] The tensions within the Mann family that would be explored in the famous and much-praised three-part TV series *Die Manns* (2001) can already be glimpsed here.

The story is framed in the family's difficult external circumstances. Germany's defeat and the Allies' demand for huge reparations have led to impoverishment and inflation. Thomas Mann was relatively—but only relatively—well off: his paternal inheritance and his own savings, along with his in-laws' wealth, went up in smoke, but he was able to earn foreign currency and kept his house in a select residential quarter of Munich.[4] Professor Cornelius, the central figure of *Disorder*, earns millions of marks from his university post, but has to pay 8,000 marks for a bottle of beer and 6,000 marks for a single egg. By the end of 1923, according to an essay about inflation that Mann published in 1942, an egg could cost 100 million marks.[5] The value of the mark against the dollar sank to 4,200 billion. The German government managed to end inflation in 1924, in part by compelling speculators to surrender their 1.5 billion worth of foreign currency, and the Republic returned temporarily to an even keel.

Cornelius, a professor of history, is uncomfortable to have history going on around him. Mann conveys his discomfort by telling the

[3] Klaus Mann later described his and his sister's pranks in *Kind dieser Zeit* (1932; repr. Munich: Nymphenburger Verlagshandlung, 1965), 134–7, insisting that they were ultimately harmless, though not everyone would regard an elaborate system of shoplifting as harmless.

[4] See the chapter 'Trillion-Dollar Eggs', in Hermann Kurzke, *Thomas Mann: Life as a Work of Art; A Biography*, trans. Leslie Willson (Princeton: Princeton University Press, 2002), 326–7.

[5] 'Erinnerungen aus der deutschen Inflation', *GW* xiii. 181–90. This essay, commissioned by the US Treasury Department, was actually written by Mann's son Golo (see *GKFA* 6/2: 59).

story in the present tense: instead of being safely past and done with, events are crowding on him unpredictably.[6] Like his creator, Cornelius is making a difficult transition from the old to the new. Mann had struggled to overcome the conservatism which had led him to support the War and had found a belated expression in *Reflections of an Unpolitical Man* (1918). In his challenging speech 'Von deutscher Republik' ('On the German Republic') on 13 October 1922 he came out strongly in favour of the Weimar Republic. His ambivalence is explored in the person of Cornelius. Like Hans Castorp in *The Magic Mountain*, published in 1924, Cornelius feels a respect for the past as such, but this feeling makes him uneasy: 'The past is immortalized, which is to say: it is dead, and death is the source of all piety and all sustaining sensibility' (p. 10). The area of the past which he especially studies is the age of Philip II of Spain (reigned 1556–98), who tried unsuccessfully to roll back the Protestant Reformation in Europe. Cornelius sympathizes with Philip's defence of a lost cause, just as an earlier Mann protagonist, Tonio Kröger, does with the tragic portrayal of Philip in Schiller's play *Don Carlos*. One of the children's friends, the actor Ivan Herzl, is currently playing the title role, that of Philip's disruptive and unruly son.

Cornelius's attachment to the past, and hence to death, plays a part in his tender love for his 5-year-old daughter Lorchen, which he knows to be unhealthy. The ritualized games he plays with Lorchen provide a refuge from the social and political change going on around him. But Lorchen cannot remain a child forever. She belongs to the younger generation, who, in the person of her elder siblings Ingrid and Bert, have thrown aside the taboos governing the society of Imperial Germany in which Cornelius grew up.

The younger generation makes its presence felt in the party which Ingrid and Bert give for their friends. It is really a very decorous party, which some guests even attend in evening dress. Even so, the dancing conveys youth, energy, enjoyment; in an unforced way, it stands for life, and the onlooker Cornelius, with his residual attachment to death, is as much an outsider as Tonio Kröger was at the hotel dance that explicitly symbolized life. The music also opens up a wider world than the Europe to which Cornelius's studies confine him.

[6] On the use of the present tense, see David Turner, 'Balancing the Account: Thomas Mann's *Unordnung und frühes Leid*', *German Life and Letters*, 52 (1999), 43–57 (50).

Besides French, Hungarian, and possibly Swedish songs, the gramophone plays 'African shimmies, Java dances and Creole polkas—wild and spicy stuff' (p. 27), not much to Cornelius's taste. Little Lorchen, however, loves it, especially as she can dance with the handsome and impeccably polite Max Hergesell. At bedtime she cries until the kindly Max comes to wish her goodnight.[7] Her 'early sorrow', fortunately easy to assuage, is the first warning that the intimate bond between her and her father is, in the long term, unsustainable.

*

Mario and the Magician (1930) is based on a holiday which Thomas and Katia took with their two youngest children, Elisabeth and Michael, from 31 August to 13 September 1926 in the Ligurian seaside resort of Forte dei Marmi. They found the atmosphere uncongenial, noting the pervasive nationalism and irritability of the Italian middle classes. When the 7-year-old Elisabeth ran naked across the beach, a scandalized crowd gathered, as in the story, and the Manns were taken to the police station and fined. They moved to a different hotel. One evening they attended a performance by the famous hypnotist Cesare Gabrielli (1881–1943) who was a Fascist sympathizer and had taken part in the Fascists' March on Rome (October 1922), which led to Mussolini's being appointed prime minister. The story improves on reality, however, by ending in violence, whereas the real-life Mario, instead of shooting the hypnotist, simply ran away.[8] His experience in Forte left Mann, previously a lover of Italy, disenchanted with the country he now called 'Mussolinien' (i.e. 'Mussolinia').[9]

Mann's transmutation of these events into fiction, and Gabrielli into the dubious Cavaliere Cipolla, has prompted questions about the 'I' who narrates them. Are we to identify him with Mann, or to see him as a fictional device whose account may be unreliable? It has been argued that in failing to remove the children from the performance,

[7] This is based on a real event, as Elisabeth Mann-Borgese stated in 1998: the children's friend Fritz Riemerschmidt (1901–78), a student at the Technical University in Munich, danced with the 5-year-old girl, and when she was too excited to settle down, he came to her bedside to calm her. *GKFA* 6/2: 76.

[8] See Mann's letters to the Viennese poet Hugo von Hofmannsthal, to the Milanese theatre critic Enzo Ferrieri, 14 April 1927, and to the schoolteacher Otto Hoerth, all quoted in *GKFA* 6/2: 93, 96–7, 98–9, and his recollections in 'Lebensabriß' (1930) (*GW* xi. 139–40).

[9] From an interview quoted in *GKFA* 6/2: 95.

the narrator is an irresponsible parent; that he, like the rest of the audience, succumbs to the hypnotist's power; and that his classical allusions ('the sun of Homer' (p. 40), 'Circe's staff' (p. 71)) reveal him as pompous and pretentious.[10] On the other hand, the narrator's vulnerability shows that even a well-educated German is not immune; and if you criticize him, you are implicitly saying 'Well, *I* wouldn't have succumbed to Cipolla if I had been there', and thus trivializing the story by underestimating Cipolla's power.[11] As for the classical allusions which add depth to the story, it seems again trivial to interpret them simply as displays of learning intended to satirize the narrator. The story reveals both the sinister power of an individual demagogue and the effect which a populist dictator, mentioned discreetly as the 'Duce', has already had on the Italian population, or at least on the middle classes.

The psychological understanding of Cipolla's sway is indebted partly to Nietzsche. In *On the Genealogy of Morals* (1887) Nietzsche undertakes to explain the power which the priest, without the aid of violence, characteristically exercises over his flock. The flock are sick; if they were healthy, in Nietzsche's view, they would not need Christianity. Far from curing them, the priest keeps them in a state of low vitality and encourages them to think they are sinful, so that they are to blame for their own sufferings.[12] Cipolla is himself sick, with a physical defect and a constant need for artificial stimulus from cigarettes and cognac, but has a powerful will. He bullies anyone who challenges him, inflicting psychosomatic pain on them, and transforms part of his audience into zombie-like creatures who dance helplessly onstage—a grotesque parody of the dance which, in Nietzsche and in other works by Mann, represents life and vitality.

Cipolla's hold over his victims is also erotic. Burdened himself with a defect, he singles out young men in the audience, taunts them with their supposed sexual prowess, and takes particular care to humiliate

[10] See A. F. Bance, 'The Narrator in Thomas Mann's *Mario und der Zauberer*', *Modern Language Review*, 82 (1987), 382–98.

[11] Or, as Eva Geulen puts it, such commentators have to invent a 'fictive reader' who 'provides the secure vantage point from which to judge and impose distance, a position of power and critical authority that is supposed to be able to resist seduction'. 'Resistance and Representation: *Mario und der Zauberer*', *New German Critique*, 68 (1996), ii. 3–29 (18).

[12] See Friedrich Nietzsche, *On the Genealogy of Morals*, trans. Douglas Smith, Oxford World's Classics (Oxford: Oxford University Press, 1996), 104–6 (Third Essay, section 15).

them. By hypnotizing Signora Angiolieri, he induces her to leave her husband and blindly follow him. Restoring her to her husband, he steps slightly out of character by issuing a warning intended for Mann's readers: 'that there are powers stronger than reason and virtue, powers that are only very rarely found coupled with magnanimity and self-denial!' (p. 69). But his erotic abuse leads to his downfall. He works out that the waiter Mario has been defeated by a rival, called simply the *giovanotto* (young man), in a contest for a girl called Silvestra. He takes pleasure in humiliating Mario publicly by claiming that he himself is Silvestra and persuading Mario to kiss him. He does not know that Mario has brought along a pistol with the presumable intention of shooting the rival suitor. Mario whips out the pistol, fires it, Cipolla collapses in a crumpled heap, and the performance is brought to an abrupt end.

We may suspect a subtext. The narrator shows great but unexplained interest in Mario. Cipolla reveals his homosexual attraction to Mario by calling him a 'Ganymede', an allusion to the beautiful boy whom the enamoured Zeus carried up to heaven to be his cupbearer.[13] Mann himself staunchly refused to yield to the homosexual longings recorded in his diaries, which often had handsome waiters as their object. Besides the erotic triangle Mario/the *giovanotto*/Silvestra, there may be a hidden one: the narrator/Cipolla/Mario.[14]

The story clearly has much to say about politics, particularly Fascism, and can be understood as a veiled warning against parallel developments in Germany. Mann was well aware of the growing influence of the National Socialist Party and warned in 1928 that anyone who criticized its extreme nationalism risked being dismissed as an old-fashioned liberal.[15] The story, however, focuses in detail on the

[13] On this and other stereotypes of homosexuality in the story, see Geulen, 'Resistance and Representation', 20–1. George Bridges, controversially, reads Mario's assassination of Cipolla as Mann's symbolic attempt 'to banish from his own life with one resolute act [. . .] the troubling and potentially destructive demon of homosexuality': 'Thomas Mann's *Mario und der Zauberer*: "Aber zum Donnerwetter! Deshalb bringt man doch niemand um!"', *German Quarterly*, 64 (1991), 501–17 (513).

[14] Mann made a handsome waiter the hero of his novel *Felix Krull*. See Jens Rieckmann, '"In deinem Atem bildet sich mein Wort": Thomas Mann, Franz Westermeier und *Die Bekenntnisse des Hochstaplers Felix Krull*', *Thomas Mann Jahrbuch*, 10 (1997), 149–65.

[15] *GW* x. 695. This does not, however, justify the claim that 'One should not be misled by the story's Italian setting into believing that it relates to Mussolini's Italy, and not to Hitler's Germany'. Anthony Grenville, 'Idealism versus Materialism in the Representation

degradation of civil life and popular consciousness wrought by the Fascists in Italy since their ascent to power in 1922. Nationalism pervades everyday life and even produces the grotesque spectacle of patriotic children. The young men do their hair in 'the fashionable style of the awakened Fatherland' (p. 49). These observations are confirmed by other visitors: 'Foreign writers noticed that people in fascist Italy smiled less readily than before, and even young children tended to adopt "a fierce and gladiatorial pose . . . as though all their sense of humour had been lost".'[16]

Although Mussolini does not appear, his presence pervades the story. Cipolla boasts that the brother of the Duce (i.e. of Mussolini) has attended his performances. He constantly asserts his patriotism, claiming with obvious mendacity that there is no illiteracy in the fatherland. In this environment of state-sponsored irrationality, the doctor who twice proves himself 'a loyal and upright servant of medical science' (p. 38, cf. p. 41) cuts an even lonelier figure than the honest travel agent who admits the existence of the cholera in *Death in Venice*.

Cipolla's death at the hands of Mario, however, is not a political act, but a response to the magician's sexual abuse. Mann's presentation of Italian Fascism foregrounds sexuality. Cipolla, the physically and sexually damaged demagogue, compensates by exercising power. The victims of his dominance, though from various social classes, merge into a homogeneous mass. In the hall where his performance takes place, the seats are not arranged in tiers, so that everyone is on a level. We are repeatedly told that many of the inhabitants of Torre di Venere belong to the middle class, suggesting a democracy of universal mediocrity. Insofar as Cipolla's dominance is sexual (bullying the cocky young men, seducing Signora Angiolieri, and humiliating Mario), the story is propelled less by political than by erotic forces.

Here we can discern traces of Mann's new-found fascination with the Swiss ancient historian and mythographer Johann Jakob Bachofen (1815–87) whose oeuvre he began reading in 1926, at the beginning

of History in Literature. The Dictator Figure in Thomas Mann's *Mario und der Zauberer* and Brecht's *Der aufhaltsame Aufstieg des Arturo Ui*', *Journal of European Studies*, 17 (1987), 77–105 (82). On the story's relation to German events, see *GKFA* 6/2: 99–100.

[16] Denis Mack Smith, *Mussolini* (London: Weidenfeld & Nicolson, 1981), 161, quoting numerous foreign correspondents in *The Times* and elsewhere. Cf. ibid. 150 and 181, on Mussolini's programme to transform the Italian character.

of his work on the *Joseph* novels.[17] As we shall soon see, Bachofen's thought is also strongly present in *The Transposed Heads*. Bachofen differed sharply from contemporary (and subsequent) historians of antiquity in his willingness to accept myths as historical evidence. From a wide variety of sources he discerned, not an ancient matriarchal society, but a primeval past in which both sexes mingled promiscuously, women were 'hetaerae' (prostitutes), social ranks were unknown, and everyone was equal. This condition, represented by the image of the swamp, was ended by male violence. What followed, however, was not crude male dominance, but a balance between male power and female religious authority: the age of 'Mother Right'. Women established marriage, agriculture, and organized religion. They guided humanity's transition from nature to culture. The cult of Aphrodite, the glorified hetaera, yielded to that of Demeter, the mother-goddess. Gradually, however, mother right was superseded by patriarchy. Abstract thought replaced intuitive knowledge. Whereas the emergence of a child from the mother's body normally has witnesses, the conception of a child has none, so that patriarchy rests on abstract reasoning, not sensuous proof. Abstraction was required for law, theology, and intellectual development. It was indispensable for the growth of civilization. In retrospect, female power was often seen as dangerous: thus, myths told how the Amazons were overcome by Theseus, the murderer Clytemnestra killed by her son Orestes, and the Furies tamed by the goddess of wisdom, Athene, who significantly had no mother but was born from the head of Zeus. How to balance loss and gain in humanity's progress has puzzled Bachofen's commentators, who note the 'problematic relation between unstinting praise of the world of Mother Right and determined affirmation of the superiority of Father Right and the order of abstract law'.[18]

[17] On Mann's reading of Bachofen, see Elisabeth Galvan, *Zur Bachofen-Rezeption in Thomas Manns 'Joseph'-Roman* (Frankfurt a.M.: Klostermann, 1996), 5–48. Mann was so attached to his three-volume selection from Bachofen's work that when he was forced into exile and deprived of his books in the summer of 1933, he asked his publisher to supply him with another set.

[18] Lionel Gossman, *Basel in the Age of Burckhardt: A Study in Unseasonable Ideas* (Chicago: University of Chicago Press, 2000), 187; Gossman provides an excellent introduction to Bachofen (111–200). See also Peter Davies, *Myth, Matriarchy and Modernity: Johann Jakob Bachofen in German Culture 1860–1945* (Berlin: De Gruyter, 2010).

In *Mario*, the town's name ('Tower of Venus') recalls Aphrodite, the goddess of Bachofen's primeval swamp; the tower no longer exists, which (if the tower can be read as phallic) suggests the destruction of masculinity. Cipolla challenges and assaults the masculinity of the young men, of the gentleman from Rome who cannot sustain his resistance, and even of a colonel. Mario himself, as Cipolla observes, bears the name of the Roman general Marius (157–86 BC). Cipolla is bent on undoing the triumph of male-inflected civilization. His riding crop, 'Circe's staff', recalls how Circe, the sorceress in the *Odyssey*, turned her lovers into swine. His magic aims to undo the hierarchies which are often thought essential to culture, wipe out the intellectual achievements of civilization, and restore a state of nature. To that extent, the story looks beyond contemporary politics and hints at a wider narrative, derived especially from Bachofen, of the rise and fall of culture.[19]

*

The Transposed Heads (1940) is an unclassifiable tale. Much too long for a short story or even a novella, but much less than a novel, it is among Mann's least read and least understood works. Mann described it in a letter to his American patroness Agnes E. Meyer as 'a mischievous being [. . .] that shimmers and oscillates and never supplies a definite meaning and slips out of your hand when you try to grasp it'.[20]

In 1939 the distinguished Indologist Heinrich Zimmer (1890–1943) sent Mann an offprint of his recently published lecture 'The Indian World Mother'.[21] The title must have appealed to Mann as a reader of Bachofen. Having recently been sidetracked from his *Joseph* project by writing *Lotte in Weimar* (published in 1939), Mann

[19] For a reading of *Mario* through the lens provided by Bachofen, see Yahya Elsaghe, 'Die "Principe[ssa] X." und "diese Frauen -!" Zur Bachofen-Rezeption in *Mario und der Zauberer*', *Thomas Mann Jahrbuch*, 22 (2009), 175–93.

[20] Letter of 18 June 1951, in Thomas Mann and Agnes E. Meyer, *Briefwechsel 1937–1955*, ed. Hans Rudolf Vaget (Frankfurt a.M.: Fischer, 1992), 290.

[21] 'Die indische Weltmutter', *Eranos-Jahrbuch 1938* (Zurich: Rhein-Verlag, 1939), 175–220. Zimmer, like Mann, was in exile. He had been dismissed in 1938 from his chair of Indian philology at Heidelberg because his wife Christiane, daughter of Hugo von Hofmannsthal, was ultimately of Jewish descent. He moved first to Oxford and then to Columbia University. Because of his premature death from pneumonia, many of his books were published posthumously, based on his lecture notes. Mann dedicated the first English translation of *The Transposed Heads* to him.

really needed to get down to the fourth volume, *Joseph the Provider*, which appeared in 1943. However, one of the Indian myths that Zimmer recounts so appealed to him that he set to work to rewrite and modernize it.

Two friends happen to see a beautiful girl bathing in a pool sacred to the goddess Kali. One of the friends falls hopelessly in love with her and eventually marries her. All three set out on a journey to visit the young woman's parents. On the way they come to a temple of Kali. The new husband enters the temple to worship Kali, but on seeing the statue of the goddess, hung with skulls, he resolves (for no very clear reason) to sacrifice himself, and contrives to cut off his own head. Wondering what has happened to him, the friend in turn enters the sanctuary, finds his friend headless, and promptly cuts off his own head. The young woman, discovering both corpses, is about to hang herself, when the voice of the goddess tells her to replace the heads on the bodies and thus bring the two back to life. She obeys, but in her confusion she puts the wrong head on each body. There the story ends. Zimmer adds brief speculations of his own about whether the woman was unconsciously motivated by desire for the other man and describes her mistake as a Freudian slip (*Fehlleistung*).

Mann's retelling goes much further in modernizing the narrative. The young woman is now called Sita, the name of the wife of the hero Rama from the ancient Indian epic Ramayana; her name also means 'furrow', with a sexual connotation. The two men are individualized as Shridaman, the intellectual merchant with refined features, and Nanda, the stocky cowherd. Despite their differences, they are close friends, each of whom feels incomplete without the other. After the exchange, Sita can no longer settle down with Shridaman (or rather, with the man who bears Shridaman's head). Sita is pregnant by her husband Shridaman: who will count as the father of the child? And since each man has some desirable attributes, Sita, making love with Shridaman, imagines herself in the arms of the physically more satisfying Nanda. Along with their small son, she goes in search of Nanda, with whom she makes love. Shridaman arrives, and the situation is resolved drastically: Shridaman and Nanda kill themselves, successfully this time, and the doubly widowed Sita commits sati.

Mann's additions can be seen as a (perhaps unconscious) homage to Goethe. He already knew a similar story that was retold by Goethe in his poem 'Legende', the central and longest portion of his trilogy about an Indian pariah or Untouchable.[22] A Brahmin executes his wife for her supposed unfaithfulness. Made remorseful by a supernatural sign, he sends his son to the place of execution to restore her to life, but the son mistakenly places her head on the body of a dead Untouchable woman, so that the revived being has the head of a high-caste Brahmin and the body of a pariah. Mann also mentions this story in *Lotte in Weimar*.[23] While in Goethe's version two women are victims of a man, in Zimmer and Mann it is two men who are manipulated by a woman.[24]

The effect in Mann's story is to cast doubt on the idea that head, mind, or spirit can be imagined as separate from the body. Body and spirit affect each other. Topped with Shridaman's head, the Nanda body becomes more like Shridaman's, and when Sita is reunited with Nanda she discovers that his features (previously dominated by a flat, goat-like nose, in contrast to Shridaman's narrow nose) have become more refined. And there is a further complication. When she transposed the heads, Sita was pregnant by Shridaman. But the body that impregnated her now belongs to Nanda. Who is the true father of the child?

To resolve the problem of paternity, the three turn, not (as in the original story) to a prince, but to a holy man, Kamadamana, who lives as an ascetic hermit in the Dankaka forest. Here he performs such feats of endurance as sitting between four fires in the heat of summer and sleeping in wet clothes in the cold season.[25] Kamadamana is a comically hypocritical figure: his privations are clearly motivated by vanity, and so far from overcoming desire, he readily starts rhapsodizing about fleshly love. Here Mann is indebted to Nietzsche's sceptical analysis of asceticism in *On the Genealogy of Morals*.[26]

[22] Johann Wolfgang Goethe, *Sämtliche Werke: Briefe, Tagebücher und Gespräche*, ed. Friedmar Apel et al., Deutsche Klassiker-Ausgabe, 40 vols. (Frankfurt a.M.: Deutscher Klassiker Verlag, 1986–2000), ii: *Gedichte 1800–1832*, ed. Karl Eibl (1988), 451–5.

[23] Mann, *Lotte in Weimar*, ed. Werner Frizen, *GKFA* 9/1 (Frankfurt a.M.: Fischer, 2007), 355.

[24] There is also a reminiscence of Goethe's novel *Die Wahlverwandtschaften* (1809). There, a husband and wife, making love, each dream of another potential partner, so that a double adultery takes place. See Goethe, *Elective Affinities*, trans. David Constantine, Oxford World's Classics (Oxford: Oxford University Press, 1994), 78–9.

[25] Mann took these details from the story, reported by Zimmer, of the hermit Kandu who was seduced by the beautiful goddess Pramlocha: see Heinrich Zimmer, *Maya: Der indische Mythos* (Stuttgart: Deutsche Verlags-Anstalt, 1936), 73–9.

[26] Nietzsche, *On the Genealogy of Morals*, Third Essay. Nietzsche mentions Indian asceticism: 'the ascetics of Vedanta philosophy' (trans. Smith, 97).

Elsewhere, too, Mann's story is light and often humorous, in contrast to Zimmer's heavy and sombre narrative, and enlivened by many colloquialisms. He found a stylistic model in the play *La Machine infernale* (1934), a modernized version of Sophocles' *Oedipus*, of which its author, Jean Cocteau (1889–1963), sent him a copy. The 'infernal machine' is fate, conceived as a mechanism operated by the gods for their own amusement. Cocteau's characters speak in modern colloquial language shot through with knowing Freudian references. Mann told the author he read it 'with a kind of tragic amusement', and that some passages made him laugh till he cried.[27] Hence Mann, writing in English to his American publisher, described his version of the story as a 'metaphysical joke'.[28]

The central relationship between Shridaman and Nanda, however, expresses a deeply serious and long-standing preoccupation of Mann's. It is a revised version of the relationship between the spirit and the body explored some forty years earlier in *Tonio Kröger*, where the intellectual Tonio is in love with the robust Hans Hansen but finds the latter, though good-natured, incapable of understanding him. Tonio briefly wished he could be like Hans. Mann himself noted the resemblance, writing to his American patroness, Agnes E. Meyer: 'Yes, Tonio, Hans and Inge are now united in a fiery grave. Peace to their ashes!'[29]

Now, in *The Transposed Heads*, the two friends, incarnating respectively the spirit and the body, are merged, but the effect, described in section XI, is saddening. Shridaman comes to regret 'that what had been strange to him had now become his and was no longer the object of his admiration, or in other words that he himself had now become what he had yearned for' (p. 125). For another Mann protagonist, Felix Krull, admiration of his own beauty is a source of happiness.[30] Here, however, the less self-centred Shridaman misses an object of yearning.

[27] Mann, letter to Cocteau, 22 February 1925, in Eva-Monika Turck, 'Der Briefwechsel zwischen Thomas Mann und Jean Cocteau', *Germanisch-Romanische Monatsschrift*, 59 (2009), 409–27 (422).

[28] Mann, letter of 15 August 1940 to Alfred A. Knopf, in *Dichter über ihre Dichtungen: Thomas Mann*, 3 vols., ed. Hans Wysling and Marianne Fischer (Frankfurt a.M.: Fischer, 1979), ii. 586.

[29] Letter of 18 June 1941, in Mann and Meyer, *Briefwechsel 1937–1955*, 290.

[30] *The Confessions of Felix Krull, Confidence Man*, was begun before the First World War. The early chapters were published in 1922. Mann returned to the novel late in life and published it, extended but still unfinished, in 1954.

The situation is summed up in a passage which, as an early commentator plausibly argues, presents 'the kernel of Mann's intent':[31]

This world is not so made that the spirit is destined only to love the spiritual, and beauty only things of beauty. It is the contrast between the two that reveals, with a clarity that is in itself both cerebral and beautiful, the destination of the world to be the unity of spirit and beauty, a bliss that is consummate and no longer divided into two, and our present story is but one example of the misadventures and failures that befall us in our attempts to reach that destination. (p. 143)

This message about the duality of spirit and body is inserted into a larger historical narrative which Mann constructs with the help of Heinrich Zimmer, himself a sympathetic reader of Bachofen and of Jungian depth psychology. Mann's story is set at an indeterminate period of ancient Indian history. The people who called themselves 'Aryas', worshippers of the thunder-god Indra, have overwhelmed an older urban culture.[32] Indra is called 'the Lord of the Thunderbolt', 'the Great Newcomer and Crusher of Cities', who 'tore down the fortresses of the dark-skinned people' (pp. 88, 89). The 'dark-skinned' people, in contrast to the light-skinned invaders, are the 'Dravidians' such as Nanda, who is stocky while Shridaman is slender, who squats while Shridaman sits, and who wishes to restore something of the earlier nature-worship, focusing on the 'Bright Peak' mountain.[33] Although the word 'Aryan' (not used in the text) may sound ominous, Mann has no truck with the pseudoscientific racial theory, developed in the later nineteenth century, which saw in the Aryans a superior race whose conquests were destined to be repeated by the Germans.[34] Shridaman and Nanda have different ethnic origins, but they are intimate friends who in the course of the story carry intimacy to a new level by exchanging bodies. The story is

[31] A. Leslie Willson, 'Thomas Mann's *Die vertauschten Köpfe*: The Catalyst of Creation', *Monatshefte*, 49 (1957), 313–21 (321).

[32] See A. L. Basham, *The Wonder that was India*, 3rd edn. (London: Sidgwick & Jackson, 1967), 29–31.

[33] This regressive tendency may be intended as an allusion to the appeal of National Socialism: see Yahya Elsaghe, '*Die vertauschten Köpfe* und Thomas Manns politische Bachofen-Rezeption', in Ulrich Boss, Yahya Elsaghe and Florian Heiniger (eds.), *Matriarchatsfiktionen: Johann Jakob Bachofen und die deutsche Literatur des 20. Jahrhunderts* (Basel: Schwabe, 2018), 221–45 (243–4).

[34] See Léon Poliakov, *The Aryan Myth: A History of Racist and Nationalist Ideas in Europe*, trans. Edmund Howard (London: Chatto, 1974).

not only anti-racist, but goes to fantastic lengths to demonstrate the unreality of racial divisions.

According to Zimmer, the pattern of Indian religious history diverges from that of Europe, inasmuch as the feminine principle is not defeated but incorporated. Many Greek myths recount in symbolic form the victory of the male principle, as when Theseus conquers the Amazons and Heracles destroys the Hydra. Christianity transforms the pagan Magna Mater into the paradoxical figure of the pure virginal mother Mary. In India, despite the Aryan conquest, the devotees of Indra have struck a compromise with the worshippers of the Great Goddess. Not only does the Great Goddess have an honoured place in the pantheon, but she is seen as embodying Shakti, the force animating the cosmos, which Zimmer explains as 'the immanent force of the transcendent god'.[35] Sexuality is not disparaged but honoured: it is sacramental and divine, symbolized by the masculine *lingam* (phallus) and the feminine *yoni*. The Great Goddess is a deeply ambivalent figure:

> the all-generating, all-nourishing one is also the devourer of all life; with her black body and wreath of skulls, she is the night of death which consumes and dissolves the mythic world day. The bloody goddess floats on her boat amid a sea of blood; it is the blood of her creatures, the dark tide of life, which feeds all things and swallows them into its depths, it is the milk of life from the veins of all creatures doomed to die, which she proffers to her own drunken lips as a sacrificial drink in an inexhaustible cup made of a skull. The body of the mother, who brings forth all things from her womb and nourishes them at her breasts, is also the grave.[36]

Mann follows this description closely in evoking the shrine of the Goddess in section V of his story. Besides floating on a sea of blood, she has eighteen arms brandishing swords and torches. She is Mahadevi, the Great Goddess, and 'Durga, the unapproachable and terrible, and Kali, the dark Mother' (p. 106); 'Kali, the All-Encompassing, the Mother of worlds and beings' (p. 82). However, Mann also makes the Goddess something of a comic figure. When Sita is about to hang herself, the voice of the World Mother gives her a sound telling-off in the tone of a bossy and imperious old lady. She

[35] Zimmer, *Maya*, 112.

[36] Zimmer, *Maya*, 48; similarly in 'Die indische Weltmutter', 188.

sounds like an extreme version of the nurse Adriatica von Mylendonk in *The Magic Mountain*.

The story continues after the deaths of the protagonists, telling us about the son of Sita and Shridaman. The boy is called Samadhi, an unusual name meaning roughly 'composure', but is later known as Andhaka, 'the blind one', because of his short sight. What are we to make of him? If we look at him through the lens provided by Bachofen, we may associate him with the earthly or 'chthonic' realm of the Great Mother, whose temples are underground. His myopia may also be connected with the imperfection of his parents' marriage. However, we are told in the last paragraph that he is physically beautiful and even develops the 'calf-lock', a lock of hair on his chest, that was formerly characteristic of Nanda and, after the transposition, grew also on Shridaman's body when it was attached to Nanda's head. He pursues intellectual goals and by the age of 20 is already reader to the King of Benares (the present-day Varanasi). So perhaps he is intended as a synthesis of all three of his parents. But the story still needs to be elucidated by further research.

*

Soon after completing his *Joseph* tetralogy, in 1942, Mann was approached by an Austrian immigrant, Armin L. Robinson, now active in American show business, who wanted to commission a collection of Bible-based stories that should serve anti-Hitler propaganda. Each story was to focus on one of the Ten Commandments and show how Hitler had violated it. Robinson had previously tried to interest Metro-Goldwyn-Mayer in a series of anti-Hitler films, but without success, perhaps because his project could only have suffered by comparison with Cecil B. DeMille's epic *The Ten Commandments* (1923). Offering a fee of one thousand dollars per contribution, Robinson managed to secure ten distinguished writers, including two Nobel laureates (Mann and the Norwegian Sigrid Undset, in exile in New York). Mann was to write about the first commandment, and his story was entitled 'Thou Shalt Have No Other Gods Before Me'. As his usual translator, Helen Lowe-Porter, was busy with *Joseph the Provider*, his German text was translated by his friend George R. Marek, a music critic.[37]

[37] See David Horton, '"An acceptable job"? The First English Translation of Thomas Mann's *Das Gesetz*', *Modern Language Review*, 105 (2010), 149–70.

Mann interpreted his task liberally. His story begins with Moses' birth and leads up to his forty-day sojourn on Mount Sinai during which he writes the Commandments on stone tablets. Descending to the plain, he finds his people worshipping the Golden Calf and smashes the tablets in his fury, after which he writes the Commandments again. Presenting the new tablets to his people, Moses universalizes the Commandments by describing them as 'the ABC of human conduct' (p. 211) and warning that an unnamed 'scoundrel' (clearly Hitler), who in future will try to destroy their authority, must be trampled down by the Lord. Part of his universal legacy is the alphabet: while on Sinai, Moses, having three languages at his disposal, is inspired to invent an alphabet which will serve for all languages.

Since 1925 Mann had been immersed in the biblical scholarship required for the *Joseph* novels. The tetralogy, however, reports only events from Genesis, whereas the story of Moses occupies the following four books of the Pentateuch, from Exodus to Deuteronomy. Besides reading them closely, Mann relied on a study by Elias Auerbach and on commentaries by canonical writers from Goethe onwards.[38] Goethe examined part of the Moses story in his essay 'Israel in the Desert', which forms part of the copious historical materials accompanying his collection of orientalizing poems, the *West-östlicher Divan* (1819).[39] Heine wrote two memorable paragraphs on the figure of Moses in his *Geständnisse* (*Confessions*, 1854). And Mann also read carefully Freud's last book, *Moses and Monotheism* (1939), as well as his earlier essay 'The Moses of Michelangelo' (1914).

The story follows the Bible with considerable freedom. The plagues of Egypt are explained as natural phenomena, apart from the tenth, the killing of the firstborn, which appears to be a deliberate massacre carried out by Moses' lieutenants Joshua and Caleb. The crossing of the Red Sea is made possible by a strong easterly wind which opens up a path and closes it again just in time to drown the Egyptian pursuers. The number of the Israelites, implausibly given in the Bible as

[38] A comprehensive overview of Mann's sources is provided by Klaus Makoschey, *Quellenkritische Untersuchungen zum Spätwerk Thomas Manns: 'Joseph, der Ernährer', 'Das Gesetz', 'Der Erwählte'* (Frankfurt a.M.: Klostermann, 1998).

[39] See 'Israel in the Desert', in Goethe, *West-Eastern Divan*, trans. Eric Ormsby (London: Ginkgo, 2019), 444–62; 'Israel in der Wüste', Goethe, *Sämtliche Werke*, iii/1, ed. Hendrik Birus (1994), 229–48.

six hundred thousand men plus their wives and children and a 'mixed multitude' (Exodus 12:37–8), is reduced to twelve thousand five hundred. Geography and chronology are rationalized. Instead of following a zigzag course through various deserts, Moses leads his people straight to the large oasis of Kadesh (Numbers 20:16), from which they expel the Amalekite occupants in a furious battle. There is no suggestion that they spent forty years in the wilderness. Goethe had already pointed out that in the Bible forty is a symbolic number, associated with periods of isolation: the Flood is produced by forty days and nights of rain; Moses spends forty days on Sinai; Jesus spends forty days in the wilderness being tempted by the Devil.[40]

Mann's demythologizing approach extends, at least by implication, to Moses' divine mission. It is suggested that his encounter with God in the burning bush is a projection of his inner ardour. Although Moses believes firmly in his mission, he is not above reinforcing his always precarious authority by occasional charlatanry. He takes advantage of a volcanic eruption to strengthen his control over the people. He allows his lieutenants to put it about that he parted the waters of the Red Sea by holding up his staff. He is also shown to have many human failings and oddities. He is inarticulate, so that his half-brother Aaron must speak for him. His nose was broken in youth by a blow from an Egyptian overseer. Besides his wife Zipporah, he has a mistress, a black African from Cush (Ethiopia), with whom he enjoys sensual pleasure as a relief from the strains of governing an unruly people.[41]

The ironic portrayal of Moses by Goethe and Mann owes much to the sceptical spirit of Voltaire. Mann, who read *Candide* just before writing it, called its spirit Voltairean.[42] To Agnes Meyer, 13 March 1943, he called it a 'bit of fun' ('Spass') with 'many ironic jokes', though with deeply serious moral intent.[43] Goethe, like Mann, is ironic about Moses' insistence on micromanagement until his

[40] Goethe, 'Israel in the Desert', 460.

[41] This Cushite woman is mentioned only briefly in the Bible (Num. 12:1). Luther's translation calls her a 'Mohrin' (Negress), and Mann adopts this word. Jewish tradition maintains that she was his wife, but the Bible also says that Moses was married to Zipporah, daughter of Jethro (Ex. 2:21). In Mann's version, Zipporah turns a blind eye to her husband's liaison with the Cushite.

[42] 'ein voltairesches Element', letter to Fred Michael, 21 December 1946, in *Dichter über ihre Dichtungen*, ii. 653–4.

[43] Mann and Meyer, *Briefwechsel*, 466.

brother-in-law Jethro advises him to delegate some of his duties, something which, as Goethe says, 'he should have thought of for himself'.[44] 'Unfortunately Moses had even less talent as a field commander than as a ruler.'[45] Hence in the battle with the Amalekites he went up a mountain to pray and let Joshua and Caleb lead the fighting. Goethe even surmises that when Moses dies, and we are told that nobody knows where he is buried, this indicates that Joshua and Caleb, tired of his incompetent leadership, secretly murdered him.[46] Mann's story ends well before Moses' death, but is full of small ironic touches. For example, when Moses' sister Miriam sings a hymn of triumph, which in the Bible is attributed to Moses (Exodus 15:1–21), we are told that she had composed it herself, but 'One has to imagine it sung to the timbrel' (p. 175) in order to appreciate it.

Mann departs from the Bible in representing Moses as the son of an Egyptian princess and a Hebrew slave who is killed immediately after the princess has enjoyed him. This responds to Freud's argument in *Moses and Monotheism* that Moses must have been an Egyptian.[47] The element '-mose' appears in many Egyptian names, meaning 'son' (e.g. Rameses, son of Ra the sun-god). Moses' biblical parents, Amram and Jochebed, would therefore have been his foster-parents. Moses might have been a high official, perhaps the governor of a province. He would have followed the Pharaoh Amenhotep IV, who assumed the name Akhenaten and tried to introduce the monotheistic worship of the sun-god. When the priests reasserted their power after Akhenaten's death, Moses led a large number of Hebrews out of Egypt to rule them in the land of Canaan. Mann compromises with Freud's construction by making his Moses only half Egyptian (and since Jewish identity is traditionally transmitted via the mother, Moses is thus not technically a Jew at all).

Mann's Moses is a deeply flawed but also profoundly impressive person, recalling the inarticulate but massive personality of Peeperkorn in *The Magic Mountain*. His charisma is crucial in controlling his followers. Mann recalls Heine's eulogy of Moses as a 'gigantic figure':

[44] Goethe, 'Israel in der Wüste', 236. The English translation is unfortunately wrong at this point.

[45] 'Israel in the Desert', 452.

[46] Deut. 34:6; 'Israel in the Desert', 454.

[47] *Moses and Monotheism*, in *The Standard Edition of the Complete Psychological Works of Sigmund Freud*, ed. James Strachey, 24 vols. (London: Hogarth Press, 1953–74), xxiii. 7–137 (8).

> How small Mount Sinai appears when Moses is standing on it! This mountain is only the pediment on which the man's feet stand while his head towers into the heavens, where he speaks with God—God forgive me the sin, but often I felt this Mosaic God was only the reflected radiance of Moses himself, who so much resembles him, in wrath and in love—It would be a great sin, it would be anthropomorphism, to assume such an identity between the god and his prophet—but the similarity is striking.[48]

Goethe likewise observes: 'as is the man, so too is his God',[49] noting the angry and cruel disposition that unites them, though elsewhere in the Bible we have the benevolent God of Abraham. And in Mann's story the people either grumble about Moses or, against his wishes, identify him with the God he proclaims.

Moses uses his charisma not only to lead the Hebrew slaves out of Egypt but also to shape them into a people. His project is 'setting his father's kin apart so that he might have them for himself and out of this indeterminate mass that he loved, carve without hindrance a holy image of God' (p. 178). He is repeatedly compared to a stonemason; his foster-mother Jochebed was the daughter of a stonemason. To this end, once they have arrived at Kadesh, Moses subjects his people to an elaborate set of hygienic, dietary, and sexual regulations. They are to wash regularly and relieve themselves in private, with a shovel to bury their excrement. They may eat creatures with fins and scales, but not camels or pigs, nor a long list of birds; least of all may they eat lizards, moles, or slow-worms.[50] They may not have sex with their mothers-in-law, sisters, aunts, boys, or cattle, and may no longer prostitute their daughters. These prohibitions, which in the story precede the promulgation of the Ten Commandments, deprive the Hebrews of many pleasures and arouse much resentment. Moses enforces his rules by telling them that the God they should worship is invisible and is watching them at all times—a primitive Orwellian Big Brother.

When rebellion breaks out, Moses is ruthless. He has a death squad led by Joshua and known as the Angels of Death who enforce his rule.

[48] Heinrich Heine, *Sämtliche Werke: Historisch-kritische Ausgabe*, ed. Manfred Windfuhr, 16 vols. (Hamburg: Hoffmann und Campe, 1975–97), xv: *Geständnisse, Memoiren und Kleinere autobiographische Schriften*, ed. Gerd Heinemann (1982), 46.

[49] Goethe, 'Israel in the Desert', 461.

[50] See Lev. 11 and Deut. 14. The slow-worm, mentioned three times in Mann's story, is not mentioned in the Authorized Version, but does appear as 'die Blindschleiche' in Luther's translation of Lev. 11:30.

After Moses smashes the Golden Calf, the three hundred leaders are executed by the Angels of Death. Moses does not witness the executions because he withdraws to the mountain to produce a new set of tablets.

This portrayal of Moses is disconcerting, though not at odds with the Bible, where three thousand Calf-worshippers are killed (Exodus 32:28). In Mann, he appears as a dictator, even, it has been said, a totalitarian: 'The Mosaic totalitarianism of the idea here makes possible a policy which brings the new human into being by means of terror and genocide.'[51] By comparison, the efforts of Mussolini to remodel the Italian character, noted in *Mario and the Magician*, appear mild.

Mann is here presenting a narrative of civilization which, unlike *Joseph* and *The Transposed Heads*, does not rely on Bachofen.[52] It is indebted rather to Nietzsche's *On the Genealogy of Morals*. Nietzsche is among many thinkers, such as Thomas Hobbes and David Hume, who have traced civilization back not to an original contract but to a primordial tyranny: 'the oldest "state" accordingly emerged and endured as a fearful tyranny, as a crushing and thoughtless machinery, until such a raw material of common people and half-animals was finally not only kneaded and malleable but also *formed*'.[53] This is how Moses moulds, sculpts, chisels his people.[54] Such a task can be undertaken, according to Nietzsche, only by someone 'who is capable of giving commands, who is a "master" by nature, who behaves violently in deed and gesture'.[55] Effective rule over a subject population, however, cannot rely on continued brute force. The population must acquiesce. And, in Nietzsche's account, they do this by acquiring a conscience. Conscience is the internalization of external pressure. God tells Mann's Moses: 'you have succeeded in giving them a conscience, so that they feel awful when doing something awful' (p. 194).

[51] Wolf-Daniel Hartwich, *Die Sendung Moses von der Aufklärung bis Thomas Mann* (Munich: Fink, 1997), 217.

[52] The Calf-worshippers who eat slow-worms and copulate with their sisters may be understood as regressing to the primordial and pre-cultural chaos imagined by Bachofen: see Yahya Elsaghe, '"Hebräer?" *Das Gesetz*, der Nationalsozialismus und Thomas Manns Bachofen-Rezeption', *Thomas Mann Jahrbuch*, 33 (2020), 159–76.

[53] Nietzsche, *On the Genealogy of Morals*, trans. Smith, 66 (Second Essay, section 17).

[54] Mann seems to have imagined Moses as resembling Michelangelo, not only as a sculptor, but also physically, with his broken nose. He was impressed by Freud's essay 'The Moses of Michelangelo' (1914). See *Standard Edition*, xiii. 211–36.

[55] Nietzsche, *On the Genealogy of Morals*, trans. Smith, 66.

Unable to vent their instincts by external action, people turned their aggression against themselves. 'Every instinct which does not vent itself externally *turns inwards*—this is what I call the *internalization* of man.'[56] Humanity thus begins to develop an inner life, which is unhappy, because awareness of one's suppressed instincts makes one feel guilty and gives rise to a whole range of religious practices. Here Nietzsche forcefully describes what Freud, apparently independently of Nietzsche, would later describe as a system of repression and displacement.

Despite all this, Mann's Moses is in one respect an enlightened figure. Although he sometimes practises terrorism, he forbids his followers to rejoice in the downfall of their enemies. And besides creating the Jewish nation, he also promotes universalism by inventing the alphabet, in which the three languages known to him, and in principle all others, can be represented.[57]

*

The Black Swan, written between May 1952 and March 1953, was the last work of fiction Mann produced (though not the last he published: that was *Felix Krull* in 1954). It has received comparatively little attention. Its readers, never numerous, have often found it distasteful and even disgusting because of its preoccupation with cancer. Yet in addressing this difficult topic, it marks the logical culmination of Mann's work, which deals throughout with fatal illnesses, often in unsparing clinical detail. In *The Buddenbrooks* Hanno dies of typhoid fever. Aschenbach in *Death in Venice* apparently succumbs to cholera. Most of the characters in *The Magic Mountain* suffer, often fatally, from tuberculosis. In *Doctor Faustus*, the central figure contracts syphilis and his 5-year-old nephew dies agonizingly of meningitis. That left cancer, a disease that is still dreaded; some varieties have subsequently been treated with increasing success, but in Mann's day it was a virtually unmentionable source of horror. Mann himself, in 1946, was successfully operated on for lung cancer brought on by his lifelong habit of heavy smoking; the causal connection between

[56] Ibid. 65.

[57] Mann's historical source, Elias Auerbach's *Wüste und gelobtes Land: Geschichte Israels von den Anfängen bis zum Tode Salomons* (Berlin: Kurt Wolff, 1932), describes the invention of the alphabet as the act of a single genius (quoted in Makoschey, *Quellenkritische Untersuchungen*, 55).

smoking and lung cancer would be established only in 1954, and accepted, despite counter-pressure from the tobacco industry, by both the UK and US governments in 1957.[58]

The taboo-breaking content of Mann's story sits oddly with its ostentatiously elaborate, old-fashioned style, which recalls that of German prose fiction around 1800. The circumstantial opening sentence is reminiscent, for example, of stories by Heinrich von Kleist (1777–1811) such as *The Marquise of O—* (1808), which begins: 'In M—, an important town in northern Italy, the widowed Marquise of O—, a lady of unblemished reputation, and the mother of several well-brought-up children, inserted the following announcement in the newspapers.'[59] In its portrayal of a middle-aged woman who hopes to recapture something of her youth, the story also pays homage to Goethe (as Mann had done most fully in *Lotte in Weimar*, 1939): the inset novellas in Goethe's last work of fiction, *Wilhelm Meisters Wanderjahre* (*Wilhelm Meister's Journeyman Years*, 1821 and 1829), include 'The Man of Fifty', in which a middle-aged officer, attracted by his young niece, improves his appearance by the skilful application of cosmetics. Mann's style, particularly the long conversations between mother and daughter, is a pastiche rather than a reproduction of classical German prose, and thus from the outset establishes an ironic distance from his characters.

One possible way into this rather opaque story is to search for autobiographical subtexts. Its central character, Rosalie von Tümmler, falls in love with a 22-year-old American, Ken Keaton, whom she employs to teach her teenage son English. It has been argued that Mann has transferred to her his tendency to become enamoured of handsome young men.[60] This conjecture is strengthened by the story's setting in Düsseldorf, a city that Mann only occasionally visited and that otherwise does not appear in his fiction. For Düsseldorf, on the lower Rhine, was the home of Klaus Heuser (1909–94), whom Mann met and fell in love with when on holiday on the north German

[58] David Wootton, *Bad Medicine: Doctors Doing Harm since Hippocrates* (Oxford: Oxford University Press, 2006), 237–41.

[59] Heinrich von Kleist, *The Marquise von O— and Other Stories*, trans. David Luke and Nigel Reeves (Harmondsworth: Penguin, 1978), 68.

[60] Similarly, in *Joseph in Egypt*, Potiphar's wife (unnamed in the Bible, but here called Mut-em-enet) falls for the younger Joseph, and in a comic yet deeply touching scene from *Felix Krull*, the middle-aged Diane Houpflé contrives her own seduction by the irresistible Felix.

island of Sylt in August 1927. Looking back in 1934, Mann described his acquaintance with Heuser as 'the unlooked-for fulfilment of a life-long yearning, "happiness"'.[61] The story, however, seems also to reflect Mann's awareness that the handsome young men to whom he felt attracted in his later years would actually have been unrewarding acquaintances. In 1950, staying in the Grand Hotel Dolder in Zurich, he was struck by a young Argentinian whom he saw playing tennis, confiding to his diary a long, lyrical description of the '"divine youth"'; but Mann's own quotation marks suggest ironic self-awareness, and when his daughter Erika later pointed out a very ordinary-looking young man in the hotel dining-room and told him that was his 'tennis god', Mann noted in his diary: 'The glow-worm on your palm! Illusion! Illusion!'[62]

The young American with whom Rosalie von Tümmler becomes infatuated likewise seems unworthy of her passion. He is an inoffensive, cheerful, enthusiastic young man, probably recalling the students to whom Mann lectured at Princeton. His surname, suggesting the comedian Buster Keaton, invites us not to take him too seriously. Although he professes to dislike America, and loves European history, his portrait implies the condescension with which Europeans often regard Americans. Although the story is set in the 1920s, Ken Keaton far more resembles the many Americans who visited Europe after the Second World War. He dresses informally, wearing a 'sweater' under his jacket, and allowing his handkerchief to hang out of his breast pocket instead of just showing its tip. When he appears in a T-shirt ('Trikothemd'), showing his brawny bare arms, he can be imagined as resembling Marlon Brando in Elia Kazan's film *A Streetcar Named Desire*; Mann saw the film in 1951 and admired Brando's 'compelling Sex appeal'.[63] Many details about Ken show how little Mann knew of

[61] Mann, Diary, 24 January 1934, in *Tagebücher 1933–1934*, ed. Peter de Mendelssohn (Frankfurt a.M.: Fischer, 1977). The diaries for the crucial period, 1927, are lost: Mann destroyed them in case they might be seized by the Nazis and the contents used to defame him and others. Interviewed many years later, the 77-year-old Heuser professed to have been unaware of Mann's feelings for him. See Karl Werner Böhm, *Zwischen Selbstzucht und Verlangen: Thomas Mann und das Stigma Homosexualität* (Würzburg: Königshausen & Neumann, 1991), 374–81, and on the relationship, Kurzke, *Thomas Mann*, 354–9.

[62] Mann, Diary, 6 August 1950, in *Tagebücher 1948–1950*, ed. Inge Jens (Frankfurt a.M.: Fischer, 1991), 238–40.

[63] Mann, Diary, 14 November 1951, in *Tagebücher 1951–1952*, ed. Inge Jens (Frankfurt a.M.: Fischer, 1993), 135; Mann writes 'Sex appeal' in English. A still from the film, showing Brando with bare arms, can readily be found on Wikipedia.

American life: his father could not have worked at a filling station before 1914; it is highly unlikely that Ken, as a manual worker, would have worn gloves; the decoration he receives for bravery, the Purple Heart, was widely awarded during and after the Second World War, but not earlier.[64] There seems no adequate reason, however, to read the portrayal of Ken as expressing the revulsion against the United States that led Mann to return to Europe in 1952. Mann certainly deplored the 'feeble and absent-minded dependence of Europe on America', was alarmed by the populism of Senator Joseph McCarthy, which he saw as portending a new Fascism, and by the presumed plans of American strategists to use Europe as terrain in a future atomic war against the Soviet Union.[65] But to see Rosalie's passion for Ken as primarily representing Europe's subservience to America is to underrate the interest of Rosalie's character and to overlook further and more important layers of meaning in the story.

Rosalie, a widow of 50, is presented as a likeable, warm-hearted person with an intense love of nature. Born in May, she particularly loves the spring. Flowering lime-trees, lilac, catkins, and above all roses send her into raptures. She is interested in how plants reproduce and knows enough botany to tell her daughter Anna that poplars have both male and female flowers. She talks lyrically about the wind carrying pollen into the flower's 'chastely expectant female stigma' (p. 219). It is obvious that although Rosalie has reached the menopause, she is still keenly interested in sex, and not altogether surprising that she falls for a young man half her age. Her daughter Anna, on the other hand, has been disappointed in love, and, since she has a club foot, has little prospect of marrying. Anna is a modernist painter, whose Cubist designs are at the furthest possible remove from the sensuous portrayals of nature which her mother wishes she would create.

Rosalie experiences nature not only by sight but, even more, through her sense of smell: she imbibes all pleasant scents 'deeply and gratefully, and with the highest sensuous reverence' (p. 220). She rel-

[64] The Purple Heart medal was established by George Washington in 1782, but only three were awarded. The decoration was revived in 1932. See George L. Schoolfield, 'Thomas Mann's *Die Betrogene*', *Germanic Review*, 28 (1963), 91–120 (101). Mann's mistakes in writing about America are listed in Wolfgang Leppmann, 'Der Amerikaner im Werke Thomas Manns', *German Quarterly*, 38 (1965), 619–29 (616–19).

[65] See 'Comprendre', *GW* xii. 973–8 (976), originally published as 'Retour d'Amérique' in the French magazine *Comprendre* in 1953.

ishes the strong scents of jasmine and buckthorn (the latter is called 'Faulbaum', literally 'rotten tree', in German). In spring she swathes herself in the scent of roses. Another smell comes her way, however, when she is out walking with Anna. They notice a strong smell of musk, which on inspection turns out to come from some rotting vegetation, the corpse of a small animal, and a heap of excrement surrounded by flies. Musk, though nowadays produced synthetically, was formerly obtained from the glands of such animals as the musk-deer and the civet cat; Shakespeare's Touchstone calls it 'the very unhealthy flux of a cat'.[66] There seems to be a close affinity between musky smells, which are often found sensually exciting, and what normally inspires disgust. This affinity brings to mind a curious footnote in Freud's *Civilization and its Discontents* (1930), where Freud observes that the sense of smell, the primary means by which many animals, such as dogs, navigate the world, yielded place to vision when humanity took to walking upright, but that smell often retains an erotic charge, even in civilized society which sets great store by cleanliness.[67]

Her responsiveness to smell implies something primitive in Rosalie, and here Bachofen may well be relevant. Bachofen's narrative of cultural advance from primeval promiscuity via maternal law to masculine, rational dominance allows for moments of regression. Rosalie's hyper-awareness of sex seems to represent such a regression. The primeval swamp, Bachofen's image for promiscuity, appears when Rosalie and her friends make an excursion to the Holterhof Palace (based on the real Schloss Benrath) and observe 'the swamp cypress' along with another primeval-sounding tree, the 'Californian giant sequoia' (p. 265). (Mann's term is 'Mammutbaum', literally 'mammoth tree'.)[68] Earlier, the smell of jasmine and buckthorn came from a hollow in the ground ('Bodenfalte'), an aperture with sexual implications. Rosalie is not promiscuous, but we are told that her late husband was. Nor is she represented misogynistically as a typical woman. The chaste Anna, whose art consists of non-sensuous abstraction, is at the opposite pole to her mother. Rosalie and she embody different stages in Bachofen's and Freud's narratives of the ascent of civilization.

[66] *As You Like It*, III. ii. 60. [67] Freud, *Standard Edition*, xxi. 99–100.

[68] See Yahya Elsaghe, *Krankheit und Matriarchat: Thomas Manns 'Betrogene' im Kontext* (Berlin: De Gruyter, 2000), 218–19.

The trip to Holterhof reveals yet another mythic dimension of the story. It is partially modelled on the story of Cupid and Psyche told in Apuleius' second-century novel *The Golden Ass*.[69] Psyche is a young woman of such surpassing beauty that she arouses the hatred of Venus, who decides to punish her by making her fall in love with a contemptible person. She tells her son Cupid to make this happen, but Cupid, overcome by Psyche's beauty, himself becomes her lover on condition that they meet only in the dark, so that she can feel but never see him. Prompted by her envious sisters, Psyche looks at Cupid by lamplight, but drops oil on him and wakes him, so that he flies away. As punishment, she is given a series of tasks which she accomplishes with magical help. As the last, she must descend into the underworld and obtain from its queen, Proserpina, a casket containing beauty lotion. On her journey she carries two coins and two barley-cakes. The coins are for the sinister ferryman Charon, the cakes are for the hellhound Cerberus. When she reaches Proserpina, she is offered a rich meal, but, as instructed, accepts only a piece of coarse bread. She returns, and although curiosity made her open the casket, the gods forgive her, appease Venus, and allow Psyche to marry Cupid and herself become a goddess.

When enthusing about roses, Rosalie recalls—an unlikely allusion from someone who is not particularly well educated, hence something Mann had to bring in at all costs—how Psyche looks at her sleeping lover by lamplight.[70] For the story's purposes, Rosalie corresponds to Psyche, Ken to the supposed contemptible lover (though hardly to Cupid); the boat trip on the Rhine corresponds to Psyche's crossing of the Styx, the sinister boatman to the mythical ferryman Charon, the hissing black swan, fed by Rosalie, to Cerberus, and the mansion, with its dark corridors and atmosphere of decay and the grave, to the underworld. Rosalie has brought bread to feed the swans with and even takes a bite of it herself, though Ken objects that it is '*old and hard*'.[71] What significance might be assigned to the swans? In Greek mythology the elegant swan is among the birds associated with

[69] Apuleius, *The Golden Ass*, trans. P. G. Walsh, Oxford World's Classics (Oxford: Oxford University Press, 1994), 75–113.

[70] The same scene is alluded to by Goethe: *Wilhelm Meisters Wanderjahre*, in Goethe, *Sämtliche Werke*, x, ed. Gerhard Neumann and Hans-Georg Dewitz (1989), 473.

[71] For these and other parallels, see Elsaghe, *Krankheit und Matriarchat*, 178–81.

Aphrodite. Zeus transformed himself into a swan to seduce Leda. The swan is a multivalent symbol of sexuality. The *black* swan, an import from Australia, was unknown in ancient times, hence the Latin poet Horace uses the phrase to exemplify something so rare as to be non-existent.

Mann was willing to let the English translation of his story be entitled *The Black Swan*.[72] The black swan, though hostile to Rosalie, may also represent Rosalie herself. Although she has reached the menopause, she believes that her love for Ken has caused her menstrual bleeding to resume. Three times in the story she compares herself to Sarah in the Old Testament, who laughed when told that she would bear a child after the menopause, yet did so (Genesis 18). Alas, the miracle that worked for Sarah does not apply to Rosalie. During the night after the excursion, she falls gravely ill and is taken into hospital. The doctors find that the bleeding results, not from any kind of rejuvenation, but from a cervical cancer that is already too far advanced to be treated. As with the fatal illness of Hanno in *The Buddenbrooks*, Mann resorts to emotionally distancing clinical details, provided by the surgeon who had operated successfully on his own cancer.[73] Yet after this almost brutally unsentimental climax, the story ends on a note of reconciliation: Rosalie affirms that she has always loved nature and been loved in return, and her actual death is gentle and apparently painless.

[72] Letter to Anna Jacobson, 3 May 1954, in *Dichter über ihre Dichtungen*, iii. 528.

[73] The long letter from Dr Frederick Rosenthal is printed in *GKFA* 6/2: 328–32. The accuracy of Dr Rosenthal's information has been severely questioned: see Arnaldo Benini, 'Die skandalöse Parabel: Thomas Manns Erzählung *Die Betrogene*', in Thomas Sprecher (ed.), *Liebe und Tod—in Venedig und anderswo* (Frankfurt a.M.: Klostermann, 2005), 227–46.

NOTE ON THE TRANSLATIONS

APPROACHING the later stories of Thomas Mann, written over three decades in very different historical and biographical circumstances, I had in mind a straightforward translation strategy, which in practice, and allowing for a degree of flexibility, has proved fairly durable. Aware as I was of the wealth, vigour, and evolution of the author's diction across a varied collection of scenes and periods, my intention has been to find a language Mann might have used if he had written these stories in English: *Disorder and Early Sorrow* in the early 1920s, *The Transposed Heads* in the late 1930s, *The Black Swan* in the early 1950s, and so on. However, I must add that this did not mean historicizing the language in the way a translator of older texts, with fortunate or unfortunate results, might seek out a historically circumscribed idiom, incorporating words and phrases used at that time but not today. Nor have I made it my purpose to modernize Mann's language in translation, to bring it up to date, so to speak. Rather, what I have done is to avoid words and idioms in English that Mann would not—indeed could not—have chosen to use, because such language was not in use when he wrote. Does that mean my chosen medium belongs to a certain period in the past and lacks the currency or modernity we would expect from a writer of Mann's status? On the contrary. While the language I found for the earliest of these stories, *Disorder and Early Sorrow*, could have been used in English in 1925, it does not—beyond reference to the cultural furniture of its own time and place—contain language that would be very out of place today. In short, my chief focus has been to avoid anachronism. I might put it this way: it has transpired, during the toil and exhilaration of translating these stories, that the linguistic resources of the English language are so voluminous and rich, and the author's work is so contemporary in appeal, that Mann's modernity and our own can cohabit in a single English idiom.

I mentioned a 'degree of flexibility' within the application of the principles outlined above. This became especially necessary when translating two of the stories, *The Transposed Heads* and *The Law*, in which Mann himself had worked in the context of historical settings and language. While translating the former, I spent long, fascinating hours informing myself of Hindu rites and rituals, as well as of Indian history and geography, while also reviewing Mann's own sources in these matters. Among the parody, religious iconography, and Sanskrit reference I found a strange and unexpectedly modern and quite daring story of quasi-Freudian psychology, openly referenced sexuality, and the kind of mind–body dichotomies that have detained philosophers for centuries and still do as our own era moves ever further into robotics, AI, reproductive technology, cloning, and experimental neurology. As for *The Law*, set in biblical times, I spent a considerable time in the Torah in Luther's translation as well as in the first five books of the King James Version, in which, rightly or wrongly, I see a work of equivalent seminal importance. Mann cites full sentences from Luther's version, sometimes from different editions, or quotes half-sentences which then continue in an offhand modern German, or he makes up comical Luther-style sentences which may or may not contain authentic Lutheran phrasing. He also uses archaic and quite rare words which are not biblical but contribute to place the text in a distant past.

A further concern has been my decision to respect and preserve, as far as possible, the specificity of Mann's syntactical control of narrative arrangement and flow, however retarding or even frustrating that may prove in English. Much has been made of Mann's 'long sentences', of German hypotaxis and English parataxis. Helen Lowe-Porter, the admirable translator of much of Thomas Mann's oeuvre during the German author's lifetime, in an essay published posthumously in 1966, puts it this way: in English 'the train of thought is likely merely to suggest where the German follows through, explaining and expounding' so that English is 'easier to read' whereas 'German constructs more relative and subordinate clauses, with longer sentences, a different order'.[1] From a comparative linguistic and cultural point of view this may well be correct, and yet, and yet . . . Are we to suppose that Thomas Mann's sentences are long solely because his language is German? Do most German writers write sentences like Mann's, then? Surely a personal choice is involved, and a personality. The rhetorical purposes of syntactical writing, the desire, within a single structure, to hold on, to

[1] The essay is cited from J. C. Thirlwall (ed.), *In Another Language: A Record of the Thirty-Year Relationship between Thomas Mann and His English Translator, Helen Tracy Lowe-Porter* (New York: Knopf, 1966), 199.

reflect, retain, complement, complicate, analyse, relativize, suppress, postpone, play, concede, reopen and tease out—who will deny that these may simply be all-too-human desiderata rather than essentially German ones? Without going into detail here, one could list any number of authors writing in languages other than German, including English, who relish the pleasures of driving a team of subordinate clauses, and many German writers who prefer shorter sentences. The more I have learned about Thomas Mann, whether through the intense, readerly work of translating or by reading criticism and biography, the more I have understood why his complex sentences are characteristically and indispensably his own; neither Proustian nor Joycean, Jamesian nor Cervantian, they are rooted in Thomas Mann's life, sensibility, and personal writing style rather than in any specific era or language.

Lastly, I should like to offer my thanks to four individuals whose support has sustained me on what has been an unexpectedly long journey—to my editor Ritchie Robertson, whose patience I tried but never exhausted; to my great friend Simon Korner, who, in questions of English style and expression, is the best reader I know; and although I do not know him personally, to David Horton, whose book *Thomas Mann in English: A Study in Literary Translation* is an excellent primer for translators, not only of Mann; finally, to Christiane Nuhn, who, against all the odds, succeeded in convincing me that I was capable of finishing this piece of work.

SELECT BIBLIOGRAPHY

Biographies

Hamilton, Nigel, *The Brothers Mann: The Lives of Heinrich and Thomas Mann, 1871–1950 and 1875–1955* (London: Secker & Warburg, 1978).

Hayman, Ronald, *Thomas Mann: A Biography* (London: Bloomsbury, 1996).

Kurzke, Hermann, *Thomas Mann: Life as a Work of Art; A Biography*, trans. Leslie Willson (Princeton: Princeton University Press, 2002).

Prater, Donald A., *Thomas Mann: A Life* (Oxford: Clarendon Press, 1995).

Critical Studies of Thomas Mann

Boes, Tobias, *Thomas Mann's War: Literature, Politics, and the World Republic of Letters* (Ithaca, NY: Cornell University Press, 2019).

Buck, T., 'Loyalty and Licence: Thomas Mann's Fiction in English Translation', *Modern Language Review*, 91 (1996), 898–921.

Heller, Erich, *The Ironic German: A Study of Thomas Mann* (London: Secker & Warburg, 1958).

Kontje, Todd, *The Cambridge Introduction to Thomas Mann* (Cambridge: Cambridge University Press, 2011).

Kontje, Todd, *Thomas Mann's World: Empire, Race, and the Jewish Question* (Ann Arbor: University of Michigan Press, 2011).

Lukács, Georg, *Essays on Thomas Mann*, trans. Stanley Mitchell (London: Merlin Press, 1964).

Reed, T. J., *Thomas Mann: The Uses of Tradition*, 2nd edn. (Oxford: Clarendon Press, 1996).

Robertson, Ritchie (ed.), *The Cambridge Companion to Thomas Mann* (Cambridge: Cambridge University Press, 2002).

Scaff, Susan von Rohr, *History, Myth and Music: Thomas Mann's Timely Fiction* (Columbia, SC: Camden House, 1998).

Disorder and Early Sorrow

Rauch-Rappaport, Angelika, 'Melancholia in Thomas Mann's *Unordnung und frühes Leid*: Feeling Envy for the Young and Dancing', *Oxford German Studies*, 34 (2005), 204–10.

Turner, David, 'Balancing the Account: Thomas Mann's *Unordnung und frühes Leid*', *German Life and Letters*, 52 (1999), 43–57.

Mario and the Magician

Baker, Geoffrey, 'Making a Spectacle of Ourselves: The Unpolitical Ending of Thomas Mann's *Mario und der Zauberer*', *Seminar*, 45 (2009), 355–68.

Bance, A. F., 'The Narrator in Thomas Mann's *Mario und der Zauberer*', *Modern Language Review*, 82 (1987), 382–98.

Bridges, George, 'Thomas Mann's *Mario und der Zauberer*: "Aber zum Donnerwetter! Deshalb bringt man doch niemand um!"', *German Quarterly*, 64 (1991), 501–17.

Geulen, Eva, 'Resistance and Representation: *Mario und der Zauberer*', *New German Critique*, 68 (1996), ii. 3–29.

Grenville, Anthony, 'Idealism versus Materialism in the Representation of History in Literature: The Dictator Figure in Thomas Mann's *Mario und der Zauberer* and Brecht's *Der aufhaltsame Aufstieg des Arturo Ui*', *Journal of European Studies*, 17 (1987), 77–105.

Hatfield, Henry, 'Thomas Mann's *Mario und der Zauberer*: An Interpretation', *Germanic Review*, 21 (1946), 306–12.

Leneaux, Grant E., '*Mario und der Zauberer*: The Narration of Seduction or the Seduction of Narration?', *Orbis Litterarum*, 40 (1985), 327–47.

Lunn, Eugene, 'Tales of Liberal Disquiet: Thomas Mann's *Mario and the Magician* and Interpretations of Fascism', *Literature and History*, 11 (1985), 77–100.

Schwarz, Egon, 'Fascism and Society: Remarks on Thomas Mann's Novella *Mario und der Zauberer*', *Michigan Germanic Studies*, 2 (1976), 47–67.

Speirs, Ronald, *Mann: 'Mario und der Zauberer'* (London: Grant & Cutler, 1990).

The Transposed Heads

Schulz, Siegfried A., 'Hindu Mythology in Mann's Indian Legend', *Comparative Literature*, 14 (1962), 129–42.

Willson, A. Leslie, 'Thomas Mann's *Die vertauschten Köpfe*: The Catalyst of Creation', *Monatshefte*, 39 (1957), 313–21.

The Law

Horton, David, '"An acceptable job"? The First English Translation of Thomas Mann's *Das Gesetz*', *Modern Language Review*, 105 (2010), 149–70.

Ziolkowski, Theodore, *Uses and Abuses of Moses: Literary Representations since the Enlightenment* (Notre Dame, IN: University of Notre Dame Press, 2016).

The Black Swan

Latta, Alan D., 'The Reception of Thomas Mann's *Die Betrogene*: Tabus, Prejudices, and Tricks of the Trade', *Internationales Archiv für Sozialgeschichte der Deutschen Literatur*, 12 (1987), 237–72.

Latta, Alan D., 'The Reception of Thomas Mann's *Die Betrogene*, Part II: The Scholarly Reception', *Internationales Archiv für Sozialgeschichte der Deutschen Literatur*, 18 (1993), 123–46.

Schoolfield, George C., 'Thomas Mann's *Die Betrogene*', *Germanic Review*, 28 (1963), 91–120.

Further Reading in Oxford World's Classics

Mann, Thomas, *The Buddenbrooks*, trans. Mike Mitchell, ed. Ritchie Robertson.

Mann, Thomas, *Death in Venice and Other Stories*, trans. Ritchie Robertson and Nicola Luckhurst, ed. Ritchie Robertson.

Mann, Thomas, *Doctor Faustus*, trans. and ed. Ritchie Robertson.

Mann, Thomas, *The Magic Mountain*, trans. Simon Pare, ed. Ritchie Robertson.

A CHRONOLOGY OF THOMAS MANN

1875 (6 June) Birth of Paul Thomas Mann to Julia (née da Silva Bruhns, b. 1851) and Thomas Johann Heinrich Mann (b. 1840), the second of five children. His siblings are Luiz Heinrich (b. 1871), Julia (b. 1877), Carla (b. 1881), and Viktor (b. 1890).

1877 Mann's father is elected to the Lübeck senate.

1891 (13 October) Mann's father dies; the family firm (Johann Siegmund Mann, Corn Merchants, Commission and Transport Agents) is liquidated and the family house sold, leaving Heinrich and Thomas with independent means sufficient to establish themselves as writers.

1893 Frau Mann moves to Munich with the three younger children (Julia, Carla, and Viktor); Thomas stays at school in Lübeck.

1894 Thomas leaves school and joins his mother in Munich, where he starts working for an insurance company, but leaves it after four months in the hope of a career as a journalist. His first story, 'Gefallen' ('Fallen'), is published in the Naturalist journal *Die Gesellschaft* ('Society').

1894–8 Thomas publishes short stories in the periodical edited by his brother Heinrich, *Das Zwanzigste Jahrhundert* ('The Twentieth Century'). The two brothers also work and travel together.

1898 Mann's first book, *Der kleine Herr Friedemann* (*Little Herr Friedemann*), a collection of short stories, is published.

1899 Beginning of friendship with Paul Ehrenberg.

1900 (May) Mann completes the novel *The Buddenbrooks*. Called up for military service, beginning on 1 October, but thanks to an inflamed tendon in his right foot he is confined to bed and given leave in December.

1901 *The Buddenbrooks* published in two volumes. This novel was the foundation for Mann's reputation and success: it sold a million copies in just over a year, and continued to have a steady sale.

1903 The collection *Tristan: Six Novellas* appears (including *Tonio Kröger*).

1905 (11 February) Mann marries Katia Pringsheim (b. 1883), daughter of a wealthy Munich mathematics professor of Jewish descent.
(9 November) Birth of their first child, Erika Mann.

1906 (18 November) Birth of Klaus Mann.

1909 (27 March) Birth of Gottfried ('Golo') Mann. Mann publishes the novel *Königliche Hoheit* ('Royal Highness'), which is judged lightweight by comparison with *The Buddenbrooks*.

1910 Mann begins work on *Confessions of the Confidence Man Felix Krull*, only to abandon it in 1911. (7 June) Birth of Monika Mann. (30 July) Suicide of Mann's sister Carla.

1911 (May) Feeling ill and depressed, Mann visits the Adriatic island of Brioni and Venice with his wife; (26 May–2 June) they stay in the Hotel des Bains on the Venetian Lido.

1912 (15 May–12 June) Mann visits Katia, who is staying in a sanatorium in Davos in Switzerland. (June) *Death in Venice* completed; (October–November) published in the journal *Die neue Rundschau* ('New Review').

1913 Mann begins work on *The Magic Mountain*, planning it as a novella similar in length to *Death in Venice*.

1914 (August) Outbreak of war; Mann shares the widespread patriotic euphoria.

1915 (November) Heinrich Mann's essay on Zola is published, with a hostile reference to Thomas Mann, who is inspired to start work on the *Reflections of an Unpolitical Man*.

1918 (24 April) Birth of Elisabeth Mann. (9 November) Proclamation of a German republic. (October) Just before the war ends, Mann publishes *Reflections of an Unpolitical Man*.

1919 (7 April) Soviet Republic declared in Munich; (1–3 May) overthrown by government and paramilitary troops. (21 April) Birth of Michael Mann. Mann continues work on *The Magic Mountain*.

1922 (24 June) Assassination of the Foreign Minister, Walther Rathenau. (15 October) Mann delivers his address, 'Von deutscher Republik' ('On the German Republic') in the Beethovensaal in Berlin; ostensibly a celebration of the dramatist Gerhart Hauptmann's sixtieth birthday, it is recognized as Mann's public avowal of support for the Weimar Republic.

1924 *The Magic Mountain* published.

1926 (31 August–13 September) The Manns take a holiday at Forte dei Marmi in Italy, where the events inspire *Mario and the Magician* (published 1930).

1927 (10 May) Suicide of Mann's sister Julia.

1929 Mann is awarded the Nobel Prize for Literature, explicitly for *The Buddenbrooks*.

His speech on Lessing, at the bicentenary of the latter's birth, marks an important attempt to reconcile myth with reason in the struggle against fascism.

1930 (February–April) Travels in Egypt and Palestine.

1932 The centenary of Goethe's death brings forth important lectures and essays.

1933 (30 January) Hitler becomes Chancellor of Germany.

(10 February) Mann leaves Germany with his wife, initially to lecture in Holland and Belgium, then to visit Switzerland; while there, his children Klaus and Erika warn him not to return. After spending the summer on the French Riviera, the Manns settle at Küsnacht outside Zurich in Switzerland. (October) Publication of *The Tales of Jacob* (first volume of *Joseph and His Brothers*).

1934 Publication of *The Young Joseph*. (May–June) Mann pays his first visit to the US; lectures on Goethe at Yale University.

1935 (June–July) Mann revisits the US and receives an honorary doctorate from Harvard.

1936 Mann is deprived of German citizenship; becomes a Czech citizen. Also deprived of his honorary degree from Bonn University. *Joseph in Egypt* is published in Vienna by Bermann-Fischer, Mann's publisher, now also in exile. (8 May) Lecture on 'Freud and the Future' delivered in Vienna to celebrate Freud's eightieth birthday.

1937 (April) Mann revisits the US at invitation of the New School of Social Research in New York.

1938 (February) returns to the US for long visit; encouraged to settle there following news of Hitler's annexation of Austria; accepts a chair at Princeton University. (1 October) German invasion of Czechoslovakia. (9 November) 'Kristallnacht': attacks on Jewish homes and synagogues throughout Germany.

1939 (3 September) Britain and France declare war on Germany after Germany invades Poland.

1941 (April) The Manns move to Pacific Palisades, Los Angeles. (December) US declares war on Japan after its attack on Pearl Harbor; Germany and Italy declare war on the US.

1943 *Joseph the Provider* published by Bermann-Fischer, now in Stockholm. (23 May) Mann begins work on *Doctor Faustus*. 'The Tables of the Law', Mann's story about Moses, is published in a book entitled *The Ten Commandments: Ten Short Novels of Hitler's War against the Moral Code*.

1944 Thomas and Katia Mann become American citizens.

1945 (12 April) Death of President Roosevelt. (7 May) Germany's unconditional surrender.
(29 May) Lecture, 'Germany and the Germans', delivered at Library of Congress; it is Mann's major statement on the German catastrophe, closely linked to *Doctor Faustus*.

1947 (May–August) Thomas and Katia visit Europe, including Britain, Switzerland, Italy, and Holland, but not Germany. Publication of *Doctor Faustus*.

1949 (21 May) Suicide of Klaus Mann. Mann revisits Germany (Frankfurt, Munich, Weimar) in connection with celebrations of the bicentenary of Goethe's birth.
(12 October) Founding of German Democratic Republic in Soviet zone of occupation.
Beginning of anti-Communist hysteria in the US, stirred up by Senator Joseph McCarthy.

1950 (2 March) Death of Heinrich Mann.

1951 Mann resumes work on *Felix Krull*.

1952 Alarmed by McCarthyism, Mann moves to Switzerland; he and Katia rent a house at Erlenbach near Zurich.

1954 The Manns buy a house at Kilchberg on Lake Zurich. *Felix Krull* published.

1955 (12 August) Thomas Mann dies in Zurich of arteriosclerosis.

MARIO AND THE MAGICIAN AND OTHER LATE STORIES

DISORDER AND EARLY SORROW

THERE was only a vegetable main course, savoy cabbage cutlets, so now there's a flummery to follow, concocted from one of those custard powders tasting of almonds and soap that people buy now, and while Xaver, the young domestic, in a striped jacket he has outgrown and wearing white woollen gloves and yellow sandals, is serving it up, the Big Ones indulgently remind their father that they have company arriving today.

The Big Ones are: Ingrid, brown-eyed and eighteen, a most delightful girl in her final school year, who, if only because she has charmed her teachers and especially the headmaster to the extent that they will allow her to get away with anything and everything, is likely to sit school-leaving exams without any intention of putting the certificate she will receive to further use, but who, on the basis of her pleasant smile and equally agreeable voice, as well as her pronounced and highly entertaining talent for parody, instead feels powerfully drawn to the theatre—and then Bert, a blond boy of seventeen, who has no desire whatsoever to see school through but plans to plunge into life as soon as possible as either a dancer or cabaret performer, or even as a waiter, and this last 'in Cairo' to boot, a destination to which he has already tried to escape once, his attempt to do so one morning at five o'clock foiled only at the last minute. Bert bears a decided resemblance to the domestic servant Xaver Kleinsgütl, who is the same age, although not because Bert looks in any way ordinary—in fact, his features are strikingly similar to those of his father, Professor Cornelius—but rather because of some convergence from the other side, or, at most, by dint of a reciprocal assimilation of their types, in which their broadly similar attire and general deportment are the determining factors. Both wear their thick hair long on top and hastily parted down the middle, the effect being that each uses the same motion of the head to flick back his hair. When either of these two leaves the house by the garden gate, bareheaded whatever the weather, a windbreaker waggishly girt with a leather thong round the waist, with a slight stoop or even his head inclined towards his shoulder, pushing or mounting a bicycle—and Xaver will use the bicycles of his masters as the whim takes him, including those of the ladies, availing himself without qualm even of the Professor's—Dr Cornelius, looking out of his bedroom window, cannot for the life of him tell which one he has before his eyes: the boy or his son. They look like young muzhiks,* he thinks, completely alike, and both are passionate smokers, although Bert lacks the means to smoke as many as Xaver, who will tally up as many as thirty a day of a brand sporting the name of a movie diva* in full bloom.

The Big Ones call their parents the 'Dotards'—not behind their backs but straight to their faces, and with great affection, too—though Cornelius is only forty-seven and his wife all of eight years younger. 'Dearest Dotard' they exclaim, or 'most Devoted Lady-Dotard', while the Professor's parents, living the confused and browbeaten lives of elderly folk at his erstwhile home, are referred to as the 'Grand-Dotards'. As for the Little Ones, Lori and Biter, eating in the upper hallway with 'Anna Blue', so named for the bluishness of her cheeks, they follow the example of their mother in addressing their father by his forename, Abel. It sounds indescribably droll when either of them speaks to him—or of him—in this rather flamboyant manner of confidentiality, especially in Eleonore's sweet tone of voice, a five-year-old who is the very image of Frau Cornelius in her childhood photographs, and whom the Professor adores above all.

'Darling Dotard,' says Ingrid amiably, placing her large but comely hand on that of her father, who, in accordance with bourgeois and not unnatural mores, heads the table during family meals, and on whose left, opposite her mother, is Ingrid's place—'Gracious Forebear, pray accept my gentle reminder, for there is something you are certain to have repressed. It was this afternoon, after all, that we were to have our little frolic, our hop with herring salad—and as for your good self, do keep countenance: despair not, for all will be over by nine.'

'Oh?' says Cornelius with a long face—'Good, good,' he says, shaking his head to show goodwill and accordance with the necessity of the thing. 'Is that already upon us, then? I thought—Thursday, ah yes. How time flies. When are they coming?'

They're due at around half past four, replies Ingrid, whose brother defers to his sister when they communicate with their father. While resting on the top floor, she continues, her father will barely hear a sound, and then, between seven and eight, he'll be taking his constitutional. If he so wishes, he could easily slip out via the patio.

'Ah', Cornelius utters glumly, as if to say, 'you exaggerate'. But now even Bert chips in:

'It's the only evening in the week when Vanya doesn't have to perform; he would need to leave at half past six on any other. That would be sad for us all, would it not?'

'Vanya', that's Ivan Herzl, celebrated young devotee of the State Theatre and good friend of Bert and Ingrid, who often go and have tea with him or visit him in his dressing room. He is an artist of the new school who, or so it appears to the Professor, stands on the stage in strange and exceedingly affected and unnatural dancing poses emitting grief-stricken shrieks. This sort of thing is thoroughly off-putting to a professor of history, but Bert has placed himself under Herzl's powerful influence, lining the lower rims of his eyelids black—the subject of several difficult but fruitless rows with his father—and, with youthful indifference to the torments of his elders, declaring that he is not only set on modelling himself on Herzl if he takes up dancing professionally, but is resolved to move exactly as he does in the event of his becoming a waiter in Cairo.

Cornelius raises his eyebrows slightly and gives his son a little bow, a gesture suggestive of the moderation and self-restraint that befits a dutiful member of his own generation. This pantomime is without detectable irony and universal in its validity. From Bert's point of view it could as easily be addressed to him as refer to the expressive talents of his friend.

'Who else is coming?' enquires the master of the house. They give him several names, names he may have heard, names from their own, well-situated, residential neighbourhood or from more urban districts, names of Ingrid's friends in the final year at her girls' grammar school… And they still have some telephoning to do, they add. They would have to phone Max, for example, that is Max Hergesell, student of engineering, whose name Ingrid pronounces in the nasal drawl which according to her is the private manner of all Hergesells, and which she proceeds to parody in the most comical and authentic style until her parents laugh so heartily that they well-nigh choke on their dismal flummery. For even in these times, one has to laugh if something is funny.

Every now and again the telephone rings in the Professor's study and the Big Ones go running in the knowledge it will be for them. Many people have had to relinquish their telephones owing to the recent price rises, but the Corneliuses have managed to hold on to theirs, if only just, in the same way as they have been able to retain their pre-war villa—all thanks to the tolerable salary he receives as a tenured professor of history, which, under the present circumstances, has been adjusted to millions. Their suburban home is elegant and comfortable, albeit somewhat run-down—material shortages making repairs impossible—and marred by iron stoves with long pipes. Still, the setting of their lives has remained that of the erstwhile upper middle class, even if the life they actually lead, impoverished and complicated, with shabby remade clothes, no longer reflects that. The children know nothing else; for them, all this is normal and orderly; they are born villa-proletarians. The question of clothing barely concerns them. This is a generation who has invented a costume to suit their times, a product of poverty and pioneer gusto, consisting in summer of little more than a belted linen smock and sandals. The older, bourgeois family members have a harder time of it.

The Big Ones converse with their friends in the other room, while their napkins hang over the backs of their chairs. It is their invited guests who are on the telephone. They wish to accept or decline their invitations or to discuss this or that, and the Big Ones deliberate with them in the jargon of their tribe, a Babel of ebullient slang and presumption of which the Dotards understand barely a word. And these, too, are engaged in discussion about what food to offer the guests. The Professor shows middle-class zeal. He would like there to be a gateau for dinner, or at least something like a gateau, to follow the Italian salad and black-bread open-faced sandwiches, but Frau Cornelius asserts that that would be going too far—the young people would not expect it, she explains, and the children agree with her when they sit down again to their pudding.

The lady of the house, whom the taller Ingrid takes after, is worn and wearied by the absurd complications of domestic economy. She feels the need for a cure, but the shifting ground under their feet and topsy-turviness of everything have made that impracticable for the time being. She remembers—and now reminds them of—the eggs that quite simply have to be purchased today at six thousand marks apiece and are only available on a particular day of the week in a particular quantity and at a particular shop fifteen minutes from here; the children, before they do anything else, must set off to procure them directly after luncheon. Danny, the neighbours' son, is coming to join them, and Xaver, too, will put on civilian clothes and accompany his young master and mistress. For the shop provides only five eggs a week to each household, and so the young people are to enter the shop individually, one after another with different fictitious names and the intention of acquiring twenty eggs in all for the Villa Cornelius. This is a main source of weekly entertainment for the entire band, the muzhik Kleinsgütl included, but especially so for Bert and Ingrid, who show a singular proclivity for baffling and duping their fellow human beings, a whim they indulge at every turn, even when no eggs are forthcoming. When travelling in trams they love to impersonate, by means of insinuation and acting, young people entirely different from their real selves. Holding long, bogus conversations with each other quite openly in a local dialect that they never normally speak, employing all the vulgarities of common parlance, they exchange the tritest of platitudes about politics, prices and make-believe people, until the whole tramcar, with sympathy but also with a dark foreboding that something is not quite right, hangs on every word of their boundlessly banal eloquence. At this point they become increasingly audacious, telling each other the most hideous stories about these non-existent persons. Ingrid—in a high, warbling and grossly chatty voice—succeeds in passing for a shopgirl who has an illegitimate child, a son with sadistic tendencies who, in the countryside, has recently subjected a cow to such 'indescribable torture' that to see such a thing was scarcely bearable for a decent Christian. Bert only just stops himself bursting into laughter at Ingrid's warbled rendering of 'torrchur'; managing to exhibit a ghoulish concern instead, he enters into a long and gruesome, albeit perverse and indeed inane exchange with the unfortunate shopgirl about the ins and outs of this morbid cruelty, until an elderly man sitting diagonally opposite, with his folded ticket protruding between his forefinger and a signet ring, decides enough is enough and loudly objects to people so young discussing themata of this nature in such detail (he actually uses the Greek plural 'themata'). Whereupon Ingrid pretends to dissolve in tears, while Bert—with clenched fists and gnashing teeth, his whole body shaking—acts as if only a supreme effort of self-restraint, a composure he will be incapable of maintaining for much longer, were preventing him from unleashing lethal fury upon the elderly gent, so that the old man, who only meant well, promptly leaves the tramcar at the next stop.

Such are the amusements of the Big Ones. The telephone plays a prominent part in these, for they phone up all kinds of people, opera singers, state officials, dignitaries of the Church, identifying themselves as shop assistants, or as Count and Countess Manndeville, and only with difficulty accepting that they have dialled the wrong number. On one occasion they emptied their parents' calling-card tray and redistributed the cards higgledy-piggledy among the letter boxes of the neighbourhood, but not without a refined sense of the confusingly quasi-probable, a move which generated considerable turmoil at the time, for heaven-knows-who suddenly seemed to have visited God-knows-whom.

Xaver, his servant's gloves removed and the yellow chain-link ring he wears on his left hand revealed, enters the room flicking back his hair and sets about clearing the table, and while the Professor finishes his weak beer (at eight thousand marks a bottle) and lights a cigarette, the Little Ones are heard larking about on the stairs and in the hallway. As usual they have come to report to their parents after table, storming the dining room, battling with the door, on whose handle they both hang by their tiny fists, then stamping and stumbling with their hurried, clumsy little legs across the carpet, their feet in red felt slippers with their socks hanging down around their ankles, calling out news and prattling with each other as they head for their habitual destinations: Biter to his mother, onto whose lap he clambers on his knees to tell her how much he has eaten and to show his full tummy as proof, and Lori to her 'Abel', so very much hers because she is so very much his, and because she instinctively feels and smilingly delights in the profound and, like all deep emotion, somewhat melancholy tenderness with which he enfolds her little-girl person in his arms, sensing too the love in his eyes and kisses as he presses his lips to her finely formed hand or her temples, where tiny blue veins are traced with such touching delicacy.

The children display a strong yet indeterminate sibling likeness, an impression augmented by the consistency of their clothing and hairstyles, yet they also show marked differences, especially those deriving from being male and female. Here, quite clearly, is a little Adam and a little Eve—on Biter's side, so it seems, emphasized by his self-assertive personality: his is certainly the stockier, sturdier, brawnier build, but he also underscores his four-year-old male dignity through posture, facial expression and his manner of speaking, and by letting his little arms, like an American athlete, hang down from slightly hunched shoulders, or by drawing down the corners of his mouth and trying to make his voice sound deep and serious. All this dignity and masculinity, it might be added, stems more from aspiration than from his true nature, for born and nurtured in times of turbulence and distress, he has acquired a somewhat unstable and irritable nervous system, and consequently suffers terribly under life's travails; he is prone to fits of temper and to stamping his feet in despair, wracked with embittered sobbing over the merest trifles, all of which make him his mother's dearest charge. He has a longish little nose, small mouth and rounded, chestnut-coloured eyes, also something of a squint, meaning he will probably need to wear correcting spectacles soon. The nose and mouth are his father's, manifestly so now that the Professor has had his pointed beard removed and goes clean-shaven. (The pointed beard was simply no longer tenable; even a man of history must make concessions to the customs of the present.) But it is his tiny daughter whom Cornelius holds on his lap, his darling Eleonor, his little Eve, so much more delicate and sweeter of face than the boy, and while holding his cigarette away from her, he allows her pretty little hands to finger his spectacles, whose lenses are divided for reading and distance, a feature that every day attracts her curiosity.

At bottom he is aware that his wife's preference is probably more magnanimous than his own, and that Biter's problematic masculinity is perhaps of greater consequence than the more even-tempered charm of his own darling. But the heart will not be swayed, he thinks, and his own heart belongs to his little girl, and has done so for as long as she's been here, in fact since he first set eyes upon her. When he holds her in his arms, he almost always remembers that first time: it was in a bright room in the Women's Hospital, where Lori had come into the world after a gap of twelve years between herself and her older siblings. He had stepped in closer, and at almost the very moment when, under her mother's smiling eyes, he had carefully pulled aside the curtains surrounding the doll's-bed-sized canopy cot next to the larger bed and caught sight of the little miracle lying there among her pillows, so well formed, so pleasantly bathed in the serenity of her harmonious proportions, with tiny hands that even then, when they were so much smaller, were just as lovely as they are now, and with her wide-open eyes, which at that time were sky-blue and reflected the brightness of the day—yes, in almost that self-same instant he had felt smitten and had bonded; it was love at first sight and it was forever, a feeling unknown to him, unexpected, unhoped for, at least in as far as his conscious thoughts were concerned, a feeling that took possession of him and which, immediately, with astonishment and joy, he understood would stay with him for as long as he lived.

Actually, Dr Cornelius knows that, examined more closely, this unexpectedness, this whole matter of the unforeseen nature of his feelings, and even of their having been entirely involuntary, is not quite correct. Underneath it all he understands that it was no accident that such emotions had overwhelmed him and taken their place in his life, and that in actual fact he had been subconsciously prepared for them, or, more correctly, been ready to receive them; something within him was poised to engender them when the right moment came and, strange to say, that something was his character as a professor of history. But Dr Cornelius does not tell anyone this, and anyway, he knows it only occasionally, with a secret smile on his lips. He knows that professors of history have no liking for history while it is happening, but only after it has happened; that they hate the upheavals of the present, considering them disorderly, incoherent and impertinent, in a word 'unhistorical', and that their heart belongs instead to the coherent, upright and historical past. For the past, the university scholar admits as he takes his walk by the river before the evening meal, is robed in the aura of timelessness and eternity, an aura with considerably more appeal to the nerves of a university professor than the effronteries of the present. The past is immortalized, which is to say: it is dead, and death is the source of all piety and all sustaining sensibility. Walking alone in the darkness, the Professor secretly accepts this. His conservative instinct, his appreciation of the 'eternal', has sought refuge from the brashness of the times in the love of his little daughter, for paternal love and an infant at its mother's breast—these are timeless and eternal, and therefore sacred and beautiful. And yet in the darkness Cornelius sees that something is not quite right and proper about this love of his—this he concedes theoretically, in the spirit of scholarly discipline. It has its roots in something tendentious, this love; it contains enmity, opposition towards history as it is happening now in favour of history that has happened, and that is death. This is strange enough, yet it is also true;

yes, in its way, true. The vehement ardour he feels for this tiny scrap of life and progeny has something to do with death; it bolsters his defence against life, and in a certain sense this is not really very good—but then it would be to take asceticism to insane lengths if, merely because of some incidental academic insight, one were to tear so pure and lovely a feeling from one's heart.

He steadies his darling daughter on his lap, her thin little legs dangling from his knees, and talks to her in a tender and playfully deferential manner, his eyebrows raised, entranced as she answers and calls him 'Abel' in her sweetly piping voice. At the same time, he exchanges meaningful glances with her mother, who is looking after her Biter and gently urging him to be sensible and control his temper, for today, exasperated by life's difficulties, the boy has been overwhelmed by another tantrum, behaving like a wailing dervish. Cornelius also throws the occasional, somewhat wary glance at the Big Ones, for he considers it not beyond the bounds of possibility that they are no strangers to certain intellectual notions entertained by him during his evening stroll. If so, they aren't showing it. Standing behind their chairs, with their arms propped on the backrests, they follow the blissful parental scene with sympathy, and some irony.

The children are wearing thick, brick-red artist's smocks with fashionably modern embroidery; these were once Ingrid's and Bert's, and are quite alike, except that in Biter's case, his short little trouser legs protrude. They also have the same pageboy haircuts. Biter's hair, an uneven blond that is gradually turning darker, sticks out at all angles; shaggy, it has the appearance of a small, comical, ill-fitting wig. Little Lori's, by contrast, is auburn, silken, fine and glossy, and just as lovely as the rest of her little person. It covers her ears, which, as everyone knows, are of different size: one of them is proportionate, the other slightly irregular, in fact decidedly too large. Her father occasionally uncovers them and exaggerates his surprise, as if noticing the tiny deformity for the first time, embarrassing Lori, but also amusing her. Set far apart, her eyes are a golden brown with a cute gleam, the sweetest gaze one can imagine. The brows above them are blond. Her nose is still quite unformed, with fairly thick nostrils whose nasal passages are almost circular, while her mouth is large and expressive, with a beautifully curved, agile upper lip. When she smiles, revealing the gapped pearls of her baby teeth (she has lost only one so far—she let her father wiggle the wobbly thing out with his handkerchief, at which she turned very pale and trembled), she has dimples, whose rather concave form, for all the infantile softness of her cheeks, derives from a slightly protruding lower face. On one cheek, near the artless tumble of her hair, she has a downy mole.

All in all, she herself is less than satisfied with her looks—a sure sign that she cares about them. Her face, she considers dolefully, just happens to be ugly; her 'little figure', however, is quite nice. She has a love of choice short, sophisticated phrases, which she strings together: 'possibly, of course, in the end'. Biter's self-critical worries have more to do with morality. He tends towards remorse, deems himself an arch-sinner because of his tantrums, and is convinced he won't go to Heaven but to 'Hole', as he calls it. Telling him that God has great understanding and knows when to turn a blind eye doesn't help at all; in his glum obstinacy he shakes his head along with its ill-fitting wig of hair and declares that for him salvation is out of bounds. If he has a cold, he seems full of phlegm; lay as much as a finger on him and he'll clatter and creak from top to bottom, his fever so dreadful he can only puff and pant. This brings out the fatalist, regarding Biter's constitution, in Nanny Anna Blue, for in her opinion a boy with 'such uncommonly fat blood' might have a stroke at any moment. On one occasion she supposed such a terrible moment to have arrived, after Biter, in a fit of rage, had gone berserk and been told as a punishment to stand in the corner with his face to the wall—which face, on random inspection, was found to have turned blue all over, much bluer than Anna's own. Soon she had the whole household up on their feet, while she announced that the boy's far-too-fat blood had brought about his final hour, and naughty Biter, to his sincere astonishment, suddenly found himself swathed in anxious affection, until it transpired that the blue of his features did not derive from apoplexy, but from paint on the wall of the nursery, whose indigo hue had smeared his tear-stained face.

Nanny Anna has come in, too, and stands by the door with her hands folded over her white apron; she has a glossy hairdo, goose eyes and a demeanour that befits the austere dignity of her limitations. 'The children', she declares, proud of her care and instruction, have done 'decipherably well'. She has recently had seventeen septic tooth stumps extracted and replaced by a uniform set of false yellow teeth with dark-red rubber gums, embellishing her peasant's face. Her thoughts are captivated by the peculiar notion that her false teeth are a widespread topic of conversation—that they are, so to speak, the talk of the town. 'There's been a lot of idle gossip', she states sternly and mystically, 'because it's well known I've had new teeth fitted.' Her speech shows a general tendency towards obscurity and vagueness, with scant concern for whether she is understood by others or not, as in the example of a certain 'Dr Bleifuss', who is 'known to every child', adding that there are 'more living in the house who pretend to be him'. One can only be indulgent in such matters. She teaches the children nice poems, for example:

Railway, railway,
Engine, steam and soot,
Puffing away or here to stay
It makes a little toot.

Or this weekly menu, full of privation as befits the times, but no less jolly for that:

On Monday we go without,
On Tuesday make do with kraut,
On Wednesday we're stuck in the middle,
On Thursday we play on the fiddle.
On Friday we wish for fish,
Saturday's gruel in a dish,
On Sundays it's cutlet for all,
And if we're good, coleslaw.

Then there is a certain four-liner of inscrutable and unsettled romance:

Open the gate, open there,
Let in the grand carriage.
Who sits in that carriage?
*A lord with golden hair!**

And finally, the unbearably jovial ballad of Marie who sat on a stone, a stone, a stone, combing her—again—golden hair, golden hair, golden hair, and of Rudolf, who pulled out a knife, a knife, a knife, and who came to a nasty end.

With her agile little mouth and sweet voice, Lori sings and recites these pieces endearingly—and much better than Biter does. She does everything better than Biter, and he sincerely admires her and defers to her in all things, except during his fits of rebelliousness and rough-and-tumble tantrums. She often takes a scientific approach, explaining the birds in their picture book, telling him their names: the cloud-eater, the hail-eater, the raven-eater. She demands he repeat them after her. She instructs him in medical matters, too, teaching him the names of illnesses such as chest-itis, blood-itis and breath-itis. If he doesn't pay attention and fails to repeat what she says, she makes him stand in the corner. She even boxed his ears on one occasion, but was so ashamed of what she had done that she went and stood in a corner herself for quite a long time.

Oh yes, they get on well together; they are the very best of friends. They experience everything together, all their adventures. They come home full of excitement, recounting as with one voice that they saw 'two moo-cows and a veal' in the lane. They are on familiar terms with the servants downstairs, with Xaver and the Hinterhöfer ladies, two formerly middle-class sisters who are 'au pairs', as the phrase goes, that is, who in return for board and lodging perform the duties of cook and chambermaid; periodically, at least, the children sense that their own relationship to their parents is similar to that of the downstairs servants. If they receive a scolding, they go to the kitchen and say: 'Master and Mistress are cross!' Nonetheless, it is still nicer playing upstairs, especially with 'Abel' when he doesn't have to read and write. He thinks of more marvellous things to do than Xaver and the ladies. When the two of them play at being 'four gentlemen' going for a walk, 'Abel' bends his knees until he's the same height as the children, and then he goes walking with them, hand in hand. They can't get enough of this; if they could, they would walk round and round the dining room with little 'Abel' all day—five gentlemen in all.

Then there is the wholly thrilling cushion game, in which one of the children, usually Lori, apparently unnoticed by Abel, sits as quietly as a mouse on one of the dining-table chairs and waits for him to come. Glancing around him and applauding with his loud voice the anticipated comforts of sitting down, he approaches the chair and takes his place on top of Lori. 'What's all this, then?' he says, shifting back and forth, deaf to the unseen and increasingly loud giggling behind his back. 'Has someone placed a cushion on my chair? What sort of a hard, lumpy, annoying cushion is this I'm sitting on, and in such obvious discomfort, too?!' And squirming about more and more vigorously on this particularly odd cushion, he reaches behind his back and finds himself grasping a rapturous bundle of giggles and squeaks, whereupon he turns around at last, and a grand finale of discovery and recognition concludes the drama. Even repeated hundreds of times, this game too loses none of its excitement.

There will be no such entertainment today. The upheaval of the imminent Big Ones' party is in the air, and before that there's the shopping trip with its apportioned roles. Little Lori has only just recited 'Railway, railway', and Dr Cornelius, to her embarrassment, has barely finished discovering that her ears are of quite different size, when in walks Danny, the neighbours' son, to pick up Ingrid and Bert; and Xaver too has swapped his striped livery for a plain jacket, which straight away lends him a somewhat rakish, albeit nevertheless smart and amiable appearance. And so the Little Ones repair with Nanny Anna to their upstairs kingdom and the Professor withdraws to his study to read, as is his wont after lunch, while his wife turns her thoughts and activities to the anchovy sandwiches and Italian salad that still need preparing for the dance party. Before the young people turn up, she also has to cycle to town with her shopping basket to purchase food in exchange for a sum of money she has in her possession, before it loses its value.

Cornelius leans back in his chair reading. With his cigar resting between index and middle finger he reads a passage in Macaulay* about the origins of English national debt at the end of the seventeenth century and then another by a French author about Spain's increasing debt accumulation towards the end of the sixteenth—both for tomorrow morning's lecture. For he wishes to compare England's surprising economic prosperity at that time with the disastrous effects of Spanish debt accumulation a hundred years earlier, and to analyse the ethical and psychological reasons for the disparity between them. This will allow him to proceed from William III's* England, the current focus of his course, to the age of Philip II* and the Counter-Reformation,* his own pet subject, about which he has written a highly regarded book—a much-cited work, to which he owes his tenured professorship. With his cigar becoming rather too pungent as it approaches its end, he runs through several faintly melancholy sentences that he intends to read out to his students: on the objectively futile struggle of the dilatory Philip against the New, the course of history, the powers respectively of the individual and of Germanic freedom, both of them conducive to the dissolution of empires, and on the doomed and godforsaken struggle of obstinate gentility against the might of progress and change. The sentences meet his approval and he continues to polish them while returning the volumes he has used to their places in the shelves and ascending to his bedroom to take his usual break, that quiet hour he needs with closed shutters and closed eyes, which today, as he recalls now that his scientific distractions are behind him, will take place under the sign of rumbustious domestic festivities. He smiles at the light palpitations this recollection induces in him; in his head the sentences he has drafted about Philip dressed in black silks mingle with the thought of the children's house ball, and he dozes off for five minutes.

Repeatedly, while lying and resting, he hears a ring at the door or the shutting of the garden gate, and each time he feels a small stab of excitement, of anticipation and trepidation at the thought that the young people are already arriving and crowding the entrance hall, and with every stab he smiles to himself, and yet even his smile is an expression of nervousness, although it does, of course, contain a portion of joy, too; for who wouldn't look forward to a party. At half past four (by now it's evening) he gets up to refresh himself at the wash-stand. For a year now its wash-bowl has been damaged. It's meant to tilt, but has broken away from its hinge at one side and can be neither repaired, there being nobody to come and fix it, nor replaced, because no shop can deliver a new one. As a makeshift solution it's been suspended above the drain at the edge of the marble top and can only be emptied by lifting it with both hands and pouring the water out. Cornelius shakes his head at the bowl, which he does several times every day, then gets ready—and takes meticulous care, too, polishing his glasses under the ceiling light until they are clean and shiny. Then he sets off downstairs.

Hearing the hubbub of voices at the bottom of the stairs and the gramophone already playing, his face assumes a socially obliging expression. 'Please don't let me disturb you!' are the words he resolves to say before heading straight into the dining room for tea. The sentence seems just right for the occasion, he thinks: nothing less than cheerful and considerate to the young folk, and a suitable bulwark for himself.

The hallway is brightly lit; all the chandelier's electric candles are glowing but for a single spent one. On one of the lower stairs Cornelius pauses and surveys the hall. It looks pretty in this light, with the Marées* copy above the brick fireplace, the softwood wainscoting too, and then the red carpet with their guests standing around chatting with cups of tea and half-slices of bread spread with anchovy paste.

There's a party atmosphere, an airy haze of clothes, hair and breath wafting over the hallway, all distinctive and unforgettable. The cloakroom door is open, for some guests are still to arrive.

Initially, company dazzles; what the Professor sees is merely the general picture. He hasn't noticed Ingrid in a black silk dress, her arms bare and a white pleated shawl thrown over her shoulders, standing right in front of him at the bottom of the stairs with her friends. She nods, smiling up at him, revealing her beautiful teeth.

'Rested?' she asks softly, so that only he hears. When, with an unwarranted start, he recognizes her, she introduces him to her friends.

'May I introduce you to Herr Huber?' she asks. 'This is Fräulein Plaichinger.'

Herr Huber is feeble-looking; Fräulein Plaichinger, however, is a Germania*—blonde, voluptuous, in a flowing robe, with a snub nose and the high-pitched voice corpulent ladies often have, as can be heard when she answers the Professor's courteous greeting.

'Ah, welcome, welcome!' he says. 'So glad you could do us the honour. You'll be taking exams with Ingrid, am I right?'

Herr Huber is a golf-club friend of Ingrid's. He's in business, employed at his uncle's brewery, and for a moment the Professor pulls his leg about the thinness of the beer, pretending to overestimate vastly young Huber's influence on its quality. 'But don't let me disturb you, will you!' he then says, making as if to cross to the dining room.

'And here comes Max,' says Ingrid. 'Now, Max, you slacker, dilly-dallying to dance and repast.'

The young ones are very familiar and informal with one other; they are on first-name terms straight away, which the older generation finds quite disconcerting: barely a trace of propriety, gallantry or decorum anywhere.

A young man with a white dicky and thin black bow tie approaches from the cloakroom to greet his friends—dark-haired, but with a ruddy complexion, clean-shaven, of course, but with a hint of whiskers near the ears, a lovely boy in fact, not pretty in a laughable or flamboyant manner, like a Gypsy fiddler, but handsome in a wholly likeable, decent and winning way, with kind dark eyes and a rather awkwardly fitting dinner-suit.

'Oh, come on, don't scold me, Cornelia. It's the stupid lectures,' he says, and Ingrid presents him to her father as Herr Hergesell.

So, this is Herr Hergesell, is it? Well-bred young man that he is, he thanks his host for the kind invitation while they shake hands. 'Yes, I'm straggling,' he says, and continues with a bit of wordplay. 'Yes, we had no bananas* today, not till after the four o'clock lecture anyway, and I still had to go home and get changed.' Then he holds forth about his pumps, which have apparently been causing him considerable distress in the cloakroom.

'I brought them in my bag,' he says. 'It certainly wouldn't do for us to come here and trample all over your carpet in our outdoor shoes, would it? But like some reckless idiot, I forgot to bring a shoehorn, and I couldn't get into them for the life of me, ha-ha, what a carry-on! In all my days I've never had such a tight pair of shoes. And you can't rely on getting the same size either, and then there's the material, it's so hard these days—just look! That's not leather, it's cast iron! My forefinger's completely squashed...' And confidingly he holds up his reddened finger while again referring to the whole incident as a 'carry-on', and a vile one at that. He really does speak like Ingrid's imitation of him: a nasal, quite distinctive drawl, which was evidently not affected at all, but was quite simply the manner of all Hergesells.

Dr Cornelius deplores the absence of a shoehorn in the cloakroom and bestows sympathy on the forefinger. 'Now you really mustn't let me disturb you any further,' he says. 'Goodbye!' And he crosses the hallway to the dining room.

Here, too, are guests, sitting around the extended family dining-table drinking tea. However, the Professor heads straight for a small recess decorated with embroidery and lit by a ceiling light, a snug with its own little round table where he usually takes tea. There he finds his wife conversing with Bert and two other young men. One of these is Herzl, whom Cornelius knows and greets. The other is called Möller, evidently the rambling Wandervogel* type, who neither owns nor cares to own the appropriately formal evening wear (which, in fact, no longer exists anyway), a young person with no intention of playing the 'gentleman' (who no longer exists, either). He is wearing a belted blouse and short trousers, has thick, stylishly swept-back hair, a long neck and horn-rimmed spectacles. He is in the banking profession, the Professor is told, but also has an artistic vein and is what one might call a folklorist, a collector and singer of folk-songs from all continents and languages. Today, too, he has responded to a request to bring along his guitar, at present still hanging in its oilcloth case in the cloakroom.

Herzl, the actor, is short and slim, but has a heavy black beard growth, discernible through the powder he has dusted on after shaving. His eyes are unexpectedly large, sultry and deeply melancholy, and yet he has not only applied plenty of shaving powder, but also, it appears, some rouge—the faint crimson of his cheekbones being of obvious cosmetic origin. Odd, thinks the Professor; you'd think it would be either melancholy or make-up. Taken together, isn't it a mental contradiction? How could a melancholic paint his face? On the other hand, that's probably where the exceptional and uncommonly psychological form of the artist shows through and makes such a contradiction possible, possibly itself actually consisting of it, no less. Interesting, and no reason to abandon common courtesy. His is a legitimate form, indeed a primordial form… 'May I offer you some lemon, Herr Hofschauspieler?'

Court actors don't exist at all any more, but Herzl is happy to be addressed so, despite being a revolutionary artist. And that's another of these contradictions that belong to his psychological type. The Professor presumes as much, and is justified in doing so, and flatters him, partly to atone for the secret umbrage he has taken at Herzl's applying a little rouge to his cheeks.

'My deepest gratitude, my dear Herr Professor!', Herzl blurts out so precipitately that only his excellent enunciation skills can prevent his tongue from tripping up. His behaviour generally towards his hosts, and in particular towards the master of the house, shows the greatest respect, in fact more than that, it demonstrates an almost excessive and obsequious politeness. It is as though he has a bad conscience on account of the rouge, which he had initially applied out of inner compulsion but has now come to disapprove of out of deference to the Professor's sensibility, and which he now hopes to make up for by virtue of his great humility towards the unrouged world.

Sipping their tea they chat about Möller's folk-songs—about Spanish and Basque folk-songs—and before long they are discussing the new production of Schiller's *Don Carlos* at the State Theatre, a production with Herzl in the title role. He talks of his Carlos. 'I hope my Carlos is all of a piece,' he says. Then they review the other members of the cast, commenting on the staging, the setting, and at this point the Professor sees that he is being steered back to his wonted course, his Spain of the Counter-Reformation, a thought he finds almost embarrassing. It isn't his fault, after all; he has done nothing to point the conversation in this direction. He fears it will look as if he has exploited the opportunity to pontificate; this surprises him, and he says nothing. He is relieved when the Little Ones, Lori and Biter, join them at the table. They are dressed in blue velvet Sunday outfits, and want, in their own way, to take part in the Big Ones' party too, until bedtime. Shy and wide-eyed, they say hello to strangers and have to recite their names and age. Herr Möller just looks at them earnestly, while actor Herzl appears wholly entranced and enraptured by them. He virtually blesses them, lifting his eyes to the heavens and folding his hands in front of his mouth. No doubt he means it sincerely, but his being used to the milieu and methods of the theatre renders his speech and gestures frightfully false, and furthermore, it looks as if his devotion to the children is also intended to make up for the rouge on his cheekbones.

The guests' tea-table has been cleared, and now there is dancing in the hall; the Little Ones run over, while the Professor makes to withdraw. 'Enjoy yourselves, won't you!', he says, shaking hands with Herr Möller and Herr Herzl, who have leapt to their feet. Then he walks across to his study, his peaceful realm, where he pulls down the blinds, turns on the desk lamp, and sits down to work.

This is work he can do at a pinch in a noisy environment: a few letters, a couple of excerpts. Of course Cornelius feels distracted. He dwells on trifling impressions: Herr Hergesell's intractable pumps, the Plaichinger girl's piping voice in her fat body. As he writes or leans back in his chair staring into space, his thoughts also return to Möller's collection of Basque songs, to Herzl's humility and exaggerations, 'his Carlos' and Philip's court. Conversations are mysterious, he finds. They are compliant; they follow our secretly dominant interests without our directing them. It's something he's often noticed, he thinks. Meanwhile, he listens to the sounds of the party beyond his door, which are actually not noisy at all. Just some talking, not even the shuffle of dancers' feet is audible. They aren't shuffling in a circle anyway, but moving about the room in a curious manner on the carpet, which doesn't bother them, while holding each other quite differently from the way they did it in his day; and they are doing so to the sounds of a gramophone, which is what he is mainly listening to, these strange tunes of the New World with their jazzy orchestration and all sorts of percussion, of which the machine gives a splendid rendering, and with that clickety-clack of castanets put to effect solely as jazz instruments, with nothing Spanish about them. No, nothing Spanish. And with that, his work thoughts take over again.

Half an hour later it occurs to him that it would be no more than friendly of him to contribute a packet of cigarettes to the revelry. It is surely not acceptable, he tells himself, for the young people to have to smoke their own cigarettes, although they probably wouldn't think twice about it. And so he enters the empty dining room and selects a packet from his personal store in the small wall cabinet—not the best, nor the brand he himself likes to smoke, but a sort that are rather too long and thin and which he wouldn't mind getting rid of on this occasion; they are young people, after all. He goes out into the hall and, with a smile on his face, lifts up the packet for all to see and places it—open—on the mantelpiece, whereupon, with scarcely a glance around the room, he sets off again for his study.

Now there's a pause in the dancing. The music machine is silent. They are all standing around chatting at the edge of the hall, or sitting at the armorial table by the windows, or on chairs in front of the fireplace. This amphitheatre of young folk also includes one or two on the worn-out plush runner of the staircase: Max Hergesell, for example, half reclined, with one elbow propped behind him on the step above and the other hand gesticulating as he speaks, while the shrill and voluptuous Fräulein Plaichinger gazes into his eyes. The main part of the floor is empty, except for the space right in the middle of the room, directly under the chandelier, where the two Little Ones in their blue-velvet Sunday attire cling to each other awkwardly, going round and round in a silent daze. Crossing the floor, Cornelius bends down and, with a kind remark, strokes their hair without disturbing them in their earnest little pursuit. But glancing back as he goes out, he catches sight of Hergesell; probably because he has been observing the Professor, the student of engineering pushes off from the stairs with his elbow and comes down into the middle of the room, where he takes Lori out of her brother's arms and begins a comical dance with her, without music. Almost like Cornelius himself when he does his walk with the 'four gentlemen', the student bends his knees and, lowering his body to where he can hold her as if she were a big girl, performs a few shimmy-steps with bashful little Lori. Anyone watching finds it highly amusing. It's a sign to set the gramophone turning again, and for everybody to return to the dance floor. The Professor, the door-handle already in his hand, continues to watch for a moment, nodding his head and laughing with his shoulders, then he enters his room. For several minutes his face mechanically retains the smile he had on outside the door.

He turns a few pages in the light of his desk lamp and writes, dealing with a few undemanding practical matters. After a while he notices that the guests have left the hall for his wife's drawing room, which is connected to both the hall and his own room. He can hear talking, and the tentative sounds of someone tuning a guitar. So Herr Möller is going to sing, and indeed has already begun. Strumming a resonant accompaniment the young bank clerk, with his powerful bass voice, sings a song in a foreign tongue—perhaps Swedish? All the way through to the end, which meets with considerable applause, the Professor is unable to identify the language with any certainty. There's a portière behind the door to the drawing room, muffling the sound. When a new song starts, Cornelius warily goes through.

The drawing room is in semi-darkness, lit only by the shaded standard lamp, near which sits Möller with one leg crossed over the other on a cushioned settle, thumbing the strings of his instrument. Since there aren't enough seats to go round, the audience has dropped any semblance of formality and assumed a makeshift, casual character. Some stand, while others, including young ladies, simply sit on the floor, on the carpet, with their arms clasped around their knees, or with their legs stretched out in front of them. Hergesell, for example, though wearing a dinner suit, is seated in the same manner at the foot of the grand piano, with Fräulein Plaichinger beside him. The Little Ones are there too: Frau Cornelius, in her armchair opposite the singer, has them on her lap, and Biter, the barbarian, starts talking loudly over the singing so that he has to be terrorized with finger-wagging and shushing. Lori, all sweetness and quiet on her mother's knee, would never be so naughty. The Professor tries to catch her eye, as if to secretly wave to his little girl, but she doesn't see him, indeed she doesn't seem to be paying much attention to the artist either. Her gaze is deeper.

Möller is singing the '*Joli tambour*':*

'*Sire, mon roi, donnez-moi votre fille—*'*

Everyone is delighted. 'How fine!' Hergesell is heard to drawl in the signally nasal and, as it were, spoilt tone of all Hergesells. Now

Möller is playing something German, for which he has composed the tune himself. It is a beggar's song, and earns the youngsters' rapturous applause:

> 'Beggar-girl will a-rovin' go,
> Tura-hi a-di tura-ho!
> Beggar-boy 'll a-courtin' go,
> Turadi-diddle-dum-dee.'

There is nothing less than jubilation following the jaunty beggar's song. 'How exceptionally fine!' opines Hergesell, again in his own way. Then comes something Hungarian followed by a hit song rendered in its wholly outlandish original language—for Möller a triumph. The Professor, too, ostentatiously joins in the applause. This impact of culture and historicizing retrospective artistry on the shimmying and socializing warms his heart. He approaches Möller and congratulates him, discusses the songs with him as well as his source materials: a songbook with scores, which Möller promises to lend him for inspection. Cornelius's affability towards him has grown because, like all fathers, he can't help comparing the talents and values of this young stranger with those of his own son, and now he feels vexed, envious and ashamed as a result. 'Here's this Möller,' he thinks, 'a hard-working bank clerk' (he has no idea whether Möller really is hard-working). 'And yet he also boasts this special talent, whose development naturally must have necessitated considerable study and energy. And then there's my poor Bert who doesn't know anything and can't do anything and whose only thought is of playing the buffoon, though I doubt he has talent enough for that either!' But he wants to be fair and, giving it his best, he tells himself that in spite of everything Bert is a fine chap, and that he may ultimately have greater resources than Möller, however successful the latter; perhaps there's a poet in him, or something, and anyway, in his dancing-waiter plans he's just a boy in troubling times chasing after some will-o'-the-wisp. But his envious father's pessimism proves stronger.—When Möller starts up with another song, Dr Cornelius retires to his room.

As he goes about his business, distractedly, as before, it turns seven; and now that he has remembered a short, matter-of-fact letter he might yet write with little effort, and since writing is a great pastime, it is soon almost seven-thirty. The Italian salad is due at half past eight; it is time the Professor went out, posted his letters, and took his portion of fresh air and exercise in the winter darkness. By this time, the ball in the hall has started up again, and he will have to pass between the dancers to reach his coat and overshoes, but that won't be of much interest to anybody this time: he is nothing but an attendant at this youthful social event; they have seen him several times already, and so he needn't worry about disturbing anyone. After tidying away his papers safely and gathering up his letters he leaves the room, and, on finding his wife sitting in an armchair near the door, even decides to stay on for a while in the hallway.

There she sits, looking on, now and then receiving visits from the Big Ones and from other young people, and Cornelius stands alongside her, watching too, smiling at the lively goings-on which have evidently now reached their peak. There are other spectators, too: Anna Blue, standing by the stairs in all her austere rigidity—because the Little Ones cannot get enough of the party and because she must pay attention that Biter does not twirl about too much because of the danger of his awfully fat blood boiling in his veins. But the downstairs world, too, wants its share of the Big Ones' dancing fun: Xaver and the Hinterhöfer ladies are standing at the pantry door enjoying the spectacle. Fräulein Walburga, the older of the déclassé sisters and the one who cooks (to avoid describing her as an actual cook, to which she objects), gazes with brown eyes through thick round glasses, whose bridge, to prevent it pressing on her nose, is padded round with a small piece of cloth, a jolly, sweet-natured sort, while Cecilia, the younger one, although not exactly young, has, as ever, a particularly smug expression on her face—her way of defending her dignity as a former member of the third estate. Cecilia suffers especially bitterly as a result of her plunge from the petit-bourgeois sphere to the lower stratum of servant status. She refuses adamantly to wear a bonnet or any other badge of the housemaid's profession, and her worst hour comes regularly every Wednesday when Xaver is off-duty and she has to do the serving. She serves with her face averted and her nose turned up, a fallen queen; it's a deeply depressing ordeal to see her humiliated so, and the Little Ones, happening to be present at dinner one evening, started weeping loudly at the sight of her, both of them at the very same moment.

Young Xaver knows no such sorrow. In fact he enjoys serving and does so with a skill as natural as it is born of practice, for he was once an apprentice waiter. Otherwise, he is a downright good-for-nothing and fully blown windbag to boot—with positive qualities, too, as his unassuming master is forever ready to admit, but an impossible windbag nonetheless. One must just accept him as he is, and not expect to gather figs from thorns. He is the child and product of unhinged times, a typical example of his generation, a servant of the Revolution, a likeable Bolshevist. The Professor often refers to him as the 'Master of Ceremonies', because he can be relied upon to hold his own when some unusual or diverting situation calls for it, generally proving himself both obliging and quick to learn. But the notion of duty is entirely unknown to him and he can no more be persuaded to fulfil humdrum everyday tasks than certain dogs can be made to jump over a stick. Evidently, and disarmingly, it would go against his nature, robbing one of the will to prosecute the matter further. He would be willing to get up at any hour of the night if it were for something unusual or intriguing. But usually he doesn't get up before eight o'clock—and that's it, he simply doesn't, he won't jump over the stick, and yet all day long the expressions of his easy-going existence—his mouth organ playing, his hoarse but passionate singing, his cheerful whistling—resound from the basement kitchens throughout the floors above, while his cigarette smoke fills the pantry. He idles, watching the declassed ladies work. In the morning, while the Professor is having breakfast, Xaver tears off the daily sheet on his master's desk calendar—otherwise, he doesn't lift a finger in that room. Dr Cornelius has often told him to leave his calendar alone because Xaver has a tendency to tear off two days at a time, with the risk of increasing disorder. But young Xaver enjoys the work of page-tearing; he refuses to give it up.

Incidentally, he is a friend to children, and that is part of his charm. Playing games with the Little Ones in the garden he is himself as childlike as can be, carving pieces of wood, using his skills to make this and that for them, and he even reads their books to them, his thick lips making it quite peculiar to listen to. He loves the cinema from the bottom of his heart, and when he has been there inclines towards melancholy, wistfulness and soliloquies. He is stirred by vague hopes of one day belonging to that world himself and of finding happiness there. He bases such hopes on the manner in which he flicks back his thick hair, on his bodily agility and daredevilry. He often climbs the ash tree in the front garden, a tall but pliant tree, scaling it branch by branch all the way up, frightening the life out of anyone who watches. Once at the top he lights a cigarette, making the whole tree sway from top to toe, and from his crow's nest keeping a lookout for any film director on his way here to hire him.

Were he to take off his striped jacket and don a plain one, he could simply be one of the others, no longer the odd one out. The Big Ones and their friends are a fairly diverse-looking bunch; some of them wear formal evening dress, but it isn't the dominant impression. There are quite a few types like Möller, the balladeer, sprinkled among them, both on the female side and amongst the young men. To the Professor observing the scene from his place beside his wife's armchair, the circumstances and social backgrounds of these members of the younger generation have become familiar through hearsay. On the female side they are shortly to sit school-leaving exams, or are already students at university or at the School of Arts and Crafts; on the male side, one or two of them lead entirely adventurous existences, unique creations of their era. One pale beanpole of a youth with pearl buttons in his shirt, the son of a dentist, is nothing but a speculator on the stock exchange and, according to everything the Professor has heard, lives the life of Aladdin with his magic lamp. He has a car, invites his friends to champagne suppers and loves to distribute gifts among them whenever the opportunity arises: small but costly keepsakes in gold or mother-of-pearl, for example. Today, too, he has brought along presents for his young hosts: a gold pencil for Bert, and for Ingrid a pair of gigantic earrings, real hoops of a barbaric size, which, thank goodness, are not for inserting through the earlobes but for clipping onto them. The Big Ones come laughing and showing off their presents to their parents, who shake their heads in admiration, while again and again Aladdin, at a distance, takes a bow.

The young folk dance with enthusiasm, in as far the actions they are performing with such quiet devotion can be called dancing. They shuffle slowly around the carpet, holding each other in their peculiar, novel posture—bellies forward, shoulders back, hips swaying somewhat—going through their paces according to some obscure rulebook, and without tiring, because this is not the sort of thing that can make one tired. No sign of heaving bosoms here, not even of rosy cheeks. Here and there two girls dance with each other, occasionally even two young men; it's all the same to them. This is their way of moving to the exotic strains of a gramophone played with needles robust enough to blare out shimmies, foxtrots and one-steps, all these double foxes, African shimmies, Java dances and Creole polkas—wild and spicy stuff with a foreign rhythm that is part languishing, part martial, a monotonous Negro entertainment dressed up in orchestral frills, drums, jingle-jangle and clickety-clacks.

'What's that record called?' Cornelius asks Ingrid as she shuffles past with the pale speculator to a piece with a particularly soulful, pressing beat, certain of whose inventive details he finds comparatively appealing.

'The Prince of Pappenheim: Take comfort, fair child,' says she, and smiles back nicely with her white teeth.

Cigarette smoke wafts beneath the chandelier. The haze of sociability has thickened—that dryly sweet, substance-rich, heady party miasma that all find so redolent of juvenile heartache, and especially those who have survived an all-too-sensitive youth… The Little Ones are still in the hallway; since they are enjoying the party so much, they are permitted to stay up until eight o'clock. The young folk have got used to them joining in; to a certain extent, and in their own way, they too are a part of it all. As a matter of fact they have separated: Biter, in his blue-velvet smock, twirls round and round on his own in the middle of the carpet, while Lori comically pursues a shimmying couple, trying to hold on to the man's dinner jacket. The jacket belongs to Max Hergesell, dancing with his lady friend, Fräulein Plaichinger. They shimmy well, a pleasure to watch. One has to admit that there is actually much enjoyment to be had from these dances of the wild new times, especially when the right people are dancing them. Young Hergesell leads admirably, apparently improvising, but within the rules. How elegant his backward steps, when the space behind him allows! But even on the packed dance floor, he acquits himself with style, aided by the suppleness of a partner who is blessed with that unforeseen grace of which corpulent women are sometimes capable. They are conversing cheek to cheek and seem unaware of Lori's attentions. Others laugh at the small girl's pertinacity, and when the group comes past, Dr Cornelius attempts to intercept his little girl and to draw her towards him. But Lori, in her consternation, twists herself free and wants none of Abel now. He is nothing to her, and she stretches her little arm out, pushing against his chest, her beloved face averted, in her state of anguish and annoyance trying to escape him, following her own fancy.

The Professor can't help feeling aggrieved by this. For a moment he hates this party whose ingredients have confused his favourite little girl and turned her heart against him. His love for her, this not entirely unselfish love, with its not entirely unobjectionable roots, is sensitive. He smiles mechanically, but his eyes have misted over and become randomly 'fixed' upon the carpet pattern in front of him between the dancers' feet.

'The Little Ones ought to go to bed,' he tells his wife, but she begs for another half an hour for the children. It was a promise, she says, since they are having such a good time. He smiles again and shakes his head, standing there for a moment or two before going to the cloakroom, which is overflowing with coats, scarves, hats and galoshes.

He has trouble digging his own things out of this jumble, and as he is trying to do so, who should enter the cloakroom but Max Hergesell, wiping his brow with a handkerchief.

'Professor—', he says in the tone of all Hergesells, and gives a youthful bow. 'Are you on your way out? This to-do with my pumps is really frightful. They pinch as badly as Charlemagne's.* The things are just too small, it turns out, quite apart from how tough they are. This one's pressing here, on the nail of my big toe,' he says, standing on one leg while holding his other foot in both hands. 'It's almost beyond words. I'm going to have to change them; my street shoes will have to serve instead after all… Oh, may I be of assistance to you?'

'Well, thank you,' says Cornelius, 'but really no need! Better to liberate yourself from those fetters of yours! Most kind of you.' For Hergesell has lowered himself on one knee and fastened the clips of the Professor's galoshes.

The Professor thanks him, touched by the young man's respectful readiness to oblige. 'Enjoy the rest of the party,' he tells him, 'once you have changed! Of course you can't be dancing in shoes that pinch. You definitely must change them. Goodbye! I must get a breath of fresh air.'

'I'm off to dance with Lori again,' Hergesell calls after him. 'She'll be a super dancer when she's old enough, that's for sure!'

'Do you think so?' Cornelius replies, looking back from the front door. 'Well, you are the expert and champion. Let's just hope that with all that stooping, you don't get curvature of the spine!'

And with that he waves and is gone. 'Nice boy,' he thinks, leaving the house. 'Student of engineering, knows what he's about, all as it should be. So good-looking and friendly, too.' Again, remembering his 'poor Bert', he is gripped by paternal envy, a disquiet that makes him paint the young stranger's life in a rosy light, and his son's, by contrast, in the murkiest colours. And thus he sets off for his evening constitutional.

He walks up the avenue, crosses the bridge and, on the other side, continues downriver along the riverbank path towards the next bridge but one. It's cold and damp with occasional snow. He has turned up the collar of his coat and holds his walking stick behind his back, with its crook over his arm. Now and then he takes a deep breath, filling his lungs with wintry evening air. As usual when walking, his mind goes to scholarly matters, to his lecture course and the passages on Philip's struggle against Germanic insurrection that he wants to recite tomorrow and intends to be imbued with fairness and melancholy. Especially fairness, he thinks. For that is the spirit of scholarship, the principle of enlightenment, and it is the light by which we should show the world to young people, not only for the sake of their intellectual development, but also for humane and personal reasons: to avoid offending them, or in order not to aggrieve them indirectly in their political sensibilities, which these days, of course, are so dreadfully riven and contrary and contain so much dynamite that one may easily attract the ire of an opposing party, or raise a scandal if you are historically biased. But taking sides, he thinks, is quite simply not the historical approach; only fairness is historical. But that said, and with all due consideration… being fair is neither hot-headedness, nor is it the bright and buoyant piety of conviction. It is melancholy, and since it is by its very nature melancholic, it will also, equally by nature, and surreptitiously, sympathize with the melancholic and unpropitious side and force of history, more than with the bright and buoyant pious side. In the end, is this sympathy what it consists of, without which it could not exist? So that, ultimately, fairness does not exist? the Professor asks himself, and is so immersed in his train of thought that he posts his letters in the letter box by the next bridge but one and begins his homeward journey wholly unconsciously. The thought he is entertaining is a disturbing one for a scholar, but it is in itself scholarly, a matter of conscience and of psychology, and it is his duty to take it up impartially, whether inconvenient or not… Such are the reveries that accompany Dr Cornelius home.

Standing under the front door arch is Xaver, who seems to be looking out for him.

'Professor!' calls Xaver with his thick lips, flicking back his hair. 'If you will, sir, go up and see Lori. She's got it bad, sir.'

'What's wrong?' asks Cornelius in shock. 'Is she ill?'

'T'ain't exactly ill, sir,' Xaver replies. 'Juss, it knocked 'er flyin', and she's cryin' 'er 'art out. It's cos of that gentleman who was dancin' wi'er, the one with the dicky-bow. Didn't want to leave the 'all, did she, tears rollin' down 'er cheeks too. Knocked 'er flyin' alright, quite bad, sir.'

'Nonsense,' says the Professor, already inside, tossing his things into the cloakroom. He says no more, opens the screened glass door to the hallway, and without even a glance at the dancers, heads straight for the staircase on the right. He takes the steps two at a time and, making his way along the upper hallway, turns down a short corridor and steps straight into the nursery, followed by Xaver, who holds back at the door.

In the nursery the lights are still burning. There is a coloured-paper picture frieze along the walls, a big shelf stuffed with toys, a rocking horse with red-lacquered nostrils bracing a hoof on one of its curved rockers, and other toys—a diminutive trumpet, building bricks, toy train carriages—all scattered across the linoleum floor. The white cot beds are not far apart: Lori's right in the corner, by the window, and Biter's a few feet away, but more towards the middle of the room.

Biter is asleep. As usual, with help from Anna Blue, he has said his prayers in his resounding voice and instantly fallen into the wild, ruddy-cheeked glow of that terrifically deep slumber of his which not even a cannon fired by his bedside could disturb; on either side of his little head his clenched fists, flung backwards onto the pillow, lie next to his sweat-matted, sleep-tousled, ill-fitting wig.

Lori's bed is surrounded by women. Besides Anna Blue, the Hinterhöfer ladies are at the cot side too, conferring with Anna as well as with each other. As the Professor approaches they stand aside, and there, sitting among her little pillows, is Lori, pale of face, weeping and sobbing so bitterly that Dr Cornelius cannot remember ever having seen her so. Her lovely little hands rest on the blanket in front of her. Her nightie, with its narrow lace border, has slipped over her lean, birdlike shoulders, and her head, that sweet little head Cornelius loves so much, with its protruding lower face so unusually flower-like on the thin stalk of her neck, is tilted back to one side, so that, with her tearful eyes directed into the corner where the wall meets the ceiling, she appears to be constantly nodding at her own great heartache, as if it were up there somewhere. For whether deliberately and expressively or because of her convulsive sobbing, her little head nods and wobbles ceaselessly, while her agile mouth, with its bow-shaped upper lip, remains parted, like that of a little *mater dolorosa*, and while tears pour from her eyes, she lets out a repetitive wailing that bears no resemblance whatsoever to the irritating and unnecessary shrieking of misbehaved children, but which comes from genuine anguish of the heart, filling the Professor, who cannot bear to see Lori weeping at any time, with an unbearable sympathy.

This sympathy is expressed in the extreme irritation he feels towards the attendant Hinterhöfer ladies.

'There must be a lot of work preparing dinner this evening,' the Professor declares impetuously. 'Can it be, I wonder, that my wife is being left to take care of it on her own?'

That is quite enough for the sensitive ears of these former members of the middle class. Thoroughly offended they make for the door, where Xaver Kleinsgütl adds insult to injury by mocking and mimicking them, he who has never been anything else but flagrantly low-born, and for whom the ladies' sense of their own comedown is forever a source of the greatest amusement.

'Oh my little one, my little one,' says Cornelius, his voice strained, while enfolding the woeful Lori in his arms and sitting down on the chair next to her cot. 'What's the matter with my little darling?!'

Her tears have wet his face.

'Abel… Abel…', she stammers, sobbing. 'Why… is… Max… not my brother? I want… Max… to be my brother…'

What a calamity! What a very awkward calamity! What part of this dance party could have concocted this! wonders Cornelius, looking up in perplexity at Nanny Anna Blue standing there in all her bigoted dignity at the foot of the cot, her hands folded before her on her apron.

'The thing here is', she says, with austere wisdom, her lower lip drawn in, 'that the child's female instincts are lookin' uncommonly lively.'

'Oh, shut your mouth, can't you!' Cornelius retorts in torment. At least he can be glad that Lori hasn't withdrawn from him, isn't turning her back on him as she did in the hallway earlier, but wants him to cuddle her and has asked him to help her, while repeating her foolish, abstruse desire for Max to be her brother, and then wailing that she wants to return to him in the hall, so that he can dance with her again. But Max is dancing in the hallway with Fräulein Plaichinger, who is a fully grown colossus of a woman and has every right to him—while to the Professor, torn apart by pity, Lori has never appeared so tiny and sparrow-like as she does now, snuggling up to him, helplessly wracked by sobs, and without the slightest notion of what is troubling her poor little soul. She doesn't know. It isn't clear to her that she is suffering because of the grown-up, fat and fully entitled Plaichinger, who is allowed to dance in the hallway with Max Hergesell, while Lori was permitted to do so only once, just for fun, as a joke, in spite of her being incomparably the lovelier of the two. However, to reproach young Hergesell on this account would be downright impossible; it would imply an insane and impertinent claim on him. No, Lori's sorrow grants her no rights and it has no hope of healing; it ought therefore to hide its face. Because it is without understanding, however, it also knows no restraint, and that is what makes it so painful. Anna Blue and Xaver have no feeling for this sort of painfulness; they are impervious to it, whether out of dullness or because they share a more down-to-earth attitude to nature. But the Professor's fatherly heart is being torn asunder by it, as well as by the mortifying horror of this hopeless, irredeemable passion.

It doesn't help to remind Lori that she already has a perfectly good little brother in the person of Biter, soundly asleep next to her. She only casts an anguished, scornful glance over at the other cot through her tears, and asks for Max. It is to no avail either when he promises her a protracted five-gentlemen walk around the dining room, or attempts to describe to her what splendid lengths they will go to when they perform the 'cushion game' before table. She has no interest in any of that, nor has she any inclination to lie down and go to sleep. She doesn't want to sleep, she wants to sit up and suffer… But then both of them, Abel and Lori, listen as something wonderful happens, something that sounds like two pairs of feet approaching the nursery step by step, something about to put in a dazzling appearance…

This is Xaver's doing—that much is instantly clear. Xaver Kleinsgütl, since mocking the expelled ladies, has not been idling by the door all this time. Instead he has bestirred himself, he has taken steps and indeed action too; he has been downstairs in the hallway tugging on Herr Hergesell's sleeve, uttering a few thick-lipped words and making a request. And now the two of them are here. While Xaver hangs back in the doorway, having completed his share of the task, Max Hergesell, in his dinner suit, with a hint of dark whisker at his ears and lovely black eyes, marches through the nursery straight to Lori's cot, and as he approaches he is visibly aware of his role as fulfiller of dreams, Fairytale Prince and Swan Knight—one who can say: 'Well now, here I am, all your sorrows have come to an end!'

Cornelius feels almost as overwhelmed as Lori.

'Fancy that,' he murmurs weakly, 'look who's here. That is extraordinarily kind of Herr Hergesell.'

'That's not exceptionally kind of him at all!' Hergesell replies. 'It's only natural that he'll drop in to see his dancing partner again and say goodnight.'

And he goes up to the bars of the cot, behind which sits little Lori who's lost her tongue but is smiling blissfully through her tears. From her mouth comes a small, high note, just one, almost like a sigh of joy, then she looks up at her Swan Knight with her golden eyes, which, though swollen and red, are incomparably more gentle than those of the stout Fräulein Plaichinger. She does not raise her arms to embrace him. Her happiness, like her pain, is without understanding, but she doesn't do that. Her beautiful little hands remain on her blanket, motionless, while Max Hergesell leans with both arms on the cot railing, as on the parapet of a balcony.

'Lest she,' he says, 'through sorrowful nights, sit weeping upon her bed!'* And he gives the Professor a knowing glance in the hope of garnering his applause for such erudition. 'Ha, ha, ha, so young too! "Take comfort, fair child!" You are good. Something will come of you. Stay just as you are; it's all you need do. Ha, ha, ha, so early too! Will you sleep now and cry no more, little Loreley, now that I've come to you?'

Lori, transfigured, gazes at him. Her sparrow-like shoulder is bare; the Professor draws the narrow lace border over it. He can't help thinking of a sentimental story about a dying child and a clown whom the child had once watched with rapturous delight at a circus, a delight that had never left her. And so they sent for the clown who came to the child's deathbed in a costume embroidered with silver butterflies, and the child died in bliss. Max Hergesell is not embroidered, and Lori, thank God, is not going to die, it's just that 'it knocked 'er flyin' '; but apart from that the story really is quite apposite, and the feelings the Professor harbours against young Hergesell, leaning on the cot with all that half-baked blether—delivered more for the father's ears than the child's, which Lori doesn't notice—are a quite peculiar mix of gratitude, embarrassment, hatred and admiration.

'Goodnight, little Loreley!' says Hergesell, offering his hand across the railing. Her pretty little white hand disappears in his large, strong, red one. 'Sleep well,' he says. 'Sweet dreams! But not of me! For heaven's sake! At your age! Ha, ha, ha, ha!' Thus he concludes his fairy-tale clown's visit, and Cornelius accompanies him to the door.

'No need for thanks! No, absolutely not, think nothing of it!' he magnanimously and obligingly protests, while they walk to the door, where Xaver joins him on his way downstairs to serve the Italian salad.

Dr Cornelius, however, returns to little Lori, who has lain down now, her cheek resting on her flat little pillow.

'That was nice, wasn't it!' he says, tidying her blanket, and she nods back at him with one last sob. For perhaps a quarter of an hour he stays seated by her cot side, watching as she leaves for the land of Nod in the tracks of her brother, who found the right way so much earlier. Her silky brown hair acquires the lovely curly fall it usually finds in her sleep; her long eyelashes reach down below her eyes, from which so much sorrow has poured; her angelic mouth with its bow-shaped upper lip rests open in sweet contentment, quivering now and then when a late sob breaks the gentle rhythm of her breathing.

And her hands, those little hands that remind him of white and rosy blossoms, lying there like that: the one on her blue quilt, the other beside her face on the pillow! A wave of tenderness fills Dr Cornelius's heart, as if it were wine.

How fortunate, he thinks, that Lethe streams into her tiny soul with every breath of her slumber; that a child's night forms such a deep and broad abyss between one day and the next! Tomorrow, and that is for certain, young Hergesell will be no more than a pale shadow, powerless to cause her heart the slightest distress, and then, in oblivious delight, and together with Abel and Biter, she will apply herself to a five-gentlemen walk and the exciting cushion game.

Thank heavens for that!

MARIO AND THE MAGICIAN

A TRAGIC TRAVEL EXPERIENCE

OUR recollections of Torre di Venere* are atmospherically unpleasant. Vexation, irritation and high tension filled the air from the beginning, and it would all end with the shock over that awful Cipolla,* in whose person, in a manner as ominous as it was humanly impressive, the peculiar maliciousness of the atmosphere seemed embodied and to an alarming degree compressed. Looking back, we felt that the horrific end* was predestined and lay in the nature of things themselves; the fact that the children had had to endure it was, aside from all else, a woeful impropriety, a misunderstanding ultimately attributable to the strange man's false pretences. Luckily, the children did not understand where the comedy ended and calamity began, and so they were left with the fond illusion that it had been theatre from start to finish.

Torre lies some fifteen kilometres from Portoclemente, one of the most popular summer resorts on the Tyrrhenian Sea, an elegant town that—with its colourful seafront hotels and shopping street, its broad beach packed with *capanne** and pennant-sporting sandcastles, its bronzed humanity and noisy bustle of amusements—stays overcrowded for months on end. And since this self-same beach, bordered by pine groves and surveyed by nearby mountains, keeps its fine-sanded, spacious and welcoming character for the entire length of the coast, it need hardly surprise us that a somewhat more peaceful rival soon set up shop further along: Torre di Venere, whose eponymous tower visitors have long sought in vain, is a touristic offshoot of the larger bathing resort and was for some years an idyll for the few, a refuge for those of a more unworldly bent. As is usual for such places, however, peace and quiet have long since moved even further down the coast—to Marina Petriera or heaven knows where. We know how all the world seeks peace only to chase it away again by leaping upon it with an absurd yearning, falsely supposing that peace and noise can be wed, and that wherever noise goes peace may also be; setting up its fairground stall where the latter lingered, the former is wholly capable of believing it is still there. And so it is with Torre: while remaining more sedate and less showy than Portoclemente, the town is increasingly frequented by Italians and foreigners. Portoclemente may no longer be as chic as it was, but if it is less so, it nonetheless remains a noisy and crowded fashionable resort, and so it is more chic now to go to nearby Torre, which is more stylish and, what is more, cheaper, and while the attraction of these qualities has persisted, the qualities themselves no longer exist. Torre now has its Grand Hotel; guest houses abound, some more sophisticated, some plainer. The owners and renters of summer houses and pinetum gardens overlooking the sea no longer have the beach to themselves, and the scene in July or August in no way differs from that at Portoclemente: the beach swarms with scolding, quarrelling, cheering bathers, the infernal blaze of the sun peeling the skin off the backs of their necks; flat-bottomed, gaudily painted boats bob on the sparkling blue, manned by children whose vigilant mothers, filling the air with their hoarse anxiety, call out their little ones' sonorous forenames, while vendors, picking their way between the limbs of reclining sunbathers, peddle oysters, drinks, flowers, coral jewellery and *cornetti al burro*,* crying their wares in the husky, unconstrained tones of the South.

Such was the beach scene at Torre on our arrival—pleasant enough, to be sure, but it was obvious to us that we had come too early. It was mid-August, after all, and the Italian season was still in full swing, hardly the best time for strangers to appreciate the town's attractions. What throngs gathered in the garden cafés along the promenade in the afternoons!—in 'Esquisito' for example, where we occasionally sat and were served by Mario, that same Mario I shall presently return to. It is virtually impossible to find a table, and the many musical ensembles, none of which pays the slightest attention to any other, cut into one another's performances willy-nilly. In the afternoons especially, there is an influx of day trippers from Portoclemente, for Torre naturally offers a popular destination to the restless guests of that pleasure dome, and owing to the Fiat motor-coach continually hurtling to and fro, the oleander and laurel bushes at the sides of the connecting trunk road are covered in an inch-thick layer of snowy-white dust—an extraordinary but disagreeable sight.

One really should travel to Torre di Venere in September when the large crowds have dispersed, or in May, before the sea has warmed sufficiently to tempt southern bathers to take a dip. Even in early or late season the place is not empty, but the mood is more subdued, and less national. English, German and French dominate under the shades of the beach huts as well as in guest-house dining rooms, whereas in August, in the Grand Hotel at least, where for want of more personal accommodation we had reserved rooms, the stranger will find that everything is still in the hands of Roman and Florentine society, so much so that he is likely to feel quite isolated, and even, on occasion, like a second-class guest.

To our chagrin, this was our experience on the evening of our arrival when we entered the dining room for dinner and were shown to a table by the waiter in charge. There was nothing objectionable about this table, but our gaze was arrested by an adjoining glass veranda overlooking the sea, as full as the main dining area but not as completely full, its smaller tables aglow with red-shaded lamps. Our little ones were clearly delighted with the merry sight, and without thinking twice we announced our preference to take our meals on the veranda—a declaration based on ignorance, as it transpired, for we were informed with somewhat abashed politeness that the cosier seating area was reserved for 'our clientele', '*ai nostri clienti*'. Our clientele? But surely that meant us. We were no chance passers-by, here today and gone tomorrow, but guests of the house booked in for three or four weeks—boarders, in fact. Incidentally, we refrained from demanding any explanation of the difference between ourselves and the 'clientele' who were permitted to dine in the glow of red lamps, and instead took *pranzo** at our table in the functionally lit common dining room—and a fairly mediocre repast it was too, with the usual insipid and unimaginative hotel food; we would soon find the cuisine far better at Pensione Eleonora,* a stone's throw further inland.

For it was to that establishment we repaired three or four days later, before we had as much as settled in at the Grand Hotel, and not because of the veranda and its little lamps; the children, who had made friends with the waiters and porters straight away and whose attention was fully absorbed by the blandishments of the seaside, had quickly forgotten those colourful attractions. But with certain members of the veranda 'clientele', or, more correctly, of the management who toadied to them, one of those disputes was quick to spring up that can spoil a holiday stay from the very first. Roman nobility was in residence, a Principe X and his family, and since these grandees had their rooms in close proximity to our own, the Principessa, a grand lady and passionate mother, was much alarmed by the residual symptoms of a whooping cough infection our little ones had recently put behind them and whose lingering but mild symptoms occasionally interfered with the otherwise unshakeable nightly slumber of our youngest. The nature of this illness is not entirely clear, leaving ample scope for superstition in this part of the world, and so we bore no grudge against our elegant neighbour, who adhered to the widespread belief that whooping cough was transmitted acoustically, and who simply feared that our bad example might infect her own little ones. In full consciousness of her social and female standing she lodged her complaint with the manager's office, which, represented in the person of the familiar frock-coated manager, hurried to convey to us its considerable regret that present circumstances dictated our unavoidable relocation to the hotel annex. We did our best to assure the aforesaid person that the infection had reached its final stages, indeed had all but fully abated, and therefore no longer posed any danger whatsoever; the only concession made to us was that our case would be brought before the medical panel and that the hotel doctor—and only he, not one appointed by ourselves—would be asked to decide. We gave our approval to this arrangement, convinced that it would put the Principessa's mind at ease and allow us to avoid the discomforts of moving. The doctor arrived and proved himself a loyal and upright servant of medical science. He examined the children and declared their malady to have passed with no further cause for concern. As far as we were concerned, then, the incident was now closed, but here was the manager telling us that even following the doctor's assessment we were required nonetheless to vacate our rooms and remove to the annex.

Such Byzantine* practices left us outraged. It is unlikely that the duplicitous intractability we met with could have stemmed from the Princess. The obsequious patron had probably not even dared to inform her of the doctor's decision. In any event we notified him that, all things considered, we preferred to leave the hotel immediately—and packed. We were able to do so with a light heart, for we had, in the meantime, already established relations with the Pensione Eleonora, whose welcoming and more private outward appearance had made an immediate impression on us as we passed by, and with whose owner, Signora Angiolieri, we had struck up a very pleasant acquaintance. Signora Angiolieri was a fine-boned, black-eyed lady of Tuscan mien, probably in her early thirties and with the faintly ivory complexion of southern women; together with her quiet, bald and neatly dressed husband, she owned a much larger boarding house in Florence, presiding over their Torre subsidiary only during the summer and early autumn. Previously, however, before her marriage, our new landlady had been the companion, fellow traveller, wardrobe mistress and indeed good friend of 'La Duse',* a period she evidently considered to have been the greatest and happiest of her life, and which she immediately gave us a lively account of during our first visit. Numerous photographs of the great actress, with cordial personal dedications, as well as other souvenirs of their life together, graced the little tables and étagères of Signora Angiolieri's drawing room, and although it was obvious that the cult of her captivating past was partly intended to heighten the appeal of her current business prospects, we nevertheless listened, while she gave us a tour of the house, with great interest and enjoyment to the tales she told in her clipped and sonorous Tuscan accent of the passionate solicitude, tender-heartedness and profound sensitivity of her immortal mistress.

It was therefore to this establishment that we had our belongings brought, much to the regret of the Grand Hotel staff, who, in typically Italian manner, had grown fond of the children. Our new accommodation was self-contained and pleasant, offering easy access to the sea and beach promenade along an avenue of young plane trees; the dining room, where Madame Angiolieri herself served up the soup every lunchtime, was cool and clean, while the service was attentive and friendly and meals were excellent. We even found some Viennese acquaintances, with whom we took to chatting in front of the house after the meal, and who introduced us to others among their acquaintance. And so everything might have gone well—we were perfectly happy with the exchange we had made, and in fact there was nothing that stood in the way of a satisfactory stay.

Yet we did not feel altogether comfortable. Perhaps it was the fatuous reason for our change of abode that haunted us—I, for one, must admit that I find it hard to digest such collisions with the all-too-human: the abuse of power, injustice, obsequious corruption. They occupy my mind for far too long, plunging me into a well of irritation, a futile state induced by the inordinate casualness and naïvety with which these phenomena occur. At the same time, it was not as if we felt we had fallen out with the Grand Hotel: the children still had their friends there, the hotel porter mended their toys, and from time to time we took tea in the gardens of that establishment, not without catching sight of the Princess, who, her lips emphasized in coral-red, came trotting daintily but determinedly into the garden to scout for her darlings whom she'd left in the care of an English governess, unaware as she was of our alarming proximity, for we had warned our own little one that, should she make an appearance, he must refrain even from clearing his throat.

The heat was extreme—is it fair to add that? The heat was African; as soon as one left the indigo-blue freshness at the sea's edge, the sun's reign of terror proved so relentless that one dreaded the few steps between beach and lunch table, even when clad in mere beach pyjamas. Would you enjoy that? For weeks on end? Of course, we are talking about the South here—its classical weather, its climate that nourished the flowering of human culture, the sun of Homer,* and so on. But after a while it is simply too much, and I tend to find it dull, and the blazing emptiness of the sky day after day becomes a burden. The strident colours and vast indomitable naïvety of the unbroken light supposedly awaken convivial emotions; they vouchsafe carefree immunity from the vagaries and setbacks of the weather. And yet without initially grasping why, one finds these features leave the deeper, less straightforward needs of the Nordic soul unfulfilled; a sense of desolation sets in, a feeling which, in time, turns into something like contempt. You are right, without that stupid business of the whooping cough, I might not have had such a feeling; but I was irritable, and perhaps I actually wanted to feel like that, and grasped, more or less unconsciously, for a suitable psychological motive, if not to induce the feeling, then at least to justify and intensify it. Anyway, this is where you can count on our bad faith—as far as the sea is concerned, and the morning spent on the fine sands in full sight of its eternal splendour, and while this kind of thing ought to be out of the question and is contrary to all our experience, we actually did feel ill at ease on that beach; we did not feel happy.

Too early, too early—as I have said, the beach was still in the hands of the country's middle class, a conspicuously pleasing breed, you are right in that, too; among the young we found much comeliness and wholesome charm, although this was inevitably offset by lower middle-class rabble and undistinguishable humanity generally, all of which, admit it, is no more fetching under this sky than under ours. What *voices* these women have!—to claim that this was the home of western vocal artistry sometimes seemed a little far-fetched. '*Fuggièro!*'*—I hear her cry still, because for twenty mornings in succession I heard her brazenly raucous and grotesquely accentuated bellow, with its blaringly open '*èh*', ring out a hundred times in close proximity, a kind of mechanical howl of despair. '*Fuggièro! Rispondi al mèno*':* they tended to pronounce the 'sp' in the German way, as a 'schp', which is particularly annoying when you are already in a bad mood. Her yelling was directed at an odious boy with a revolting sunburn between his shoulders, whose impudence, unruliness and sheer malice were as bad as anything I had seen, and who, besides all else, was a great coward, capable with his outrageous whining of throwing a whole beach into turmoil. One day, for instance, a crab pinched his toe in the water, and the scale of wailing he raised over this tiny mishap, like some grieving antique hero, was blood-curdling, making us think some dreadful accident had occurred. He evidently believed the injury had poisoned him. Crawling to the shore he proceeded to roll about in apparently unbearable agony, crying '*Ohi!*' and '*Oimè*', legs and arms flailing as he fended off the tragic appeals of his mother and the assurances of bystanders, for spectators had arrived from all around. A doctor was fetched, the same doctor who had provided such a sound judgement on our whooping cough, and who now proved himself once again to be a reliable man of science. With his good-natured manner he offered the consoling news that there was nothing at all to worry about, advising his patient to return to the water to cool his tiny pincer wound. Instead of which, like someone who had drowned or taken a fall, Fuggièro was carried from the beach on a makeshift stretcher at the head of a large entourage—only to return to his antics of pretending accidentally to demolish other children's sandcastles on the following morning. In other words, a little monster.

And yet this twelve-year-old was but one of the leading promoters of the elusive and unsettling public mood that would spoil what might have been a charming holiday. Somehow, the atmosphere was constrained, lacking in innocent abandon; there was a great deal of insistence on respect, although it was difficult at first to know for what exactly, or in what sense; the public stood on its dignity, and, whether for its own benefit or in front of foreigners, flaunted its earnestness; it made much of comportment and maintained a more than keen sense of honour—but why? It soon became apparent that it was about politics, and that it also involved the notion of the nation. The fact was that the beach was teeming with patriotic children—an unnatural and depressing sight. For aren't children a human species and society of their own, their own nation, so to speak? Because they have a common way of life, wherever they happen to be, they find it easy and indeed essential to come together, even if their limited vocabularies belong to different languages. Our own, too, played with both native and foreign children. However, they manifestly suffered disappointments they found puzzling. There were sensitivities, expressions of assertiveness that seemed too touchy and didactic to wholly deserve that name; there were clashes over flags, disputes over prestige and precedence. Parents intervened, less to assuage than to judge, or to defend their own principles; set phrases were declaimed about the greatness and majesty of Italy, phrases that were not much fun and spoiled games. We saw how our children were affected by this and how they withdrew at a loss, and we were hard put to offer them a plausible explanation of the circumstances. These people, we told them, were passing through a phase, a condition, something like an illness.

It was our own fault; owing to our carelessness we became involved in a conflict—or rather, another conflict—with the very 'condition' we had identified and appraised; it appeared that the earlier conflicts had not been completely the product of chance. Anyway, in a word, we offended public morals. Our little daughter, who was eight years old, but in physical development a year younger and as thin as a sparrow, had taken a long bathe in the sea owing to the heat and had gone back to playing in her wet swimming suit, and we had then permitted her to go back into the sea to wash off all the sand that had stuck to her costume, following which she was to put it back on and try to keep it cleaner. Anyway, naked now, she ran the few metres to the sea's edge, rinsed her tricot in the water, and came back to us. Ought we to have known what a flood of derision, resentment and protest her conduct, or rather our conduct, would excite? I don't wish to be dogmatic, but everywhere in the world attitudes to the naked body and our feelings towards it have changed completely during recent decades. There are matters we 'no longer give a thought to', and these include the freedom we had allowed this anything-but-provocative child's body. But it was considered provocative here. The patriotic children jeered. Fuggièro whistled through his fingers. An incensed conversation among adults nearby grew ever louder and boded nothing good. A gentleman in dress coat and particularly unsuitable bowler on the back of his head assured his scandalized womenfolk that he was intent on taking corrective action; so he came over and took his stand before us, whereupon a philippic rained down on our heads in which all the pathos of the sensuous South was placed at the service of an inflexible discipline and prudish morality. The indecent act we had been guilty of, he declared, was all the more worthy of condemnation for being at the same time an ungrateful and disrespectful abuse of Italian hospitality. This was a breach not only of the letter and spirit of the public bathing regulations, but also a wicked violation of his country's honour, and in order to protect that honour he—the gentleman in the dress coat—would be taking appropriate steps to ensure that our offence against the dignity of Italy would not go unpunished.

We did all we could to follow this harangue, and nodded our heads respectfully. To contradict this furious person would undoubtedly have meant falling from one error into another. However, we did have one or two things on the tips of our tongues, for example, that the word 'hospitality', when all circumstances were taken into account, was not strictly speaking the mot juste, and that we, to put it plainly, were not guests of Italy but those of Signora Angiolieri, who some years ago had exchanged her role as confidante to Eleonora Duse for the profession of hospitality. We also felt like answering that we had been quite unaware that morals in this beautiful country had fallen into such neglect as to make this relapse into prudery and oversensitivity both self-explanatory and inevitable. But we restricted ourselves to the reassurance that any provocation or lack of respect on our part had been entirely unintentional, and pointed out the mitigating circumstances of the little miscreant's tender age and slight physique. To no avail. Our assurances were rejected as false, our defences as irrelevant, and the setting of an example deemed necessary. I believe someone then informed the authorities by telephone, and one of their officials appeared on the beach claiming the case was very serious, '*molto grave*', and that we should follow him up to the *municipio** on the town square, where a superior official proceeded to confirm the provisional verdict of '*molto grave*' and held forth in the same clearly normal didactic jargon concerning our offence as had the gentleman in the bowler, before imposing on us an atonement fine of fifty lire. We considered this contribution to the Italian budget worth our adventure, and so paid and left. Shouldn't we have departed altogether?

If only we had done! Had we departed, we could have avoided the fatal Cipolla, but several things conspired to impede any such decision to move elsewhere. A poet* once said that it is indolence that detains us in distressing circumstances—our own perseverance might be explained in the same light. In any case, one does not gladly beat an immediate retreat after such an experience; one hesitates to admit one has behaved unacceptably, especially if one's defiance is bolstered by encouragement from without. In the Villa Eleonora, the verdict on the injustice of our misfortune was unanimous. Our Italian after-dinner acquaintances believed that it was detrimental to the reputation of their country and declared their intention to take their countryman, the gentleman in the dress coat, to task. On the following day, however, the gentleman and his party were not on the beach—not on our account, of course, although it may well be that anticipation of his pending departure had lent vigour to his actions. At all events, we were relieved to see he had gone. And to complete the picture: we remained because we had begun to view our stay as something remarkable, and remarkableness has a worth in itself, quite separate from comfort or discomfort. Are we to strike our colours and avoid an experience as soon as it no longer guarantees us enjoyment and assurance? Are we to simply 'depart' when life turns out to be a little uncanny, alarming or somewhat embarrassing or even aggrieving? Of course not! You should stay where you are, take a good look at it, put yourself in its path; that way one may even learn something. And so we remained, and reaped as the cruel reward of our steadfastness the impressive and ill-fated appearance in our lives of Cipolla.

I have not mentioned that in practically the same instant as we were being reprimanded by the authorities, the after-season began. The grim gentleman in the bowler hat who denounced us was not the only guest to leave the seaside resort; for most it was time to depart, and we saw a good many luggage barrows on their way to the station. The beach became less nationalistic; life in Torre's cafés and along the paths in the pine groves became both more familiar and more European; we could probably have taken our meals in the glass veranda at the Grand Hotel, yet refrained from doing so, feeling perfectly content as we did at Signora Angiolieri's table—'content', that is, within the shadows cast by the demon of the place. No sooner had this welcome turn of events transpired when the weather changed, its well-nigh punctual transformation in seeming accordance with the public's holiday calendar; the sky clouded over, not that it had grown cooler, but the blazing heat that had prevailed since our arrival eighteen days earlier (and probably for some time before that) gave way to a sticky sirocco sultriness, and from time to time a few faltering raindrops moistened the velvety sand of our mornings. Moreover, two-thirds of our planned stay in Torre had passed; the listless, colourless sea in whose shallows languid jellyfish now floated was at least something different; it would have been silly to crave the return of a sun whose overweening sway had provoked so many sighs.

It was at this juncture that Cipolla first advertised his presence: Cavaliere* Cipolla, as he was called on posters that were put up everywhere from one day to the next, even in the dining room at the Pensione Eleonora—a travelling virtuoso, an artiste, or, in his own words, *forzatore*, *illusionista* and *prestidigitatore*,* who proposed to entertain the highly esteemed public of Torre di Venere with several extraordinary phenomena of a mysterious and astonishing nature. A magician! The announcement alone was enough to turn our little ones' heads. They had never seen such a performance before and now our holiday trip was to grant them this unknown excitement. Straight away they began to badger us to acquire entry tickets for the conjurer's evening performance, and although we had initial reservations about the lateness of the hour at which the event was due to commence, to wit nine o'clock, we gave way on the understanding that we could easily go home as soon as we had received an impression of Cipolla's probably quite modest artistry and that the children would be able to sleep later on the following morning; the upshot was that we purchased our four tickets from Signora Angiolieri herself, who had taken a number of preferential seats in commission for her guests. She was unable to vouch for the man's performance, and we were hardly expecting much ourselves, but we did feel a certain need for diversion, and the children's insistent curiosity somehow proved contagious.

The Cavaliere's spectacle was to take place in a hall that had served during the high season as a cinema with a weekly changing programme. We had never been there before. You reached it by passing the 'Palazzo', a dilapidated fort-like building that had ostensibly seen grander days and was now for sale, and following the town's main street, where a chemist's, hairdresser and the usual types of shop were to be found and which led, one might say, from the feudal via the commons to the plebeian; for it ended between the humble dwellings of fisherfolk where old women sat on their doorsteps mending nets, and it was here, too, in this proletarian quarter, that the 'Sala', which was hardly better than a wooden shed, albeit a capacious one, was situated, its large entrance decorated inside and out with layers of brightly coloured posters. Shortly after dinner on the appointed evening, then, we made our way there in the dark, the children dressed up for the occasion and delighted to be doing something special. It was sultry, as it had been for days; there were occasional flashes of summer lightning and a few drops of rain. We walked under our umbrellas. It took us a quarter of an hour.

Once our tickets had been checked in the entrance passage, we were expected to find our own seats. They were in the third bench on the left, and on taking our places it became obvious to us that the starting time for the performance, for all it was disconcertingly late, would nonetheless be treated with laxity: it was only very gradually that an audience, seemingly quite intent on arriving late, began to fill the parterre, to which, there being no boxes, the auditorium was restricted. This tardiness made us feel slightly anxious. The pinkness of our children's cheeks owed as much to exhaustion as to exhilaration. On our arrival only the standing room at the back and along the side aisles had been fully occupied, and here stood, their bare arms folded over striped pullovers, Torre di Venere's autochthonous manhood, local fishermen, young go-getting lads; and while we were perfectly happy to see these local folk, whose presence always adds colour and humour to such events, the children were simply delighted with them. For among these people they had friends, acquaintances they had made during afternoon walks further along the beach. Often, returning home at the hour when the sun, weary with its gigantic efforts, sank into the sea and turned the foam on the incoming surf a golden red, we had happened upon rows of bare-legged fishermen who, heaving and bracing their feet on the sand, hauled in their nets with long-drawn-out cries, collecting their generally skimpy catch of *frutti di mare** in dripping buckets; and the little ones had watched, tried out their scraps of Italian, helped pull on ropes, and had found chums. Now they were exchanging greetings with the standing-room company; here was Guiscardo, there was Antonio, they knew their names, waving and calling over to them sotto voce and receiving a nod back, or a laugh displaying a mouthful of very healthy teeth. Look, there's Mario from 'Esquisito' even, Mario who brings us chocolate! He wants to see the magician too, and he must have arrived early; he's almost standing at the front, but he hasn't noticed us; he isn't paying attention—that's typical of him, despite being a waiter. Instead we wave to the man who hires out the paddle-boats on the beach and is also there, right at the back.

By this time it was 9.15, and then almost 9.30. You can understand our nervousness. When would the children get to bed? It had been wrong to bring them here, for to expect them to interrupt their enjoyment when it had hardly begun would prove hard indeed. In time the parterre was quite full: it seemed all Torre was present, the guests of the Grand Hotel, the Villa Eleonora guests as well as those of other boarding houses, faces we recognized from the beach. We heard English and German. We heard French of the kind spoken by Romanians when addressing Italians. Madame Angiolieri herself was sitting two rows behind us beside her taciturn, bald husband, who was busy stroking his moustache with the middle fingers of his right hand. They had all come late, but nobody was too late; Cipolla kept us waiting.

He kept us waiting, and that is probably the right expression for it; he heightened the suspense by delaying his appearance. We ourselves appreciated the point of this behaviour, but there were limits. Towards half past nine the audience began to clap—it was a nice way of expressing legitimate impatience, especially since it also showed a willingness to applaud. For the little ones, joining in was part of the fun. All children love to clap. From the popular section of the audience someone shouted: '*Pronti!*' and '*Cominciamo!*'* And what do you know: whatever had blocked the start of the show for so long now conveniently vanished. A gong sounded, to which the many standing members of the audience responded with a unanimous 'Ah!', whereupon the curtains parted. They revealed a stage whose furniture was more in keeping with a schoolroom than the setting for a conjurer's spectacle, a scene principally suggested by the blackboard on an easel in the foreground, stage left. Besides this were an ordinary yellow clothes rack, one or two customary wicker chairs and, further to the rear, a small round table on which stood a bottle of water and a glass and, separately on a tray, some liqueur glasses and a flacon of amber liquid. We were granted only two seconds to take in these paraphernalia. Then, without the lights going down, Cavaliere Cipolla took the stage.

His entry at quick march was calculated to show deference to the wishes of the audience and presented the illusion of someone who had hurried at this speed from quite some distance to appear before the present gathering, while in fact he had been standing in the wings.

Cipolla's attire gave support to the fiction of his arrival from afar. A man of indeterminate age, albeit anything but young, with an angular, ravaged face and piercing eyes, a wrinkled mouth and tight lips, a thin, black, waxed moustache and a so-called imperial mouche in the curve between chin and lower lip, his dress had the complicated elegance of evening streetwear. He wore a broad, velvet-collared cape and pelerine with satin lining, which, when the use of his arms was restricted, he held together at the front with white-gloved hands, also a white scarf round his neck and a tilted top hat with swooping brim pushed over his brow. To this day, and perhaps more so than anywhere else, the eighteenth century is alive in Italy and with it that peculiar kind of charlatan, that garish buffoon so characteristic of the epoch, tolerably well-preserved specimens of which one can only encounter in this country. Cipolla's general manner and appearance had much of this historical figure, and the sense of grotesquery and garish tomfoolery found in the traditional type was immediately conveyed by the higgledy-piggledy way in which his pretentious clothing, with its wrongly placed creases and badly set tucks, sat—or, in effect, hung—upon his body: whichever angle you looked at him from, there was something that was not quite right about the figure he cut—later, this would become clearer. Nevertheless, I must emphasize that there was nothing in the least bit jocular or clownish in his bearing, air or behaviour; on the contrary, there was a stern seriousness about him, with no attempt at anything comic, an occasionally cross-tempered sense of pride too, as well as that kind of dignified and self-satisfied air peculiar to the cripple—none of which, however, stopped his behaviour from provoking laughter in some quarters of the hall, to begin with at least.

His manner now had lost every last vestige of deference; the alacrity of his stage entry turned out to have been solely an effusion of energy in which servility had played no part. Standing front stage and removing his gloves by nonchalantly plucking at their fingers to reveal his long yellowish hands, one of which sported a signet ring with a prominent lazurite stone, he let his small hard eyes with puffy bags under them roam around the hall, assessing what he saw—not swiftly, but pausing here and there to examine a single face, his gaze supercilious, his mouth pinched, and speaking not a word. With a dexterity as astonishing as it was casual he tossed his rolled-up pair of gloves some distance to land in the water glass on the small round table and, mutely casting his eyes around as before, produced a cigarette packet from an inside pocket—the cheapest brand of the state monopoly, as the wrapper showed—from which, without looking, he drew forth a cigarette with his fingertips, lighting it with an instantly flaming petroleum lighter. With his lips drawn back in an arrogant grimace and one foot softly tapping on the stage, he blew out a grey spout of deeply inhaled smoke through teeth that were worn-down and broken.

The audience were scrutinizing him as keenly as he had them. Among the standing young people one saw puckered brows and piercing stares on the lookout for the weakness this all-too-cocky fellow was sure to betray. He showed none. When taking out and replacing his cigarette packet and lighter, his clothes had proved awkward, and in so doing he had drawn back his evening coat to reveal, rather incongruously, a riding whip with a silver, claw-like, crook handle that hung by a leather thong attached to his left forearm. It further became apparent that Cipolla was not wearing a dress suit but a frock coat; in lifting this aside, too, he had revealed, partially hidden by his waistcoat, a multicoloured sash about his body, which members of the audience speaking in undertones behind us held to be a Cavaliere's badge of honour. Whether that be the case I shall leave undecided, for I have never heard of any such badge of honour linked to the title of Cavaliere. Perhaps the sash was simply humbug, not unlike the conjurer's way of just standing there saying and doing nothing but idly and pompously puffing his smoke at the audience.

There was laughter, as I have mentioned, and the mirth became almost universal when a loud, deadpan voice in the standing sector called out: '*Buona sera!*'*

Cipolla pricked up his ears. 'Who was that?' he fairly snapped. 'Who was it spoke just now? Well? First so bold, now so scared? *Paura, eh?*'* His voice was high-pitched and slightly asthmatic, also metallic. He waited.

'That was me.' The young man, responding to the challenge to his sense of honour, spoke into the silence—a handsome fellow in a cotton shirt with his jacket slung over his shoulder, quite close to us. His thick, black, wiry hair stood high and wild on his head, the fashionable style of the awakened Fatherland; it distorted his looks somewhat, giving him an African appearance. '*Bè*... that was me. Actually, it should have been your job, but I decided to lend you a hand.'

The laughter sparked up again. The boy had a quick tongue. '*Ha sciolto lo scilinguágnolo*,'* said someone near us. That jibe from the standing section was well deserved, after all.

'Ah, bravo!' answered Cipolla. 'I like you, *giovanotto*.* Believe me, I had noticed you already. I have a particular affection for people like you, people who are useful to me. You're obviously quite a chappie. You do as you like. Or have you ever not done as you like? Or even done something you didn't want to do? Where it wasn't you who wanted it? Listen, my young friend, you need to take it easy, not always playing the tough man and doing double time: wanting *and* doing. Division of labour's the thing—*sistema americano, sa'*.* Do you, for example, want to show this select and venerable audience your tongue, I mean your whole tongue, right down to its roots?'

'No,' the lad answered belligerently, 'that's not what I want. It wouldn't speak much for my upbringing.'

'It wouldn't speak for anything at all,' Cipolla answered, 'for you would merely be *doing* it. With all due respect for your upbringing, my own opinion is that before I count to three you will turn to your right and stick out your tongue at the present company, and you'll stick it out further than you've ever thought you could.'

As he looked at him, Cipolla's piercing eyes seemed to sink deeper into their sockets. '*Uno!*', he said, and made his riding whip, whose thong he had let slip from his forearm, whistle once through the air. The boy turned to face the audience and stuck out his tongue as far as it would go and made such a great effort that there could be little doubt that it was the very longest of tongue-lengths he had to offer. Then, with a blank face, the young man resumed his former position.

'That was me,' Cipolla mocked, jerking his head towards the boy a couple of times. '*Bè*... it was me.' Whereupon, leaving the audience to reflect, he turned to the small table and poured himself a glass of what appeared to be cognac from the flacon, then knocked it back with a practised hand.

The children laughed heartily. Of the verbal exchange they had understood practically nothing; but the fact that something perfectly droll was already going on between the strange man up there and someone in the audience was something they found highly amusing, and since they had had no notion of what could be expected from the performance we had promised them, they were happy to find this a delightful start to the evening. As for ourselves, we exchanged a glance, and I remember my lips involuntarily imitating the sound Cipolla had made in the air with his riding whip. In any case, it was obvious that people did not know what to make of such a muddled beginning to the magician's soirée, and they could not understand what had driven the *giovanotto*, their spokesman so to speak, to turn his insolence against them: the public. They found his behaviour foolish and ignored him, turning their attention instead to the artist, who, after fortifying himself at the small table, came back to the front and addressed the audience thus: 'Ladies and gentlemen,' he began in his asthmatic, metallic voice, 'you will surely have noticed that I reacted somewhat sensitively just now to the instructive remarks with which this hopeful young linguist (*questo linguista di belle speranze*—the audience laughed at the pun) saw fit to caution me. I am a man of some self-esteem; please accept that! I take no pleasure in being wished a good evening unless it is done genuinely and politely—there is no need to do so in any other way. In wishing me a good evening you wish yourself one, for the audience will only have a good evening if I have one myself, and that is the reason this darling of the girls of Torre di Venere' (he couldn't stop taunting him) 'did well to deliver proof that I shall have one tonight and can therefore proceed without accommodating his wishes. I can pride myself on having nothing but good evenings. There is the odd bad one, it's true, but that happens rarely. My profession is hard and my health is not the most robust; I have a small bodily imperfection that prevented me from participating in the war for the glory of the Fatherland. It is solely thanks to my mental and spiritual powers that I master life, which only ever means mastering oneself, and I can flatter myself that my work has attracted the respectful attentions of the educated public. The leading newspapers have been full of appreciation for it; the *Corriere della Sera** did me the justice of calling me a phenomenon, and in Rome I had the honour of seeing the Duce's* brother among the visitors to one of my evenings. Even so, I did not expect, on coming to a relatively insignificant place such as Torre di Venere' (laughter erupted at the expense of poor little Torre), 'to have to renounce or lay aside such petty quirks and inclinations as were generously forgiven me by the good people of that sublime and radiant city, especially not on account of the pointed remarks of persons who seem to have been spoiled with the favours of the fair sex.' Once again the young man had to pay for it; Cipolla never missed an opportunity to portray him as a *donnaiuolo** and rustic Lothario. At the same time there was a striking disproportion between, on the one hand, the dogged resentfulness and sheer animosity of his repeated attacks, and on the other, his displays of self-esteem and the claims to worldly success of which he boasted. In all likelihood the youth had simply served as another source of amusement such as Cipolla probably selected to poke fun at every evening. The sharpness of his jibes, however, contained genuine venom, the personal dimension of which should have been obvious to anyone who compared their physiques, even if the deformed older man had not repeatedly played on the handsome young man's putative success with women.

'Now that we are about to begin this evening's entertainment, allow me to make myself a little more comfortable!'

And he went over to the clothing rack to remove his outer garments.

'*Parla benissimo*,'* somebody sitting near us said. Thus far the man had achieved nothing, and yet his talk itself had been acknowledged as an achievement; he had managed to impress the audience. As far as the inhabitants of southern countries are concerned, language contributes to life's enjoyments, and they have a far livelier social respect for it than northerners. The national bond of the mother tongue is cherished by these peoples in the most commendable manner, and there is something positively exemplary in the gratifying reverence they accord its forms and phonetic rules. They speak with pleasure, they listen with pleasure—and they listen with discrimination. For the way a person speaks is considered a measure of rank; carelessness and crudeness breed contempt, while elegance and mastery bring social standing, which is why a person of lower status, if his purpose is to create an effect, will try out refined phrases and take great care in using them. In this respect, at least, Cipolla had won his audience over, although he could hardly be counted among the class of men whom the Italian, in a peculiar mingling of moral and aesthetic sensibilities, deems '*simpatico*'.*

After divesting himself of his silk hat, scarf and coat he returned to the front while adjusting his jacket, pulling down his cuffs with their large cufflinks and straightening his humbug sash. He had particularly ugly hair, that is, the crown of his head being practically bald, his hair had the appearance of a narrow, dyed-black flap stuck on between nape and forehead and parted down the middle, while the hair at his temples, also dyed black, was brushed sidewise towards the corners of his eyes—it resembled the hairstyle of an old-fashioned circus director, preposterous in its way, yet eminently suited to Cipolla's offbeat style and worn with such confidence that the audience responded with mute restraint to its comic appearance. The 'small bodily imperfection' of which he had warned was all too visible now, although its nature was still not entirely clear: his chest was too high, as is common in such cases, but the corresponding affliction of the back seemed not to sit in its usual place between the shoulders, but lower down on the hips or buttocks, and while this did not exactly hinder his gait, it gave him a grotesque appearance and each of his steps a strangely lurching motion. Nonetheless, adverse reaction to his condition had been obviated by his having already mentioned it, and now that he was before them, a delicate but palpable sense of civility prevailed in the hall.

'At your service!' said Cipolla. 'If you have no objection we shall begin the evening with one or two arithmetical exercises.'

Arithmetic? That didn't sound like conjuring tricks. We began to suspect that the man was sailing under a false flag, although it still wasn't obvious what the right one was. I began to feel sorry for the children, but for the time being they were happy merely to be there.

The numbers game that Cipolla now set in motion was simple and, in its outcome, astounding. He began by fastening a sheet of paper to the top right corner of the blackboard with a drawing pin and then, lifting up the paper, writing something in chalk on the board underneath. He spoke incessantly while doing so, his constant flow of commentary and clarification designed to prevent his presentation from becoming tedious, although he was actually an eloquent master of ceremonies and never at a loss for a chatty witticism. That he persisted in diminishing the gap between stage and auditorium, initially bridged through his curious skirmish with the young fisherman, by coercing members of the audience into mounting the stage while for his part descending into the public space to seek personal contact with his guests—all this belonged to his working style and added much to the children's enjoyment. I find it hard to say to what extent his immediately entering into quarrels with various individuals was also deliberate and a part of his method, although there was no interruption of his serious and querulous manner, but the audience, at least in its more demotic sector, did seem to think it was part of the act.

For after he had finished writing and hidden what he had written under the sheet of paper, he expressed his wish that two people come up to the stage in order to help him carry out the calculation. It wasn't going to be anything difficult, and even those who were less confident with numbers could easily participate. As usual, nobody volunteered, and Cipolla was wary of disturbing the more genteel members of his audience. His focus was on the common people, and addressing two stalwart young bumpkins in the standing room at the back, he both dared and encouraged them to join in, finding it reprehensible that they were standing there idly gaping instead of serving the general good, and sure enough he succeeded in setting them in motion. Treading awkwardly they made their way up the central aisle to the stage, took the steps and, grinning gauchely amid the '*bravi*' calls of their peers, placed themselves in front of the blackboard. Cipolla joked with them for a few minutes, praising the heroic firmness of their limbs and the size of their hands, all highly suited to rendering the required service to the present company, whereupon he handed one of them the piece of chalk and told him simply to write down the numbers that were called out. But the man declared that he could not write. '*Non so scrivere*,'* he said in his rough voice, and his companion added: 'Neither can I.'

God knows if they were telling the truth or merely trying to tease Cipolla. In any case, the latter was far from sharing the mirth their confession gave rise to. He was offended and disgusted. There he sat on a straw chair centre stage, with his legs crossed and smoking another of his cheap cigarettes, which probably tasted better for his having poured himself a second cognac while the simpletons tramped up to the stage. Again, he let a stream of deeply inhaled smoke pass out between his exposed teeth, and like a man withdrawing from something utterly abhorrent to stand on his dignity and own resources, he gazed with an expression of austere disapproval, his crossed foot all the while bobbing up and down, past the two disreputable clowns and over the heads of the audience into empty space.

'Scandalous!' he exclaimed with haughty disdain. 'Go back to your places! Everybody in Italy can write; there is no room in this great country for benighted ignorance. To utter such an indictment before an international audience—a slight by which you not only humiliate yourselves but also deliver the government and your country to idle rumour-mongers—is a cheap joke. If Torre di Venere really is our

Fatherland's most provincial backwater, the refuge of ignoramuses in the most basic fields of knowledge, then I ought to be ashamed of coming here, although I am sure I must have been aware of one or two respects in which the place doesn't quite measure up to Rome...'

At this point he was interrupted by the fellow with the Nubian* haircut and jacket slung over his shoulder, whose pugnacity, as soon became evident, had only temporarily abated, and who proceeded to set himself up as the true and valiant champion of his home patch.

'That's enough!' he shouted. 'Enough of these jokes about Torre. We're all from here and won't stand by and see the town ridiculed in front of foreigners. And these two are our friends. They may not be scholars, but these lads are more honest than a certain person in this room who may brag all he wants about Rome, but didn't found it.'

This was marvellous. The young man certainly had a quick tongue. The audience found such histrionics entertaining, even if they continued to delay the onset of the actual programme. It is always engrossing to listen to two people arguing. There are people who simply find it amusing; their detachment allows them a sort of malicious pleasure; others feel flustered by it, uneasy, and to a great extent I share their misgivings, although at the time I was under the impression that it all rested on a kind of agreement, the two illiterate oafs and the *giovanotto* in the jacket more or less in cahoots with the artist in order to produce a lively show. The children fully enjoyed listening. They understood nothing, but the inflection of the voices kept them on the edge of their seats. So this was a 'magic evening', or at least an Italian one. They expressly found it 'very nice'.

Cipolla had got up and with two of his lurching steps reached the front of the stage.

'Well, look here,' he said with grim cordiality, 'if it isn't our old friend! A youth who wears his tongue on his sleeve!' (Instead of '*lingua*' he used the word '*linguaccia*', meaning 'big mouth', sparking general amusement.) 'Off you go, my friends!' he said, turning to the two bumpkins. 'That's enough of you! I need to deal with this gentleman now, *con questo torregiano di Venere*, this tower watchman of Venus, who no doubt has his eye on various sweet expressions of gratitude for his vigilance...'

'*Ah, non scherzamo!* Let's talk seriously!' shouted the young man, his eyes flashing, and it really did look as if he were about to throw his jacket aside and engage in a more direct form of combat.

Cipolla was not particularly troubled by this. We exchanged worried glances, but unlike us the Cavaliere was dealing with a fellow countryman and had native soil under his feet. He remained unperturbed, flaunting his total superiority. With his gaze fixed on the audience he grinned, flicking his head sideways at the young gamecock as if calling on the house to share in his malicious glee at the way his adversary's rowdiness merely betrayed the lad's crudity. And then, yet again, something strange happened, casting Cipolla's superiority in an uncanny light while reducing the belligerent tension the scene exuded to a humiliating and mystifying travesty.

Staring into his eyes in a peculiar manner, Cipolla drew closer to the young fellow. He even came halfway down the steps to our left that led down to the auditorium, stopping only when he was directly in front of the troublemaker, and slightly above him. The riding whip hung on his arm.

'You are not in the mood for jokes, my son,' he said. 'That is hardly surprising, for anyone can see that you are not feeling well. Even your tongue, whose cleanliness left much to be desired, indicated an acute disorder of the gastric system. One ought not to attend an evening entertainment if one feels as you do, and indeed it is clear that you yourself were unsure whether it might not have been better to make a poultice for your stomach and take to your bed. It was reckless of you to drink so much of that dreadfully sour white wine this afternoon. And now you have the gripes and wish you could just bend over with the pain. Don't be shy, go ahead! Allowing your body to yield in that way to intestinal cramp does have a certain soothing effect.'

He uttered these words with calm intensity and a kind of stern sympathy, while his eyes, piercing those of the young man, seemed at once to wilt and to burn above the upper lids—they were especially strange eyes, and you could tell it was not only manly pride that prevented his counterpart from looking away. Soon, there was no trace of the arrogance that had previously characterized the young man's bronzed face. Gazing at the Cavaliere, his mouth had fallen open, a mouth that formed a smile that was distraught and pitiful.

'Double over!' Cipolla repeated. 'What else can you do? With cramps like that you have to bend double. Surely you won't resist a natural reflex simply because somebody else has recommended you follow it.'

Slowly, the young man raised his forearms, and as he pressed them across his stomach his body stooped to one side and bent over more and more, until finally, feet pointed inward and knees facing each other, a picture of writhing torment, he was practically crouching on the ground. Cipolla left him hunkered in that position for a few moments, then making a little cut through the air with his riding whip, he lurched back to the small round table and poured himself a cognac.

'*Il boit beaucoup*,'* a lady behind us declared. Was that all she had noticed? We were unsure how far the audience understood what was going on. The lad himself, who was standing upright again, smiled awkwardly as if he did not really know what had happened to him. The public, following the events with bated breath, applauded when they came to an end, yelling both '*Bravo, Cipolla!*' and '*Bravo, giovanotto!*' Apparently, the outcome of the altercation was not judged a personal defeat for the young man; instead the audience encouraged him as one might an actor who had played a lamentable character commendably. And it was true that his manner of squirming with stomach pain had been particularly expressive; its vivid allure, one might say, was calculated to appeal to the gallery, and it was, so to speak, a brilliant performance. Nevertheless, I am not sure whether the audience's behaviour had been governed solely by that humane sense of tact in which the South surpasses us, or to what extent it in fact rested on insight into the true nature of things.

The Cavaliere, reinvigorated, had lit another cigarette. The mathematical experiment could recommence. Without further difficulty a young man was found in the back rows who was willing to write dictated numbers on the blackboard. And we knew who he was; knowing the faces of so many of the participants had made the whole entertainment all the more familiar. He worked at the colonial goods and vegetable store on the main street and had served us very nicely on several occasions. He handled the chalk with businesslike dexterity, while Cipolla, who had descended to our level, moved with his crooked gait through the audience collecting two-, three- or four-digit numbers which those asked were free to choose and which the Cavaliere relayed to the young shopkeeper, who, in turn, wrote them down one beneath the other. All this, calculated to produce general amusement, jokes and rhetorical digression, was conducted in a spirit of mutual consent. Inevitably, the artist came across foreigners who had difficulty with Italian numbers, and with these he went to inordinately chivalrous lengths to show his patience; this sparked the polite merriment of the natives, whom he then embarrassed by demanding they translate numbers given in English and French. Some of the numbers recalled significant years in Italian history; these were immediately taken up by Cipolla, who delivered a running commentary on their national importance. Somebody called out 'One!', to which the Cavaliere, with scarcely a backward glance, seriously affronted as ever when anyone attempted to pull his leg, retorted that the number given was one fewer than two digits, whereupon another joker shouted, 'Number Two, then!', raising the laughs that casting innuendoes upon bodily functions are always sure to win among southerners. The Cavaliere alone maintained a dignified restraint, although it was he who had provoked the insinuating remark in the first place; nonetheless, with a shrug of his shoulders, he asked his scribe to record this item, too.

When about fifteen numbers in variously long sequences of digits were on the board, Cipolla asked everyone to add them together. Adept reckoners might do so in their heads, but others were at liberty to use a pencil and pocketbook. While the audience were calculating, Cipolla sat on his chair beside the blackboard, smoking and grimacing with the smugly superior air of the cripple. A five-digit figure was soon to hand. Someone announced it, a second confirmed it, the sum calculated by a third was slightly different, while that of a fourth was in agreement with the first two. Cipolla stood up, knocked some ash off his coat and lifted up the piece of paper in the top right corner of the board to reveal what he had written underneath. The correct sum, close to a million,* was there. He had set it down in advance.

Astonishment and loud applause. The children were overwhelmed. How had he managed to do that, they wanted to know. We informed them that it was a trick and could not be easily understood; after all the man was a magician. So now they knew: this was what a conjurer's soirée was like. First there was the way the fisherman had got stomach pains, and now the result already written on the blackboard—it was wonderful, and we saw with some alarm that for all their eyes were hot and tired, and despite the hands of the clock being at almost half past ten, it was going to be very difficult to persuade them to leave. There would be tears. Still, it was obvious the hunchback was not performing magic, or at least not in the usual sense of an artistic skill, and that what he was doing was not suitable for children. For that matter, I have no way of knowing what the audience really thought of it, but there was plainly some reason to doubt its members had actually been 'free to choose' the numbers that were added up; perhaps one or two of those asked really did think a number up, but in general it was obvious Cipolla had selected his own people, and that the procedure in its entirety, aimed at producing the predetermined result, was subject to his control—at the same time, one nevertheless had to admire the keenness of his arithmetical skills, even if the rest showed a curious propensity to elude one's admiration. All that patriotism, and his tetchy sense of dignity, too: while the Cavaliere's fellow countrymen may have felt at home with all this and been ready for more harmless larks, to outsiders the mixture felt oppressive.

Incidentally, Cipolla himself saw to it that the character of his art was obvious to anyone who had the slightest notion of such things, without of course putting anything into words. Or probably he did speak of it, because he spoke perpetually, if only in vague, bumptious, self-promoting phrases. He continued for a while on the same experimental tack, first of all complicating the calculation by introducing other forms of calculus besides addition, then making them look utterly simple in order to show how it was done. He got people to 'guess' numbers he had previously written down under the piece of paper. It worked almost every time. One person admitted having actually wanted to name a different figure; because the Cavaliere's riding whip had whistled through the air right in front of him at precisely the same moment, however, he had let a number slip out that was then found on the blackboard. Cipolla's shoulders shook with apparent laughter. He feigned admiration for the ingenuity of the participants; his compliments nonetheless had something derisive and degrading about them, and I cannot think his experimental subjects took very much pleasure from them, even if they did smile and felt that at least some of the applause was intended for them. Nor did I gain the impression that the artist was popular with his audience. One sensed a certain revulsion, a latent rebelliousness; but while common courtesy might curb such stirrings, Cipolla's prowess and austere self-assurance proved formidable, and even his riding whip, I think, did much to ensure that the rebellion stayed under the surface.

Following his experiments with numbers he changed to cards. He took two packs of cards out of his pocket, and I remember the basic procedure of his card experiments as follows: he would remove three cards from the first pack and, without looking at them, secrete them in the inside pocket of his frock coat; he would then hold the second pack in front of the subject of the experiment, who would then draw the same three cards—it was not always three correct cards, for sometimes only two were right, but Cipolla nonetheless triumphed in the majority of cases, revealing the three cards for all to see and graciously thanking the audience for the applause with which, for better or worse, they acknowledged his powers. A young man in the front row, to our right, an Italian with sharp and proud facial features, called out that he had resolved to arrive at a clear decision based on his own free will and was determined to reject any sort of influence whatsoever. Under these circumstances, what did Cipolla think would be the upshot?—'You will make my task more difficult,' the Cavaliere replied, 'but your resistance will not alter the outcome. Freedom exists, and so does the will, but freedom of the will does not exist, for a will that aims at being free grasps at empty space. You are free to draw a card or not to draw one. But if you do draw, you will draw the right one—and the more wilfully you do so, the surer will be the outcome.'

One had to admit that he could not have chosen better words to sully the waters and muddle the mind. The defiant young man hesitated nervously before making a move. He drew a card and immediately demanded to see if it was among the concealed ones. 'But what for?' replied an amazed Cipolla. 'Why do things by halves?' But because the man was stubborn enough to insist on proof in advance: '*È servito*',* said the conjurer with an unusually servile gesture, and without looking at them himself, he revealed the three cards in the shape of a fan. The card on the left was the one the young man had drawn.

Amid the applause of the audience, the furious freedom fighter resumed his seat. The devil knows to what extent Cipolla supported his innate talents with mechanical props and duplicitous legerdemain. Even if we assume such a combination of factors to be the case, the audience's boundless curiosity had in any case united it in the enjoyment of an exceptional piece of entertainment, and its acknowledgement of the artist's professional skills was unequivocal. '*Lavora bene!*'* was an observation made here and there by people sitting near us, and what that meant was that objective fairness had triumphed over antipathy and silent indignation.

Cipolla's first action in the wake of this latest success, which was no less impressive for being a partial victory, was to fortify himself with another cognac. He certainly did 'drink a lot', and it was an unpleasant thing to witness. But he plainly needed liquor and cigarettes to maintain and renew his vigour, upon which, as he had said himself, all manner of powerful demands were made. Now and then he really did look sick, run-down and hollow-eyed. But a glassful always restored him to his spirits, and as the smoke he had inhaled flowed from his lungs in a grey stream, his speech poured out too, just as it had before, animated and arrogant. I distinctly remember him progressing from card tricks to the kind of parlour games that rely on human powers that are above or below the level of conscious perception, on intuition and 'magnetic' transference, in short upon a subliminal sort of revelation. What I can no longer recall in detail is the order in which his performances followed. And I won't bore you with descriptions of his experiments—we all know them, we have all taken part at some time or other in the discovery of hidden objects or blindly carried out a series of actions, instructions for which pass from organism to organism along obscure paths. We have all gained our little insights, whether driven by curiosity or contempt, into the ambiguously impure and complex character of the occult, and we have all shaken our heads at the all-too-human tendency to bolster its promotion by means of perplexing humbuggery and underhand manoeuvres, although such traits offer no proof of the inauthenticity of the other elements in this dubious amalgam. All I can say is that there is, of course, a proportionate amplification, with impressions gaining in depth in every direction, when a man like Cipolla is both the director and leading actor in such a murky business. Facing away from the audience, he sat at the back of the stage smoking, while somewhere in the auditorium the plans were secretly laid that he was to obey, and the object was passed from hand to hand that he would discover in its hiding place, and that he would use in an action that had already been agreed upon. The sight he typically presented when—at the hand of someone leading him who was in the know and had instructions to move in full compliance with the Cavaliere while keeping his mind on the agreed objective—he zigzagged through the auditorium with his head thrown back and free hand outstretched, was that of a figure groping forward in fits and starts, then faltering and stopping to listen, then setting off again, only to halt abruptly and correct his course. The roles now seemed reversed, with the current passing in the opposite direction, as the artist, in the unremitting flow of his monologue, did not hesitate to emphasize. He who had for so long been the commanding, insistent one, was now the suffering, receiving part who carried out orders, whose will had been suppressed, and who instead carried out a voiceless common will that seemed to reside in the air; but he stressed that it came to the same thing. The ability to surrender one's self, he said, to become a tool, to obey in the fullest and most absolute sense of the word, was merely the reverse of that other capacity to will and command, in fact they were one and the same; commanding and obeying consisted of a single principle, an indissoluble unity; a person who knew how to obey also knew how to command, and vice versa; each notion was implicit in the other, just as the People and the Leader were immanent in each other, but the achievement itself, that highly disciplined and gruelling achievement, was always his, the leader's and organizer's, in whom the will became obedience, the obedience will, whose person was the birthplace of both, and who therefore laboured under a heavy burden. He asserted this forcefully and often, emphasizing that he was subject to considerable hardship, probably to explain his need for fortification and the frequent refilling of his glass.

He padded about as if in the throes of a vision, guided and borne forward by the mysterious common will. He removed a bejewelled needle from an Englishwoman's shoe, where it had been hidden, and carried it in stops and fitful starts to a different lady—who happened to be Signora Angiolieri—and handed it to her on bended knee accompanied by a sentence it had been agreed he would say, words that seemed obvious enough but that were difficult to utter, for he was to say them in French: 'I present this to you as a token of my veneration', was what he was supposed to say, and to us it seemed there was malice in such a harsh stipulation; it showed a contradiction between an interest in seeing something miraculous succeed, and the desire to see this pretentious man suffer a defeat. But the really curious thing was the way Cipolla, on his knees before Madame Angiolieri and making several attempts to speak, struggled to understand the task he had been assigned. 'I must say something,' he uttered, 'and I have a clear notion of what it is I am supposed to say. Nevertheless, I also feel it would be wrong if the words were to pass my lips. Beware of helping me unintentionally!' he called out, although, or rather because, that was probably exactly what he was hoping for. '*Pensez très fort!*'* he suddenly cried in bad French, whereupon he burst out with the sentence he had actually been ordered to say, albeit in Italian, although he did say the final and most important word of the sentence in the sister tongue, a language with which he was probably entirely unacquainted, instead of *venerazione* saying *vénération*, and ending it with an impossibly nasal vowel—a partial success then, which, after his preceding achievements—the finding of the needle, his approaching the woman who was due to receive it and kneeling before her—appeared almost more impressive than an outright victory would have been and elicited a round of admiring applause.

Cipolla, rising to his feet abruptly, wiped the sweat from his brow. You will understand that, in telling you about the needle, I am relating only one example of the manner in which he worked—an example that particularly stuck in my memory. However, he changed his original method on several occasions, introducing new and improvised variations which came to him at every turn by way of his contact with the audience, all of which took a considerable amount of time. He seemed to take especial inspiration from our landlady; she succeeded in eliciting from him some uncanny instances of second sight. 'It has not escaped my notice, Signora,' he said to her, 'that there is something special about you, something honourable. Anybody who has eyes to see will notice the radiance emanating from your delightful brow; if I am not mistaken it was once stronger than it is today, a gradually fading glow… Say nothing! Don't help me! Your husband sits by your side—am I right?' he declared, turning to the quiet Signor Angiolieri. 'You are this lady's husband, and your happiness is complete. But memories enter your happiness… royal memories… it seems to me that the past, Signora, plays an important role in your present life. You knew a king… Didn't a king once cross your life's path?'

'No,' whispered the dispenser of our midday soup, and her golden-brown eyes shimmered in the noble pallor of her face.

'No? No, no king; I only suggested it in a rough, more general sense, so to speak. No king, and no prince—yet a prince nonetheless, the prince of a more sublime realm. A great artist it was at whose side you once… You wish to gainsay me, and yet you cannot do so wholly; only in part. Well, then! It was a great, indeed a world-famous *woman* artist; you enjoyed her friendship in tender years and her sacred memory overshadows and transfigures your life to this day… Her name? Is it necessary to put a name to the artist whose fame has long been joined with that of the Fatherland and is just as immortal? Eleonora Duse,' he concluded, quietly and solemnly.

Overwhelmed, the small woman nodded to herself. The applause was like a nationalist rally. Almost everyone in the auditorium knew of Signora Angiolieri's important past and was thus in a position to appreciate the Cavaliere's intuition, especially the guests of the Casa Eleonora. The only question was how much of this he had already been acquainted with, or what he had found out when making his initial professional enquiries on arriving at Torre… But I have no reason whatsoever to cast rationalistic suspicion on talents which, before our very eyes, led to the man's undoing.

Moreover, there was now an interval, and our lord and master withdrew. I must admit that I have dreaded reaching this point in my account almost since I began setting it down. It is generally not hard to read people's thoughts, and in our case it is fairly easy. You will inevitably want to ask me why we did not finally leave—and I cannot give you an answer. I don't understand it myself, and I don't know how to explain it. By this time, it must have been all of eleven o'clock, indeed even later. The children were asleep. They had found the most recent series of experiments too boring, and Nature had prevailed with barely a struggle. They slept on our laps, our little girl on mine and the boy on his mother's. Yes, this was reassuring, but it was also a reason to sympathize with them, an injunction to take them to their beds. I can assure you that we wanted to comply with that touching counsel; we really did. We woke the poor things with the announcement that it was now high time to go home. But their plaintive resistance began the moment they came to their senses and, as you know, the abhorrence children feel towards leaving some form of amusement early can only be broken, not subdued. It was wonderful to see the magician, they wailed, and after all, we didn't know what to expect next, we should at least stay and find out what he starts off with after the break, they could sleep a little bit from time to time, but not go home, not go to bed while the lovely evening is still going on without us!

We acquiesced, if only, as far as we knew, for the moment—just for a short while more, just for the time being. There is no excuse for our staying on, nor can I explain it. Did we think that having said A, and making the mistake of bringing the children here in the first place, we were now obliged to say B and let them stay? No, that won't do at all. Was it that we ourselves were having fun? Yes and no; we had very mixed feelings about Cavaliere Cipolla, but if I am not mistaken, everybody in the room shared the same feelings, and yet nobody left.

Or had we succumbed to a certain fascination that emanated from this man who had such a peculiar way of earning his living, a fascination capable of paralysing our resolve even beyond his stage routine and tricks? Or perhaps we can put it down to sheer curiosity. One simply wanted to know how, after all that had already happened, such an evening might proceed, and Cipolla, for that matter, had indicated during his stage exit that his box of tricks was by no means empty, and that even more sensational effects were in the offing.

But all that isn't it—or rather, it isn't all of it. The proper thing would be to answer the question of why we were not leaving now with another question: why hadn't we left Torre earlier? For these, to my mind, are one and the same question, and if I am to wriggle my way out of this quandary, I might as well say that I have already provided the answer. The fact is that what happened in the hall was just as strange and dramatic, just as uncomfortable, mortifying and oppressive as events had been in Torre generally, or indeed more so, for it was in this hall that all the abnormality, disquiet and tension with which the atmosphere of our sojourn had seemed charged came together, and the man whose return we now awaited seemed the very personification of all that; and since the whole hadn't led to our departure, it would seem illogical if this part of it had. You may accept that as an explanation for our immobility, or you may not! I'm afraid I cannot offer you anything better—

Anyway, there was an interval of ten minutes, which grew into almost twenty. The children, still awake and delighted by our indulgence, fully enjoyed the time granted, renewing their acquaintance with the locals, with Antonio, Guiscardo and the man with the paddle-boats. Through cupped hands they hailed the fishermen with well-wishing messages, whose Italian wording they had obtained from us: 'Lots of fish tomorrow!', 'Full nets!', and to Mario, the young 'Esquisito' waiter: '*Mario, una cioccolata e biscotti!*'* And this time, he paid attention, answering with a smile: '*Subito!*'* We would have reason to remember this amicable and somewhat preoccupied, melancholy smile.

Thus the break came to an end; the gong sounded, the gossiping audience regathered, the children sat up eagerly with their hands in their laps. There had been no curtain. Cipolla entered the open stage with his lurching gait and, in the manner of a compère, immediately proceeded to introduce the second part of his show.

Allow me to summarize: this self-assured, misshapen man was the most powerful hypnotist I had ever come across. Duping the public by advertising his performances as those of a conjurer was evidently a ruse to circumvent police regulations that strictly prohibited the commercial practice of such powers. Perhaps formal obfuscation in such cases was customary, and to some extent officially tolerated, or partly so. Be that as it may, the conjurer had from the beginning made no secret of the real nature of his activities, and indeed the second half of his programme now openly and exclusively concentrated on the special experiment of demonstrating the suspension and coercion of the human will, while at a purely rhetorical level retaining its focus on circumlocution. In a protracted series of experiments that were by turns humorous, exciting and astonishing, and were still in full swing by midnight, we were shown everything, every sort of marvel from the unremarkable to the monstrous, that this natural and uncanny field had to offer, while for their part the audience laughed and shook their heads, slapping their thighs as they applauded every grotesque detail, thoroughly under the spell of an austere and self-assured personality, although it seemed to me, at least, that they were not without feelings of defiance towards the unique form of humiliation which, for each individual and for all, lay in Cipolla's triumphs.

Two things played leading parts in these triumphs: the cognac glass and the claw-handled riding whip. The role of the first was to fire up his demonic energy, for it seemed that without it exhaustion beckoned, and this could have engendered a humane fellow feeling for the man among the audience, were it not for the second feature, his whistling scourge, that offensive symbol of mastery whose arrogance kept us down and whose application kept at bay any gentler sentiments than those generated by our bewildered and peevish submission. Did he miss them? Did he even want our sympathy? Did he want our all? A remark of Cipolla's that has stuck in my mind did suggest such covetousness. He made it at the height of his experiments when he had, by means of stroking and breathing on a young and obviously highly susceptible volunteer, put him into a such a deep catatonic trance that he was able not only to prop up the young man's extended body at the neck and feet between the backs of two chairs, but also to sit on his rigid torso without its giving way. The sight of this monster in a frock coat squatting on the young man's stiffened frame was beyond belief and ghastly, and the audience, supposing that the victim of this scientific diversion must be suffering, expressed its sympathy. '*Poveretto!*'—'Poor fellow!' kindly voices called out. '*Poveretto!*' an embittered Cipolla sneered back. 'You've got the wrong man, ladies and gentlemen. *Sono io, il poveretto!* I am the one who has to suffer.' The audience had a lesson to learn. All right then—perhaps it was Cipolla himself who had borne the cost of our entertainment and taken upon himself the stomach cramps to which the *giovanotto* had supplied the tormented faces. But appearances spoke otherwise, and one is not inclined to say *poveretto* to someone who suffers in his effort to debase others.

I have jumped ahead of my story and tossed the proper sequence of events aside. Even today my memory is filled with the facts of the Cavaliere's sufferance, but I find it impossible to order them properly, which is of no importance anyway. What I do know, however, is that the larger and more elaborate efforts, those that received the most applause, impressed me less than certain smaller ones that were quickly over. The phenomenon of the youngster transformed into a bench came to mind just now only because of the rebuke it gave rise to... That an elderly lady asleep in a straw chair should be lulled by Cipolla into the illusion that she was on a journey to India and in her trance be capable of a lively account of her adventures on land and at sea, detained me less, and I found it less sensational, than the incident immediately following the interval when a tall, well-built man of military aspect was unable to lift his arm merely because the hunchback had given notice that he would be unable to do so, underlining this remark with a single flick of his whip. I can still see the face of that stately, moustachioed *colonnello* before me, and I can still see the way he grinned and clenched his teeth as he wrestled to recover his freedom of movement. What a muddle! He appeared to want to act, but not to be able, yet his real difficulty was probably that he was simply unable to want, for the ruling factor here was the will's entanglement with itself leading to a paralysis of freedom, just as our taskmaster had sneeringly predicted to the Roman gentleman.

And I am even less able to forget the comic but also touching and ghostly scene involving Signora Angiolieri, whose ethereal lack of resistance to his powers the Cavaliere would certainly have noticed during his first, brazen survey of the auditorium. In an act of pure sorcery he literally pulled her out of her seat, drew her away from her row and took her with him, while beforehand, so that his light might shine all the brighter, he had asked Signor Angiolieri to call to his wife by her forename and to throw the weight of his own existence and marital rights in the balance, so to speak, demanding that he appeal with his husband's voice to everything in his wife's soul that might protect her virtue against evil magic. Yet how futile this proved! Cipolla, standing at some distance from the couple, let his whip whistle once, with the effect that our hostess gave a violent start and turned her face towards him. 'Sofronia!' Signor Angiolieri now called (we had no idea that Signora Angiolieri's forename was Sofronia), and how right he was to start calling so soon, for it was clear to everybody that there was no time to lose: his wife's face remained unwaveringly fixed on the cursed Cavaliere. With his riding whip hanging from his wrist, Cipolla, backing away from his victim step by step, began to make beckoning and pulling gestures with his ten long, yellow fingers. At this point the pallid, shimmering figure of Signora Angiolieri arose from her seat, turned fully towards her charmer and began to float along in his wake. What a ghostly and dire sight! With a moonstruck expression on her face, arms stiff, her lovely hands raised a fraction at the wrist, her feet seemingly together, she appeared to glide slowly from her bench and to follow her tempter… 'Call her, Sir, you must call her now!' the horrible man urged, and Signor Angiolieri's weak voice called out: 'Sofronia!' Oh, but he called her name several times, and since his wife was drifting ever further away from him, he even cupped one hand around his mouth, waving to her with the other as he called. But that poor voice of love and duty faded unheard as his lost one went from him: moonstruck Signora Angiolieri, enchanted and unhearing, sailing away, passing into the central aisle and along it towards the beckoning hunchback, towards the exit. The effect was consummate; there could be no doubt that if her master had willed it, she would have followed him to the ends of the earth.

'*Accidente!*'* yelled Signor Angiolieri in genuine dismay, leaping to his feet as they reached the door of the hall. But in the same instant the Cavaliere cast aside his victor's laurels, so to speak, and broke off. 'Enough, Signora—and thank you,' he said, offering the astonished woman now coming to her senses his arm with comedic chivalry, before leading her back to Signor Angiolieri. 'My dear Sir,' he greeted her husband, 'here is your wife! I return her into your hands unharmed, and with my compliments. With all the powers of your manhood cherish this treasure that is entirely yours, and inspire her vigilance with the knowledge that there are powers stronger than reason and virtue, powers that are only very rarely found coupled with magnanimity and self-denial!'

Poor Signor Angiolieri, so quiet and bald! He did not look like a person who could protect his happiness even against demonic powers far weaker than those displayed here, which added mockery to terror. With an air of gravity and self-satisfaction the Cavaliere resumed his place on the stage accompanied by applause which, in response to his eloquence, had grown twice as loud as before. It was this triumph more than any other, if I remember correctly, that boosted his authority to the point where he would make his audience dance—yes indeed, dance. This should be taken quite literally, and it added a certain degeneracy to the proceedings, a certain unhinged, late-night, topsy-turvy dissolution of whatever critical resistance had until then restrained the unpleasant man's influence. He naturally had to fight hard to perfect his supremacy, especially against the recalcitrance of the young gentleman from Rome whose moral rigidity threatened to set a public example endangering that supremacy. However, the Cavaliere knew all about the importance of examples; clever enough to attack the weakest link in the chain, he made the feeble and easily entranced young man whom he had previously made stiff as a board lead off the dancing orgy. The latter had a way of reacting as if struck by a bolt of lightning whenever his master as much as glanced at him, throwing back his shoulders, placing his fingers along his trouser seam and falling into a state of military somnambulism, so that one could easily see that he would be willing to fulfil any task that was asked of him, however ridiculous. He also seemed to be quite content with his submissive role and glad to be rid of his wretched freedom of will, for he was always offering his services as the subject of experiments and plainly staked his honour on presenting the perfect example of obliging soullessness and spinelessness. Now, too, he climbed to the stage, and it required only a single flick of the whip in the air to make the young man follow the Cavaliere's instruction to execute a so-called 'step-dance',* which meant closing one's eyes and letting one's head bob up and down while flinging one's puny limbs about in a kind of self-contented frenzy.

This was apparently enjoyable, and it was not long before the young man was joined by two other youngsters, one in simple attire and the other well dressed, who proceeded to step-dance on either side of him. It was at this point that the gentleman from Rome raised his voice and defiantly enquired whether the Cavaliere meant to teach him to dance, too, even if he did not want to.

'Even if you do not want to!' Cipolla retorted in a tone of voice I shall not forget; his dreadful '*Anche se non vuole!*' rings in my ears to this day. Then the struggle began. After pouring himself a glassful and lighting a fresh cigarette, Cipolla told the Roman to stand in the central aisle with his face to the exit and, after taking up a position himself some distance behind him, let his whip whistle through the air to the command: '*Balla!*'* His antagonist did not move. '*Balla!*' repeated the Cavaliere sharply, flicking his whip. You could now see the young man's neck begin to move inside his collar, and at the same moment one of his hands lifted at the wrist, and a heel twisted outward. But this went on for some time: there were quivers and twitches—indications that he was about to succumb, signs that seemed now to grow stronger only to be suppressed again. It was plain to all that what we were seeing here, and what Cipolla would have to defeat, was a deliberate commitment to resistance, a heroic obstinacy. This courageous being, in attempting to save the honour of mankind, was twitching but not dancing, and since the experiment had been dragging on for a long time, the Cavaliere was forced to divide his attention and turned now and then to the stage, to the dancers flouncing about, disciplining them with a whistle of his whip, but not without simultaneously informing the audience 'aside' that the frolickers would not in the least be weary after this, no matter how long they went on for, since it was in fact not they who were dancing, but he himself. Then his eyes would return to the Roman, boring their way into the back of his neck, assaulting that firmness of will which defied his command.

You could see it falter, his firmness of will, under the Cavaliere's whip-cracks and constant solicitations—one watched it matter-of-factly, if to some extent with sympathy and sadness, and with a cruel form of gratification. If I understood these events correctly, then the fellow was constrained by the negativity of his defensive stance. In mental terms, it is probably impossible to live by not wanting something; in the long run, not wanting to do something simply cannot be one's purpose in life; between not wanting to do something and no longer wanting at all, and therefore succumbing to a demand nevertheless, there is probably too little space for the idea of freedom not to feel squeezed, and so it was precisely in this direction that the Cavaliere's coaxing—woven in between his whistling whip and his commands—pressed, combining interventions that were known only to himself with those of a bewildering psychological nature. '*Balla!*' he said. 'Who would accept such torture? Is this self-violation what you mean by freedom? *Una ballatina!** Your arms and legs are dying for it. How good it will feel to let them do what they want at last! But look, you already *are* dancing! That isn't fighting now—it's pleasure!' And indeed it was. The stubborn young man's twitching and stretching got the better of him; he raised his arms, lifted his knees, and suddenly his joints relaxed and he flung his limbs in every direction—and he danced, and it was in this state, and to the applause of the audience, that the Cavaliere led him onto the stage to join his other marionettes. Once there, the subjugated man's face became a public spectacle: he had a broad grin, his eyes were half closed while he 'enjoyed himself'. It was a kind of consolation to see that he was happier now than he had been in the hour of his pride.

His 'fall' marked an epoch: the ice was broken; Cipolla's triumph had reached its high point; Circe's* staff, that whistling leather whip with its claw handle, reigned supreme. At the time I have in mind, which must have been long after midnight, between eight and ten people were dancing on the small stage, but there was all manner of activity in the auditorium too, and an English lady with a pince-nez and long teeth, without receiving the least encouragement from the Cavaliere, had left her row to perform a tarantella* in the central aisle. Meanwhile Cipolla was slouching on a straw chair stage left, gulping down his cigarette smoke and smugly blowing it out again through his nasty teeth. Tapping his feet and occasionally shrugging his shoulders, he gazed into the carefree audience, now and then letting his whip whistle backwards behind him at one of the dancing puppets who, out of sheer enjoyment, was slacking off. The children were still awake at this hour. I mention them with shame. This was not a good place to be, for them more than for anyone, and the only reason I can think of for our having not yet removed them from the scene was that the infectious carelessness which affected everyone had taken hold of us too at that late hour. For by that time it made no difference. At least, and thank God, they had no sense of the disreputable nature of the evening's entertainment. Their innocence showed itself again and again in their delight at being so exceptionally permitted to be present at such a spectacle, a magician's soirée. Repeatedly, they had fallen asleep on our laps for a quarter of an hour at a time, and now, with red cheeks and their eyes full of sleep, they laughed with all their heart at the way the master of the evening made the people jump about. It hadn't occurred to them that it would be so hilarious, and with their inept little hands they gladly participated in every round of applause. But they jumped from their seats with joy when Cipolla beckoned their friend Mario, Mario from 'Esquisito'—beckoned him like a figure in a cartoon, raising his hand in front of his nose and, by turns, stretching out his index finger and curling it back to form a hook.

Mario obeyed. I see him still, climbing the stairs to the Cavaliere, who continued to beckon him with his index finger in that grotesquely characteristic manner. I also remember quite clearly that for an instant the young man hesitated. For much of the evening he had leant with crossed arms or his hands in the pockets of his jacket against a wooden pillar in the side aisle to our left, where the *giovanotto* with the bellicose haircut stood, and, as far as we could see, had followed the performance attentively but without much enjoyment and God knows how much insight. After all that, he evidently found his being coerced into participation an unpleasant prospect. It was nonetheless only understandable that he obeyed the call. His profession had made him used to doing so, and apart from anything else, how was a simple young fellow like him supposed to summon the wherewithal to spurn the bidding of a man as crowned with success as was Cipolla at that hour. Whether he liked or not, he moved away from his pillar, thanking those standing in front of him who turned as he made for the stage, stepping aside to let him pass, and climbed the steps, a sceptical smile around his protruding lips.

Picture him as a stocky, twenty-year-old youth with closely cropped hair, a low forehead and heavily lidded eyes of an indeterminate grey colour, shot with green and yellow. This I know so precisely because we often spoke to him. His upper face with its flat nose, which carried a saddle of freckles, receded in relation to the lower half, whose thick lips, between which moist teeth were visible, were the dominant feature, and these thick lips together with his hooded eyes lent his features an unsophisticated wistfulness, which was the reason we liked Mario from the first. His conduct showed not an ounce of grossness; it would otherwise have been at variance with the unusual slenderness and delicacy of his hands, which even southerners found genteel, and which it was a pleasure to be served by.

We knew him humanly, without knowing him personally, if you will permit me to make that distinction. We saw him practically every day and had developed a certain sympathy for his dreamy, frequently absent-minded ways, which he would hastily correct by adjusting to an especially obliging mode. His manner was serious, and only the children could make him smile; it was not surly, but neither was it ingratiating, and was without forced affability, or rather, it eschewed affability altogether and seemingly did not aspire to being liked. We would have remembered his person in any case, as one of those unremarkable memories of travel that sometimes come to mind more easily than the principal ones. Of his circumstances we knew only that his father was a lowly clerk in the *municipio*, and that his mother was a laundress.

The white jacket he wore as a waiter sat better than the shabby pin-striped suit in which he went up now, with a watered silk neckerchief instead of a collar, its ends tucked under his closed jacket. He now approached the Cavaliere, who, however, did not stop the motions of his finger under his nose, so that Mario had to draw closer still, right up to the powerful man's legs and the chair where he was sitting, whereupon Cipolla stuck his elbows out and took hold of him, turning him so that we could see his face. Cheerfully, with a casual imperiousness, he inspected him from head to toe.

'What's all this, *ragazzo mio*?'* he said, 'How come we have taken so long to get acquainted? But please believe me, I have already made your acquaintance... Oh yes, I have had my eye on you for some time and assured myself of your admirable qualities. How could I have forgotten you again though? So many meetings, you know... Tell me, my boy, what do they call you? It is only your first name I want.'

'My name is Mario,' the youth answered quietly.

'Ah, Mario, very good. Yes, there is such a name. A common name. An ancient name,* one of those names that keep the heroic traditions of the Fatherland alive. *Bravo. Salve!*'* And he stretched his arm and flat hand out diagonally from his bad shoulder in a Roman salute.* If he was a little drunk, that was hardly astonishing, but he nevertheless spoke very distinctly, emphatically and volubly, although by now a certain smugness had crept into his demeanour and intonation, a kind of lolling, pasha-like arrogance.

'All right then, my Mario,' he continued, 'it is good that you have come here this evening and have even donned such a dashing neckerchief, which suits your face handsomely and will stand you in good stead with the girls, those delectable maidens of Torre di Venere…'

A laugh sounded from the standing room, roughly from where Mario had been earlier—it had come from the *giovanotto* with the warrior's haircut; he stood there, with his jacket over his shoulder, and again gave a crude and rather sneering laugh.

Mario shrugged his shoulders; at least I think that is what he did. Anyway, he shrugged. Or perhaps he cringed, and the jerking of his shoulders was a belated disguise, as if he wanted to say that both his neckerchief and the fair sex were of no importance to him.

The Cavaliere gave a downward glance.

'We needn't worry about him,' he said. 'He is jealous, probably of the success your neckerchief gives you with the girls, or maybe, too, because of the friendly chat we are having up here, you and I… If he wants I could remind him of his stomach cramps. It would be no trouble to me. Tell me, Mario: you are enjoying yourself this evening… and during the day you work in a shop selling dry goods?'

'In a café,' the young man corrected.

'Better in a café, then! Cipolla got it wrong for once. So you are a *cameriere*,* a cup-bearer, a Ganymede*—I'm happy with that, another reminder of antiquity—*salvietta*!'* To the amusement of the audience the Cavaliere once again stretched out his arm in a salute.

Mario smiled, too. 'Although before that,' he added parenthetically, 'I did serve for a while in a shop in Portoclemente.' Something in his remark suggested how human it is to want to help a prophecy along, to find something in it that is correct.

'Aha, aha! In a dry goods shop!'

'There were combs and brushes,' Mario replied evasively.

'Didn't I say that you weren't always a Ganymede, didn't always serve with a napkin? Even when Cipolla makes a blunder, he does it in such a way as to inspire trust. Tell me, do you trust me?'

An indefinite gesture.

'Not exactly a proper answer,' the Cavaliere observed. 'It is clearly difficult to gain your trust. I must admit that even I am having difficulty.

In your features I see reserve, sadness, *un tratto di malinconia**… But tell me,'—and he took hold of Mario's hand encouragingly—'are you distressed?'

'*Nossignore!*'* Mario answered swiftly and assertively.

'You *are* distressed,' the magician insisted, high-handedly over-riding the young man's assertion. 'You don't want me to see that? Go on, try fooling Cipolla! Of course, it's girls, isn't it? It's a girl: you're lovesick.'

Mario shook his head vigorously. At the same moment, close by, the *giovanotto*'s heartless laugh rang out, catching the Cavaliere's attention. The latter's eyes glanced upward, wandered about in the air, but he kept his ear cocked to the source of the laughter and, just as he had done once or twice while talking to Mario, he let his whip whistle over his shoulder towards his marionettes, making sure none of them flagged. In doing so, however, he almost lost his conversation partner, because Mario suddenly started and, turning away from Cavaliere, attempted to slip away via the steps. He was red around the eyes. Cipolla only just managed to hold him back.

'Hold your horses!' he said. 'What's up? You're bolting, are you, Ganymede? And with things now at their best, too, or about to be at their best. Just stay here, will you, for I promise fine things; I promise to convince you that there is no reason for your distress. This girl you know, and whom others know, this—now what was her name? Wait! I see her name in your eyes, it's on the tip of my tongue, and I see you, too, are about to utter it…'

'Silvestra!' called the *giovanotto* from below.

The Cavaliere kept a straight face.

'Aren't some people rude?' he asked, without looking down, or rather, without allowing the disturbance to interrupt his conversation with Mario. 'Those truly impertinent cockerels that crow at all hours of the day and night? And that was one of them, stealing her name from your lips and mine, so vain he probably believes he has a special right to it. Let's leave him behind. Silvestra, on the other hand, your Silvestra, yes, what a girl, eh?! A real treasure! She's so lovely, it makes your heart stand still just to see her walk, breathe, laugh. And then her round arms when she washes and tosses her head back and flicks the hair out of her eyes! An angel from paradise!'

Mario leaned his head forward and stared at him. He seemed to have forgotten the audience and where he was. The red blotches around his eyes had become larger and looked as if they were painted on. I have rarely seen anything like it. His thick lips were parted.

'And this angel of yours is making you suffer,' Cipolla continued, 'or rather, you are making yourself suffer on her account… That is different, my friend, a significant difference, believe me! There are misunderstandings in love—indeed that is where misunderstanding feels most at home. You might ask what Cipolla, with his small bodily imperfection, can know about love? And you would be mistaken; he knows a great deal about it; he has a powerful and comprehensive understanding of all it entails, and it would be very worth your while to follow what he has to say about it. But let us not bother with Cipolla; we shall leave him out of it altogether and think only of Silvestra, your own delightful Silvestra! What? She would give some crowing fool preference over you, so he may laugh and you must weep? Preference over you, such a soulful and likeable lad? That is somewhat unlikely, is it not? Impossible, in fact. And Cipolla and she know better, they do. If I were she, you see, and had the choice of some smeary Jack Tar, some bit of salt cod, some shrimp—and a Mario, a Knight of the Serviette, moving among ladies and gentlemen, skilled in the arts of serving refreshments to foreign visitors, and who loves me with true, passionate feeling—upon my soul, making this decision isn't hard for my heart, for it knows whom alone I shall give it to, and blushing have already given it to. It is time for my chosen one to see it, and to understand. It is time for you to see me, Mario, and to know me, my love… Tell me, who am I?'

It was horrid to watch the way this imposter made himself seem charming, coyly turning his sloping shoulders, pining with his puffy eyes, his mawkish smile baring his splintered teeth. Oh, but what had his deceiving words done to our Mario? It is as hard for me to put it into words as it was to watch, for it was an exposure of his innermost being, the public exhibition of a disconsolate and rapturously delusional passion. He folded his hands in front of his mouth, his shoulders heaving with every violent breath. Doubtless he could not trust his eyes or ears for joy, but there was one thing he had overlooked: he really could not trust them. 'Silvestra!' he breathed, overcome, from the bottom of his heart.

'Kiss me!' said the hunchback. 'You can, believe me! I love you. Kiss me here,' and lifting his hand and arm up and sticking his little finger out, he pointed with the tip of his forefinger to his cheek, next to his mouth. And Mario bent down and kissed him.

A hush fell over the room. The moment was grotesque, monstrous and enthralling—the moment of Mario's bliss. And yet a sound broke that dreadful interlude, that hiatus in which all the confusions of joy and illusion pressed so heavily on our emotions, not heard at first, but coming immediately after the unhappy, bizarre union of Mario's lips with the repugnant flesh that foisted itself upon his tenderness; it was the sound, to our left, of the *giovanotto* laughing, and it alone was heard amid the suspense of that moment—brutish, yes, and gloating too, and yet, if I was not much mistaken, it also contained an undercurrent of compassion towards so much wistful misfortune, nor could one deny that it was reminiscent of that cry '*poveretto!*' which the magician had earlier deemed to have been addressed to the wrong person and which he claimed should rightly apply to himself.

Barely had the laughter subsided, however, when the recipient of the caress made his whip whistle through the air, lower down this time, next to the leg of his chair, and Mario, coming to himself, started up and back. He stood in that position and stared, his upper body leaning backwards as he pressed one hand over the other to his abused lips, then, beating his temples with the knuckles of both hands several times, turned on his heels and dashed down the steps while the audience applauded Cipolla, whose hands lay in his lap and whose shoulders shook with laughter. Reaching the bottom and still in full fling, Mario wheeled around with his legs apart and threw up his arm, and two flat-sounding detonations crashed through the applause and laughter.

There was immediate silence. Even the step-dancing puppets came to a standstill and gawped. In a flash Cipolla had leapt up from his chair. And there he stood with his arms spread out in front of him as if to fend off some danger or shout 'Stop! Silence now! Get away from me! What is happening?', only to slump back on his chair an instant later, his head lolling on his chest, and in the next instant to tumble sideways off the chair to the floor, where he lay motionless, a jumble of clothes and twisted limbs.

The pandemonium knew no bounds. Ladies shuddered and buried their faces in the chests of their companions. Someone called for a doctor, another for the police. Some people stormed the stage and others, in the crush, threw themselves upon Mario to disarm him, to wrench from the hand hanging by his side the small, tarnished metal mechanism that barely resembled a pistol and whose almost non-existent barrel had set Fate in such a disconcerting direction.

We took the children—yes, at last—and dragged them towards the exit, passing a pair of *carabinieri* who had just arrived. 'Was that really the end?' they wanted to know, just to be sure… 'Yes, that was the end,' we assured them. A horrific end, a thoroughly dire end. And yet a liberating end nonetheless—I could not help but feel that, and still do!

THE TRANSPOSED HEADS

AN INDIAN LEGEND

I

Whoever hears the tale of Sita* of the beautiful hips, daughter of Sumantra, a cow-breeder and scion of the warrior caste, and that of her two husbands (if one may say as much), a story as bloody as it is bewildering, will face the greatest of challenges to their emotional fortitude and mental capacity to resist the ghastly beguilements of Maya.* It is thus to be hoped that listeners will follow the resolute example of the narrator, for it almost requires more courage to tell such a story than to hear it. How it came about, from first to last, is nevertheless what follows.

In days when memories would arise in people's minds as if a sacrificial cup were slowly filling with an intoxicating drink or with blood, a time when the womb of a stern and patriarchal piety opened to the seed of the Primeval Being, when nostalgia for the Mother drew rejuvenated fervour to the ancient symbols, swelling the pilgrim caravans that thronged in spring to the dwelling places of the great World Nurse:* it was then that two young men, in years and caste not far apart, but different in physical type, had a close friendship. The younger of the two was called Nanda, the somewhat older, Shridaman. The first was eighteen years old, while Shridaman had already turned twenty-one, and each of them, wearing the sacred thread, had been initiated on his appointed day into the community of the twice-born.* They hailed from the same settlement, a temple village called Welfare-of-Cows, which, at the behest of the gods, had been founded long ago in the land of Kosala,* where it still stood. The village lay enclosed by a cactus hedge and wooden palisade, the posts and crossbars of whose gates, facing the four points of the compass, a wandering seer and initiate of Sarasvati,* the goddess of speech—a man who never spoke a false word and was fed by the villagers—had described in his blessing as oozing with honey and butter.

The friendship between the two young men rested on the disparity of their I-and-my-feelings, with those of the one aspiring to those of the other, and vice versa. For incarnation gives rise to separation,

separation to difference, difference to comparison, comparison to disquiet, disquiet to amazement, amazement to admiration, while admiration leads to a desire for interchange and union. *Etad vai tad.** This is that. This is a doctrine that especially applies to youth, when the clay of life is still soft and the I-and-my-feelings have not yet hardened into fragments of the One Being.

Young Shridaman was a merchant and merchant's son, Nanda a blacksmith and cowherd, for his father Garga wielded a hammer and fanned his forge with birds' wing feathers while also keeping cattle in a pen and putting them out to pasture. As for Shridaman's begetter, Bhavabhûti by name, he traced his paternal lineage to a Brahmin line versed in the Vedas,* which Garga and his son certainly could not. Yet they were not Shudras* either, and for all their slightly goatish noses, it was to human society that they belonged. And as for Shridaman and indeed for Bhavabhûti, too, their Brahmanical affiliations were little more than a memory, for Bhavabhûti's father had knowingly remained at the life stage of householder, which follows on from that of student, and, during all his lifetime, had not proceeded to the stages of hermit or ascetic. He had disdained to live solely from pious gifts paid in tribute to his knowledge of the Vedas, or perhaps he thought there would not be enough to eat, and had begun an honest trade in lint, camphor, sandalwood, silk and chintz. And thus his son, Bhavabhûti, begotten to serve the gods, also became a *vanija*, or merchant, in the village settlement called Welfare-of-Cows, and then there was his son, Shridaman, who had followed in the same footsteps, albeit not without devoting several years of his youth, under the aegis of a guru and spiritual master, to the study of grammar, astronomy and the rudiments of the knowledge of essences.*

Not so Nanda, Garga's son. His karma* was different and he had never, whether by dint of tradition or descent, concerned himself with matters of the mind; he was just as he was, a son of the people, a cheery fellow with Krishna's looks, for he had dark hair and skin and even had Krishna's lucky calf-curl on his chest.* Smithing had given him sturdy arms and his work as a cowherd had shaped him, too, for his body, which he liked to rub with mustard oil and to adorn with garlands of wild flowers and gold jewellery, was comely, in keeping with the sweetness of his beardless face, and even if his lips were a little thick and his nose, as already indicated, bore some resemblance to that of a goat, these were endearing features, and his black eyes almost always smiled.

And all this, when he compared it to himself, was pleasing to Shridaman, whose limbs and hair were several shades lighter than Nanda's and whose facial features also differed. The ridge of Shridaman's nose was as thin as a knife blade, and he had eyes that were gentle in pupil and lid and a soft, fan-shaped beard on his cheeks. His limbs, too, were soft, not shaped by cow-herding and smithery, but more like those of a Brahmin or merchant, with a narrow, rather flabby chest, and a modicum of lard on his little belly—but he was otherwise flawless, with fine knees and feet. It was a body well suited to serving as accessory and appendage to a noble and knowledgeable head, which of course was the main part of the ensemble, whereas in all of Nanda (so to speak) the body was the main thing, while the head was merely a pleasant appurtenance. All in all the two were like Shiva when he appeared in two forms, one as a bearded ascetic lying as if dead at the goddess's feet, the other, however, as a standing figure in the bloom of youth facing the goddess, his limbs outstretched.

But since they were not One—unlike Shiva, who is both life and death, world and eternity in the Mother—but constituted separate beings here below, they appeared to each other as images. Each of their my-feelings found itself boring, and although aware that all beings consist of shortcomings, they observed each other with interest because they were different. Shridaman, with his fine mouth and fine beard, took pleasure in thick-lipped Nanda's uncultivated Krishna features, while Nanda, who was partly flattered by this—and more so because Shridaman's lighter colour, noble head and refined way of speaking, which, as we know, had gone hand in hand with wisdom and the knowledge of essence from the very beginning, had made a great impression upon him—loved nothing better than to consort with Shridaman, and so it was that they became inseparable friends. At the same time, their affection for each other contained a degree of mockery, too, with Nanda poking fun at Shridaman's pale flab, thin nose and genteel speech, while Shridaman would secretly scoff at Nanda's goatish nose and rough and ready affability. But this kind of discreet mockery belongs to the disquiet that derives from comparison, implying a tribute to I-and-my-feelings, and does not in any way impair the desire for Maya that accrues from it.

II

Now it came to pass one delightful springtime when the air was mellifluous with birdsong, that Nanda and Shridaman undertook a cross-country journey together on foot, and each had a particular reason to do so. Nanda had received instructions from his father, Garga, to barter for a quantity of raw iron with folk of humble standing whom Nanda would know how to talk to, people who wore only aprons made of rushes and were skilled and well practised in ironstone smelting. They lived in homesteads several days' journey to the west of the friends' home village, not far from the small town of Kuruksheta,* which in turn was situated some distance north of the populous city of Indraprastha,* by the Yamuna* river, and which was where Shridaman also had work to do. The latter's task was to visit a business friend of his family there, a Brahmin who had likewise not moved beyond the stage of householder, and, to his best possible advantage, to barter a parcel of brightly coloured yarn, which the women at home had spun from fine thread, for rice pestles and a particularly practical sort of firelighter, for there was a shortage of both items at Welfare-of-Cows.

After walking for a day and a half, amid other travellers on rural roads or alone through woods and wasteland, each with his burden on his back—Nanda with a box of betel nuts, cowrie shells and Alta-red* on bast paper to grace the soles of feet, goods with which he intended to pay the lowly folk for their ore, and Shridaman with his yarn sewn into a deerskin, which, however, Nanda too, out of friendship, sometimes carried on his back—they came to a holy bathing place sacred to Kali, the All-Encompassing, the Mother of worlds and beings, who is the dream-drunkenness of Vishnu, and this site was on the banks of a stream called the Goldfly, which, like a colt let loose, gleefully springs from the womb of the mountain but soon slows and at a holy place joins the river Yamuna, which in its turn, and at a place even holier, feeds into the eternal Ganga, which enters the sea by many mouths. Copious bathing places, highly renowned, purging all stains, where scooping up the waters of life and immersing oneself in their womb one may receive rebirth—many such sites lie along the river-banks and estuaries of the Ganga and at places where other rivers flow into the earthly Milky Way and where still others join with those rivers, as does the Goldfly, daughter of the abode of the snows, with the Yamuna, and in all these places you will find sites of purification and union with the divine that are convenient to all who bring offerings or seek communion and which are furnished with consecrated steps for access, so that the devout need not splash through reeds and lotus without decorum or sanctity to enter the holy womb, but can step forward with dignity to drink and sprinkle water on themselves.

Now, the bathing place the two friends had come upon was not one of those larger ones to which both lowly and noble flock (albeit at different hours) and where countless offerings are brought, and whose miraculous qualities are proclaimed by the pandits. It was an unassuming, tranquil, hidden place, not situated at the confluence of two rivers but erected at a spot of no particular importance on the Goldfly riverbank, which rose several steps from the riverbed and whose high point was also the site of a small, merely wooden and rather ramshackle temple devoted to the goddess of all desires and pleasures, a shrine sporting many vivid carvings, with a sprawling hunchbacked tower above the cella.* The steps leading down to the womb, too, were wooden; they were damaged, but nonetheless adequate for a dignified descent.

The youths expressed their joy at finding a spot offering an unexpected opportunity for prayer, refreshment and relaxation in the shade. It had grown quite hot by midday; the heavy summer threatened to be early this spring, and a grove of bushes and trees stretched from the little temple along the ridge of the riverbank—mango, teak and kadamba, magnolia, tamarisk and tala palm, offering protection from the sun and a good place to rest and have breakfast. First, the friends fulfilled their religious obligations, as well as the circumstances permitted. There was no priest present to provide them with oil or clarified butter with which to anoint the stone lingam-idols positioned on the small terrace in front of the temple. Using a ladle they found there they scooped water out of the river and, murmuring the appropriate words, did their good deed. They then stepped down into the greenish womb, their hands cupped together in front of them, drank, sprinkled an appropriate amount of water over themselves, dipped under the surface and gave thanks, after which, out of sheer enjoyment, they stayed on to bathe a little longer than was spiritually necessary, and, with the blessed sensation of union with the divine in their limbs, proceeded to their chosen resting place under the trees.

Once there, they shared their provisions with each other like brothers, shared them although each could have eaten his own and although each had nothing but what the other also had. When Nanda broke a barley cake, he straight away passed half to Shridaman, saying: 'Here you are, my friend', and when Shridaman cut a piece of fruit, he handed half to Nanda with the same words. Shridaman sat to eat with his legs to one side and feet together on the fresh green grass, which was as yet unscorched. Nanda, on the other hand, squatted in the common manner, with his knees drawn up and feet placed in front of him, a posture hard to maintain for long if it does not run in the blood. They had adopted these positions unconsciously and without thinking, for if they had attended to their way of sitting, Shridaman, following his liking for the primitive, would have drawn up his knees in front of him, whereas Nanda, desiring the opposite, would have sat sideways. The latter wore a cap on his wet, black, plain hair, a loincloth of white cotton, rings around his upper arms, and hanging from his neck, framing the lucky calf-curl on his chest, a necklace of stone beads held together by gold ribbon. Shridaman had wound a white cloth around his head and was dressed in white cotton, too—a short-sleeved tunic in whose open neck an amulet-pouch hung on a thin chain, and which fell over a puffed, apron-like breechcloth wound around the lower body. As a sign of their piety, each wore a mineral-white mark on his forehead.

When they had finished eating, they put aside the leftovers and talked. It was so pretty here that no prince or king could have been more fortunate. Between the trees—tall bamboo and calamus stalks whose leaves and clusters of blossom faintly stirred on the downward slope—they could see water and the lower steps leading down to it. Thick green garlands of creeper plants hung gracefully from branch to branch. The chirping and warbling of invisible birds mingled with the buzzing of golden bees, which darted back and forth in their urgent visits to the blossoming grasses. The spot was fragrant with the cool freshness and warm scent of plants, with the intense perfume of jasmine and distinctive scent of the tala fruit, with sandalwood, and also the aroma of mustard oil, which Nanda had rubbed into his skin after their cleansing river communion.

'Being here it's as if we were beyond the six waves of hunger and thirst, old age and death, suffering and delusion,' said Shridaman. 'It is so extraordinarily peaceful here. As if we'd left life's restless bustle and been placed at its tranquil centre, and could breathe at last. Listen, how hushful it is! I use the word "hushful" deliberately, because when there's a hush we listen more intently, and this place is full of the hush that makes us listen for anything inside it that is not completely hushed and where stillness speaks as in a dream, which we hear too as if we were dreaming.'

'It is just as you say,' replied Nanda. 'You don't do much listening in a noisy marketplace, but there again, the only kind of stillness that's like your "hushful" is one where there's something or other to listen to. The only real stillness, one that is full of silence, is Nirvana,* which is why you could never call it hushful.'

'No,' Shridaman answered, and had to laugh. 'I don't suppose anyone so far has thought of calling Nirvana hushful. And yet you did so, after a fashion, in negative terms at least, when you maintained that you can't call it that, thereby choosing from among all the negative statements about Nirvana it is possible to utter—for of course it is only possible to speak of Nirvana in negative terms—the one that is funniest. You often say such clever things—if indeed we may use the word "clever" for something both true and absurd. It's something I like very much because it tends to make the top of my tummy vibrate, which is a bit like sobbing. It makes you see how related laughing and weeping are, and that we are quite deluded to see an essential difference between pleasure and pain, cherishing the one while disliking the other, when in fact both can be called good or bad. However, among the emotions we experience in life there is a combination of weeping and laughing that deserves more than any other to be cherished and called good. We call it "sympathy", which is the name for a kind of cheerful commiseration, and the reason why my tummy's vibrating and sobbing feel so similar is that I am moved to that kind of commiseration, which is to say that your cleverness makes me feel sorry for you.'

'But why do I make you feel sorry for me?' asked Nanda.

'Because you are ultimately a true child of Samsara* and of life's preoccupation with itself,' replied Shridaman, 'and not at all one of those souls who are driven by a desire to emerge—like lotuses rising above the flood and offering their open cups to the heavens—from this dreadful ocean of weeping and laughing. On the contrary, you are quite happy to stay in the depths where myriad entwining shapes and masks teem in the flux, and because you are happy to be there it makes others feel happy too at the sight of you. But now you have stubbornly set your mind on adding to the negative definitions of Nirvana with your comment that it is not hushful, which is funny to the point of tears, or, if we use the appropriate term, induces sympathy by making one commiserate with your so refreshing happiness.'

'Just listen here!' Nanda answered. 'What exactly are you telling me? If you felt sorry for me because I was gulled by Samsara and didn't have the knack of turning into a lotus, I could accept that. But commiserating with me just because I try my best at thinking a little bit about Nirvana—well, I might well feel offended by that. And I am going to say so: you make me feel miserable, miserable for you.'

'And why is that—why do you feel sorry for me, too?' asked Shridaman.

'Because it's true you've read the Vedas and know a thing or two about essence,' retorted Nanda, 'but for all that, you've fallen for illusions even more willingly and easily than those who haven't read them. That's what tickles my ribs in sympathy, or in "cheerful commiseration" as you put it. Because as soon as it's a bit hushful, like it is here, you're deceived straight away into thinking it has something to do with peace, and then off you go, dreaming you are over the six waves of hunger and thirst, imagining yourself at the tranquil centre of life's bustle. And yet the hushfulness is right here, and the fact that there are things to hear in this hush is proof that there is a lot going on in there, a lot of bustle, and that all your notions of peace are in fact an illusion. Those birds are only cooing to each other because they want to make love; the bees, dragonflies and flying beetles are fluttering about because they're hungry; the grass is swarming with the sounds of thousands of invisible creatures just struggling to survive, and those lianas so gracefully garlanding the trees seek only to choke their sap and life's-breath so that they themselves can become fat and strong. This is the true knowledge of essences.'

'I am well aware of that,' said Shridaman, 'and am not deluding myself, or only momentarily and of my own free will. For truth and the knowledge that comes with understanding are not everything; there is also an intuitive insight into the ways of the human heart that is like allegory and deciphers the handwriting of phenomena not only according to its primary, more mundane sense, but also at a secondary and higher level, which it uses to facilitate a vision of purity and the spiritual. How can you expect to arrive at a perception of peace and to experience the joy of quiescence in your soul without allowing a Maya-image—which, of course, itself is neither joy nor peace—to offer you a way in? It is permitted and given to mankind to see truth by using reality, and "poetry" is the word that language has coined for this gift and this permission.'

'Ah, so that's what you think, is it?' laughed Nanda. 'Accordingly, if one goes by what you have to say, poetry is the stupidity that comes after cleverness, and so if someone is being stupid, you would have to ask them whether they were still stupid or had become so again. I must say, you bright boys don't make it easy for us. Now, there was me thinking how important it was to be clever, but before you can get that far someone comes along and tells you how important it is to be stupid again. You shouldn't be telling us about this new, higher stage in case we lose our courage to climb the one below it.'

'It wasn't me who told you that you should become clever,' said Shridaman. 'Come, now that we've eaten let us stretch out on the soft grass and look into the sky through the branches of these trees. What a remarkable visual experience it is to be in a position that doesn't force us to look up, but in which our eyes are already directed upwards, so that we can behold the sky as does Mother Earth herself.'

'Siyâ, let it be so,' Nanda agreed.

'Siyât!' Shridaman corrected him according to the pure and correct language, and Nanda laughed at him and at himself.

'Siyât, siyât!', he repeated. 'Such a quibbler! Leave me my own patter! Whenever I speak Sanskrit it sounds like a snuffling heifer with a rope strung through its nose.'

Shridaman had to laugh heartily, too, on hearing Nanda's rustic comparison, and then they stretched out as he had suggested and looked straight ahead through twigs and swaying clusters of blossom into Vishnu's sky-blue, at the same time, with the help of leaf fronds, warding off the red-and-white flies, said to be under Indra's protection, that were attracted to their skin. Nanda had agreed to lie down, not because he was particularly interested in contemplating the sky as did Mother Earth, but merely because he was cooperative. It wasn't long before he sat up again and, with a flower between his teeth, took up his Dravidian* squatting posture.

'Indra's fosterling is damn annoying,' he said, treating the many flies darting around them as if they were one and the same individual.

'He's probably keen on that good mustard oil of mine. But it could be he has been given the task of tormenting us as a punishment by his protector, the Elephant-rider, the Lord of the Thunderbolt, the Great God—and I'm sure you know why.'

'That needn't concern you,' replied Shridaman, 'for under the tree last autumn you were in favour of celebrating Indra's thanksgiving in the old—or actually new—way, following spiritual rituals and Brahmanical observance; you may therefore wash your hands of our decision in council to break with Indra and turn to a newer, or rather older, form of thanksgiving that is more in keeping with our village ways and more natural to our religious feelings than the claptrap of Brahmin ceremonies for Indra the Thunderer, who brought down the fortresses of the ancient people.'

'Indeed, it is as you say,' Nanda acknowledged, 'and to this day I feel ill at ease because of it, for though it's true I spoke in favour of Indra under the tree, I worry that, having been deprived of his festival, he is unlikely to be bothered with such details and will instead hold us all responsible in our Welfare-of-Cows. I don't know how or where from, but suddenly it enters people's heads that thanksgiving to Indra is no longer right, at least not for us cowherds and farming villagers, and instead we should contemplate simpler pieties. What, they ask, has great Indra to do with us? The Brahmins, with their knowledge of the Vedas, may bring offerings to him while reciting endless sayings. But we want to sacrifice to the cows and mountains and woodland pastures because these are our right and proper gods, and we have this feeling that we used to do exactly that before Indra turned up, he who came before the new people and smashed the fortified cities of our native peoples, and even if we no longer remember how these things are done, they will return to us and our hearts will teach us how. We wish to render homage to the pastures on "Bright Peak" mountain, which is not far from here, and to do so with pious rites that are new only in so far as we have had to summon them from such memories as our hearts have stored. Our wish is to sacrifice pure beasts to "Bright Peak" mountain and to bring offerings of soured milk, flowers, fruits and fresh rice. Afterwards, our herds, garlanded with autumn flowers, can wander the mountain with their right flanks turned to him, bellowing to him with the thunderous voice of clouds heavy with rain. This, they say, is the nature of our new and ancient reverence to the mountain. But so that the Brahmins have nothing to complain about, we shall feed a few hundred of them, bringing milk for them from all our folds so that they may eat their fill of soured milk and rice pudding and be satisfied. That's what some who were under the tree said, and others agreed, while still others did not. I voted against paying homage to the mountain from the start, because I fear Indra and have great respect for him who tore down the fortresses of the dark-skinned people, and because I disapprove of reviving things we no longer truly understand. But you spoke in pure and proper words—and I mean "proper" with regard to your use of the language—in favour of the new way of ordering festivals and, over Indra's head, of restoring homage to the mountain, and so I grew silent. For I thought to myself, if those who went to school and learned a thing or two about the nature of essence are now speaking out against Indra and for simplification, then who are we to talk. And we can only hope that the Great Newcomer and Crusher of Cities shows some understanding, and that he is satisfied with the feeding of so many Brahmins and doesn't smite us with droughts or excessive rainfall. Perhaps, I thought, he himself is bored of his festival, and would find it more entertaining to have a mountain sacrifice and the procession of cows. We simpletons held him in great respect, but recently, perhaps, he hasn't had that much respect for himself. In the event, I actually liked the revived rituals and enjoyed helping to drive the garlanded cows around the mountain. But I was thinking just now when you corrected my Prakrit* and wanted me to say "siyât", how strange it is that you lent your support to the cause of simplification with such proper, educated words.'

'You have nothing to reproach me for,' replied Shridaman, 'because you spoke in your own vernacular when you favoured the Brahmanical sayings. No doubt the pleasure of doing so made you feel happy. But I can tell you: it is far more exhilarating to plead in truly cultivated words on behalf of simplicity.'

III

THEREUPON they fell silent for a while. Shridaman, still lying on his back, looked up at the sky. Nanda, still squatting, had wrapped his sturdy arms around his knees in front of him and was looking through the trees and bushes on the slope towards the bathing place sacred to Kali, the Mother.

'Psst! Whoopee! Well I'll be blowed!' he suddenly whispered, putting a finger to his thick lips. 'Shridaman, my brother, sit up quietly and have a look at that! I mean, at who's going down to bathe. Open your eyes, it'll be worth the trouble! She can't see us, but we can see her.'

A girl stood at the lonely shrine and was in the process of carrying out her bathing devotions. She had laid her sari and her bodice on the steps that led down to the water and stood there, fully nude, attired solely in some chain jewellery around her neck, dangling earrings and a white band wrapped around her thick, tied-up hair. The loveliness of her body was stunning. Made of Maya, it seemed, and with the most fetching skin tone, neither too dark nor overly white, but with something of the golden hue of polished bronze, and how gloriously she was formed after Brahma's design, with the sweetest, childlike shoulders and her delightfully curved hips enclosing the generous expanse of her belly, and with her youthfully firm, budding breasts and splendidly broad buttocks, narrowing to the most slender, delicate back that appeared to curve supplely inward as, raising her lissom arms, she held her hands clasped at the nape, opening to view her delicate, darker armpits. The most impressive feature in all this, the aspect that most closely accorded to Brahma's thoughts, notwithstanding the ravishing sweetness of her breasts that can only win the soul over to the world of appearances, was the combination of her marvellous behind with the slim pliability of her elfin back, a conjunction granted and consummated by way of the additional contrast between the curvature of her hips, so worthy of eulogy, and the dainty slenderness of her midriff above them. The heavenly damsel Pramlocha,* whom Indra sent to the great ascetic Kandu to prevent him from attaining godlike powers through his exceptionally intense asceticism, cannot have been much different.

'Let's leave,' said Shridaman quietly, having sat up, his eyes glued to the girl's appearance, 'it isn't right that she cannot see us and we see her.'

'Why not?' replied Nanda in a whisper. 'We were here in this hushful place first, listening to anything and everything there was to listen to; it's not our fault. So let's stay here, for wouldn't it just be awful if we were to clear out crashing through the undergrowth and she noticed she'd been seen without her seeing. I like watching her. Don't you? Your eyes have gone all red, like when you're reciting verses from the Rig Veda.'*

'Be still!' Shridaman cautioned him in turn. 'And be earnest! Her appearance is serious and sacred, and our attending to it is only excusable if we do so in a serious and pious manner.'

'Well of course!' replied Nanda. 'This may not be a laughing matter, but it is nevertheless enjoyable. You wanted to gaze up to the heavens lying on the flat earth. Now you see that sometimes you get the best view of heaven by standing up and looking straight ahead.'

Whereupon they were quiet for a while, watching without moving. Just as they had done earlier, the golden girl held her cupped hands together in front of her and prayed before seeking union with the sacred stream. They could see her a little from the side now, and it did not escape them that not only her body but her face, too, between her dangling earrings, was of singular sweetness—her little nose, lips, brows and, above all, the long curves of her lotus-petal eyes. When she turned her head slightly, startling the friends who feared that she might have noticed their attentions, it became obvious that her delightful figure had not been debased or robbed of its meaning by an ugly face, but that harmony prevailed, the grace of her countenance confirming that of her physique as a whole.

'But I know her!' Nanda murmured suddenly, snapping his fingers. 'I've only just recognized her; up until now I hadn't seen her real self. It's Sita, Sumantra's daughter, from a village called "Home of the Hump-backed Bull", not far from here. Obviously she comes from there to bathe and purify herself. And why wouldn't I recognize her? After all, I swung her up to the sun.'

'You swung her?' asked Shridaman, quietly and quite inquisitively. And Nanda responded:

'Not half! I swung her with all the strength of my arms, and in front of the whole village. If she had been dressed I would have recognized her immediately. But who'd recognize someone in the nude straight away? It's Sita from Home of the Hump-backed Bull all right. I was there last spring visiting my aunt, and it just happened to be time for the festival of aid for the sun, but she…'

'Tell me later, please!' Shridaman interrupted him, whispering nervously. 'The good fortune of our being able to see her close up is matched by the possible ill fortune of her quite easily hearing us. Not a word more, or we may startle her!'

'Then she might run away and you wouldn't see her any more, which you haven't had your fill of yet, have you?' Nanda teased him.

But his friend indicated that he really should be silent, and so they went back to sitting quietly and watching Sita of Home of the Hump-backed Bull performing her bathing devotions. After finishing her prayers, bowing and lifting her face to the sky, she stepped gingerly into the river's embrace, scooped up some water, drank, then dipped in properly, immersing herself so that all of her that was visible was the hand she had placed on the crown of her head, and deciding to stay on for a while to enjoy the refreshing river, she gracefully ducked in and out, cupping the water to her breast on one side then the other, until finally, having done what she came to do, she climbed back onto dry land, a cool and dripping beauty. But even now, the fortune granted to our friends at this place had not entirely run out, for after purifying herself in the sacred stream, the girl sat down on the steps to dry herself in the sun, while the natural charm that life had bestowed on her, carefree in the delusion that she was alone, led her to adopt first this then that pleasing posture, and only when that had run its course, and without the least bit of haste, she put on her clothes again, and, climbing the steps, passed from view towards the temple.

'Well, that's that then,' said Nanda. 'At least we can talk again now and stretch our legs. After a while it gets a little boring, pretending that you're not there.'

'I don't understand how you can speak of boredom,' answered Shridaman. 'Is there a more blissful state than losing yourself in a Maya-image and existing solely within it? I would have liked to hold my breath for the entire duration, not because I feared losing sight of her, but because I feared depriving her of her belief that she was alone; I trembled for that belief, and to it I feel bound by a sacred debt. She is called Sita, you say? I feel better for knowing it; it consoles me for the debt I owe her that I can have her with me and honour her by name. And you know her from having swung her?'

'Well, it's just as I told you,' Nanda asserted. 'It was last spring when I was at her village, and she'd been chosen as the Sun Maiden, and so I pushed her swing to help the sun, and I pushed her so high up into the sky that you could hardly hear her screams. And anyway, they were drowned by the shrieks of the crowd.'

'You were lucky,' said Shridaman. 'You are always lucky. It must have been because of your sturdy arms they chose you to swing her. I can see her now, climbing up and up, soaring into the blue. In my imagination, the image of her flying merges with our shared image of her standing piously, bowing in prayer.'

'At all events,' added Nanda, 'she has reason to pray and do penance, not because she's done anything wrong—she's a very respectable girl—but because of her looks, which she can't do anything about, of course, but for which, strictly speaking, she still somehow carries responsibility. A comely figure, they say, is captivating. But why captivating? Well, because it imprisons us in the world of desires and delights, enmeshing the beholder ever more deeply in the constraints of Samsara until he is drained of consciousness in the same way as a person can run out of breath. That's its effect, if not its intention, although the way she has elongated her eyes to make them look lotus-leaf-shaped does rather suggest intention. It's all very well to say that her comely figure was given to her, and that she did not wilfully take it on, and that she therefore doesn't need to pray or do penance, yet sometimes there is no real difference between "given" and "taken", and she knows that herself and probably prays for forgiveness that she is so captivating. But she did accept the comeliness, not in the way one accepts a gift, but in the sense that she fully embraced it, and no purifying bath can alter that: the captivating behind she came out with was the same as the one she went in with.'

'You oughtn't to speak so coarsely of such a delicate and sacred spectacle,' Shridaman upbraided him heatedly. 'True enough, you've had a brush or two with the nature of essence, but I have to tell you that it's all so uncouth when you spout it, and the way you use what you've learned betrays that you were not worthy of the vision that came before us, when in fact the whole encounter depended on our proving ourselves worthy of it, that is on the spirit in which we attended to the spectacle.'

Nanda humbly accepted Shridaman's rebuke.

'Then teach me, Dau-ji,' he requested, addressing his friend as 'older brother', 'in which spirit you yourself attended and in which I, too, should have attended!'

'Behold,' said Shridaman, 'all beings have two forms of existence: one for themselves and one for the eyes of others. They exist, and they exist for the beholder, are soul and image, and it is always immoral to be affected solely by the image, while paying no attention to the soul. It is necessary to overcome our feelings of disgust at the image of a mangy beggar. We shouldn't stop at the effect it has on our eyes and senses, for what affects us in this way is not full reality and we need to go behind that, so to speak, in order to attain to the knowledge that every image, every spectacle, lays claim to, which is to be more than image, so that our task must be to seek its true being, the soul behind the image. But not only should we not stop at the feeling of disgust the image of misery instils in us, but we should equally not, indeed even less so, allow ourselves to be detained by the pleasure that an image of beauty inspires in us, for this too is more than image, although the senses may be more tempted to take it at face value than would be the case with the revolting image. For it seems that beauty makes no claims at all on our conscience and no demand that we proceed to its soul, while the image of the beggar, because of its very miserableness, does. And yet we make ourselves culpable, too, if we delight in the sight of beauty without enquiring into its being, and it seems to me that we make ourselves especially indebted to it if we see it without it seeing us. You should know, Nanda, that it was a great gift to me when you were able to tell me the name of the girl we beheld, Sita, Sumantra's daughter, for that expanded my knowledge to something that is more than the image, since a name is part of the essence and the soul. But how pleased I was when I heard you say that she was a respectable girl, which surely means that it will be easier to find one's way behind her image and to get to know her soul. And what it also means is that it is only conventional, and nothing to do with morality, if she elongates her eyes to resemble lotus leaves and maybe puts a little eye make-up on, too, and that she does so innocently, because morality is also dependent on following civilized codes of behaviour. For after all, beauty has obligations towards its image, and by fulfilling those, it perhaps intends merely to stimulate enquiry into its soul. How happy it makes me to think that she has an upright father in Sumantra, and a caring mother, too, both of whom brought her up to be well behaved, and I can envision her life and work as a daughter of the house, grinding cornmeal on a stone or preparing porridge at the hearth or spinning wool to a fine thread. Duty-bound by having spied on her, my whole heart desires nothing more than to see her image turn into a person.'

'I can understand that,' replied Nanda. 'However, bear in mind that I would not feel so vigorous a desire as you, because she had already become more of a person to me when I swung her up to the sun.'

'Well, I do bear that in mind, I certainly do,' Shridaman retorted with a certain quiver that had entered his voice during this exchange. 'Yes, I do, obviously, because the familiarity of which you were deemed worthy—whether rightly or wrongly I cannot tell, because it was because of your robust arms and indeed whole body that you earned it, not because of your brain and thoughts—this familiarity, in your mind, seems to have made of her a totally material individual and to have blunted your regard for the higher meaning of such an apparition, else you would not have spoken so inexcusably coarsely of the comely figure it has adopted. Do you not know, then, that *she* hides in every female figure, whether maid, mother or dotard: she who gives birth to and nourishes all existence, Shakti, the Great Goddess, from whose womb come all things and into whose womb all things do pass, and that it behoves us to honour and venerate every manifestation that bears her sign? She has revealed herself to us in her most gracious form, here on the Goldfly riverbank, and shall we not then be most deeply moved by her self-revelation in the aspect she chose, to the extent, as I now realize, that my voice is quivering a little as I speak, although that is partly out of indignation at the way you spoke—?'

'And your cheeks and forehead too have turned red, as if from sunburn,' said Nanda, 'and your voice, though shaking, is fuller than usual. By the way, I have to admit that I too, in my own way, was quite affected.'

'Then I don't understand how you could speak in such an inadequate manner,' Shridaman answered, 'and how you could accuse her of a comeliness that enmeshes creatures in constraints that drain them of the breath of consciousness. That is to have a reprehensibly one-sided view of things and to show that you are wholly lacking in any sense of the true and perfect entity who revealed herself to us in her sweetest image. For she is All and not a single thing: life and death, madness and wisdom, enchantress and liberator—is this unknown to you? Do you only see her beguiling and enthralling the regiment of creatures, and not that she also guides them through the darkness of disorientation to knowledge of the truth? Then you know little and have failed to grasp a secret that is admittedly hard to grasp: that the drunkenness with which she vexes us is at the same time the rapture that carries us to truth and freedom. For the fact is that what chains us also frees us, and that it is enthusiasm that links sensual beauty with the spirit.'

Nanda's black eyes glistened with tears, for he was easily moved and was almost incapable of listening to metaphysical language without weeping, especially now, with Shridaman's otherwise somewhat thin voice suddenly assuming an impassioned fullness that greatly affected him. And so he sobbed slightly through his goatish nose and said:

'What words, Dau-ji! I don't think I have ever heard you speak so solemnly; it touches my heart. I really should ask you not to continue—it affects me so deeply. But please do, please go on talking about chains and the spirit and the All-embracing One!'

'So now you see what a peculiar matter this is,' answered Shridaman in his exalted tone, 'and that she not only dupes us but makes us wiser. If my words move you, that is because she is the goddess of the great river of speech, which flows as one with Brahma's wisdom. We must recognize her by her doubleness, for she is the wrathful one, dark and horrifying, who drinks the blood of creatures from a steaming bowl, but who is also the sacred and gracious one, from whom all existence springs and who lovingly harbours all forms of life at her nourishing breasts. She is Vishnu's great Maya and holds him in her arms, and he dreams in her, but we dream in him. Many rivers flow into the eternal Ganga, but the Ganga flows into the sea. Thus do we flow into Vishnu's world-dreaming godhead, which however flows into the sea of the Mother. But know this: we came to the mouth of our life-dream at a sacred bathing place, and it was there that she who gives birth to all and who devours all, in whose womb we bathed, appeared to us in her sweetest form to amaze us and enthuse us, presumably to reward us for honouring and anointing her generative symbol. Lingam and Yoni*—there is no greater mark and no greater hour in life than when the appointed one with his Shakti* walks around the sacred wedding fire, when their hands are joined by the garland and he says the words: "I have received her!" When he accepts her from her parents' hands and speaks the royal words: "Here am I, there are you; I am the sky, and you are the earth; I am the melody, you are the words; thus we embark on the journey together!" When they celebrate their coming together—no longer mortals, no longer he and she, but the great pair, he Shiva, she Durga, the sublime goddess; when their words become deranged and are no longer *their* words but a stammering from inebriate depths as they fade into the highest reaches of life in the bliss of their embrace. This is the sacred hour, immersing us in the Vedas and, in the Mother's womb, endowing us with release from the delirium of Self. For just as beauty and spirit flow together in delight, so do life and death in love!'

Nanda was completely enraptured by Shridaman's metaphysical words.

'No,' he said, shaking his head as tears rolled down his cheeks, 'the way the goddess's speech is so lovely to you and bestows upon you Brahma's wisdom—it's almost too much for me to bear, and yet I wish I could go on listening to you forever. If I could only sing and recite a fifth of what your head comes up with, I would love and respect myself with every bone in my body. That's why I need you, my elder brother, because what I do not have, you have, and you being my friend is almost as if I had it myself. For as your bosom friend, a part of you is in me, and I am partly Shridaman, but without you I would only be Nanda, and couldn't cope. I shall be frank: I would not wish to survive for a moment if we were parted, but would seek to build a pyre to burn myself. Well, that's that. Take this before we go!'

And he delved into his travel bag with his dark beringed hands and pulled out a sheaf of betel of the kind people like to chew to freshen their breath after meals. With his tear-streaked face averted, Nanda handed the roll to Shridaman. For these are revered as a gift, and as a means of sealing an agreement or a friendship.

IV

AND so they continued on their way, the transactions they were intending to conduct taking each on a different route, for on reaching the Yamuna river with its throng of sails and seeing on the horizon the outline of the town of Kurukshetra, Shridaman was to continue with the ox-carts along the wide road until he reached the bustling alleyways of the town and the house of the man with whom he wished to bargain for rice pestles and firelighters, whereas Nanda had to take a narrow path branching off from the main road that led to the homesteads of the humble folk who would give him raw iron for his father's smithy. They blessed each other as they took their leave and arranged to meet again three days later at a certain hour at the same crossroads and, their business behind them, to return by the same route to their home village.

Now that the sun had risen three times, Nanda—astride a grey donkey he had also purchased from the humble folk and onto which he had loaded the iron—had to wait for a while at their appointed place of parting and meeting because Shridaman was late, and when, with his pack of wares, Shridaman finally did come along the wide road, his steps were weary and sluggish, his cheeks hollow beneath his soft, fan-shaped beard, and his eyes full of despondency. He showed no joy at seeing his friend again, and when Nanda hurried to relieve him of his burden by loading that, too, onto his donkey, Shridaman's manner showed no sign of changing and, no less glumly or drooping than before, he trudged along beside Nanda uttering little more than 'Yes, yes', even when he should have said 'No, no', which in fact he did say occasionally, albeit only when it would have been the right time to say 'Yes, yes', for example when they stopped to rest and fortify themselves and Shridaman declared that he neither wanted to eat nor was capable of doing so, then added, when asked, that he was also unable to sleep.

It all pointed to an illness, and when, under a starry sky on the second evening of their journey home, the anxious Nanda finally managed to get Shridaman to speak a little, he not only admitted that he was sick but added with a lump in his throat that he was suffering from an incurable illness, a sickness unto death,* such that he not only must die, but also wanted to die, and that 'must' and 'want' in his case were entirely intertwined and indistinguishable, but that taken together they engendered a compulsive desire by which 'must' unavoidably led to 'want' and 'want' to 'must'. 'If you are serious in your friendship,' he said to Nanda in his choked and wildly emotional voice, 'then do me a final favour and build me a funeral hut that I may sit inside it and burn in the fire. For I am in such torment from the incurable sickness that burns me from within that the consuming heat of the flames will be like a soothing oil to me and a refreshing bath in the holy waters.'

'By the great gods, what's got into you?' thought Nanda, after listening to this. It must be said, however, that Nanda, despite his goat's nose and a physique that placed him squarely between the humble ones, from whom he had bought his iron, and Shridaman, the grandson of a Brahmin, rose laudably to the occasion and did not lose his head in the face of his friend's morbid grandiloquence, but used the advantage a hale body naturally has over the infirm under such circumstances, loyally placing his capabilities at the service of his ailing friend and, suppressing his dismay, addressing him indulgently and prudently.

'Please feel reassured', he began, 'that should your illness—as I have no reason to dispute following your assertion—indeed prove incurable, I shall not hesitate to carry out your instructions and build you a funeral hut. Indeed I shall make it large enough for me to join you there once I have set fire to it, for I do not intend to part from you for a single hour, but shall accompany you into the flames. Because that is so, however, and because the matter is of such great concern to me, you must be sure to tell me what is actually wrong with you and to give your illness a name, if only to convince me of its incurable nature, and so that I can get on with preparing our joint immolation. You must admit that what I am asking is perfectly fair, and if even I with my limited wits find it just, how much more must you as the cleverer one approve. When I put myself in your position and attempt to think for a moment with your head—as if it were sitting on my shoulders—I can't help agreeing with myself that my—or rather, your—conviction that your illness is incurable needs to be investigated and confirmed by others before we take the far-reaching steps you intend. For that reason, speak to me!'

For some time the hollow-cheeked Shridaman refused to talk, stating only that the fatal hopelessness of his suffering required no proof or discussion. Eventually, however, after repeated prodding, and with his hand covering his eyes so he did not have to look at his friend while speaking, he brought himself to utter the following confession.

'Since the day when we watched that girl who was naked yet modest at Devi's bathing place,' he began, 'I mean the girl you swung into the sun, Sita, the daughter of Sumantra, a torment arising from her nakedness and also her modesty, and whose roots are in both equally, has planted itself in my soul and grown there by the hour; it has worked its way through all my limbs and into the finest branchings of their fibres, draining me of my mental powers, robbing me of sleep and appetite and slowly but surely causing my ruin.' And this affliction, he continued, was a fatal illness and without hope, because its cure—the fulfilment of wishes grounded on the girl's beauty and modesty—was simply unthinkable and unimaginable and reckless to a degree, in short, far beyond anything deserved by mankind. It was obvious that any man must perish who was tormented by desire for a happiness whose fulfilment—even if his very survival depended upon it—only a god might imagine. 'If I can't have her,' he continued, 'Sita of the partridge-eyes, she of the lovely colour and magnificent hips, then my vital spirits will simply evaporate. So go and build my pyre hut, for only through fire is there salvation from the conflict between the mortal and divine. However, should you wish to sit beside me in the flames, though I may regret the loss of your youth and cheerfulness and lucky calf-curl, I shall also consider it fair, because the thought alone of you swinging her upwards makes the fire in my soul burn all the hotter, and I would be loath to leave anyone behind on earth to whom such a privilege had been granted.'

Nanda, after hearing his deeply serious friend out, and to Shridaman's utter amazement and incomprehension, burst out laughing, and then still in stitches, by turns embraced his friend or danced and jumped up and down on the spot.

'In love, in love, in love!' he cried. 'And that's all! That's what your sickness unto death is about! What fun! What larks!' And he began to sing:

'The wise man, the wise man,
How his thoughts astonished!
But now his brain is not so sane
Enlightenment has vanished.

A girl it was who caught his eye
And turned his sage's head,
A monkey fallen from a tree
Could hardly look so wretched.'

He was in stitches after that, too, and with his hands on his knees exclaimed:

'Shridaman, my brother, how glad I am that it's nothing serious and that you are only going on about pyres because your heart's straw hut has gone up in flames! The little minx spent too long in your line of sight and the god Kama struck you with his flower arrow—for what sounded to us like the humming of honeybees was in reality the whirr of his bowstring, whereupon Rati, the sister of springtime and goddess of love and desire, reached you. Which is all quite common and jolly, an everyday event, and in no way goes beyond what mankind deserves. For if it seems to you that only a god could dare imagine the fulfilment of your desires, then that's just because of their ardour, but also because they do indeed come from a god, namely from Kama, and not because your desires befit him, but because it was he who sent them to you. I don't mean to be unkind, but only to cool the heat of your lovelorn senses a bit, when I say that you are exaggerating things far too much in thinking only gods but not mortals have a right to the fulfilment of their wishes—whereas in fact nothing is more human and more natural than your desire to sow in that furrow.' (He put it like that because the word Sita means a 'furrow'.) 'But there is an adage that truly applies to you: "By day the owl is blind, by night the bee, but he whom love blinds, nor night nor day can see." I confront you with this maxim, hoping you will recognize yourself in it and reflect that Sita of Home of the Hump-backed Bull is by no means a goddess, although in the nude at Durga's bathing place she may have appeared like one to you, but a completely normal, albeit unusually pretty little thing who lives as others do, grinding cornmeal, preparing porridge and spinning wool, and whose parents are like other folk, even if her father Sumantra does boast a smidgeon of warrior blood in his veins—from a time so far back though, you could say it was far-fetched! In short, these are people you can talk to, and what's the point of having a friend like your Nanda if he can't set this perfectly ordinary and feasible matter in motion to make your wish come true? Well? Hey? What do you say, you dunderhead? Instead of erecting a hut to set ablaze with me sitting inside it beside you, what I want is to build you a marital home where you can live with your lovely-hipped bride!'

'Your words', replied Shridaman after a moment's silence, 'contained much that grieved me, and I won't even mention your song. It is offensive to call my tormented desires commonplace and mundane when I find them overwhelming, when they tear me apart, and when it's entirely correct to describe a yearning that is stronger than us, indeed too strong for us, as being improper for mortals and fitting only for a god. But I realize you mean well by me and wish to console me, and I forgive the vulgar and ignorant manner in which you spoke of my deathly illness. And not only do I forgive you, but your last words seem to suggest a possibility that makes my heart leap with renewed vigour when it had all but resigned itself to death—and this is only the result of imagining its possibility, belief in which I am incapable of. Actually, I do have an inkling that somebody who is not immediately affected by my state of mind may be capable of judging my predicament more clearly and rationally than I. But then again, I immediately mistrust any state of mind that is not my own, which I do believe in, although it points to my death. After all, isn't it quite probable that the divine Sita was married while still a child and is soon to be united with a husband with whom she grew up—a thought that fills me with such cruelly burning anguish that I have no other option but to flee to the cooling pyre hut?'

But Nanda swore by his friendship with Shridaman that the latter's fear was entirely unfounded and that Sita was not bound by child marriage. Indeed her father Sumantra had rejected one such proposal, mainly because he was against exposing her to the ignominy of widowhood should the boy-groom die at an early age. And of course she could never have been chosen to be a Swing-Maiden if she had been wedded as a young girl. No, Sita was free and available, and with Shridaman's good caste, his domestic circumstances and knowledge of the Vedas, all it would take to make a happy ending as good as certain was for him, Shridaman, to charge his friend formally with taking the matter in hand and setting the negotiations between the two families in motion.

Shridaman's cheek had twitched in pain at the repeated mention of the swinging incident, but out of gratitude for his friend's willingness to help he gradually let himself be swayed by Nanda's dependably sound reasoning away from his yearning for death to the conviction that the fulfilment of his longing to take Sita in his arms as his bride was neither beyond the realms of possibility nor exceeded his licence as a mortal being, without however jettisoning his demand that Nanda, should the courtship fail, build the pyre hut with his stout arms and without further ado. Garga's son reassured him that he would keep his promise to do exactly that, while drawing his friend's attention to the series of steps such a courtship procedure would require them to take, whereby Shridaman's role was simply to step back entirely and wait for the success of their undertaking: first Nanda would inform Bhavabhûti, Shridaman's father, of his son's intentions and advise him on taking up negotiations with the girl's parents; then, as the appointed representative of the suitor and as matchmaker, Nanda would travel to Home of the Hump-backed Bull and, in his capacity as a friend, continue to act as intermediary in bringing the couple together.

No sooner said than done. Bhavabhûti, a *vanija* of Brahmin stock, was delighted by the news conveyed by his son's friend. Sumantra, the cattle breeder of warrior descent, was not displeased with Nanda's overtures, nor with the handsome gifts that accompanied them.

Nanda sang the praises of his friend in the house of wooing in a conventional yet convincing manner. The return visit by Sita's parents to Welfare-of-Cows, which served to verify the matchmaker's honesty, was equally propitious. And as the days passed and one step followed another, the girl learned from afar to see in Shridaman, the merchant's son, her destined husband and master. The marriage contract was drawn up and its signing celebrated with a hospitable feast and the exchange of auspicious gifts. The day of the wedding, carefully chosen under counsel of those schooled in celestial omens, came ever closer, and Nanda, who knew it was approaching and that Shridaman's union with Sita depended on him—a fact that prevented Shridaman from believing it would come at all—performed his role as wedding inviter, running about and informing kith and kin of the approaching occasion. A local Brahmin recited texts, and while layers of dried cow-pat were stacked to build the sacred fire in the inner courtyard of the bride's family, Nanda put his sturdy arms to good use.

And so the day came when lovely-limbed Sita—her body anointed with sandal, camphor and coconut oils, painted and adorned with jewels, wearing a drape sari with bespangled bodice, and her head enveloped in a sheer veil—first beheld her appointed husband (whereas he, as we know, had already set eyes on her) and addressed him by name for the first time. The hour had been long in coming, but finally arrived in the present when he spoke the words 'I have received her', when he accepted her from her parents' hands during offerings of butter and rice, calling himself the sky and her the earth, himself the melody, her its words, and when, to the women's singing and hand-clapping, he walked with her three times around the blazing pile, following which, behind a team of white bulls, he drove her ceremoniously to his home village and his mother's bosom.

Once there, even more auspicious rites had to be performed: they walked around the fire; he fed her with sugar cane, and let the ring drop into her robe; they sat down to a banquet with family and friends. But when they had eaten and drunk and been sprinkled with Ganga water and attar of roses, they were escorted by the assembled company to a room that had been given the name 'Chamber of the Happy Couple' and where a bed decorated with flowers awaited them. There, amid kisses, jokes and tears, everybody took leave of them—Nanda, who had been with them throughout, was the last to tarry on the threshold.

V

It is only to be hoped that the listener, misled by the hitherto pleasant course of this tale, has not succumbed to deception over its true character! For while we were silent the story turned its face away for an instant, and when we see that face again it will not be the same: it will be contorted to a hideous mask, a disturbing, petrifying visage that instils terror and a wild willingness to sacrifice, a mask such as Shridaman, Nanda and Sita caught sight of on their journey, and which… But let us take one thing at a time.

Six months had passed since Shridaman's mother had held lovely Sita on her maternal lap and since Sita had granted the full enjoyment of conjugal bliss to her thin-nosed husband. The sultry summer had run its course, and the rainy season that floods the sky with a sea of clouds and covers the earth with freshly sprouting flowers was nearly over too; the tent of heaven was without blemish and the autumnal lotus was in bloom when the newly-weds, in accord with friend Nanda and with the permission of Shridaman's parents, decided on a journey to visit Sita's parents, who had not seen their daughter since she had embraced her husband and who wished to assure themselves that she had taken to marital life. Although Sita had begun of late to look forward to the joys of motherhood, they had decided to venture on the trip, which was not very long and, in the cooling season, not particularly arduous.

They travelled in a covered and curtained cart drawn by a zebu and a dromedary, friend Nanda holding the reins. He sat in front of the married couple, cap askew on his head and legs a-dangle, too preoccupied with keeping pace and track, so it seemed, to give much consideration to turning and chatting with those behind him. He spoke the odd word to the animals, and from time to time, his voice quite loud and clear, he would burst into song, although every time he did so, only a few notes would come out before his song shrivelled to a hum and ended with a softly spoken command to the beasts. His harsh and sudden manner of delivering these first notes, as if from a constricted breast, was startling; the swift dying of his voice no less so.

Behind him, the married couple sat in silence. Because he was in front of them, their gaze, should they have looked ahead, would have fallen on the back of Nanda's neck, and that, now and then, was precisely what the young woman's eyes did, rising slowly from her lap and, after resting briefly on the spot aforementioned, returning swiftly to their point of departure. Shridaman altogether avoided looking in that direction, instead turning his face sideways towards the hanging sackcloth. He would have preferred to change places with Nanda and steer the wagon himself, so he would not—as did his wife beside him—have Nanda's brownish back with its visible backbone and restless shoulder blades before him. But that was out of the question, for the arrangement he envisaged, which might have brought him some relief, was not appropriate. And thus they continued along the road in silence, albeit all three with quickened breath as if after running, and with red veins in the whites of their eyes, which is always a bad sign. Indeed, a person gifted with second sight would have noticed the black wings hovering over their covered wagon as they passed.

They preferred to move under the cover of darkness, or rather, in the early hours before daybreak, as one might well do to avoid the burden of the midday heat. But they had other, more personal reasons for doing so. Now that confusion dwelled in their souls, and since darkness favoured aberration, they had, unbeknownst to themselves, made use of the opportunity at hand to project their inward confusion onto the space around them, and lost their way. Nanda, with the excuse that it was a moonless night lit solely by the stars, failed to steer the zebu ox and dromedary off the road where he should have done to reach Sita's home village, instead turning off at a place where the track he followed was soon no track at all but merely something resembling one, a clearing between individual trees that at first stood apart but soon increased in number and became a dense forest enclosing them, so that they could no longer find the clearing they had initially followed into the trees, by which they might have got out again.

It was impossible to drive their cart any further forward through the surrounding tree trunks and on the soft forest floor, and they admitted to one another that they had lost their way, but not that the situation they had brought about matched the confusion of their own thoughts and feelings; for Shridaman and Sita, sitting behind the driver Nanda, had not been asleep at all, but had knowingly allowed him to lead them astray. There was nothing for it but to make a fire just where they were, the better to protect themselves against dangerous animals, and wait for sunrise. At dawn when the sun lit up the forest, they inspected the scene around them, let their animals walk unharnessed and, with a great deal of effort, heaved their wagon criss-cross wherever they could find a space between the teak and sandalwood trunks until they reached the edge of the forest where a bushy but nonetheless passable gorge opened in front of them, which Nanda claimed would be sure to lead them to their destination.

Jolting and wobbling along the track in the gorge, they came upon a temple hewn out of the rock which they recognized as a shrine for Mahadevi, who is Durga, the unapproachable and terrible, and Kali, the dark Mother; and following an inner impulse Shridaman expressed a desire to get out and show reverence to the goddess. 'All I want is to take a look, offer a prayer and be back in a jiffy,' he told his companions. 'Just wait here a moment!' And leaving the wagon, he climbed up the roughly hewn steps to the temple.

This temple was of no greater importance than the house devoted to the Divine Mother at the secluded bathing place on the banks of the Goldfly stream, and yet its pillars and sculptural decorations had been sculpted to a devout opulence. The heft of the rugged mountain bore down on an entrance supported by columns and guarded by snarling leopards, and to the right and left of the entrance, chiselled out of the rock face, were painted scenes, and then again, on both sides within, a history of life in the flesh, a life consisting of bones, skin, sinews and marrow lumped together with semen, sweat, tears and rheum, faeces, urine and gall, and all of it fraught with passion, anger, madness, lust, envy and despair, with severance from loved ones and bonds that are unwelcome, with hunger, thirst, age, sorrow and death, and all sluiced through and through with hot, sweet rivers of blood, a life that suffers as it revels in a thousand shapes, devouring itself while it swarms, everything changing into everything else, so that in the all-embracing flux and ferment of estates human, animal and divine, an elephant's trunk seems to be a man's arm and a boar's head replaces a woman's. Shridaman paid no attention to these shapes and imagined he hadn't seen them, but as he walked through, and his bloodshot eyes skated over them in passing, they entered his soul, preparing it for the sight of the Mother, arousing tenderness, giddiness and compassion.

Twilight reigned in the rock-hewn house; the only daylight fell through the mountain above into an assembly hall, through which he walked to access an adjoining, lower antechamber. From here he descended some more steps through a deeply set doorway, and the core of the house opened before him, the womb of the Divine Mother.

Reaching the bottom of the steps he shuddered and staggered backwards, his hands grasping the two lingam stones on either side of the entrance. The image of Kali was terrifying. Was it only because of his red-veined eyes, or had he really never seen the Furious One take such a triumphantly blood-curdling form before? Framed in an arch of skulls and hacked-off hands and feet, wearing a glittering crown, clad in the bones and severed limbs of her subjects, the idol stepped out from the rock face at the centre of the whirling wheel of her eighteen arms in colours that stole all light only to hurl it away again in every direction. The Mother wielded swords and brandished torches in her many hands; blood steamed in the skull that one of her hands held to her lips, a pool of blood spread out at her feet—the Terrifying One stood in a boat that was afloat on the sea of life, on an ocean of blood. The smell of real blood, too, wafted past Shridaman's thin-ridged nose; it was an oldish blood, sweet in the stagnant air of the mountain cave, this underground slaughterhouse, whose floor runnels, sticky and clogged, had been cut to channel away the quickly draining lifeblood of beheaded animals. Four or five animal heads—buffaloes, pigs and goats, their eyes open and glazed—were stacked in a pyramid on the altar in front of the picture of the Unescapable, and a sword, used to cut their throats, sharp and shining albeit spotted with dry blood, lay at the side on the flagstones.

Shridaman's initial horror as he stared into the wildly gaping countenance of the Demander of Sacrifice, the Death-Bringing Giver of Life, and at her whirling arms, the sight of which made his mind go round in drunken circles, surged from moment to moment into a high pitch of enthusiasm. He pressed his fists against his heaving chest and one immense shudder after another, both hot and cold, overcame him, filling the back of his head, the pit of his stomach and his forlornly excited sex with the urge to engage in extreme action against himself and in the service of the eternal womb. His lips, already bloodless, mouthed a prayer:

'You who have no beginning, who existed before all else! Mother without man, whose dress nobody lifts! You, who embrace all desire and horror, sucking back all the worlds and images you bring forth! The people venerate you with countless offerings of living beings, for all lifeblood is your due! Shall I not know your favour and find my salvation, if I offer myself to you? I know very well that I cannot escape life that way, desirable as that might be. But let me come back to you again through the gateway of your maternal body that I may be rid of this self and no longer be Shridaman, for whom all desire is confounded because it is not he who bestows it!'

He spoke these dark words, seized the sword on the ground and severed his own head from his body.

That is quickly said, and it could only be done quickly, too. And yet here the storyteller has but one wish: that the listener will not accept this assertion indifferently or unthinkingly as something quite usual or natural just because it has been recorded so often and because reports claim it was normal for people to cut off their own heads. An individual case is never normal: how very common it is for people to think or speak of death or birth, but be present at a birth or death and ask yourself, ask the woman in the pangs of childbirth or the mourners taking leave, if what they are going through is normal! A self-decapitation, however often it may have been reported, is a practically impossible feat; to do so, immense ardour and a staggering concentration of vital force and willpower must be brought to bear on the moment of consummation, and that the Brahmin merchant Shridaman with his gentle contemplative eyes and all-but-sturdy arms was able to accomplish as much should not be taken for granted but acknowledged with incredulous astonishment or disbelief.

It is doubtless enough to say that he carried out this horrific sacrifice in the twinkling of an eye: there lay his head with its softly bearded cheeks and here was the body, which was the less important appurtenance of his noble head, and whose two hands still clutched the grip of the sacrificial sword. Blood gushed from his torso and crept across the barely sloping floor through slant-sided runnels to accumulate in a pit under the altar—not unlike the little Goldfly river dashing like a colt let loose out of Himavant's* Gate, only to follow its course ever more serenely towards the estuary.

VI

If we now leave the womb of the rock-hewn temple and return to the pair waiting outside, we should hardly be surprised to find them—in silence at first, but soon in conversation—wondering about

Shridaman's whereabouts; for somebody who had wanted to pay brief homage within, he was taking rather a long time. Lovely Sita, sitting behind Nanda, had, by turns, gazed at the back of his neck and down at her lap, and had kept as quiet as he had, with his goatish nose and thick plebeian lips directed forwards towards his team. Eventually, however, they began to shift back and forth on their seats, and after a while Nanda came to a decision and, turning to his friend's young wife, asked:

'Have you any idea why he has kept us waiting for so long or what he's up to in there?'

'It's quite beyond me, Nanda,' she retorted, in precisely that warbling, sweet sounding voice he had been afraid to hear; he had even been afraid she would unnecessarily use his name, although it wasn't any less unnecessary than if he had asked, 'What's keeping Shridaman?' instead of simply asking, 'What's keeping him?'

'Much as I've tried,' she continued, 'I can't come up with an answer, dear Nanda, and if you had not turned round to me and asked just now, I should have very soon put the same question to you.'

He shook his head, partly mystified by his friend's tardiness, partly to fend off the superfluous things she kept saying; saying 'turned round' would have been quite sufficient, while adding 'to me', even if obviously correct, was unnecessary and downright risky—spoken as it was in her warbling and slightly precious manner while waiting for Shridaman.

He fell silent, afraid to speak in case he too spoke in an affected tone of voice and chanced to address her by her name, which, following her example, he felt a certain temptation to do; and so it was she who, after a pause, came out with a suggestion:

'You know what, Nanda, why don't you go after him and find out what's keeping him, and give him a shake with your strong arms if he's forgotten himself in prayer—we can't wait any longer, and it's peculiarly odd of him to leave us sitting here wasting time under the rising sun when our getting lost has already made us late and my parents may be starting to get worried about me, because they love me above all things. Could you go and fetch him, please, Nanda! Even if he doesn't want to come yet and refuses to leave, just bring him here anyway! After all, you're stronger than he is.'

'All right, I'll go and get him,' Nanda replied, 'but of course I'll be kind. All I need to do is remind him of the time. And for that matter, it was my fault that we lost our way and nobody else's. In fact I had already considered going after him myself, and was only worried that you might be frightened to stay here all on your own. But it's only for a couple of minutes.'

With that, he lowered himself from his driver's perch and went up into the temple.

And we who know what a sight awaits him there, we must accompany him through the assembly hall where he suspected nothing, and through the vestibule where, too, he was wrapped in ignorance, and finally down into the core, the womb of the Great Mother. Well, now he stumbled and staggered, a muffled cry of horror on his lips, and made an attempt to steady himself by gripping the lingam stones, just as Shridaman had done before him, but Nanda did not do so because of the image that had appalled Shridaman and then enthused him, but because of the gruesome sight on the floor. There lay his friend, his waxen head with loosened kerchief severed from his torso, his blood creeping in two separate streams across the floor to the pit.

Poor Nanda quivered like an elephant's ear. He held his dark, beringed hands to his cheeks, and his friend's name, half stifled, squeezed its way out between his plebeian lips, again and again. Bending over, he helplessly prodded Shridaman's two sundered parts on the ground, for he did not know which he should turn to, embrace, address: the body or the head. In the end he decided on the latter because it had always, and so decidedly, been the most important part, and kneeling down to the pale head, his goat-nosed face contorted by bitter tears, he spoke to it, while at the same time keeping one hand on the body and occasionally turning to it.

'Shridaman,' he sobbed, 'my dear friend, what have you done, and how could you bring yourself to do it, and indeed how could you have done it at all with your own arms and hands—such a difficult feat to accomplish! It wasn't the sort of thing you'd do! But even if nobody could have expected it of you, you managed it! I have always admired your intellect, but now, even in my wretchedness, I must admire you for your bodily abilities, too, because you succeeded in this most difficult of all deeds. What must have befallen your soul for you to have been capable of doing it? What sort of sacrificial dance must generosity and despair, hand in hand, have performed in your breast for you to slay yourself like this! Ah, woe, your fine head severed from your fine body; your tummy fat still where it used to be, but without sense or meaning now, cleft from your noble head. But tell me, is this my fault? Am I to blame for your deed by simply being, if not by my actions? You see it is your thoughts I follow, in as far as my head can still think at all—for perhaps your understanding of essence might have led you to conclude that the guilt of being was more essential than the guilt of doing. But what more can a man do than avoid doing? I have kept silent to avoid speaking with a lovey-dovey voice. I have never said anything superfluous, nor added her name when speaking to her. I am my own witness, and it's true I have no other, that I did not approve when she favoured me with a dig at you. But what use is any of this if I am guilty simply by virtue of existing in the flesh? I should have gone to the desert and followed the strict observance of a hermit's life. That's what I should have done without you asking me to, I'm sorry to admit; but in my defence I can at least say that I would have certainly done so if you had asked me. Why didn't you ask me, then, dearest head, before you were severed and lay down here instead of staying atop your body? Our heads have always spoken to each other, yours clever and mine simple, but as soon as it became serious and dangerous you said nothing! Now it's too late; you didn't speak but acted both magnanimously and cruelly, showing me how I must act. For surely you didn't believe I would hang back and allow my strong arms to refuse a deed that your delicate arms have accomplished? I have often told you that I had no intention of surviving you, and when you were lovesick and commanded me to build a funeral hut, I declared that, if at all, I would build one for two and accompany you into the fire. What must happen now I already know, although it's only now I am able to extricate it from the turmoil of my thoughts, for as soon as I entered and saw you lying there—I say you, and mean your body and your head next to it—my decision was instantly made. I wanted to burn with you, so now I shall bleed with you, for there is nothing else I can do. Or am I supposed to go out and tell her what you have done and then to listen out for secret glee mixed in with the cries of horror she will emit? Am I to go around with a tarnished name and let people gossip, as they surely will: "That villain Nanda maltreated his friend, murdered him out of lust for his wife"? No, not that! Not ever! But I shall follow you, and may the eternal womb drink my blood with yours!'

This said, he swivelled from the head to the body, loosed the sword grip from his friend's already stiffening hands and, with his sturdy arms and great thoroughness, carried out the sentence he himself had pronounced, so that his body, to speak of that first, fell across Shridaman's, and his nice head rolled over to where his friend's lay, coming to a halt with its eyes rolled upwards. But his blood, too, initially gushed forth like a wild spring before creeping sluggishly through the runnels to the mouth of the pit.

VII

MEANWHILE Sita, the 'furrow', was sitting alone outside in her covered cart, and the longer there was no neck in front of her to look at, the more time seemed to drag on. What had befallen that neck while she was abandoning herself to her everyday impatience was something she could not have dreamt of, unless in her innermost soul, in depths far beneath her disgruntlement—which, while lively enough, was merely concerned with a world of harmless practicalities such as made her stamp and shuffle her little feet—an inkling of something truly horrendous stirred, something that accounted for her having to wait here but which at the same time meant her impatience and annoyance were inappropriate responses, because that something belonged to an order of possibility that made the stamping and shuffling of feet entirely irrelevant. And it is to be expected that the young wife was secretly prone to such disquiet, because she had lived for some time in conditions and been exposed to experiences of an order that, to say only this much, were not without a certain affinity with the excessive and extreme. But in things she said to herself, suchlike was not to be found.

'This is unspeakable,' she thought, 'and hardly bearable. These men, they are all alike; one shouldn't give precedence to this one or that, because none is reliable. One of them makes you sit with the other, and I don't know what he deserves for that, but if you send the other you end up all alone. And all the while the sun is rising because we've wasted so much time by getting lost. It's almost enough to drive you mad! Among all that's reasonable or permissible I can find no plausible explanation and no excuse for first one of them staying away and then the other, who is supposed to go and fetch him, also failing to materialize. The only thing I can think of is that they have argued and got into a fight because Shridaman was so absorbed in prayer that he wouldn't leave and then Nanda tried to force him to but didn't dare use his full strength out of consideration for my husband's delicate constitution, because if he wanted to Nanda could carry him out here to me like a child in those arms of his, which feel as hard as iron if you accidentally touch them. That would be mortifying for Shridaman, but the humiliation of having to wait here has almost made me wish Nanda would do exactly that. Let me tell you something: it would serve you two right if I took the reins and drove on my own to my parents' house, and when you came out the place would be empty. If it weren't going to be such a dishonour to turn up without a husband or friend because they'd left me in the lurch, I would do that without a second thought. But as it is, I have no other choice now (and the moment for this has definitely come) but to get up and go after them and find out what in the world they are up to. It's no wonder I feel somewhat anxious, poor pregnant woman that I am, when I think there must be something abnormal behind this baffling behaviour of theirs. But the worst thought in the end is that for a reason that someone else may be able to fathom, they have quarrelled, and that their strife has kept them where they are. Well, I'm going to intervene and set their heads straight.'

Whereupon lovely Sita got out of the cart, too, and made her way to the Divine Mother's house, her hips swaying under her sari—and fifty breaths later she was confronted with the most ghastly sight imaginable.

She threw up her arms, her eyes bulging in their sockets, and slowly slumped to the ground in a faint. But what good was that? The ghastly sight had time to wait, and did wait, just as it had while Sita believed she was waiting; and she could stay like that for as long as she liked, but when the unhappy woman came to herself again, nothing had changed. She tried to faint again but thanks to her strong constitution, failed. So she cowered on the stone floor, her fingers buried in her hair, staring at the severed heads, the bodies lying across each other, and all that creeping blood.

'You gods, spirits and great ascetics,' her bluish lips whispered, 'I am lost! Both men, and both at once—it's the end of me! My lord and husband who walked around the fire with me, my Shridaman with his adorable head and body that was at least warm, who taught me desire, as far as I know it, in nights of holy wedlock—his revered head severed from his body, dead and gone! And the other gone and dead, too, Nanda, who pushed my swing and wooed me for Shridaman, his body bloodily severed from his head, and there he lies, his lucky calf-curl still on his cheerful breast, with no head—and so what now? I could touch him, could feel the power and beauty of his arms and thighs, if I felt like it. But I don't; bloody death has raised a barrier between him and such wantonness, just as honour and friendship did before. They cut each other's head off! For a reason I can no longer hide from myself, their anger flared up like a fire when butter is poured on it, and they got into such a terrible row that it came to this bloody exchange—I see it as if with my own eyes! Yet there is only one sword here—and it's held by Nanda? How could these furious boys fight with a single sword? Shridaman, forgetting all his usual gentleness and wisdom, took up the sword and cut off Nanda's head, who then—but no! Nanda, for reasons that make my skin crawl, beheaded Shridaman, who then—but no, but no! Stop thinking!—nothing at all can come of it but the bloody darkness that already surrounds me here, and if one thing is obvious, it's that they behaved like wild men and didn't think of me for a moment. Or rather, they did think of me, because their abominable male exploit was all about my poor person, and it sends a shiver down my spine to think it, but they were only thinking of me with regard to themselves, not with any regard for me or for what was going to become of me—they cared about that just as little in their fury as they do now, lying there motionless without their heads and leaving it up to me to decide where to go from here! Where to go? There is no going anywhere from here, because here is the end. Am I supposed to go through life as a widow abhorred for the abomination of having cared so little for her lord and master that he perished? That is what a widow faces as it is, but what stigma will attach to me when I come alone to the houses of my father and father-in-law? There was only one sword there, and they cannot have killed each other with it; a single sword is not enough for two. So that leaves one other person, and that person is me. They'll call me a licentious woman who murdered her husband and his chosen brother, my brother-in-law—the chain of evidence is conclusive. It is wrong, but it is conclusive, and they'll brand me in my innocence. No, not innocence, no; there would be some sense in lying, it would be worth lying if everything were not at an end, but there's no sense in it now. I'm not innocent, have not been for some time, and as for the licentiousness, there is even some truth in that—a lot, a lot indeed, only not as people will think, and so is there mistaken justice, then?—I must prevent that and do justice on myself. I must follow them—there's nothing else left for me to do in this world. I can't wield the sword with these little hands, which are too small and fearful to destroy the body to which they belong, which may be full and enticing, but is all weakness. Ah, it's such a pity about its sweetness, for it must nonetheless become as stiff and senseless as these here, and never again awaken desire or suffer lust. That is what must happen, though the number of victims will rise to four. What would it get out of life anyway, the child of a widow? It would certainly be crippled by its misfortune; wan and blind it would be because my heartache made me pale, even as I felt pleasure, and I closed my eyes to the man who gave me it. They left me to decide where to go from here. Just watch me find the way!'

So she picked herself up and, staggering somewhat to begin with, stumbled up the steps and ran back out through the temple into the light, her gaze fixed on destruction. A fig tree with lianas hanging from its boughs stood in front of the shrine. She caught hold of one of the green vines, made a noose, put it around her neck and was on the point of throttling herself.

VIII

AT that moment a voice spoke to her from above that could only be the voice of Durga-Devi, the Unapproachable Kali, the Dark One, the voice of the World Mother herself. It was a deep and harsh voice, motherly and resolute.

'Stop that at once, you silly goose!' the voice said. 'I suppose it wasn't enough to let the blood of my sons spill in the pit, and that is why you want to spoil my tree and hang your own body—which is a rather pretty version of my own essence—out for the crows, along with that dear, sweet, warm, tiny germ of life that's growing inside it? Haven't you noticed you've missed your monthly, you nitwit, and that you are expecting my son? If you can't even count to four in women's matters, feel free to go hang yourself, but not on my patch, or else it'll look as if life itself is going to rack and ruin and isn't welcome here, and all due to your stupidity. I've heard quite enough rubbish anyway from those preachy philosophers claiming human existence is an illness infecting one generation after another through lust—and now you, fool, trying to play games with me. Just take your head out of that noose, or I'll box your ears for you!'

'Holy Goddess,' Sita replied, 'of course, I obey. I hear your thundering voice and at your command I have broken off my desperate act straight away. But I must nevertheless protest that it is not true that I did not know of my condition and had not noticed that you had stopped my cycle and blessed me. I only thought it would be blind and wan and crippled by misfortune.'

'Be so good as to let that be my concern! First of all, that's just women's silly superstition, and secondly, my work needs pale and blind cripples to exist, too. Better to explain yourself and confess to me why the blood of my sons flowed down the runnels towards me, both of whom, each in his own way, were excellent boys! Not that their blood was unpleasant to me, but I would have preferred to leave it in their perfectly good veins for a while. So tell me about it, but be honest! It won't have escaped you that I see everything anyway.'

'They killed each other, Holy Goddess, and abandoned me. They had a violent quarrel about me and, using the same sword, they chopped each other's—'

'Fiddlesticks! Really, only a wench could spout such outright twaddle! Each of them, one after the other, sacrificed himself to me in manly piety, just so you know. But why did they do it?'

Lovely Sita began to weep and answered, sobbing:

'Ah, Holy Goddess, I know why, and confess I am guilty, but can I help it? It was such a misfortune, though possibly unavoidable; it was Fate, if you will permit me to call it that' (here she sobbed several times), 'and it was such a calamity, such snake poison to me to become a woman instead of the sheepish, frivolous girl that I was, ignorant of the world, tending my father's fire in peace, before I knew man or was initiated into your concerns—for your blithe little girl it was as if she had swallowed deadly nightshade, and since then she has been an entirely different person, and sin with its irresistible sweetness has power over her freshly receptive mind. Not that I'd wish to go back to my blithe and frivolous ignorance—I can't, not even that is possible. All I remember is that I didn't know men then, didn't actually see them in those days, nor did I care about them, and my soul was free of all burning curiosity about them and their mysterious ways, and so I could tease and mock them and continue on my cheeky, haughty way. Had the sight of a young man's chest ever thrown me into confusion, or had looking at his arms and legs made me feel weak at the knees? No! In those days it was as if they weren't there at all; my haughty coldness was barely affected, because I wasn't developed. Then a boy came along with a flat nose and black eyes, a fine body, and it was Nanda from Welfare-of-Cows, and he pushed me into the sun on my swing, but I didn't feel hot. I felt warm, but that was the air caressing my skin and only that, and to thank him I tweaked his nose. Then he returned as a matchmaker for Shridaman, his friend, after his parents and mine had agreed he could. By that stage things had possibly changed somewhat, maybe my unhappiness goes back to the time when he wooed me for another man who was ready to embrace me as a husband but was not there; only Nanda was there.

'He was always there, before the wedding and during it, when we walked around the fire, and after that, too. I mean he was there in the daytime, not at night, of course, when I slept with his friend Shridaman, my husband, and we met as the godlike couple we had been on the bed of flowers during our wedding night when he unlocked me with his manly vigour, making me a woman and putting an end to my inexperience and the prickly haughtiness of my early years. He was good at that, and why shouldn't he be, he was your son after all, and he went about our loving union in a very tender way—there was nothing that could have stopped me loving, honouring and fearing him, and oh no, dearest Goddess, I am not so depraved that I could not love my lord and husband and, what's more, fear and honour him, with his face so fine and wise, and his beard as soft as his gleaming eyes and his eyelids so gentle, and with the body they belonged to. And yet for all I held him in such high esteem, I always wondered whether it really suited him to make a woman of me and instruct the fearless but detached person I was in the sweet and scary seriousness of sensual love; I always felt it didn't befit him, as if it weren't worthy of him, as if his head wasn't in it, and when his flesh rose to meet me in our nights of wedlock, I felt ashamed on his behalf as if his refinement were debased by it—and that brought shame and humiliation to me, too, in my arousal.

'Eternal Goddess, that is how it was. Scold me, punish me, I, your creature, shall confess to you without reservation in this awful hour how it all came about, knowing full well that all things are manifest to you anyway. Bodily love did not become my husband, not his head and not even his body, which is, as I am sure you will admit, the capital factor if things are to go well, so that the latter, now severed so wretchedly from the head that belonged to it, was unable to conduct our physical union so that my heart was in it, whose desire he aroused but could not satisfy. Have mercy, O Goddess! The desire of your wakened creature was greater than its joy, and its longing greater than its pleasure.

'During the day, however, and in the evening before we went to bed, I saw our friend with the goatish nose, Nanda. I didn't only see him, I watched him, and did so in the way that holy wedlock had instructed me to observe and appraise men, and the question sneaked into my thoughts and dreams as to how he would conduct the loving union and what that holy encounter might be like with him, who cannot speak anywhere near as well as Shridaman, instead of with my husband. No different, you miserable worm, you shameless hussy, disrespectful wife that you are! That's what I told myself. It will just be the same as it always is, and how can Nanda—who has only friendly words and admirable limbs, while your husband may be described as nothing less than distinguished—how would Nanda know how to make a better job of it? But that didn't help me; the question of Nanda, and the thought that bodily love must surely become his head and limbs without shame or debasement, and that he might be the very man to marry my arousal with bliss in equal measure—that idea lodged itself in my flesh and soul like a hook in a fish's gullet, and to pull it out was out of the question because the hook was barbed.

'How was I supposed to tear it from flesh and soul when Nanda spent so much time with us, and when Shridaman and he, precisely because of their difference, were unable to be apart? I couldn't help but see him during the daytime, and then I would imagine being with him at night instead of with Shridaman. Whenever I saw his chest with its lucky calf-curl, his narrow hips and very small buttocks (while mine are so large and Shridaman's hips and posterior are roughly speaking in the middle between Nanda's and mine), I lost my composure. When his arm touched mine, the thrill made the hairs on my skin stand on end. When I saw him walk and I thought how his magnificent pair of legs, the lower half of which were covered with black hairs, might embrace me in our love play, I felt dizzy with rapture and my breasts dripped with tenderness. Each day that passed made him more beautiful to me and it now seemed incomprehensible to me how unalert I had been to him and to the mustard-oil aroma of his skin at the time when he pushed my swing; he appeared to me now like the Gandharva prince Citraratha* with his unearthly allure, like the god of love in his sweetest form, blessed with youth and beauty, entrancing to the senses and adorned with celestial jewellery, garlands of flowers, fragrance and every grace—Vishnu, come down to earth in his incarnation as Krishna.

'For that reason, when Shridaman drew close at night, I paled with regret that he was the one who was doing so and not his friend, and closed my eyes to help myself imagine Nanda embracing me. But because on occasion I could not help murmuring the name of the one I wished were pleasuring me, Shridaman knew that I was committing adultery in his gentle arms. What's more, I also talk in my sleep and my dream-talk must have betrayed everything to his cruelly aggrieved ears. I assume that was so because he went about in a gloomy mood and became distant and wouldn't even touch me. But Nanda didn't touch me either—not that he wasn't tempted to—he was tempted, he was definitely tempted; there is no way one could say that he was not sorely tempted! But he stood up to that temptation out of steadfast loyalty to his friend, and I too, believe me, Eternal Mother, for I should like to believe so myself—if his temptation had become an attempt, I too would have sent him on his way out of reverence for my husband and the head of my household. But the upshot was that I had no husband at all, and all three of us found ourselves in a state of self-deprivation.

'It was under these circumstances, World Mother, that we set out on the journey we owed my parents and unintentionally came upon your house. As we passed, Shridaman said he wanted to go inside for a very short time to show his reverence to you. But in your slaughter-cell, hard pressed by distress, he did the gruesome deed and robbed his limbs of their adored head, or rather robbed his highly revered head of its limbs, plunging me into the misery of widowhood. He did so in grief-stricken self-denial, and out of sentiment for me, criminal that I am. At any rate, great Goddess, excuse my speaking the truth: it was not to you he sacrificed himself, but to me and his friend, so that we might henceforth spend our time in full enjoyment of the pleasure of our senses. Nanda, however, who went to look for him, would not stand for Shridaman's sacrifice and also hacked his own head from his Krishna limbs, so that now they are worthless. As a result, my life is worthless, too, indeed less than worthless, and I, too, am as good as beheaded, namely without husband or friend. The blame for my unhappiness I must probably attribute to my deeds in an earlier existence. But after all I have said, how can you be surprised that I had decided to put an end to my present one?'

'You are nothing more than a nosy goose,' said the goddess with her thundering voice. 'It's absurd what your curiosity has done with this Nanda fellow, who in fact was completely normal in every way. Millions of my sons run around with arms and legs like that, but you turn him into a Gandharva prince! It's really quite touching,' the thunderous voice of the goddess added, more gently. 'As the Mother, I do find carnal lust quite touching, and it's my opinion that people generally tend to make too much of it. But of course, order must prevail!' And all of a sudden her voice returned to its previously harsh and blustery tone. 'It's true, I am Disorder itself, but it's precisely for that reason that I resolutely insist on order, and so mark my words—I demand that the institution of marriage remain inviolate! It would all be topsy-turvy if I allowed my good nature to have its sway. But as for you, I am more than dissatisfied. You serve me this shambles, and then comes your impertinence, telling me my sons didn't sacrifice themselves to me so I could receive their blood, but instead the first sacrifice was for you, and the second for the first. What sort of tone is that? How could a man chop off his own head—I don't just mean slitting his throat, but slicing his head off according to the proper sacrificial rites—and a man of learning to boot, like your Shridaman, who didn't even show much skill as a lover—what I am saying is, how could he cut off his head without drawing the necessary strength and ferocity from the rapture I instilled in him? I won't tolerate you speaking to me like that, irrespective of whether there is any truth in your words or not. For the truth of the matter may be that mixed motives led to the deed, in other words, the reason for the deed is unclear. My son Shridaman did not sacrifice himself to me solely to gain my grace; in fact he also did so in anguish over you, whether he himself was aware of it or not. And little Nanda's sacrifice was only the inevitable consequence of that. For which reason I do not feel particularly inclined to accept their blood offering and agree to their sacrifice. So if I were to compensate for the double sacrifice and restore everything to what it was before, might I presume to hope that you will behave respectably in future?'

'Oh, sacred Goddess and dear Mother!' Sita cried out tearfully. 'If you were able to do that, if you could undo those dreadful deeds and give me back my husband and friend so that everything could go back to the way we were—how I would bless you and even master the words of my dreams so that Shridaman need no longer worry! I would be grateful to you beyond all description if you could manage to do that and return everything to its former state! For even if it had taken such a sorry outcome by the time I stood at your bosom and surveyed the horrible mess, and though I realized quite clearly that it could not have turned out in any other way, it would nonetheless be a wonderful thing if it were in your power to cancel that final scene so the ending could be happier next time!'

'What are "if you were able" and "if it were in your power" supposed to mean?' retorted the divine voice. 'With the power I have, it would be a mere trifle, and I hope you don't doubt it! I have proven it more than once in the course of world history. But I do feel sorry for you, although you don't deserve it, with that pale, blind, little seed in your womb, and I feel sorry for the two boys inside my house, too. So open your ears and pay attention to what I have to say! Leave that creeper stalk right there and get yourself back into my temple in front of my image where you left that shambles. Once there, don't play squeamish or faint, but pick up the heads by their hair and fit them back onto those poor bodies! As you do so, bless the cuts with the sacrificial sword, holding the cutting edge downward, each time calling out my name—you can call me Durga or Kali or simply Devi, it makes no difference—and you will find the boys healed. Have you understood me? Do not bring the bodies and heads together too quickly though you feel the powerful attraction between torso and head; it's important the spilled blood has time to return and be sucked back in. It happens as quick as magic, but it does still need a moment or two. I hope you've been listening? Then off you go! But do it properly, and don't put their heads on back to front in your haste or they'll end up the laughing stock of all and sundry, going about with eyes in the backs of their necks. Hurry up now! If you wait until tomorrow it will be too late!'

IX

THE lovely Sita said nothing more, uttering not even a 'thank you', but sprang to her feet and ran as fast as her sari would let her back to the Divine Mother's house. After running through the assembly hall and antechamber she entered the Divine Womb and, in a feverish burst of activity and under the eyes of the dreadful goddess, swiftly set about the task prescribed to her. The force of attraction between heads and trunks was not as strong as Devi's words might have led one to expect. It was palpable, but not so powerful as to pose a danger to the timely reflux of blood up the runnels, which proceeded as quick as magic and with vividly audible slurping noises as head and body approached each other. Meanwhile, the sword blessing together with the name of the Divine—which Sita, her voice growing hoarse with jubilation, called out three times in each case—did not fail to deliver their promised effect: heads firmly attached, without a mark or a scar, the two young men rose before Sita, alternately gazing at her and down at their bodies; or rather, by doing exactly that, they were in fact looking down at each other, for to look down at themselves they would have needed to look ahead at each other—such was the nature of their manufacture.

Sita, what have you done? Or what has happened? Or what in your slapdashery did you cause to happen? Or to cut it short (and to phrase the question so that it takes due account of the fluid border between happening and doing): what happened to you? It's understandable that you were acting in a state of excitement, but couldn't you have kept your eyes open while you were completing your task? No, you didn't put your boys' heads on back to front so their faces were at the backs of their necks—that was not what happened. But if we are to tell it straight and call the baffling facts of what happened to you by their name, in other words name your mishap, your calamity, your mess, or whatever the three of you want to call it, then you have fitted onto each of them the other's head and made it stick with a blessing—Nanda's head onto Shridaman, if his torso without its capital feature can be called Shridaman, and Shridaman's head onto Nanda, if the headless Nanda still was in fact Nanda; in short, your husband and friend did not arise before you as they had been before, but as reconfigured entities: behold Nanda—if the one with Nanda's pleasant head is indeed Nanda—wearing the smock and breechcloth enswathing Shridaman's fine and plump body, and behold Shridaman—if we may thus refer to the figure furnished with his so gentle head—who stands before you on Nanda's well-shaped legs, the lucky calf-curl framed by the stone-bead necklace on 'his' broad brown chest!

What a mess—and all as a result of haste! The sacrificial victims were alive again, but they lived transformed: the body of the husband with the head of the friend, the friend's body with the head of the husband. No wonder that for several minutes the rocky womb echoed with the astonished cries of the three! Touching the limbs he now possessed, the one who had Nanda's head examined the body that had once belonged, as a mere accessory, to Shridaman's noble head; the latter, that is Shridaman (if we go by the head), full of consternation, inspected the body, now his own, that had been the decisive feature when Nanda's nice head had sat on its shoulders. As for the prime mover in this new disposal, she hurried from one to the other uttering cries of joy, lamentation and self-recrimination, alternately throwing her arms around them and prostrating herself at their feet, begging forgiveness and between sobs and laughter confessing what had happened and the mistake she had made.

'Forgive me if you can!' she cried, 'forgive me, my dear Shridaman,' turning emphatically to the head of the latter and deliberately ignoring the Nanda-body it sat on; and you too, Nanda, forgive me!'—again addressing the respective head, which, despite its insignificance, she treated as if it were the capital member, while the Shridaman-body on which it sat remained to her the indifferent appendage it always had been. 'Ah, you should bring yourselves to forgive me, for if you consider the hideous deed you brought upon yourselves in your previous life as well as the despair you plunged me into as a consequence; when you consider that I was on the very point of strangling myself and then almost lost my mind in an exchange with the thundering voice of the Unapproachable, you should surely understand that I neither had my wits about me nor was I in full possession of my powers of discrimination when I went to carry out her orders—everything swam before my eyes and I could barely see clearly whose head or limbs I held in my hands, so that I had to leave it to Fortune to see that each part found its appropriate place. There was half a chance they would, and half a chance they wouldn't—and that's how it turned out, and this is how you have turned out, for how could I know whether the force of attraction between heads and limbs was the right one, even if it was certainly quite strong, although perhaps it would have been even stronger in a different combination. And the Unapproachable shares some of the blame because she only warned me to make sure your faces weren't at the backs of your necks, and so I did pay attention to that, but the Sublime One did not consider that it might all turn out like this! Tell me, are you distraught over the manner of your revival and will you curse me for evermore? If so, I shall go out and complete what I was about to do when she who has no beginning interrupted me. Or are you two inclined to forgive me, and do you think it possible that under the circumstances that blind chance has brought about, a new and better life might begin between us three—I mean a better life than would have been possible if our former state, which had such a woeful ending to it and therefore in all probability would have ended in the same way again, had simply been restored? Tell me, sturdy Shridaman! Let me know your thoughts, nobly built Nanda!'

Rivals in proclaiming their forgiveness, the switched-headed lads bent down and picked her up, each with the arms of the other, and then all three stood there laughing and weeping, their arms embracing one another in a tightly knit group, whereby two things became clear. Firstly, it turned out to have been quite right for Sita to address the resurrected young men according to their heads, for the heads were what counted, and it was undoubtedly their heads that determined their I-and-my-feelings, so that the one who now knew and felt himself to be Nanda was the one whose narrow, light-coloured shoulders carried the plebeian head of Garga's son, and the one on whose magnificent dark shoulders the head of a Brahmin's grandson sat, took for granted that he was Shridaman. The second thing that became obvious was that neither of them was angry with Sita because of her mistake; on the contrary, they were really quite pleased with their novel condition.

'Providing', said Shridaman, 'that Nanda is not ashamed of the body Fate has bestowed on him, and does not overly miss Krishna's chest-curl, which would make me feel very sad, I can only say that as far as I am concerned, I feel I am the happiest man alive. I've wanted a body like this all my life, and when I examine my arm muscles, take stock of my shoulders and look down at my splendid legs, I feel overcome by irrepressible joy, and I tell myself that from now on I shall hold my head high in a completely different way, firstly because I am conscious of my strength and beauty, and secondly, because my mental inclinations are now in harmony with my bodily constitution so that there will no longer be anything unseemly or preposterous in my allowing myself to speak in favour of simpler matters and, under the tree, to approve the procession of cows around "Bright Peak" mountain instead of reciting Brahmanical texts, because now it befits me, and what once was foreign now is mine. My dear friends, there is unquestionably a degree of sadness in the fact that this otherness now belongs to me and can no longer be an object of my longing or admiration, except that I may now admire myself, and I no longer need to serve others in promoting homage to the mountain instead of the Festival of Indra, but rather serve what I am. Yes, it's true, I admit I do feel this sadness, a sadness in being what I once yearned for. But it is totally eclipsed by the thought of you, sweet Sita, and that comes long before any thought of myself, and I mean the thought of the benefit arising to you from my new constitution, which, in advance, makes me inexpressibly proud and happy, so that for my part, I can only bless this whole miracle with the words: Siyâ, let it be!'

'Well, you might at least say "siyât", which would be the correct way,' said Nanda, who had lowered his gaze during his friend's last words, 'instead of letting your mouth be ruled by your rustic limbs, which I have to say I don't envy you—I've had them long enough. And Sita, I too am not in the least angry with you, and I likewise say "siyât" to this miracle, for I have always wanted to have as graceful a body as I have now, and if in future I defend the reciting of Lord Indra's proverbs against simplification, then it will become me better than it did before, or at least my body, which to you, Shridaman, was a mere appurtenance, while to me it is of capital importance. I am not surprised for a moment that our heads and bodies, in the manner in which you, Sita, fitted them together, exerted such a palpably forceful gravitational attraction on each other, for this force of attraction was the manifestation of the friendship that joined Shridaman and myself, and I only hope that no harm will have come to it because of what has happened. There is one thing I must say, however: my poor head cannot help thinking for the good of the body bestowed on it or wanting to exercise its rights, which is why I am astonished and distressed, Shridaman, at the way some of your words take Sita's conjugal future for granted. I can't get those words into my head because in fact none of this can be taken for granted, and instead there's a big question, and my head has a different answer to that question than yours seems to have.'

'But why?' Sita and Shridaman cried out, as if in unison.

'But why?' repeated the lithesome friend. 'How can you even ask me? To me, it's the body that's the main thing, and in that regard my thoughts are in line with the meaning of marriage in which the body is also the main thing, for children are conceived with the body and not the head. I'd like to see someone try to deny that I am the father of the tender fruit Sita bears in her womb.'

'Get your head in order, man,' shouted Shridaman, his powerful limbs shifting involuntarily, 'and remember who you are! Are you Nanda, or who are you?'

'I am Nanda,' he answered, 'but as truly as I call this husband's body my own and say "I" with it, as surely too is the lovely-limbed Sita my wife and the fruit of her womb sired by me.'

'Is that so?' Shridaman retorted, a slight tremor in his voice. 'Is it really? I wouldn't have dared claim as much even when your present body was still mine and lay beside Sita. For it was not that body she was really embracing, as emerged to my infinite sorrow from her whispering and babbling, but the one I now call my own. It is unkind of you, my friend, to touch on these painful matters and force me to talk about them. How can you insist in this way on having your head, or rather on that being your body, then pretend you have become me, and I you? Surely it's obvious that if there had been a swap of that kind and you had become Shridaman, Sita's husband, while I had become Nanda—then there wouldn't really have been an exchange at all, so that everything would be just like it was before. The happy miracle is that it was only an exchange of heads and bodies that took place in Sita's hands, which pleases our heads, as our defining features, and, more importantly, is certain to bring pleasure to Sita of the beautiful hips. But in your persistence on invoking the rights of your present body, that of a married man, thereby raising yourself to the status of her husband while allocating to me the role of friend, you exhibit reprehensible egotism, for you are concerned solely with yourself and your alleged rights, but not with Sita's happiness and the benefits that will accrue to her from the changes made.'

'Benefits', Nanda retorted not without bitterness, 'which you are ready to boast because they will also be your benefits, and in that it is your egotism that is revealed. For the truth of the matter is that I am not invoking the rights of the married body I have inherited, but those of my accustomed and very own head, which you yourself declare to be the defining feature, and which, even in conjunction with my new and finer body, mean I am Nanda. You are completely wrong to imply that I am not at least as concerned as you about Sita's happiness and benefit. Recently, whenever she looked at me and spoke to me in her sweetly undulating, dulcet tone of voice—which I feared to acknowledge because of the danger I might adopt her tone and answer in a similar manner—she looked straight at my face, indeed into my eyes, trying with her own eyes to read mine and at the same time calling me "Nanda" and "dear Nanda", which seemed excessive, although it is clear to me now that it was not excessive at all, but rather of the greatest significance. For this was her way of expressing that she was not referring to my body, which in itself does not deserve the name anyway, a fact of which you yourself offer the best proof, since you are now in possession of it and are nevertheless still called Shridaman. I did not respond to her, and to avoid falling into her own dulcet tones, barely uttered the most necessary things and did not call her by her name, keeping my eyes averted so that she could not read in them—and all this out of friendship towards you and respect for you as her husband. But now that the head into whose eyes she gazed so deeply and inquisitively and to which she said "Nanda" and "dear Nanda" has passed to the husband's body and the husband's body is in receipt of Nanda's head—now the situation has plainly altered fundamentally, and altered in Sita's and my favour. And especially in hers! For if we put Sita's happiness and satisfaction above all other things, then surely there cannot be circumstances more pure or more perfect than I portray.'

'No,' said Shridaman, 'I would not have expected anything like this from you. I feared you might be ashamed of my body, but then surely my former body could as easily be ashamed of your head for all the contradictions you have entangled yourself in, asserting now the head and now the body as the main thing in marriage—just as it suits you! You were always a modest boy, and yet here you are, suddenly scaling the summits of insolence and egocentricity, declaring your own circumstances to be the purest and most perfect in the world to ensure Sita's happiness, and yet surely it is patently obvious that I am the one who has the best possible—that is at once the happiest and most reassuring—circumstances to offer her! But there is no point or purpose in exchanging further words. Here is Sita. Let her say to whom she belongs and be the judge over us and her own happiness.'

Sita looked in perplexity from one to the other. Then she hid her face in her hands and wept.

'I can't,' she sobbed. 'Please don't force me to decide—I'm just a poor woman and it's too hard for me. True, it seemed easy at first, and much as I was ashamed of my blunder, it at least made me happy, especially when I saw you were happy. But your talk has muddled my head and split my heart in two, so that one half counters the other, just as you two have done. There is much truth in your words, dearest Shridaman, and you didn't even make use of the argument that I can only go home with a husband who has your features. But I also feel touched by Nanda's views to some extent, and when I remember how wretched and paltry his body seemed to me when it was headless, then I have to agree with him that I partly, indeed perhaps mainly, meant his head when I said "dear Nanda" to him on one occasion. But when you speak of "reassuring" me, dear Shridaman, of offering me an assured happiness, then the question of whether my husband's head or my husband's body would bring greater assurance to my happiness is indeed a terribly difficult one to answer. No, do not torture me, for I am completely incapable of settling your dispute and of judging which of you is my husband!'

'If that is how matters stand,' said Nanda after a baffled silence, 'and Sita is unable to decide between us and settle our dispute, then judgement must come from a third, or to be more precise, fourth party. When Sita mentioned just now that she could only go home with a man who has Shridaman's features, my first thought was of a solution to suit myself, where she and I would not return home but instead live in seclusion, that is, if she found her happiness assured with me, her bodily husband. I have long harboured thoughts of seclusion and wilderness, and I often considered becoming a forest hermit when Sita's voice made me fear for my loyalty as a friend. For that reason I decided to approach an ascetic who is highly disciplined in self-mastery, called Kamadamana,* and to consult him on how to live in uninhabited places, and so I visited him in the Dankaka* forest, where he lives, and where many other holy men live, too. The name he was born to is Guha, but he wants people to call him by the ascetic name Kamadamana, in so far as he lets anyone speak to him at all. He has lived in the Dankaka forest for many years, observing strict rules on bathing and silence, and I believe he cannot be far from attaining spiritual enlightenment. Let us travel to meet this wise man, who knows life and has overcome it; let us tell him our story and make him the judge over Sita's happiness. He shall decide, if you accept my proposal, which of the two of us is her husband, and his verdict shall prevail.'

'Yes, yes,' Sita cried with relief, 'Nanda is right, let's set off for the holy man!'

'Since I realize', said Shridaman, 'that we are faced with an objective problem here that cannot be solved from within but only by means of a verdict from without, I also accept your proposal and am prepared to submit myself to the wise man's judgement.'

Agreed on this, they now left the Divine Mother's house together and returned to their cart, which was waiting for them down on the gorge track. Once there, the question immediately arose as to which of the men was to take the reins and assume the role of driver, for this was work for both body and brain equally, and while Nanda knew the way to the Dankaka forest two days' journey away, and had the route in his head, Shridaman, due to his bodily constitution, was now better suited to taking the reins, which was why Nanda had hitherto occupied that position. But now he ceded it to Shridaman, taking his place behind him next to Sita and prompting him on what route he should take.

X

THREE days later the friends reached the lush green Dankaka forest, which, while a large number of holy men lived there, was large enough to provide each hermit with sufficient seclusion in an area of grim desolation. It was by no means easy for our pilgrims to ask their way from one seat of solitude to the next in their effort to find Kamadamana, the vanquisher of desires. For each of the hermits they encountered refused to hear of any other, and each was adamant in his claim of being alone in that mighty forest, surrounded by nothing but unpeopled wilderness. These places of seclusion were inhabited by men holy in varying degree: some had passed through the householder stage and were now, sometimes even accompanied by their wives, devoting their lives to a regime of moderate contemplative observances; others were yogis of a truly wild kind, who, bent on attaining extreme spiritual purity, had as good as curbed the stallions of their senses and, by means of mortification and abstinence, were engaged in a fight to the bitter end with their flesh, enduring the most horrendous privations to fulfil their unsparing vows. They fasted cruelly, slept naked on the ground in the rain and restricted themselves to wet clothing in the cold season. In the hot summers, by contrast, they would take their place between four fires whose purpose was to consume their earthly substance, some of which dripped off them, melting in the desiccating heat, while afterwards they would subject their bodies to further chastisement by rolling about on the ground for days on end, or continuously standing on their tiptoes, or maintaining constant motion by standing up and sitting down in rapid succession. If, while engaging in such practices, they fell seriously ill and felt spiritual liberation might be nigh, they set off on their final pilgrimage in a straight north-easterly direction, no longer nourishing themselves with herbs and roots, but only with water and air, until finally their bodies collapsed and their souls became one with Brahman.

Thus the friends, in their quest for directions, met holy men of one kind or another during their wanderings through the provinces of solitude (they had left their cart at the edge of the ascetics' forest with a hermit family who, not entirely without contact with the world of humans outside, led a comparatively comfortable life there). As mentioned earlier, the three had difficulty locating the uninhabited patch in which Kamadamana dwelled, for while Nanda had found his way to him through this trackless desert on an earlier occasion, he had done so with a different body, which meant his sense of orientation as well as his natural resourcefulness were now restricted. At the same time, the tree and cave dwellers of the forest pretended ignorance, or really were ignorant, and it was only with the help of the kind-hearted wives of some former householders, who gave them directions behind the backs of their masters, and only after searching for another whole day and spending a night in the wilderness, that they were lucky enough to reach the holy man's domain, catching sight of his white-washed head with its bulge of braided hair and his arms, raised to the sky like dry branches protruding from a swampy pool of water where he had stood up to his neck for who knows how long, his spirit tapering to a pinnacle.

Reverence for the prodigious fervour of his asceticism prevented them from calling out to him; instead they waited patiently for him to conclude his exercise, which, however, whether because he had not noticed them or precisely because he had noticed them, did not happen for some time. Keeping a respectful distance from the rim of the waterhole, they had to wait for the best part of an hour before he emerged; he was completely naked, his beard and bodily hair matted with dripping mud. Since his body was practically devoid of flesh and consisted mainly of skin and bones, his nakedness was fairly unremarkable, so to speak. As he walked towards the waiting visitors he swept the ground in front of him with a broom he had picked up at the edge of the water, a means, they realized, of avoiding treading on any secretive creature that happened to be in his path. He did not, at least not to begin with, behave as gently towards his uninvited guests, but raised his broom against them threateningly as he approached them, so that they might easily, during these moments, have been to blame for something irreparable happening under his feet, as he shouted:

'Away with you, gawkers and idlers! What are you doing in my solitude!'

'Kamadamana, Vanquisher of Desires,' replied Nanda in all humility, 'forgive us for approaching you so boldly in our need! The fame of your self-mastery tempted us, but what finally drove us here were the hardships of our lives in the flesh, in which, O Great Bull among the wise, we seek your advice and count on your sound judgement, should you condescend to help us. Pray be so kind as to remember me! I dared approach you once before to be blessed with your guidance in the matter of living in seclusion.'

'It is possible that you do look familiar to me,' said the hermit, his eyes glaring at Nanda from deep cavities under his menacingly bristly eyebrows. 'That goes for your facial features at least, while as for the shape of your body, it appears to have undergone a certain process of refinement since then, which I suppose I may attribute to the visit you paid me at the time.'

'It did me a lot of good,' Nanda replied evasively. 'But there is a different reason for the change you have noticed in me; it has to do with a story full of distress and wonder which is the story of the three people in need you see before you. It has confronted us with a question we are unable to answer ourselves, so that we urgently need your ruling and judgement. We wonder whether your self-mastery might be so great that you could bring yourself to listen to us.'

'It might well be,' replied Kamadamana. 'Nobody shall say it was not great enough. My first impulse was certainly to run you out of my hermitage, but that was naught but another urge that needed denying and a temptation I intend to resist. For as much as it is ascetic to avoid people, it is even more so to take them in. Believe me, your proximity and the reek of life you exude weigh heavily on my breast and bring unpleasant heat to my cheeks, as you would see for yourselves were it not for the white ash I have seen fit to daub on my face. However, I am ready to endure your visit and your fumes, especially since, as was soon obvious to me, one of you three is a woman of such proportions as delight the senses, as slim as a vine, with soft thighs and full breasts, oh yes, oh fie! Lovely is her belly, her face adorable and partridge-eyed, and her breasts, to utter this once again, are full and firm. Greetings, woman! It's true, isn't it, when men see you their body hair stands on end with pure lust, and this distress of theirs is indubitably of your making—you piece of sugarplum bait! Greetings to you, I say! I'd probably have sent those two boys packing, but since you have come along with them, my dearest, please do stay, stay here for as long as you wish—and in the spirit of true courtesy I invite you in to sit in front of my hollow tree and partake of the jujube berries I have gathered together in leaves—not to eat them, but in order to keep them in sight while I go without them and eat earthy roots instead, for these bones of mine do still need to be fed now and then. But as for your story, I shall listen despite the suffocating fumes of life it will doubtless engulf me in, indeed I shall listen to every word, for nobody should accuse Kamadamana of fearfulness. Of course, distinguishing between courage and curiosity is difficult, but the insinuation must be rebutted that I only want to listen to you because my sojourn in solitude has made me hungry and lustful for stories with the smell of real life, along with any further insinuation that my rebuttal or repression of such an objection comes merely to license curiosity, so that actually it is the latter I should be repressing—but then what of my courage? It's just the same with the jujube berries. It's tempting to think that I put them where I can see them not as the objects of my renunciation, but to enjoy the sight of them—to which I unblinkingly retort that it is precisely the sight of them that might tempt me to eat them, so I would be making life too easy for myself if I did not put them where I can see them. But the suspicion certainly also needs quashing that I have only thought up that retort, too, so I can enjoy the delicious sight of the berries, just as I might also, even if I didn't eat the berries myself but gave them to you to eat, relish the sight of you three snacking on them, which—considering the illusory character of the profusion of effects in the world and of the distinctions between "I" and "you"—is almost the same as me eating them myself. In short, asceticism is a bottomless pit whose unfathomability is the result of temptations of the spirit mingling with the temptations of the flesh and causing a degree of toil and trouble, rather like the snake that grows two heads for every one you cut off. But then again, that's just how it ought to be, and the most important thing when all is said and done is courage. So come along now with your stench of life, you steamy folk of both sexes, come with me to my hollow tree and tell me as much of life's filth as you like—it will add much to my mortification to listen to you, all the while repudiating the slightest insinuation of my doing so for my own entertainment—oh, there cannot be enough repudiation!'

That said, the holy man, constantly sweeping the earth before him with his broom, led them some distance through the undergrowth to his dwelling, a mighty and very old kadamba tree, which was still green, albeit yawningly hollow, and whose earthy, mossy interior Kamadamana had chosen as a home, not because it offered him protection against the weather, to which he exposed his present incarnation perpetually, bolstering the heat with firebrands and the cold with wetness, but only in order to know where he belonged and to store in that hollow what he needed in the way of roots, tubers and fruit to eat, as well as firewood, and also flowers and grass to scatter as an offering.

Here he asked his guests to sit down, and while they, knowing now that they were mere objects of his asceticism, did what they could to behave with the greatest humility, he gave them his jujube berries to eat as promised, which they found most refreshing. In the meantime, he adopted an ascetic attitude known as the Kayotsarga posture: motionless limbs, arms pointing rigidly downwards and legs straightened, while at the same time managing in a peculiar manner to splay not only the fingers but also the toes. And he stayed in this position, with his unremarkable nakedness and his spirit tapered to a pinnacle, while the splendidly formed Shridaman, to whom the office had devolved by virtue of his fine head, recited the story that had brought them here because of its culmination in a dispute that could only be settled from without, by a king or a holy man.

He told it truthfully, as we have already told it, and partly in the same words. To explain what the argument had been about, it would have been enough to recount only its final stages, but wishing to offer the holy man in his solitude something worthwhile, he told it straight from the beginning, just as we have here, starting with Nanda's and his own way of life, the friendship between them, their stopping for a rest by the little Goldfly river, then his lovesickness, courtship and marriage, at the same time finding opportunities to skilfully weave in things that had happened earlier, such as Nanda's swing-pushing acquaintance with the charming Sita, while allowing only sad glimpses and subtle hints of others, such as the bitter experiences of his marriage—not so much to spare himself, for his, now, were the sturdy arms that swung Sita to the sun, and his was the living body she had dreamed of in his former arms, but out of concern for Sita, for whom none of this could be pleasant and who, for the duration of the story, veiled her head in her embroidered shawl.

The able-bodied Shridaman proved a good and artful narrator, thanks to his head. Even Sita and Nanda, who knew everything already, enjoyed hearing their story again from his lips, dreadful as it was, and it is to be assumed that Kamadamana, too, although his Kayotsarga posture let nothing show, was captivated by it. After describing Nanda's and his own gruesome deed, Sita's pardon by the goddess and her forgivable blunder during her task of restoration, Shridaman at last reached his conclusion and posed the question.

'And thus it came about', he said, 'that the husband's head was allotted to his friend's body, and the husband's body to his friend's head. Be so kind in your great wisdom, holy Kamadamana, as to pass judgement on our confused state! As you decide, so shall we be bound and shall act accordingly, for we ourselves are unable to work it out. Whom does this wholly fine-bodied woman belong to, and who is her rightful husband?'

'Yes, do tell us that, Vanquisher of Desires!' cried Nanda with ostensible confidence, while Sita merely hastily removed the veil from her head and turned her lotus eyes expectantly on Kamadamana.

The latter brought his fingers and toes together again and gave a deep sigh. Then he took hold of his broom and swept a place on the ground free of vulnerable creatures and sat down in front of his guests.

'Phew!' he exclaimed. 'You three really are a fine bunch! I was ready for a story full of steaming life, but with yours I can feel the very fumes spew from your pores, and I find it easier to endure my four firebrands in the heat of summer than stomach that fug. If it weren't for my ashen make-up you would have seen the red flush it kindled in my respectably emaciated cheeks, or rather their bones, while I was listening so ascetically. Ah children, children! Like the blindfold ox turning the oil mill, you turn round and round on the wheel of becoming, moaning with the fervour of it as the six mill-churls serving the passions prick your quivering flesh. Can't you leave off? Do you have to go on ogling, licking, salivating, going weak at the knees with lust at the sight of the object of your delusion? Ah yes, ah yes, I know all this! Body of love, dewy with bitter lust—under silken skin gliding limbs thrust—lovely domes of arching shoulders—questing mouths and nuzzling noses—sweet breasts with tender stars fair—armpits damp with sweat-soaked hair—grazing lands for hands that wander—on lissom back, belly, hips, and under—gorgeous thighs, the bliss-embrace of arms—buttocks' cool and fleshly charms—till from all this in hot arousal—coital tools in sultry dark carnal—show each other in apprehension—and fly on them to seventh heaven—and here and there and that and this—ah yes, ah yes, I know all this…'

'Yes, but so do we, we know all that ourselves, and of our own doing, great Kamadamana,' said Nanda, suppressed impatience in his voice. 'Won't you be so kind as to arbitrate in the matter we have brought and advise us on who Sita's husband is, so that we know the answer at last and can live by it?'

'My verdict', the holy man replied, 'is as good as decided. It is actually quite obvious, and I am surprised you are not well enough instructed in law and order that you need an arbitrator in such a self-explanatory matter. The sugarplum over there is of course the wife of him who has his friend's head on his shoulders. For during the marriage ceremony one holds out one's right hand to the bride, but that belongs to the body, which in turn is the friend's.'

With a cry of joy Nanda sprang to his finely formed feet, while Shridaman and Sita, motionless, remained sitting, their heads bowed.

'That, however, is only the precedent,' Kamadamana continued, his voice raised, 'which a subsequent clause will elevate, compensate and substantiate—if you will kindly wait a moment!'

Whereupon he stood up and went over to his hollow tree, from which he took a rude garment of sorts, an apron made of thin bark with which to cover his nakedness. He then declaimed:

'The husband is he, who has the husband's head.
My ruling is strict, and must be taken as read.
For as woman is the height of bliss, the source of songs,
Among the limbs, kingship to the head belongs.'

Now it was Sita and Shridaman's turn to raise their heads and gaze at each other in delight. Nanda, however, who had expressed his great happiness a moment ago, was now despondent:

'But what you said before was quite different!' he said.

'What I said last', replied Kamadamana, 'is what counts.'

And so now they had their decision, and newly refined Nanda was the last who had the right to complain about it, for he himself it was who had set in motion asking the holy man to be their arbitrator—quite apart from the impeccably chivalrous manner in which Kamadamana had delivered the reasoning behind his verdict.

All three bowed their heads before Kamadamana and put his homestead behind them. After walking together in silence for a while through the lush green Dankaka forest, Nanda stopped in his tracks and took his leave of the others.

'All the best!' he wished them. 'I shall go on alone. I shall seek a place of solitude and become a forest hermit, just as I intended. Besides, in my present incarnation I feel myself a little too good for the world.'

Neither of them could fault his decision; in a slightly saddened way they supported it and bade him farewell with the kindness one might well show towards someone who had drawn the shorter straw. Shridaman patted him encouragingly on a shoulder he knew so well and advised him—out of habitual devotion, and with a degree of solicitude rarely found between two beings—not to be too hard on himself in his asceticism and to go easy on the roots, for he knew that a diet of such monotony would disagree with him.

'Let me be the judge of that,' Nanda replied dismissively, and even when Sita tried to say a few comforting words, all he could do in his bitter sadness was shake his goat-nosed head.

'Don't take it too much to heart,' she said, 'and always keep in mind that actually you yourself were nearly the one to share henceforth with me, in wedlocked nights, the joys of the marital bed! Be sure that I shall cover what once was yours with sweetest tenderness from top to bottom and, with hand and mouth, shall show my gratitude for every joy in ways so exquisite that only the Eternal Mother can teach me them!'

'That won't do me any good,' he replied stubbornly. And even when she secretly whispered: 'I'll dream of your face sometimes too,' he didn't budge but merely answered sadly and gruffly: 'That won't either.'

Thus they parted, the one and the other two. But turning again, Sita went back to Nanda when he was already a short distance away and threw her arms around him.

'Farewell,' said she. 'You were my first husband really, the one who aroused me and taught me desire, as far as I know it, and however that scraggy holy man might wish to pronounce and poetize on wives and heads, the tiny fruit under my heart is in reality yours!'

With that she ran back to her sturdy Shridaman.

XI

ONCE they had returned to Welfare-of-Cows, Sita and Shridaman spent their time fully enjoying the pleasures of the senses, and at first no shadow marred the cloudless heaven of their happiness. That little phrase 'at first', which admittedly runs like a faint, premonitory impurity across the clarity of their sky, is an insertion from outside the story; those living inside it, whose story it was, had no knowledge of any such 'at first', but were aware only of their bliss, which both sides regarded as profound.

Truly, it was happiness of a kind existing hardly anywhere on earth, a kind that belongs only to paradise. The happiness commonly found on earth, the satisfaction of desire as experienced by the great mass of human beings and permitted under conditions of law, order, piety and moral coercion, is narrow and moderate, hedged in on all sides by prohibition and inevitable self-denial. Making do, privation, abstinence—such is the common lot. Our desire is boundless, its fulfilment severely limited, and its urgent 'if only we could' encounters everywhere an unbending 'can't be done', the arid 'put up with it' of life. Some things are granted, most are denied, and the hope that what is denied today will tomorrow be granted almost always remains a dream. A paradisial dream—for the delights of paradise must surely be such that what is permitted and what is forbidden, which are such very different things in our world, in that place merge into one, so that the beautiful forbidden wears the ethereal crown of permissibility, while all that is permissible also gains the charm of the forbidden. How else is starving humanity to imagine paradise?

Now, it was exactly this unearthly kind of happiness that a capricious fate had bestowed on the married lovers who had returned to Welfare-of-Cows, a happiness they were enjoying greedily and giddily—at first. For Sita, the awakened one, her husband and his friend had been two people, and now they had become one, which, blissfully, had taken place in such a way—and indeed could not have taken place in any other way—that the best of both, and what had been the most important thing in each of their erstwhile onenesses, had combined to form a new entity that satisfied all desires. At night, on their lawful bed, she nestled in the sturdy arms of Shridaman's friend and welcomed his rapture, just as she had once dreamt of doing when snuggling up to her husband's delicate chest, albeit with her eyes closed, and yet now she also kissed the head of the Brahmin's grandson in gratitude—and thus she was the most favoured woman in all the world, for she was now in possession of a husband who, if one may say as much, consisted of nothing but essentials.

And Shridaman, for his part—how proud he was and happy with the change! Nobody need have worried that his transformation could have made anything but a pleasant impression on Bhavabhûti, his father, or on his mother (whose name is not mentioned here because she really only played a modest role), and the same goes for other members of the Brahmin merchant's family and inhabitants of the temple village. The notion that there was something dubious or unnatural about the way his bodily features had altered so favourably (as if only the natural counted as right!) might more easily have arisen if a similarly altered Nanda had appeared at his side. Nanda, however, had disappeared from sight, now that he had become a forest hermit, some inclination for which he had previously declared on occasion; his own transformation, which might have been conspicuous in the company of his friend, had been noticed by no one, and only Shridaman presented himself to view—with his bronzed, stronger and more shapely limbs, features one might well credit to the enhancing effects of married bliss on masculine development, if one were to notice them at all. For it goes without saying that Sita's husband, as before, dressed according to the conventions proper to his fine head; far from going about in Nanda's loincloth, arm-rings and stone-bead ornaments, he continued to wear the puffed, apron-like breechcloth and cotton tunic that had always been his costume. But what all this undeniably and quite plainly showed was the decisive importance of a human being's head to their sense of self. Just imagine your brother, son or a fellow citizen coming through the door with his familiar head on his shoulders and—even if there was something that seemed not quite right about the rest of his appearance—feeling the slightest doubt that this individual was not that brother, son or fellow citizen!

Eulogies of Sita's wedded bliss have predominated in this account, just as Shridaman, following his transformation, straight away placed the benefits his darling would reap from his change before all other concerns. However, it should be understood that his own happiness was just as great as hers, indeed to a degree only possible in paradise. One cannot but urge our listeners to put themselves in the incomparable position of a lover who, in deep despondency, had shrunk from his beloved, forced to realize that she craved the embrace of another, and who was now in a position—and nobody else but he—to offer her everything to fulfil all her mortal desires. In directing the listeners' attention to Shridaman's happiness, one is tempted, in fact, to regard it as even greater than that of the delightful Sita. The love for Sumantra's golden child that had seized hold of Shridaman after eavesdropping on her ritual bathing, a love so passionate and serious that for him, and to Nanda's plebeian amusement, it had assumed the nature of a sickness unto death, instilling in him the conviction that he must surely die of it—this violent, anguished and yet sensitive emotion, kindled in him by the charming image of a person whose personal dignity, nonetheless, he had immediately and emphatically striven to maintain—in short, this ardour born of the marriage of sensual beauty and reasoning and therefore involving his entire personality—was, of course, first and foremost in keeping with his Brahmanical head, which had been endowed by Sarasvati, the goddess of speech, with great fervency of thought and imagination, and for which the bland appendage of his body had been anything but an even match, as must have been obvious during his marriage. Now, however, we are urgently called upon to share in the joy and satisfaction of a character, to whose spirited, delicate and deeply serious head a blithe and ordinary body had been added, a body replete with bovine strength, created to be adequate, bones and all, to the impassioned enthusiasm of its head! It is futile to imagine the delights of paradise, such as life in the divine grove 'Joy', in any other way than as the image of this perfection.

Even that troubling 'at first', which admittedly does not arise in the above, creates no distinction between here and there; it does not belong to the consciousness of the character enjoying the state described, but only to the controlling mind of our narrator, and therefore betokens solely an objective disturbance, not a personal one. And yet it must be said that it soon, in fact from very early on, had begun to creep into the realm of the personal, too, indeed from the beginning had played its part in setting earthly conditions and limitations that had no place in paradise. We must concede that the lovely-hipped Sita made a mistake when carrying out the gracious orders of the goddess in the way she did—a mistake not only in so far as she carried it out in blind haste, but also in so far as she did not exactly carry it out in blind haste alone. This sentence is well considered and needs to be well understood.

Nowhere does the world-preserving magic of Maya, life's fundamental principle of delusion, deception and imagination, which holds all mortal beings under its spell, manifest itself more powerfully and mischievously than in the longing for love, the tender desire of one creature for another, which in reality is the epitome and prime example of all the bonding, embracing and entanglement, all the beguilement that keeps life going and coaxes it to continue. No wonder Lust, the love-god's crafty spouse—no wonder this goddess is referred to as 'gifted with Maya', for she it is who makes mere appearances so charming and desirable, or rather makes them appear so, and indeed this can be found in the word itself—in 'apparitions' for example, those startling semblances and glimmering spectres. It had been Lust, the divine juggler, who had made Sita's body appear so shimmeringly lovely, so awe-inspiring and adorable, to the youths at Durga's bathing place, and especially so to the enthusiastic Shridaman. However, one only has to observe how glad and grateful the friends were when the bather turned her head and they discovered that her little nose, lips, brows and eyes were equally delightful, so that her charming figure had not been deprived of its value and meaning by an ugly face—one only has to think back to this to appreciate how infatuated people are, not just with the object of their desire, but with the state of desiring itself, in that they strive not for disillusionment, but for intoxication and yearning, fearing nothing as much as disenchantment, in other words: to be deprived of enchantment.

Now, please take note of how the young friends' concern to assure themselves that the face of the woman they were spying on was pretty, again proves the dependence of the body, in terms of its Maya value and meaning, on the head it belongs to! Kamadamana, the vanquisher of desires, had been right to declare the head the superior part of the body and to base his judgement on the same. For it is indeed the head that determines the aspect and loveworthiness of the body, and it doesn't go far enough to say simply that the latter will be different if joined to a different head—oh no, let only a single feature, an expressive wrinkle in the face be different, and the whole will not be the same! Herein lies the error that Sita committed in error. She counted herself blessed for having committed it because to her it seemed paradisial—and had perhaps already seemed paradisial beforehand—to have Nanda's body under the sign of her husband's head, but she had not foreseen, and in her happiness may initially have been unwilling to believe, that the Nanda-body in conjunction with the thin-nosed Shridaman-head, his thoughtfully gentle eyes and the soft, fan-shaped beard on his cheeks, was not the same body: it was no longer Nanda's sprightly body, but another.

It had become a different one immediately, from the first moment, in accordance with its Maya. But the latter is not our only concern here. For in time, the time Sita and Shridaman had spent at first in full satisfaction of the pleasures of their senses and in the incomparable joy of love together, the body of Shridaman's friend, which Sita had desired and won (if it is still acceptable to call Nanda's body—now under the influence of Shridaman's head—the body of the friend, when in fact it was the distant body of the husband that had now become the friend's body)—in time, then, indeed not in very much time, the Nanda-body, now crowned with the revered husband's head, and quite aside from any Maya, had of itself changed, and under the influence of the head and its laws had gradually become more like the husband's body.

Such is fate and the usual effect of married life: Sita's gloomy experience was not very different from that of many other women who fairly soon find it difficult to recognize in their nonchalant spouse the lithe and passionate youth who once wooed them. In this particular example of the normal human lot, however, the explanation and accentuation of it are surely quite special.

The prevailing influence of Shridaman's head, which, as we noted, manifested itself in the way Sita's husband dressed his new body just as he had his former one, rather than taking on Nanda's style, also expressed itself in his refusal to rub mustard oil into his skin as Nanda had done, for his head intensely disliked the smell of it on his body, and he therefore avoided using the cosmetic altogether, which in turn meant a certain disappointment to Sita. She was possibly also slightly disappointed that Shridaman's posture when sitting on the ground was determined, as need hardly be said, not by his body but his head, so that he spurned the commonplace squatting position Nanda had habitually assumed, instead sitting with his legs to one side. But these things were merely trifles at the beginning.

Even with his Nanda-body, Shridaman, grandson of a Brahmin, continued to be what he always had been and to live as he had always lived. He was neither a blacksmith nor a shepherd but a *vanija* and the son of a *vanija* who helped his father in a respectable trade and would take over the family business when his begetter grew weary. He was not wont to wield a heavy hammer, nor did he drive the cattle to graze on 'Bright Peak' mountain, but bought and sold lint, camphor, silk and chintz, also rice pestles and firelighters, which he could provide to the people of Welfare-of-Cows, while in his spare time reading in the Vedas; it is no wonder, then, much as this tale is full of wonders, that Nanda's arms soon lost their sturdiness and grew thinner, while his chest narrowed and he again accumulated a little tummy fat, in short, that his body became increasingly husband-like. Even his lucky calf-curl fell out, if not completely; it thinned and was barely recognizable as the mark of Krishna—as Sita, his wife, noticed with sorrow. At the same time, however, there is no gainsaying the fact that his actual and not merely Maya-bound re-formation, which extended as far as a lighter skin tone, was combined with a refinement or, if you like, improvement—using the word in a partly Brahmanical, partly mercantile sense; his hands and feet became finer, his knees and ankles more delicate, and all in all, the lusty body of the friend, which had played the chief role in its previous ensemble, was becoming the bland appurtenance and accessory of a head whose noble-minded ideas it was soon no longer desirous or capable of representing with paradisial perfection and was instead reduced to accompanying with a certain lassitude.

Such was Sita and Shridaman's marital experience following the incomparable joys of their honeymoon. It did not go as far as Nanda's body changing back into Shridaman's completely, which would mean everything being exactly the same as before. That was not the case. This story does not set out to exaggerate but to draw attention to what determines the body's transformation and the way that is limited to factors that are unmistakable, and it does so in order to clear a space for the understanding that this involves an interaction between head and body, and that Shridaman's head, which determined his I-and-my-feelings, was thereby also subject to shifts in alignment, which might be explicable to natural philosophy as deriving from an interrelationship of the humours between head and body, but to a knowledge of essences as belonging to higher coherences.

There is a beauty of the mind and a beauty that speaks to the senses. Some would prefer to attribute beauty wholly to the world of the senses and to exclude the intellect completely, so that the world is seen as divided into opposing categories of mind and beauty. This is also the basis for the teachings of the Vedic fathers: 'Only two kinds of bliss can be experienced in the worlds: the joys of this body and the redeeming peace of the spirit.' But it follows from this doctrine of blissfulness that the spirit is not actually contrary to beauty in the same way as ugliness is, and that whether it is the same as the latter depends on certain conditions. The intellect is not synonymous with the ugly, or not necessarily so, for it embraces beauty through its recognition of beauty and love for it, which expresses itself as spiritual beauty and is therefore by no means an extraneous or hopeless kind of love, because beauty, too, according to the law of the attraction of opposites, aspires to the spiritual, venerates it and welcomes its wooing. This world is not so made that the spirit is destined only to love the spiritual, and beauty only things of beauty. It is the contrast between the two that reveals, with a clarity that is in itself both cerebral and beautiful, the destination of the world to be the unity of spirit and beauty, a bliss that is consummate and no longer divided into two, and our present story is but one example of the misadventures and failures that befall us in our attempts to reach that destination.

Shridaman, son of Bhavabhûti, had, by dint of an error, received a beautiful, sturdy body for his noble head, a head that manifested his love of beauty, and because he was a man of spirit, he immediately felt there was a kind of sadness in the fact that what had been strange to him had now become his and was no longer the object of his admiration, or in other words that he himself had now become what he had yearned for. This 'sadness' unfortunately carried over into the changes his head was subjected to in connection with his new body, for they were of the kind that will occur in a head that through the possession of beauty more or less loses its love for it, and thereby loses spiritual beauty, too.

It is open to question whether this process would not have taken place anyway, even without the exchange of bodies, solely as a result of Shridaman's marital possession of the beautiful Sita; we have already emphasized the general applicability of such a fate, and that its impact in this case was intensified and sharpened due to the special circumstances. In any case, to the listener who is an objective observer of human nature this is merely an interesting fact, but for Sita it was a source of distress and disillusionment to see how her husband's previously fine, narrow lips grew thicker and fuller behind his beard, how they began to protrude and form a rubbery bulge, how his nose, once as thin as a knife blade, grew fleshier and acquired an undeniable propensity to droop, verging on the goatlike, and how his eyes adopted a sort of mindless cheerfulness. When all was said and done, this was a Shridaman with a finer Nanda-body and a coarser Shridaman-head; there wasn't much that was right about him. It is for this reason that the speaker would appeal to listeners to show particular understanding for the feelings that took hold of Sita on finding that she could not but deduce from the changes she had witnessed in her husband that corresponding changes might meanwhile have taken place in her husband's distant friend.

When she considered her husband's body, which she had embraced on a wedding night that had been sacred and arousing if not exactly blissful, it was a body she no longer possessed, or, if you like, since it was his friend's body now, still did not possess, and she saw no reason to doubt that the Nanda-body's Maya would since have passed into it; she also had no doubt where the lucky calf-curl could be found now. She was quite sure, too, that the friend's faithful head, which in the meantime crowned her husband's body, must have undergone a process of refinement corresponding to that experienced by the friend's body, which was currently adorned with her husband's head, and this idea, more than the other, moved her deeply and gave her no rest, whether by day or by night, even in her husband's modest arms. In her mind's eye she saw how the lonely, attractively enhanced body of her husband together with the poor, refined head of his friend were united in spiritual anguish from being separate from her, and a wistful pity for this distant figure grew in her, so that she closed her eyes in Shridaman's conjugal embrace and in her lust turned pale with sorrow.

XII

WHEN her time was come, Sita bore Shridaman the fruit of her womb, a little boy they called Samadhi, meaning 'bringing together'.*

They waved the tail of a cow over the newborn to ward off evil and applied the cow's dung to his head to the same end—as is right and proper. The joy of the parents (if that is the right word) was great, for the boy was neither pale nor blind. But he was nevertheless quite light-skinned, which may have stemmed from his mother's descent from Kshatriya—or warrior—ancestors, and he was also, as they gradually discovered, particularly short-sighted. Thus are prophecies and folk omens fulfilled; they fulfil themselves by way of suggestion and blurring; you could say they've come true, and you could say that they haven't, as you think fit.

Later, because of his near-sightedness, Samadhi was also called Andhaka (blind one), a name that gradually prevailed. However, the trait gave his gazelle-like eyes a soft and lustrous allure, making them even more beautiful than Sita's, which they resembled, and indeed the boy had very little likeness to either of the fathers, but took decidedly after his mother, who, after all, was the defining and conclusive side of his provenance, which is probably why his whole bodily development seemed to rely on her formative influence. And this made him quite a beauty, and as soon as he had outgrown the period of soiled nappies and bow legs his frame became longer, stronger and pleasingly symmetrical. Shridaman loved him like his own flesh and blood, and feelings of resignation, an inclination to withdraw from life and live instead through his son, loomed in his soul.

The years in which Samadhi-Andhaka developed in sweetness at his mother's breast and in his cradle hammock, however, were also those in which the re-transformation of Shridaman's head and limbs took place, so that when his character as a whole reverted to that of the husband, Sita could no longer endure it and her sympathy for the distant friend, in whom she saw the begetter of her boy, became overpowering. The desire to see him again, to find out how he, too, might have changed under the law of convergence, consumed her entirely, and she also wanted to show him her little one so that he too could delight in him, but she did not dare communicate any of this to the husbandly head. And so when Samadhi was four years old, and the name Andhaka had more or less caught on, and the boy could run or rather scamper about, and while Shridaman was away on a business trip, she decided to up and leave and, cost what it may, find the hermit Nanda and console him.

One spring morning before sunrise, under the light of the stars, Sita donned her walking shoes and took up a long staff in one hand while her other held her little son's, whom she had dressed in his smock of calico from Calicut, and, with a bundle of provisions on her back for the journey, they set off unseen and hoping for the best, leaving home and village behind them.

The bravery with which she withstood the difficulties and dangers of her expedition bore witness to the determined urgency of her desire. Her warrior blood, dilute as it was, may have stood her in good stead, too, as undoubtedly also did her beauty and that of her little boy, for everybody took pleasure in helping such a charming pilgrim and her bright-eyed companion with advice and good deeds. She told people she was on her way to find the father of her child, her husband, who, with an irrepressible will to study the essence of things, had become a forest hermit, and that she was taking his son to him that he might teach and bless him; this too softened people's hearts, making them respectful and kind towards her. In villages and hamlets they gave her milk for her little one, and there was almost always a place to sleep for each of them in a barn or on the earthen banks of fireplaces. Often, jute and rice farmers would take them for long distances on their carts, but if she found no such means of transport, Sita kept walking undaunted with her staff, the child at her hand in the dust of the road taking two steps to her one, with only a very small stretch of the road visible to his lustrous eyes. She, however, gazed far ahead into the distance they must walk through, her eyes fixed on the goal of her pity and yearning.

Her wanderings took her to the Dankaka forest, for she guessed that her friend could have sought a place of solitude for himself there. But following enquiries with the holy men, she was told he was not there. Many refused to give her any more information, but several of the hermits' wives, who cuddled little Samadhi and fed him, were kind enough to go further, in fact telling her where he was. For the recluse's world is no different from any other world, where if you belong to it you will know what is what, a world where there is much gossip, criticism, jealousy, nosiness and rivalry, and where a hermit is bound to know where another dwells and what he is up to. And so it was that these good women could reveal to Sita the location of the haven the solitary Nanda had found for himself near the river Gomati or 'Cow river', seven days' journey to the south and west, and that this was a heart-warming spot with many trees, flowers, vines and creepers, full of singing birds and troops of animals, and that the banks of the river were plentiful with roots, tubers and fruits. All in all Nanda had chosen a place of seclusion that was all too pleasant, so that the more austere among the holy men were unable to take his asceticism very seriously, especially since aside from bathing and silence, he did not observe much in the way of vows and fed on whatever fruits came to hand in the forest, with wild rice in the rainy season and occasionally even a roast bird or two, while the extent of his contemplation was limited to that of a man who was merely aggrieved and disappointed. As far as her route was concerned, it was without particular misgiving or hardship, apart from the pass of the robbers, the gorge of the tigers and the valley of snakes, where one certainly ought to take care and muster one's courage.

Their advice in mind, Sita took leave of these helpful women of the Dankaka forest and, with her hopes revived, continued her journey in her wonted manner. From day to day she met the various challenges successfully, and perhaps it was Kama, the god of love, together with Shri-Lakshmi, the goddess of good fortune, who watched over their progress. She put the narrow pass of the robbers behind her without threat or hindrance, friendly shepherds showed her an indirect route around the gorge of the tigers, and in the valley of the vipers, which was unavoidable, she held little Samadhi-Andhaka in her arms all the way.

On reaching the Cow river, however, she again led him by the hand, her other hand managing her staff. She arrived on a dew-spangled morning. For a while she strode along the flowery riverbank, then, following the directions she had received, turned inward across the meadows towards a stretch of forest behind which the sun was rising and which blazed with the fiery red blossom of ashoka and kimshuka trees. At first the brilliance of the morning light dazzled her, but shading her eyes with her hand she made out a hut thatched with straw and bark at the edge of the forest, and behind it a youth wearing a bast smock, girt with grass, repairing timberwork with an axe. And as she drew even closer she noticed his arms were sturdy, like those that had swung her into the sun, but that his nose sloped to his only moderately bulging lips at an angle one would not call goatish but rather noble-looking.

'Nanda!' she called, as her heart leapt with joy. For to her he seemed like Krishna, overflowing with the juice of a powerful tenderness. 'Nanda, look, it's Sita coming to see you!'

He dropped his axe and ran to meet her, and on his chest was the lucky calf-curl. He welcomed her with a hundred pet names and greetings for he had longed for her and everything about her with all his body and soul. 'Have you come at last,' he called, 'you mellow moon, partridge-eyed one, you all-round lithe-limbed, beautifully coloured you, Sita, my gloriously hipped wife? In how many nights have I dreamt you would come across country to your outcast, lonely man like this, and now you are really here, and have overcome the robbers' ravine, the tigers' jungle and the valley of snakes, all of which I deliberately put between us in my rage against that fateful verdict! Oh, you are such a wonderful woman! And who is that you have brought with you?'

'That', she said, 'is the little fruit you gave me on our sacred wedding night, when you were not yet Nanda.'

'That can't have been very special,' he said. 'What is he called?'

'His name is Samadhi,' she replied, 'but he has gradually become known as Andhaka.'

'Why is that? he asked.

'Don't think it's because he is blind!' she reacted. 'He is no more blind than he is pale, in spite of his fair skin. But even so, he is quite short-sighted; in fact he can barely see three paces ahead of himself.'

'That is not without its advantages,' Nanda said. And they set the boy down in the fresh grass some distance away from the hut and gave him flowers and nuts to play with. Now Samadhi was occupied, while what they played themselves, fanned by the fragrance of mango blossom, which enhances the desire for love, and to the sweet calls of the kokil* in the sunlit treetops, was beyond his horizon.

* * *

The story now goes on to relate how the wedded bliss of the lovers lasted only one day and one night, for the sun had not risen again above the blazing blossoms of the forest by Nanda's hut when Shridaman arrived; on returning to his deserted home it had been obvious to him straight away where his wife must have gone. The members of his household at Welfare-of-Cows, who hesitated initially to inform him of Sita's disappearance, had probably expected his anger to flare like a fire doused with butter. That did not happen, and he had merely nodded like a man who knew what was coming; he did not leave in pursuit of his wife in anger or thirst for revenge, but set off promptly, albeit without haste, for Nanda's hermitage. For he had long known where the spot was, and he had kept it a secret from Sita in order not to expedite his fate.

His arrival was quiet; riding a pack animal, a yak, with his head bowed, and dismounting under the morning star in front of the hut without the slightest disturbance to the couple inside, he sat and waited for the day to loosen their embrace. For his jealousy was not of the ordinary kind where estranged beings snort and suffer, but was refined by the consciousness that it was his own former body Sita had resumed her marriage with, which could just as well be called an act of fidelity as one of betrayal, and his knowledge of essences had taught him that it was irrelevant whether Sita slept with him or with his friend, for even if one of the two got nothing out of it, she would always be doing it with both.

And this was the reason for his lack of haste in undertaking the journey and his calm and patience as he sat in front of the hut waiting for dawn. Why Shridaman nevertheless was disinclined to let matters take their course we shall learn as the story progresses. When Sita and Nanda, with towels around their necks because they intended to bathe in the nearby river while little Andhaka* was still asleep, emerged from the hut as the first ray of morning light shone upon the earth, they saw their friend and husband, who, sitting with his back to them, did not turn round as they came out, and so they went over to him, greeting him humbly, and, in what followed, united their own will with his, in that they conceded that the solution to their triple confusion that Shridaman had worked out during his journey was indeed a necessary one.

'Shridaman, you my lord and revered husband-head!' said Sita, bowing down before him, 'greetings—and do not think your arrival here is excruciating to us or that you are unwelcome! For when two of us are together, we shall always miss the third, and therefore forgive me that I could not stay with you any longer, and that pity drew me to our lonely friend-head!'

'And to your husband-body,' replied Shridaman. 'I do forgive you. And I forgive you too, Nanda, just as you for your part may forgive me for insisting on the holy man's judgement and taking Sita for myself, allowing only my own I-and-my-feelings to count, but ignoring yours. What is true is that you would have acted in the same way if the holy man's final judgement had been in your favour. For the delusions and discord of this life mean it is the lot of beings to stand in one another's way, and it is vain that the good long for a life in which the laughter of one is not the weeping of another. I was too uncompromising about having my own head and letting it enjoy your body. For with these arms, which have grown somewhat thin now, you had swung Sita into the sun, and during our most recent severance I flattered myself that I could offer her everything she wanted. But love wants it all. And so I was forced to discover that our Sita insisted on your head, and left me and our home. If I could only believe that she would find lasting happiness and satisfaction with you, my friend, then I would get going on my way and make of my father's house a hermitage of my own. But I don't believe it, for just as she longed for the friend-head atop the husband-body when she already had the husband-head atop the friend-body, it won't be long before she feels pity and longs for the husband-head atop the friend-body again, and she'll end up with no peace at all and no satisfaction, for the distant husband in her eyes will always be the friend she loves, and she will take our little son Andhaka along with her to see him, because in him she recognizes his father. But she can't live with both of us, because polyandry is out of the question among superior beings. Am I right in what I say, Sita?'

'What you say is what is true, alas, my lord and friend,' replied Sita. 'However, my regret, expressed in the little word "alas", refers only to a part of what you have said, but not to the fact that the abomination of polyandry is out of question for a woman like me. I have no "alas" to say to that, and am proud of it, because some of my father Sumantra's warrior blood still flows through my veins, and everything in me rises up against something as vile as polyandry: in all the weakness and confusion of the flesh, we should still have some pride and honour as superior beings!'

'I expected nothing less,' said Shridaman, 'and you may rest assured that I have anticipated your cast of mind, independent of the weakness of your sex as it is, in my thoughts on this. Since you cannot live with both of us, I am certain that this youth here, Nanda, my friend, with whom I have exchanged heads, or rather bodies, if you like, will agree with me that we cannot live either, and that nothing remains for us but to leave our current distribution of divisions behind us and reunite our essence with the universe. For when the individual being enters such confusion as we have, it is better he melt in the flame of life like an offering of butter in the sacrificial fire.'

'You are quite right, Shridaman, my brother, to expect my agreement with what you say,' said Nanda. 'It is indeed wholehearted. I really don't know what's left for us to do, as far as the flesh goes, since we've both satisfied our desires and lain with Sita: it was granted to my body to enjoy her in the consciousness of your head, and to yours in the consciousness of mine, just as she was able to enjoy me under the sign of your head and you under the sign of mine. Our honour, however, may be considered intact, for I have only betrayed your head with your body, which is compensated for in a certain sense by Sita of the beautiful hips having betrayed my body with my head; there was an occasion before that, however, when I, who had shared the betel sheaf with you as a sign of loyalty, would have betrayed you with her as the Nanda who still had his own limbs and head, and Brahma fortunately saved us from that. Nonetheless, we can't carry on like this honourably because our station in life is too high for polyandry or for the community of women: Sita's certainly is, and also yours, even with my body. But mine is too, especially with yours. For that reason I agree unreservedly with everything you say about smelting our essences and offer my services to build our pyre hut with these arms that have grown stronger in this wilderness. You will remember that I have shown willing to do this before. You will also remember that I was always resolved not to survive you and followed you to death without hesitation when you sacrificed yourself to the goddess. However, I only betrayed you after my husband-body gave me a certain right to do so and Sita brought little Samadhi to see me, as whose bodily father I see myself, just as I am happy to respect the paternal rights that accrue to you from the head.'

'Where is Andhaka?' enquired Shridaman.

'He is lying in the hut,' replied Sita, 'gathering strength and beauty for his life to come. It was high time we came to speak about him, for his future is surely more important to us than the question of how we are going to get out of this mess honourably. But these two matters are closely linked and by preserving his honour, we shall preserve our own. If I were to stay behind with him when you return to the allness, as indeed I would like to, he would go through life as the miserable offspring of a widow, bereft of all honour and joy. Only if I follow the example of the noble Satis* who accompanied their dead husband's body into the fire of the funeral pyre and who had stone slabs and obelisks erected to their memory at the site of their immolation—in other words, only if I go with you two and leave him will his life be honourable and will he enjoy favour and popularity. For which reason I, daughter of Sumantra, demand that Nanda build the pyre hut for three. Just as I have shared the bed of life with both of you, so shall the firebed of death unite us three. For in the first of these, we were actually always three.'

'I would never expect anything less of you,' said Shridaman, 'and from the start counted less on the weakness of your flesh than on your innate conscientiousness and pride. In the name of our son I thank you for your plan. But in order truly to restore honour and human pride and rescue them from the confusion the flesh has cast us into, we must pay due heed to the form of their restoration, and in that respect the thoughts and ideas I developed on my journey here differ from your own. Yes, the noble-minded widow immolates herself with her dead husband. You, however, are no widow as long as one of us two remains alive, and it is highly questionable that you would become a widow by sitting in the burning hut and dying with us. So in order to make you a widow Nanda and I will have to kill ourselves, by which I mean we shall have to kill each other, for in our case "ourselves" and "each other" are both correct terms and one and the same. Like two stags battling for a hind we must fight with two swords, which we have to hand, attached to my yak saddle. But the point of this is not that the winner survives and carries off our lovely-hipped Sita; that would bring no improvement, because the dead would forever be the friend for whom she pined, and she would pale in her husband's arms. No, both of us must fall, pierced to the heart by the other's sword—for only the sword belongs to the other, not the heart. Doing it this way would be better than if each of us turned their sword against what is his own currently severed part; it seems to me that our heads do not have the right to decide the death of the body attached to them, just as our bodies have no right to the bliss and marital lust of heads that do not belong to them. It will undoubtedly be a sore fight, in as far as the head and body of each of us will need to take care not to fight for itself and for sole ownership of Sita, but to concentrate on the double aim of delivering and receiving the fatal blow. But this two-sided suicide can hardly be harder than cutting off one's own head, which both of us, after all, have brought ourselves to do.'

'Go and get those swords, then!' exclaimed Nanda. 'I'm game for the fight, and it's a fair way of dealing with our rivalry in this matter.

It is fair because the appropriation of each other's bodies by our heads has made our arms more or less equally strong: mine are slighter on you, and yours sturdier on me. I shall offer you my heart with joy because I betrayed you with Sita, but I shall pierce yours so that she doesn't grow pale in your arms for love of me but can join us in the fire as a twofold widow.'

Since Sita had also given her assent to this order of things—which, as she put it, appealed to her warrior blood so that she had no intention of absenting herself but would be present without flinching—the fight to the death took place straight away in front of the hut in the flowery meadow where Andhaka lay asleep between the Cow river and the red-blossoming stretch of forest, and where the two youths now sank down into the flowers, each of them pierced through the other's heart. Their obsequies, however, because the holy event of a widow's self-immolation was combined with them, turned into a great festival, and thousands gathered at the site of the burning to watch little Samadhi—who was called Andhaka and was the male next of kin—hold his short-sighted face up close and set his torch to the pyre's mango and fragrant sandalwood logs, the gaps between which were chinked with straw that was thoroughly soaked in melted butter, so that the hut, in which Sita from Home of the Hump-backed Bull had found her place between her husband and his friend, would go up in flames more quickly. The pyre hut blazed to a height rarely witnessed, and if lovely Sita did scream for a while—because unless you are dead fire causes horrendous pain—her voice was drowned out by the shrilling of conch horns and clashing of drums, and it was therefore as if she hadn't screamed at all. But the story claims, and we might want to believe it, that the heat was cool to her because of the joy she felt at being united with her lovers.

An obelisk was erected on the spot in memory of her sacrifice, and what was left of the bones of the three that was not entirely consumed by the fire was collected, soaked in milk and honey, and kept in an earthenware pitcher until it was sunk in the waters of the holy Ganga.

But Samadhi, their little fruit, who was soon only known as Andhaka, had a splendid life on earth. Having won fame at the pyre festival, and as the son of a memorial-stone widow, he was treated with benevolence by all, and this grew to be a genuine affection as he became ever more handsome. By the age of twelve he was like the incarnation of a Gandharva in grace and bright vitality, and the lucky calf-curl had begun to show on his chest. His purblindness, meanwhile, far from proving disadvantageous, stopped him from dwelling all too much on the body and induced in him a preference for intellectual matters. When he was seven a Brahmin steeped in the Vedas took him under his wing and taught him correct and cultivated speech, grammar, astronomy and the art of thinking, and he was not older than twenty years old when he became Reader to the King of Benares. Then he would sit on a splendid palace terrace, attired in fine garments under a white silk parasol, reading in his engaging voice from writings both holy and profane, holding the book very close to his radiant eyes.

THE LAW

I

His birth was disorderly, which was why he passionately loved order, inviolability, edict and interdict.

He had killed early on in an outburst of anger, which is why he knew better than anyone who lacked such experience that while killing was delectable, having killed was detestable, and so you shouldn't kill.

He was sensual, which is why he yearned for the spiritual, pure and sacred—as well as the invisible, which to him seemed spiritual, sacred and pure.

Among the Midianites, a tribe of industrious herdsmen and traders who had spread across the desert, whose asylum he had been forced to seek after killing a man in Egypt, the land of his birth (more on this later), he made the acquaintance of a god you could not see although he could see you, an invisible mountain dweller who sat on a portable ark in a tent, where he delivered oracles by casting lots. For the children of Midian this numen,* whom they called Yahweh, was one god among others; they were not particularly attentive in serving him and did so only to be on the safe side—just in case. For it had occurred to them that among the gods there might be one they couldn't see, a shapeless one, and so they made sacrifices to him to avoid omission or causing offence or attracting bother from some quarter.

Moses, by contrast, because of his craving for purity and holiness, was deeply impressed by Yahweh's invisibility; he reckoned no visible god could compete with an invisible one when it came to holiness, and he was amazed the children of Midian attached so little importance to a characteristic that to him seemed full of implications beyond measure. Thinking long and hard while tending his Midianite wife's brother's sheep in the desert, shaken by visions and revelations—which in one case even escaped from within him, haunting his soul as a flaming external visage and literally imprinting its manifestation and unshirkable mission upon him—he came to believe that Yahweh was none other than El Elyon, or 'God Most High', El Roi, the 'God Who Sees Me', the god who had always been known as El Shaddai, or the 'Lord Almighty' and 'God of the Mountain', as El Olam, the

'God of the World and of Time Everlasting', or, in other words, was none other than Abraham's, Isaac's and Jacob's God, the God of the fathers, which is to say the God of his own poor, benighted, uprooted and enslaved kin at home in the land of Egypt, who in matters of worship were by now quite confused, and whose blood on his father's side flowed in his own—in Moses'—veins.

For that reason, full of the discovery he had made, his soul heavy with the mission he'd been charged with but also trembling with the desire to fulfil it, he broke off his years-long sojourn among the children of Midian, and, setting his wife Zipporah (a woman of some nobility, being the daughter of Reuel, the priest-king of Midian, and the sister of his son Jethro, who had flocks and herds) upon a donkey, and taking with him his two sons, Gershom and Eliezer, travelled west for seven days through many deserts and returned to the land of Egypt, that is, to the fallow lowlands where the Nile branches and where, in a region called Kesem, or variously also Gesem, Gosen or Goshen, his father's kindred dwelt and laboured.

Once there, and wherever he went or stood, whether in their huts or workplaces or on their pastures, he immediately began to expound to these kinsfolk the great things he had learned, at the same time holding his arms to his sides in a peculiar manner and making his fists tremble and shake. He informed them that the God of their fathers had been rediscovered on Mount Horeb in the desert of Sin, and that He had revealed Himself to him, Moshe ben Amram, from a bush that burned and was not consumed, and that the God's name was Yahweh, which meant 'I am that I am, from everlasting to everlasting', but also: a wafting breeze and a great roaring; furthermore, that He delighted in their blood and was prepared under certain circumstances to establish a covenant by which He would choose them from among all peoples, on condition that they pledged themselves exclusively to Him, and that they swore an oath of allegiance with one another to serve, without recourse to images, the Invisible One alone.

In this way he impressed himself upon them, his fists trembling at the end of his unusually thick wrists. He wasn't entirely honest with them, however, and for fear of unnerving them avoided disclosure of several of the matters on his mind, including the most important matter of all. For he told them nothing of the implications of invisibility, in other words of spirituality, purity and holiness, and chose not to point out that as sworn worshippers of the Invisible One they would have to become a separate people devoted to spirituality, purity and holiness. He kept these things to himself so as not to alarm them, for the kin of his father's flesh and blood were a miserable, oppressed lot who were exceedingly muddled in their ways of worship, and he mistrusted them, although he also loved them. Indeed, when he proclaimed to them that Yahweh, the Invisible One, delighted in them, he attributed this to the god, inserting things that doubtless came from Him, although to at least an equal degree, they were Moses' own, for it was he himself who delighted in the blood of his father's kin, just as the stone carver delights in the raw block he intends to chisel to a finely shaped, imposing figure, the work of his own hands—and it was for this reason that he had been filled with such a trembling desire, together with the vexation instilled in him by God's command, on his departure from Midian.

But what he also held back was the second part of the command, for the command was of a double kind. Not only must he announce to the tribes the rediscovery of the god of their fathers as well as His delight in them, the children of Israel, but he was also to lead those children forth out of the Egyptian house of bondage and into the open, and to guide them across many deserts to the Promised Land, the land of their fathers. This charge was tied to, and inextricably linked with, the part he had already proclaimed to them. God—and their deliverance to return home; the Invisible One—and shaking off the yoke of exile: these two were one and the same to him. He did not reveal these things to the people yet, however, because he knew that one thing would lead to the other, hoping as he did that, as far as the second matter was concerned, he would reach agreement on his own terms with Pharaoh, the king of Egypt, to whom he was not unclose.

But whether it was because the people disliked his speech, for he spoke badly and falteringly and was often unable to find the right words, or because his trembling and fist-shaking gave them a premonition of the implications of both invisibility and the proffered covenant—that is, the people suspected that he was trying to lure them into matters that were arduous and dangerous—they were sceptical, stiff-necked and fearful in the face of his persistence and, with a glance at their Egyptian overseers, snarled:

'What are you spewing words for? And what sort of words are they anyway? Has someone made you our headman, or our judge? Who could that have been?'

This wasn't new to him. He had already heard suchlike from them some time ago, before he fled to Midian.

II

HIS father wasn't his father, and his mother wasn't his mother—this is how disorderly his birth was. Under the protection of her armed guards, the Pharaoh Ramessu's* second daughter was amusing herself in the company of her female servants in the Royal Gardens by the Nile. A Hebrew labourer who was fetching water there caught her eye, and she was filled with desire for him. He had sad eyes, a youth's beard on his chin and strong arms, as she noticed while he drew water. He toiled by the sweat of his brow and had his own worldly cares, but for Pharaoh's daughter he was the picture of beauty and desire, and she commanded that he be brought to her in a pavilion; there, she ran her precious fingers through his sweat-soaked hair, kissed the muscles of his arms, and with her teasing awakened his manhood so that he, the foreign slave, took possession of a royal child. Having got what she wanted, she let him go, but he didn't get far; after thirty paces he was slain and quickly buried, and nothing remained of the sun-daughter's pleasure.

'The poor man!' she said, when she heard of it. 'You are always so overzealous. He would have held his tongue. He loved me.' But later it transpired she was pregnant and, after nine months had passed, she gave birth in all secrecy to a boy, whom her maidens put in an ark of bulrushes daubed with pitch and hid in the flags at the water's edge. Then they found it again and called out, 'Oh, what wonders! A foundling, a boy of the rushes, an abandoned child! It is like the ancient legends, like Sargon,* whom Akki, the drawer of water, found in the rushes and brought up in the goodness of his heart. These things will keep happening, won't they! What are we going to do with our find? The most sensible thing would be to give him to a mother of low estate who is nursing but has milk to spare, so that he can grow up her son and that of her honest husband.' And they delivered the child to a Hebrew woman, who brought him to the land of Goshen, to Jochebed, the wife of Amram, an authorized immigrant who belonged to the tribe of Levi.* She was nursing her son Aaron and had milk to spare; for that reason, and because good things from above would, from time to time, secretly arrive at her hut, she brought up this unaccountable child, too, in the goodness of her heart. And so Amram and Jochebed became known as his parents, and Aaron as his brother. Amram had cattle and pasture, and Jochebed was a stonemason's daughter. However, they didn't know what to call this enigmatic little boy, so they gave him a name that was half Egyptian, or rather, was half an Egyptian name. For the sons of the land were often called Ptach-Mose, Amen-Mose or Ra-Mose; they were named as sons of their gods. Now, Amram and Jochebed preferred to omit the god's-name part and just called their boy Mose. Thus he was simply a 'son'.* The only question was: whose?

III

He grew up as one of the authorized and expressed himself in their tongue. Once, in time of drought, their tribal ancestors had been permitted by the border authorities to enter the country as 'starving Bedouins of Edom', as Pharaoh's scribes called them, and had been allotted grazing land in the district of Goshen, in the lowlands. Anyone who imagines they were allowed to graze their cattle there for free cannot know their hosts very well, the children of Egypt. Not only was an excruciating tribute levied on their cattle, but every one of them who was physically capable was pressed into work, forced to labour on the various construction sites that were always underway in a land such as Egypt. But especially when Ramessu, the second of his name, became Pharaoh in Thebes, the construction became extravagant, for that was his delight and royal pleasure. He built sumptuous temples throughout the land; in the estuarine lowlands he not only had the long-neglected canal connecting the eastern arm of the Nile with the Bitter Lakes rebuilt and very much improved, thus joining the Great Sea with the tip of the Red Sea, but also erected two whole store-cities along the canal, called Pithom and Ramses, and it was into these projects that the children of the immigrants, the Ibrim, were conscripted to bake and haul bricks and to toil in the sweat of their bodies under the Egyptian rod.

This rod was little more than an emblem carried by Pharaoh's overseers; the labourers were not unduly beaten with it. They also had enough to eat while they worked: plenty of fish from the Nile, bread, beer and beef, enough to feed them well. In spite of that, labouring was neither to their taste nor their satisfaction, for they were a nomadic people whose traditions derived from wandering freely, and they found regular hours and work that made them sweat offensive, and alien to their nature. However, these tribes were too loosely bonded and insufficiently conscious of their lot to form an alliance or come to any agreement over their discontent. Having lived in tents for several generations in a land of transit between the home of their fathers and Egypt proper, their souls were without form—they lacked any firm doctrine and were of fickle spirit; they had forgotten many things and had only a rough grasp of some, but lacking a true centre they had no trust in their own feelings, not even in their resentment against the hard labour, and were beguiled by the fish, beer and beef.

Now Moshe, allegedly Amram's son, was supposed to start making bricks for Pharaoh when he outgrew his boyhood. That is not what happened, however; instead, the youth was taken away from his parents and deposited at a school in Upper Egypt, an elite boarding school where the sons of the rulers of Syrian city states were brought up alongside the offspring of the local nobility. This is where they put him, too, for his natural mother, Pharaoh's child, a wanton creature who nevertheless had a heart and who, having given birth to him among the flags, had continued to bear him in mind for the sake of his hurriedly buried father—the water-bearer with his little beard and sad eyes—did not want him to remain with savages but to be brought up as an Egyptian and attain courtly office, in discreet semi-recognition of his divine semi-royalty. Thus Moses, clothed in white linen, a wig on his head, studied astronomy and geography, calligraphy and law, but he was unhappy among the dandies at his genteel boarding school and felt quite alone, full of disdain as he was for all their Egyptian refinement, from whose lust he had sprung. The blood of the hastily buried man who had been pressed into serving this lust was stronger in him than his Egyptian side, and in his soul he preferred the poor, formless souls back home in Goshen, who did not have the courage to show their wrath—he preferred them, that is, to the lascivious arrogance of his mother's side.

'What's your name again?' his schoolmates probably asked him.

'I'm called Moses,' he answered.

'Ach-Moses or Ptach-Moses?' they asked.

'No, just Moses,' he replied.

'That's pathetic, and odd too,' the prigs declared, which made him so furious he could have killed and hastily buried them. For he saw that the point of these questions was only to poke around among the disorderly facts of his life, the vague outlines of which were generally known. For how could he himself have known that he was merely the discreet fruit of Egyptian pleasure had it not been a matter of common, albeit mostly imprecise, knowledge—knowledge that reached all the way up to Pharaoh, who was no more oblivious to the dalliances of his daughter than was Moses to the fact that such vile pleasures and murder had rendered Ramessu, the Builder, his grandfather-by-lechery. Yes, Moses knew these things and knew that Pharaoh knew them, too, and the thought of that made him nod threateningly in the direction of Pharaoh's throne.

IV

AFTER living for two years among the coxcombs of his Theban school, he could stand it no longer and escaped one evening by scaling the wall and heading home to Goshen and his father's kinsfolk. There, he was wont to prowl around among them with a resentful look on his face, and one day by the canal, near the new buildings at Ramses, he saw an Egyptian overseer beating a labourer, who had probably been lazy or unruly, with his rod. With a pale face and flaming eyes he asked the overseer what he thought he was doing, but instead of an answer the overseer gave him such a punch that the bone of Moses' nose was smashed flat against his face and remained broken for the rest of his life. But Moses grabbed the overseer's rod and taking an almighty swing, shattered the man's skull, killing him outright. He didn't even look round to see whether anyone was watching. It was a secluded spot and nobody else was about. Alone therefore, he buried the man he had slain, since the one to whose defence he had come had taken to his heels—and it seemed to him as if murdering and burying had been something he had always wanted to do.

His hot-blooded crime remained hidden, at least from the Egyptians, who couldn't work out where their man had got to, and days and years passed over the deed. Moses continued to wander around among his father's people, and to intervene in a peculiarly high-handed manner in their squabbles. On one occasion he came upon two Ibrim labourers who were quarrelling and all but coming to blows. 'Why are you arguing? You even look ready to have a brawl?' he asked. 'Aren't you miserable and down at heel enough to want to side with your own people instead of baring your teeth against one another? He's in the wrong—I saw what he did. Now let him yield and humble himself, but the other should not show triumph.'

But as often happens, both of them were suddenly united against him, saying, 'What are you doing, barging into our affairs?' The one he had said was in the wrong was particularly snappy, and raising his voice said, 'Well, that really is the limit! Who do you think you are, sticking your goatish nose into things that are none of your business? Aha, it's Mosheh, is it not, Amram's son, but that isn't saying much, since nobody really knows who you are, not even you do. As for us, we're curious to know who appointed you as master and judge over us. Were you thinking of strangling me too, then, like you strangled and buried that Egyptian a while back?'

'Keep quiet, won't you!' exclaimed Moses, shocked, and he thought to himself, 'How has that got out?' And on the very same day it became clear to him that this was no place for him to stay, and so he left the country in a place where there was no fixed border, and crossed the mudflats at the Bitter Lakes. And he wandered through the many deserts of the land of Sinai until he came to Midian, to the Midianites and their priest-king Reuel.

V

WHEN he returned to Egypt, filled with missionary zeal and the discovery of God, he was a man in his best years, sturdy, with a flattened nose, prominent cheekbones, a parted beard, wide-set eyes and thick wrists, which were especially evident when he mulled over something, as was often the case, with his right hand covering his mouth and beard. He went from hut to hut and from workplace to workplace, shaking his fists by his thighs and speaking of the Invisible One, and God the Father who was ready to make a covenant with them, although he couldn't really speak properly. For his whole nature was awkward and faltering, and when he became agitated, he tended to trip over his tongue, although in fact he was not really at home in any tongue, and when speaking would fumble his way through three: Aramaic Syro-Chaldean, the language of his paternal ancestors, which he had learned from his parents and which had been overlaid by Egyptian, the language he had been made to learn at his boarding school, and then there was Midianite Arabic, which he had spoken for quite a long time in the desert. So he kept on getting them muddled up.

His brother Aaron, a tall, gentle man with a black beard and black ringlets at the back of his neck who kept his arched eyelids lowered out of piety, was a great help to him. Moses had initiated him into everything, winning him over to the Invisible One and all the implications thereof, and since Aaron had the ability to speak through his beard with unctuous fluency, he generally went out with Moses to promote the cause and spoke in his stead, albeit with somewhat lisping, oily articulation, a manner hardly captivating, so that Moses would attempt to put more fire into his words by accompanying him with his shaking fists and interrupting him with a potpourri of Aramaic, Egyptian and Arabic.

Aaron's wife was called Elisheba, Amminadab's daughter; she was party to the sworn oath and took part in the propaganda, too, as did a younger sister of Moses and Aaron, Miriam, a spirited woman and a singer who could play the timbrel. But Moses was especially taken with a youth who, for his part, stood body and soul by Moses and his proclamation and plans, and never left his side. His real name was Osea, son of Nun (meaning 'fish'), of the tribe of Ephraim, but Moses gave him the name Jehoshua, or Joshua* for short, and the latter wore his new name with pride—he was a young sinewy lad with an erect posture and curly hair, a prominent Adam's apple and a pair of distinctly etched creases between his eyebrows, and he had his own view of the project, viewing it as less religious than military, for in his view, Yahweh, the God of the fathers, was above all the God of hosts, and the idea linked with His name, namely that of escaping from the house of bondage, was in turn bound to the conquest and possession of new settlement areas for the Hebrew tribes—inevitably so, because they would have to live somewhere, and no land, be it promised or not, would come to them as a gift.

Joshua, young as he was, had all the relevant facts stored in his clear-sighted, wide-awake curly head and discussed them unceasingly with Moses, his oldest friend and master. While lacking the means to conduct an exact population count, he had calculated the membership sum of the tribes tenting in Goshen and living in the royal storage cities of Pithom and Ramses, and including those who were scattered as slaves throughout the land, to come to around twelve or thirteen thousand people, meaning a force of about three thousand men-at-arms. Later the numbers were exaggerated, but Joshua's assessment was more or less correct, and it did not make him feel very happy. Three thousand men was hardly a terrifying force, not even if you were anticipating that once you were on your way, you could probably count on all manner of kin who were wandering about in the desert to join the core group in the hope of acquiring land for themselves. Any larger operations would be out of the question if based solely on a force of this size, and deploying it to invade the Promised Land would prove unfeasible. Joshua understood that, and he therefore tried to find an open space where his kindred could settle for a while, and where, under tolerably favourable conditions, it might be allowed time to increase its number naturally, which, if Joshua knew his people well, would mean an annual rate of two and a half in every hundred. So Joshua was on the lookout for a place to nurture and secure the growth of their armed force, and discussing his idea with Moses, he proved that he had a surprisingly clear picture of how one place related to another in the world, and that in his head he had a kind of map of the most suitable stretches of land with regard to distances, daytime marches and watering holes, and especially in respect of the bellicosity of their inhabitants.

Moses appreciated what he had in Joshua and knew he would need him, and he loved his zeal, although its immediate objects did not concern him greatly. With his right hand covering his beard and mouth he listened, while thinking of other things, to the youth's strategic comments. Although for Moses, too, Yahweh was synonymous with departure from Egypt, it was less the military campaign of gaining land that concerned him than the project of going forth into open land and finding a place of seclusion, where, out there in the open air, he could have them to himself—that whole mass of bewildered, vacillating flesh that had no idea which culture it belonged to, all those begetting men, suckling women, dabbling youths, snotty-nosed children, in short, the kin of his father—and where he could implant in their souls the holy and invisible God who was pure and spiritual, thus making Him their convening, formative centre, and, what was more, where he would be able to shape them in His image, a people different from all others, belonging to God, defined and formed by the holy and the spiritual, distinguished by awe, forbearance and fear of God, that is to say: fear of the thought of purity, of the statute of restraint which, since the Invisible One was in fact the God of all the world, would at some future point be binding for all, but was in the meantime decreed for them alone: their exacting privilege over heathens.

This was Moses' delight in the blood of his father, his delight as a creator, which itself was at one with God's gracious election and willingness to enter into a covenant, and since it was his belief that such formation in God's purpose must come before all undertakings of the sort young Joshua had in mind, and further, that this would require time, free time out in the open, he was not disappointed that Joshua's projects were not going according to plan and had come up against the insufficient numbers of men capable of bearing arms. Joshua needed time for the people to multiply by natural means, and he also needed time to grow older, old enough to establish himself as commander in the field, while Moses needed time too, time for his own work of creation, which he yearned to fulfil in God's name. And so they were in agreement, albeit from different points of view.

VI

In the meantime, however, the chosen one and his closest disciples, the eloquent Aaron, as well as Elisheba, Miriam and Joshua—as well as a certain Caleb, who was Joshua's bosom friend and the same age, a similarly strong, straightforward and brave young man—had not been idle, but had spent each and every day spreading the message among their own people of Yahweh, the Invisible One, and His approving offer of a covenant, while at the same time stoking the people's bitterness at having to labour under the Egyptian rod and planting in their minds the idea of shaking off their yoke and departing. Each contributed to these aims in his or her own way: Moses with faltering words and shaking fists, Aaron with his fluent, somewhat lisping articulation, Elisheba garrulously persuasive, Joshua and Caleb in commanding tones and curt slogans, and Miriam, who was soon known as 'the prophetess', in a more exalted tone, to the accompaniment of her timbrel. Nor did their homilies fall on barren ground. The idea of pledging allegiance to Moses' covenanting God, of dedicating themselves to the Imageless One as His own people and of setting out for open land with Him and His proclaimer, struck root among the tribes and began to forge a convening centre—all the more so because Moses promised, or rather proffered as a hopeful possibility, that he would negotiate with the highest authority in the land to obtain permission for the departure of their entire people from Egypt, so that no desperate uprising would be required to fulfil their wish and their plan could instead go ahead on the basis of an amicable agreement. They were already aware, albeit vaguely, of his semi-Egyptian birth among riverbank flags, and they knew about the refined education he had enjoyed for a time, and also about the obscure relations he maintained with the court. What once had been a reason for mistrusting and opposing him, namely his mixed ancestry and his having one foot in Egypt, had now become a source of trust and lent him authority. Certainly, if there was anyone capable of standing before Pharaoh and pleading their cause, Moses was their man. And so they assigned to Moses the task of attempting to obtain from Ramessu, the master builder and their oppressor, their release to open land—that is, to Moses and also his milk-brother Aaron, whom Moses had decided to take with him, firstly, because he himself was unable to speak coherently, while Aaron could, but also because Aaron had certain tricks up his sleeve which they hoped to present at court and thereby make an impression in Yahweh's honour, for by squeezing its neck Aaron could make a cobra become as stiff as a rod, but if he threw the rod to the ground, it formed coils and 'turned into a serpent'. Neither Moses nor Aaron had anticipated that Pharaoh's magicians would be equally acquainted with this wonder, and that it could therefore not serve as terrifying evidence of Yahweh's powers.

In fact they would have no luck at all—this much said in advance—despite all the cunning that had gone into the strategy they had forged during a war council with the youths Joshua and Caleb. For it had been decided that they would only apply to the king for permission for the Hebrew people to assemble and trek for three days beyond the border and into the desert, where they would celebrate a sacrificial feast to the Lord their God who had called them, before returning to work. They had hardly expected Pharaoh to fall for such a ruse and believe they would come back; it was only meant to be a gentler, more polite way of putting forward their request for release. But the king showed them no gratitude for their niceties.

Where the brothers were successful, however, was in entering the Great House and reaching Pharaoh's throne, and that not only once but again and again, for these were tough negotiations, held over a long period. In that sense Moses had not promised his people too much, reliant as he was on Ramessu being his secret grandfather-by-lechery, and on them each knowing that the other also knew that. This gave Moses a powerful bargaining tool, and even if it was not powerful enough to extract the king's consent to their exodus, it meant Moses was a negotiator to be taken seriously, and it assured his repeated admittance to the potentate, who feared him. Certainly, the fear of a king can be dangerous, and Moses was playing a risky game the entire time. He was brave—how brave he actually was, and what impression he made on his own folk, we shall find out fairly soon. It would have been easy for Ramessu to have him quietly strangled and hastily buried, so that at last there would have been nothing left at all of his child's carnal whim. But the princess retained a sweet memory of that brief tryst, and did not want her bulrush-boy to be harmed—he stood under her protection, however little thanks he had shown for her benevolence and plans for his education and advancement.

Thus Moses and Aaron were granted audiences with Pharaoh, who, however, rejected out of hand any talk of the sacrificial, open-air festival which their God had allegedly called for. There was no use in Aaron's speaking with unctuous coherence or in Moses shaking his fists passionately by his thighs. And nothing was gained by Aaron turning his rod into a snake, for Pharaoh's magicians were able to perform the same trick straight away, thereby proving that no superior powers could be imputed to the Invisible One in whose name the two brothers spoke, and that Pharaoh need not heed that lord's voice. 'But our kin will be struck down by pestilence or with the sword if we do not go three days' journey into the desert and hold a feast unto our Lord,' said the brothers. But the king replied, 'This is not our concern. You are people enough, more than twelve thousand, you could probably bear some thinning-out, be it by pestilence, the sword or hard labour. You, Moses and Aaron, all you really want is to indulge your people's idleness and to free them from the labour they owe me. I cannot tolerate that and will not permit it. I am presently building a number of tremendous temples and also want to build a third storage city besides Pithom and Ramses, and in order to do so I need your people's hands. I thank you for your eloquent submission, and Moses, I dismiss you for better or for worse, and with all goodwill. But I'll hear no more of desert holidays!'

That concluded the audience, with not only nothing good coming out of it, but with things resulting from it afterwards that were decidedly wicked. Wounded in his passion for building and disgruntled because he couldn't very well strangle Moses without his daughter making a scene, Pharaoh gave orders to force the Goshen people to work even harder than before, and not to be squeamish about using the rod if workers slacked; on the contrary, they were to be driven until they dropped, and until all thought of desert feasts to honour their god were dispelled. And so it came about. As a result of Moses and Aaron speaking to Pharaoh, the toils of their people became harsher from one day to the next. Straw, for example, which they needed to burn the bricks, was no longer delivered; instead they had to go to the stubble fields themselves to gather what they needed, and yet there was no reduction in the number of bricks they had been commanded to produce; they had to fulfil the same quota or have the rod dance on their poor backs. And it was in vain that the Hebrew officers who had been told to supervise the workers complained to the authorities that their demands were excessive. The response was, 'You are idle, idle and nothing else, which is why you whine and say, "We want to leave and celebrate a sacrifice." The order is final: you shall gather the straw yourselves and produce the same number of bricks.'

VII

To Moses and Aaron, this was no small embarrassment. The foremen said to them, 'That's that, then! And it's all the result of this covenant with your God and because of Moses' connections. The only thing you've accomplished is to make our reputation stink in the noses of Pharaoh and his servants, and to put a sword in their hand to slay us.'

There was little he could say in response, and Moses had a hard time of it alone with the God of the thorn-bush, remonstrating that he, Moses, had been against this mission from the start, and from the outset had requested that whoever God sent, it should not be him, because he was no good at talking. However, the Lord had said to him that Aaron, on the other hand, spoke well. And fair enough, Aaron had indeed done the talking, but he had an oleaginous way of doing so, and it had soon become obvious how misguided it had been taking on a cause like this if you had a slow tongue and someone else had to stand in to help you with the rhetoric. But within Moses' breast, God both comforted and chastised him, and again from within, retorted that he should be ashamed of his faint-heartedness; his excuses were in reality pure affectation, for he himself had burned for this mission, and delighted in the people and the thought of forming them just as much as He did, indeed Moses' own delight was entirely indistinguishable from God's, in fact it was one with it; it was God's delight that had driven him to take on the task, and Moses should be ashamed to despair at the first setback.

Moses accepted this, all the more so for having determined in the war council together with Joshua, Caleb, Aaron and the spirited women, that the increased oppression, even if it had caused bad blood, was on closer consideration not such a bad start after all, for the ill feeling was directed not only against Moses, but above all against the Egyptians, and that would make the people all the more receptive to the call of God the Deliverer, and to the thought of going forth into open land. And that is exactly what happened: the issue of straw and bricks fomented unrest among the labourers, and the accusation that Moses had caused them to be abhorred before Pharaoh and done them nothing but harm receded behind a desire for Amram's son to use his good offices and approach Pharaoh yet again.

This he did, this time no longer with Aaron but alone, and careless of the mess his tongue might make of it; he shook his fists in front of Pharaoh's throne and in a sputtering torrent of words demanded permission for his people to go forth into the open land under the aegis of celebrating sacrificial rites in the desert. And he did this not merely once, but as many as ten times, for Moses' connections were such that Pharaoh could not very well refuse him admission to the throne. A struggle, dogged and protracted, ensued between Moses and the king, which, although Pharaoh at no time consented to Moses' requests, meant that there came a day when the people of Goshen, rather than being released, were hustled out of the land, for in the end the authorities were simply glad to see the back of them. Many rumours surround the nature of this struggle as well as the means that were deployed to assert pressure on a stubborn and reluctant Pharaoh, rumours that are not entirely unfounded, yet equally not devoid of embellishment. Ten plagues Yahweh is said to have visited upon Egypt, one after another, wearing Pharaoh down while at the same time deliberately hardening his heart against Moses' cause, thereby giving Him an opportunity to show His power with ever new plagues. Blood, frogs, vermin, wild beasts, boils, pestilence, hail, locusts, darkness and death of the firstborn—such were the names of these ten plagues, and any one of them may well have happened; the question is whether any of them—with the exception of the last, a peculiarly opaque phenomenon that has never been fully explained—significantly contributed to the final outcome. Under certain circumstances, the Nile can take on a blood-red hue; its water becomes undrinkable and fish die. It is also not unknown for frogs to breed excessively in the swamps, or for lice, always present, to proliferate to the extent of an infestation. Lions, too, still roamed in considerable numbers at the edge of the desert, lurking in the jungle beside the oxbow lakes, and when rapacious attacks on humans and cattle increased, it is easy to see why they might be called a plague. And are not scabies and sores commonly found in the land of Egypt, and how easily uncleanliness may give rise to a pestilence of boils with evil blains that fester among the people? The sky there is generally blue, and so how deep must be the impression left by a rare and grievous thunderstorm, with its fire descending from the clouds mingled with the coarse grain of the hail whipping crops and tearing at trees, without there being any apparent reason for it. The locust is an all-too-familiar guest and the human race has invented various means of repulsion and barriers against their massed advance; such measures, however, are generally defeated by the insects' voraciousness itself, with whole regions stripped bare. And one need only once have experienced the gloomily eerie mood that a cosmically shaded sun can induce on earth to understand how a people blessed by light might call such a darkness a plague.

And that completes the list of reported curses, for the tenth plague, the death of the firstborn, does not really belong in this count; instead it constitutes a somewhat ambiguous concomitant of the exodus itself, and exploring its depths can be uncanny. Some of the others may have happened, or even all of them spread over a longer period; one should consider their names as more or less florid circumlocutions for the only real means of pressurizing Ramessu that Moses had in his hand, namely the simple fact that Pharaoh was his grandfather-by-lechery, and that Moses was in a position to put this about whenever he wanted. More than once the king was on the point of giving in to this pressure; at the very least he made considerable concessions. He was content to allow the men to go forth to sacrifice, but the women, children and herds were to stay behind. Moses did not accept this; they must go forth with young and old, sons and daughters, flocks and cattle, for at stake was a festival of the Lord. And so Pharaoh allowed women and offspring too, but made an exception of their livestock, which must remain behind as a pledge. But Moses asked in return, how they could procure sacrificial beasts and burnt offerings to serve their Lord, if they couldn't take their livestock? And he demanded that not a hoof be left behind—which made it quite clear this was not about a holiday, but an exodus.

The matter of hooves turned out to be the final straw before a last stormy scene took place between the Egyptian Majesty and Yahweh's officer. During the negotiations, Moses had shown great patience, but fist-shaking wrath was also in his nature. This went so far that Pharaoh couldn't bear it any longer and literally marched him to the door. 'Out!' he cried, 'and take heed not to come before my eyes again. If you do so, you shall die.' At that moment Moses, who had been so very angry, grew quite calm and simply answered, 'You have spoken. I will go and never again come before your eyes.' The thoughts that came to him as he took leave with such awful calm were not to his liking. But they were certainly to young Joshua's and Caleb's liking.

VIII

THIS is a dark chapter, one that can only be recounted in broken, veiled words. There came a day, or rather, a night, a merciless Vespers massacre night,* when Yahweh, or rather the Angel of Death, His destroyer, went about visiting the tenth plague upon the children of Egypt, or upon a part of them, the Egyptian element among the inhabitants of Goshen and the cities of Pithom and Ramses, while sparing and passing over those huts and dwellings whose doorposts, as a token, had been painted with blood.

What did He do? He brought death, the death of the Egyptian first-born, which in turn meant that he fulfilled the secret wishes of other Egyptians, helping them to assume rights they would otherwise have been denied. It is worth noticing the distinction made between Yahweh and His destroying angel here; it demonstrates that it was not Yahweh Himself who went about, but His Destroyer—or more precisely, a whole band of them, carefully selected. If, however, one finds it expedient to reduce such a company to a single figure, then it would seem appropriate to imagine Yahweh's destroying angel as a lad with erect posture and curly hair, a prominent Adam's apple and distinct creases between his brows, in other words as the kind of angel who is always glad when useless negotiations end and the time comes for deeds.

There had been no lack of preparing decisive deeds during the dogged negotiations between Moses and Pharaoh; as far as Moses himself was concerned, who expected events to take a difficult turn, these were restricted to sending his wife and two sons secretly back to his brother-in-law Jethro in Midian, so that he would not be burdened with their care when things grew serious. Joshua, on the other hand, whose relationship to Moses was unmistakably similar to that of the Destroyer to Yahweh, had acted according to his wont, and, with neither the means nor yet the standing to put three thousand kinsmen-at-arms on a war footing under his command, had at least selected his own gang—arming, drilling and disciplining them so that they could act effectively from the outset.

What actually happened back then is shrouded in darkness—in the dark Vespers night that the children of Egypt had assumed would be a celebratory night for the enslaved tribes who lived among them. It had seemed the tribes intended a festival of lanterns and banqueting for their god, a festival that would take place where they actually lived—in compensation for the sacrificial celebration in the desert that had been forbidden them; they had even borrowed gold and silver vessels, apparently for that purpose, from their Egyptian neighbours. As it happened, or rather instead of that happening, the Destroyer passed through, and the firstborn perished in every house that had not been daubed with blood using a bunch of hyssop—a visitation that brought with it a confusion of such magnitude and such a sudden overthrow of legal entitlements and property relations that, from one hour to the next, not only did Moses' people find the border gates opened for them, but they were positively bundled through them; as far as the Egyptians were concerned, they could not depart fast enough. In fact it seems that the second-born were less eager to revenge the deaths of those whose positions they now assumed than to expedite the departure of the architects of their elevation. The traditional slant put on this state of affairs is that it was the tenth plague that finally broke Pharaoh's pride, to the effect that he released Moses' paternal kin from bondage, and promptly sent an armed division in pursuit, which, however, miraculously met with disaster.

Be that as it may, the departure most certainly took the form of an expulsion, and the haste with which this occurred is underlined by the fact that nobody had time to leaven their loaves for the journey; instead they had only makeshift unleavened flatbreads, whose consumption Moses would later turn into a commemorative, celebratory custom for all time. Otherwise, whether big or small, all of them were quite ready to leave. While the Destroyer went about, they were already sitting by their loaded carts, loins girded, shoes on their feet and staves in their hands. Also loaded for the journey: the gold and silver vessels they had borrowed from the children of Egypt.

My friends! Going forth from Egypt involved both killing and stealing. However, Moses firmly determined that this should be the last time. How were people supposed to wrest themselves from impurity without offering one last sacrifice to it and defiling themselves again properly as they did so? Now Moses had the flesh-and-blood object of his creative desire before him, this formless humanity, the blood-kin of his father, free and out in the open, and freedom to him was a space for sanctification.

IX

THE wandering mass of people that now went forth—fewer than legend would have it, but nonetheless hard to handle, guide and provide for, and burdensome enough for anybody who carried responsibility for their fate and progress out in the open—took a route whose practicality was self-evident if, for good reason, one intended to avoid the Egyptian border fortifications north of the Bitter Lakes; the route led through a region of brackish lakes fed by the greater, more westerly of the two Red Sea arms that make of Sinai a peninsula. Moses knew this region, having passed through it on his flight to Midian and later again on his return. He knew it better than young Joshua did, who had only abstract maps in his head, and he was familiar with the nature and peculiar features of the reedy tidal mudflats that at times formed an open passage connecting the gulf and the Bitter Lakes, across which, under certain conditions, one could reach the land of Sinai dry-shod. If a strong easterly wind prevailed, driving an especially low tide, the mudflats permitted an open crossing, and it was in just such a state, thanks to Yahweh's favourable dispensation, that the refugees found the Sea of Reeds when they reached it.

It was Joshua and Caleb who spread the news among the multitude that Moses, appealing to God, had stretched out his rod over the waters and caused them to part, clearing the way for his people. And that is probably what he actually did, helping the east wind along with a grand gesture invoking Yahweh. At any rate, the people's faith in their leader was in dire need of a boost and needed it here and now more than ever before, as their faith was about to be subjected to a severe endurance test. For it was here that the might of Pharaoh's army, his men and chariots—chariots fitted with scythes, as they well knew—caught up with the fugitives and came within a hair's breadth of putting their journey to God to a bloody end.

The news of their approach, announced by Joshua's rearguard, induced utter terror and wild despair among the people. There was an immediate outpouring of hot-tempered regret that they had followed 'this man Moses', and a diffuse groaning and griping set in, a grumbling of the kind that, much to Moses' sorrow and bitterness, would repeat itself whenever anything went wrong. Women moaned, men cursed, holding their shaking fists by their thighs just as Moses did when he was agitated. 'Were there not graves in Egypt', people declaimed, 'where we might have lain in peace when our hour came if only we had stayed at home?' All at once it was Egypt that was 'home', while previously they had complained of their exile in a strange land and slave labour. 'It would surely be better for us to serve the Egyptians than to perish by the sword in the wilderness!' Moses heard this said a thousand times, and he still felt bitter about it after they were rescued, even though their deliverance was such an overwhelming event. For when everything went well, he was praised as 'the man Moses who led us out of Egypt'. But as soon as it went badly, things took on a different hue and the same phrase became a murmur of resentment, with the spectre of a stoning never far away.

In the event, following a short period of trepidation, it all went embarrassingly and implausibly well. Through God's miracle, Moses grew enormously in stature and was again 'the man who led us out of Egypt', albeit this time spoken in praise. The children of Israel squelched across the drained mudflats pursued by the might of the Egyptian chariots. Suddenly the wind dropped, the tide rushed in, and horse and rider gurgled and perished in the engulfing flood.

The triumph was beyond compare. Miriam, the prophetess, Aaron's sister, took a timbrel in her hand, and led the women in a round dance as she played and sang: 'Sing ye to the Lord—a glorious deed—the horse and his rider—thrown into the sea.'* She had composed this herself. One has to imagine it sung to the timbrel.

The people were deeply moved. The words 'powerful, holy, fearful, praiseworthy, and doing wonders' passed their lips endlessly, and it was unclear whether they were referring to God or Moses, the man of God, whose rod they assumed to have brought the drowning floods down on the power of Egypt. Getting the two confused was a constant risk. Whenever the people were not complaining, Moses had a hard time trying to prevent them from seeing him as God, the One he was proclaiming.

X

ACTUALLY, this was not entirely absurd, for what he had begun to expect of these poor souls went beyond normal human ways and means, and could hardly have been conceived in the head of a mortal. It made your jaw drop. Straight after Miriam's song and dance he forbade all further jubilation over the Egyptians' demise. He announced that Yahweh's heavenly host itself had been about to join in the victory anthem when the Holy One rebuked them: 'What? My creatures sink into the depths, and the best you can do is sing?' Moses spread this short but astonishing story among the people, adding, 'Thou shalt not glory in the fall of thine enemy; thine heart shall not rejoice in his adversity.' It was the first time the entire throng—twelve thousand and several hundred people, including the three thousand who were fit to bear arms—had been addressed as 'thou', an element of speech that embraced them in their entirety while at the same time paying attention to each as an individual, whether man or woman, young or old, as if every single person were being prodded in the chest by a finger. 'Thou shalt not shout with joy over the perdition of thine enemy.' This was completely unnatural. Apparently, however, this unnaturalness was connected with the invisibility of Moses' God, who wanted to be *our* god. It began to dawn on the more alert members of the brown rabble what it meant—and how uncanny and challenging it was—to have sworn allegiance to an invisible god.

They were now in the land of Sinai, in fact in the Shur desert, a disagreeable terrain they could only leave by entering an equally deplorable one, the wilderness of Paran. Why these deserts had different names was unfathomable; they abutted each other in a single, godforsaken stretch of stony barrenness and desolate hills that went on for three days with neither water nor vegetation, then went on for a fourth day, then a fifth. Moses had been well advised to rapidly make use of the esteem that had accrued to him at the Sea of Reeds to inculcate the supernatural dimension; for it wasn't long before he had again become 'that man Moses who led us out of Egypt', meaning 'led us to our ruin', and a loud grumbling pained his ears. After three days there was little left of the water they had brought with them. Thousands suffered from thirst, the relentless sun beating down on their heads and the sheer desolation of the Shur desert—or maybe it was already the wilderness of Paran—under their feet. 'What are we supposed to drink?' they cried aloud, without regard for the suffering of their leader under his burden of responsibilities. He wished he could be the only one to go without water—he'd have nothing to drink if only they could have something and he didn't have to hear them say, 'Why did you make us go out from Egypt?' Suffering alone is easily borne compared to the torment of having to provide for a horde like this one, and Moses was a very troubled man, and remained so all his life—more troubled than any man on earth.

Very soon there was nothing left to eat either, for how long could they expect their hurriedly packed flatbread to last? 'What shall we eat?' Now this cry went up too, weeping and scolding, and Moses spent several difficult hours in communication with God, reproaching Him for being so harsh towards His servant by laying the burden of this entire people upon his shoulders. 'Have I conceived this people? Have I begotten them', he asked, 'so that You may say to me, "Carry them in your bosom!" Where am I supposed to find food for them all? They come to me weeping, crying, "Give us flesh, that we may eat!" I cannot bear this whole people alone, for it is too heavy for me. And if You are going to deal thus with me, then strangle me instead, that I need not see my wretchedness and theirs.'

Yahweh didn't leave him in the lurch—not entirely. On the fifth day, crossing a plateau, they discovered a spring by some trees, which, incidentally, was marked as 'Mara Spring' on the map Joshua carried around in his head. It is true that the water tasted disgusting; something unpalatable had contaminated it, provoking bitter disappointment and a grumbling that never stopped. But Moses, made inventive by necessity, applied a kind of filter device that held back the vile impurities, if not completely, then at least to an acceptable degree, so that now the spring had become the scene of a miracle, transforming complaints into cheers of adulation and restoring his reputation considerably. The phrase 'who led us out of Egypt' immediately resumed its more rosy hue.

And as for feeding them, yet another miracle occurred, eliciting—at first—joyful astonishment. For it turned out that large areas of the wilderness of Paran were covered with an edible lichen, the manna-lichen, a sugary felt-like substance that was small and round, like coriander seed and bdellium, and extremely perishable, too, so that it started to smell foul if not consumed at once, but otherwise, ground or crushed and baked as ash-cake, it made quite passable contingency fare, and some found it tasted almost like rolls with honey, others like oilcake.

This was the initial, favourable verdict, but it didn't last long. Soon, after just a few days, people were fed up, tired of filling their bellies with manna; it was their only food and they quickly found it repellent and sickening. They complained, 'We remember the fish which we ate in Egypt for free, the marrows and sugar melons, leeks, onions and garlic. But now our souls are dried away, for our eyes see nothing but manna.'

It pained Moses to hear this, accompanied, as always, by, 'Why did you make us go out from Egypt?' What he asked God was, 'What shall I do with these people? They won't eat manna any more. Just see, it won't be long before they stone me.'

XI

HOWEVER, he was really quite well protected from such a fate by his youthful disciple Jehoshua, whose armed troop, put together in Goshen, formed a ring round the deliverer as soon as any threatening grumbling arose in the multitude. It was a small troop, and for the time being consisted of young men, with Caleb as their lieutenant, but Joshua was waiting for the first opportunity to prove himself as the commander and spearhead of all who were fit to fight, three thousand men under his orders. He knew such an occasion would soon present itself.

Moses owed a great deal to the young man to whom he had given God's name; without him he would often have been lost. Moses was a spiritual man, and his manliness, strong and sturdy as it was, with his wrists as thick as a stonemason's, was spiritual and inward-looking, a manliness both thwarted and fuelled by God's fierce flame, estranged from quotidian things, solely concerned with the holy. With a kind of blithe simplicity that stood in peculiar contrast to the periods of solemn reflectiveness when he covered his mouth and beard with his hand, all his thoughts and effort were concentrated on setting his father's kin apart so that he might have them for himself and, out of this indeterminate mass that he loved, carve without hindrance a holy image of God. He had given little or no thought to the dangers freedom might pose, to the difficulties of the desert, or to how such a multitude were to be guided through it safely, nor even to where he wanted to take them, and he was in no way prepared to assume leadership in practical matters. For that reason he was rightly grateful to have Joshua at his side, who, for his part, revered Moses' virile spirituality, and who was thoroughly committed to placing his own upstanding and extroverted youthful virility at Moses' disposal.

It was thanks to Joshua that they were able to make purposeful progress in the wilderness at all, and that they did not wander about aimlessly. He plotted their direction of travel according to the stars, calculating the distance they needed to march each day, making sure they were able to reach watering places at tolerable—if sometimes only just tolerable—intervals. It was he, too, who had discovered that the roundish lichen on the ground was edible. In other words, he looked after the Master's reputation as a leader and ensured that when people started using the phrase 'who led us out of Egypt', it took on its laudatory sense again. Their destination was clear in his head, and with Moses' approval, he let the stars guide him towards it by the most expeditious route. For they both agreed that it was necessary to fix a primary destination, a sound if preliminary abode, lodgings where life would be liveable and they could gain time, indeed a considerable amount of time, partly (in Joshua's view) so that the people could multiply and supply him in his growing maturity with a greater number of men fit to fight, and partly (in Moses' view) so that he could finally mould the unruly mass in the image of God, carving something holy and decent out of it, a work that was pure and dedicated to the Invisible One, for this was what his spirit and wrists yearned for.

Their destination now was the oasis of Kadesh.* Just as the desert of Shur abutted the wilderness of Paran, so Paran abutted the wilderness of Sin in the south—albeit not everywhere and not directly. For somewhere between them lay the oasis of Kadesh, a comparatively luscious plain and green source of relief in an otherwise arid land, with three powerful springs and a number of smaller ones, measuring a day's march in length and half a day's march in breadth, covered with fresh pasture and earth fit for cultivation, in other words an inviting swathe of land, rich in wildlife and fruit, and large enough to accommodate and sustain a company such as theirs.

Jehoshua knew of this small and alluring stretch of land; it was marked quite clearly on the map he carried in his head. Moses knew of it too, but the fact that Kadesh was their destination and that they were heading there now was Joshua's doing. Here was the opportunity he'd been waiting for. It goes without saying, however, that a pearl like Kadesh could not be without its owner. It was in firm hands—not too firm, Joshua hoped. If they wanted it, they would have to fight with whoever owned it, and that was Amalek.

A branch of the Amalek tribe held Kadesh and was bound to defend it. Joshua made it quite clear to Moses that it would come to war, a battle between Yahweh and Amalek was inevitable, even if it meant eternal enmity between them, from one generation to the next. They must take possession of the oasis; it was a province predestined for growth and sanctification.

Moses was doubtful. For him, one of the implications of the invisibility of God was that one should not covet one's neighbour's house, and he confronted his disciple over it. But Joshua answered that Kadesh was not Amalek's house. He knew not only about places, but also about times past, and he knew that Kadesh was once—he couldn't say exactly when—inhabited by Hebrew people, close relatives, descendants of the fathers, and that these had been scattered by the Amalekites. Kadesh was stolen from them, and what has been stolen can be stolen back.

Moses had his doubts about that but had his own reasons for thinking Kadesh was strictly speaking Yahweh's land, and that anyone who had pledged himself to Yahweh therefore had a right to it. For it was not only from its natural charm that Kadesh derived its name, which meant 'sanctuary'. In a certain sense it was a holy place of the Midianite Yahweh, whom Moses had recognized as the God of the fathers. Not far away, towards the East and Edom, was Mount Horeb, one of a line of peaks, a mountain that Moses had visited from Midian and on whose slopes God had revealed Himself to him from a burning bush. Horeb, the mountain, was Yahweh's seat—or at least one of them. His original seat, as Moses knew, was Mount Sinai, in the range that lay towards the deep noon. But there was a close link between Sinai and Horeb, the site of Moses' instruction, in that both were Yahweh's seats; they were, in a sense, equals, and you could say that Horeb was Sinai, and that Kadesh was called what it was called because, to put it somewhat loosely, it lay at the foot of the holy mountain.

And so Moses accepted Joshua's proposal and asked him to make preparations for Yahweh's battle with Amalek.

XII

THE battle took place, a historical fact. It was a very hard battle, surging back and forth, but Israel emerged victorious. Beforehand, Moses had conferred upon his people the name 'Israel', meaning 'God wages war', in order to strengthen their resolve, explaining that it was a very old name that had fallen into oblivion; their forefather Jacob had been honoured with it in his time, and had passed it on to his kin. The people benefited from this; the tribes had been loosely connected, but now they were all called 'Israel' and could fight under this iron-clad name united, assembled in ranks and led in the field by Joshua, their youthful commander, and Caleb, his lieutenant.

The Amalekites had no illusions as to the motives of the approaching mass of nomads; approaches of this kind could only mean *one* thing. Without waiting for an attack on the oasis, their clamouring regiments, greater in number than Israel and better equipped, sallied forth into the desert amid high clouds of dust, battle-cries and hurly-burly; thus the struggle commenced, whereby Joshua's men had the added disadvantage of being tortured by thirst and having for many days eaten nothing but manna. That said, they had Joshua directing their movements, the young man whose gaze never strayed from his goal, and Moses, the man of God.

At the beginning of the fray, Moses had withdrawn to a hill overlooking the battlefield, together with his half-brother Aaron and Miriam, the prophetess. His kind of manliness was not suited to warfare. Rather, it was his business as a priest—and everyone agreed without hesitation that this should be his sole duty—to harangue

God with arms raised and inflammatory language, such as, 'Rise up, O Yahweh of the myriads, of the thousands of Israel, let Thine enemies be scattered and those who hate Thee flee before thy face!'

They did not flee, nor were they scattered, or only did so temporarily here and there, for while it is true that Israel was enraged with thirst and sick of eating manna, the myriads of Amalek were nevertheless greater in number, and their brief periods of demoralization were always followed by advances, some of which came dangerously close to the observation point on the hill. It transpired, however, that as long as Moses held his arms up in prayer, Israel prevailed, but if he let his arms sink, Amalek gained the advantage. For that reason, and because Moses did not have the strength to hold up his arms incessantly, Aaron and Miriam propped him up at the armpits, and took hold of his arms, too, to keep them raised. What that entailed may be gauged if you consider that the battle raged from morning until evening, in all of which time Moses had to maintain his painful position. Thus we see how hard it is for the spiritual type of manliness up there on its hill of prayer—a good deal harder than for the manliness destined to engage in the cut and thrust of the turmoil below.

Nor was it possible to carry on doing this all day long; occasionally, his supporters had to lower their master's arms for a moment or two, but the immediate effect of this was always its cost in blood and affliction to Yahweh's militant champions. So Moses' supporters hoisted his arms anew, and their comrades below drew renewed courage from the sight. They also benefited from their commander Jehoshua's tactical prowess in bringing the battle to a favourable conclusion. A youthful and instinctive strategist with his own ideas and objectives, he invented manoeuvres that were wholly new and untried at the time, at least in the desert; he was also a commander whose nerves were strong enough to stand by and watch a temporary surrender of terrain. He assembled a selection of his best fighters, his angels of death, on the enemy's right flank, harried it determinedly and forced the enemy back, achieving a victory there, although in the meantime Amalek's main force had enjoyed a clear advantage over Israel's ranks and was able to take ground from them by means of a fierce forward charge. His breakthrough on the flank, however, had put Jehoshua in a position to cut through behind Amalek's rear, forcing the latter's soldiers to turn round to fight him, while also having to continue their struggle against the initially battered, now resurgent and advancing main force of Israel's soldiery, to the effect that the Amalekites panicked and finally despaired. 'Treachery!' shouted Amalek. 'All is lost! Have no hope in victory! Yahweh has overcome us, a god of fathomless perfidy!' And with this despondent cry, Amalek's sword slipped from his grasp and he was cut down.

Only a few of his people managed to flee to the north, where they were united with the main part of their tribe. Meanwhile, Israel occupied the oasis of Kadesh, which turned out to be traversed by a wide rushing stream, planted with cultivated shrubs and fruit trees and full of bees, songbirds, quails and hares. The Amalek children, left behind in their tent villages, swelled the numbers of Israel's own progeny. The Amalek women became Israel's wives and maidservants.

XIII

MOSES, although his arms continued to ache for some time, was a happy man. In due course we shall see that he also remained a most troubled man, more troubled than any man on earth. To begin with, however, he was very pleased with such a favourable turn of events. The exodus had been a success, Pharaoh's avenging host had sunk in the Sea of Reeds, the journey through the desert had passed off well, and the battle at Kadesh had been won with Yahweh's help. He could now stand proudly before his father's kin, bathing in the esteem that comes from success, as 'the man Moses who led us out of Egypt', and that was just what he needed to begin the work he yearned to do, his work of purifying and moulding in the name of the Invisible One, of gouging, rending and shaping in flesh and blood. He was glad to have this flesh to himself, set apart and out in the open of the oasis called 'Sanctuary'. This was his workshop.

He showed them the mountain that stood among others to the east of Kadesh beyond the desert; it was Horeb, also known as Sinai, whose lower two-thirds were covered with bushes and whose summit was bare, the abode of Yahweh. And this seemed plausible enough, for it was a peculiar mountain, distinguished from its neighbours by a cloud that never moved but lay atop the summit like a roof; the cloud appeared grey during the daytime, but at night it glowed. It was there, the people were told, on the bushy slope of the mountain below the rocky summit, that Yahweh had spoken to Moses out of the midst of a burning thorn-bush and tasked him with leading them out of Egypt. They listened to him with fear and trembling, for they were not yet ready to feel awe and reverence. In fact all of them, even the bearded men, had a habit of trembling at the knees in a particularly faint-hearted manner when Moses pointed out the mountain and showed them the everlasting cloud, intimating to them that what they saw was the dwelling-place of God, that same God who delighted in them and wanted to be their only God, and so Moses, shaking his fists, berated them for their unworthy behaviour and decided thereupon that it would be his concern to make them feel more trust in Yahweh, more at home with Him, and to that end he would erect a shrine to Him right in their midst, in Kadesh itself.

For Yahweh had a mobile presence—and this was connected, as was much else, with his invisibility. His seat was on Sinai, His seat was on Horeb, and barely had His people settled themselves in the tent villages of the Amalekites in Kadesh than Moses made a home for Him there too, a tent near his own that he called the meeting or congregation tent, and also the tabernacle,* and in which he kept holy objects that were of use in worshipping the Imageless One. These were mainly items Moses took from his memories of the cult of the Midianite Yahweh; of special importance was a kind of coffer with staves to bear it, on which, according to Moses—and he should know, after all—the invisible godhead was enthroned, and which they could carry out before them into the battlefield, if Amalek, for example, should show up again bent on taking revenge. He also kept a brass rod with a serpent's head next to the ark, known as the 'Brazen Serpent', to commemorate Aaron's attempted trick before Pharaoh, but with the added reference to the rod Moses had held out to divide the waters of the Sea of Reeds. But Yahweh's tent importantly also harboured the so-called ephod* tunic with its pocket from which the oracular 'Urim and Thummim'* lots were shaken to determine a yes or no, a right or wrong, a good or evil, whenever, during difficult disputes that were insoluble to human judges, it became essential to seek Yahweh's arbitration directly.

Usually, in the various legal disputes and other controversial matters that arose among the people, it was Moses himself who presided as judge in Yahweh's stead. In fact, the first thing he did in Kadesh was to establish a tribunal where, on certain days, he would resolve disputes and administer justice; the place where he did this was the site of the strongest spring, a place that had always been called 'Me

Meribah', that is 'strife-water', and it was here he adjudicated, letting holy justice flow just as water flowed from the earth. However, if one considers that a total of twelve thousand five hundred souls were subject to his jurisdiction, then one may appreciate just how troubled a man he was. The fact that justice was a new phenomenon to the forlorn and forsaken of the tribal kin, who had no knowledge of anything like it, meant that more and more of them came to see him to appeal for their rights at the site-by-the-spring, where the first thing they learned was that justice is directly related to, and protected by, the invisibility and holiness of God, and secondly, that it encompassed not only right but also wrong, which the uneducated people took a long time to grasp. For they thought that wherever justice was forthcoming, everyone must be in the right, and to begin with they refused to believe that receiving justice could also mean being judged in the wrong and having to shuffle away with a long face. If that happened, the recipient might well regret not having settled the matter with his adversary according to the old method of the stone in the fist, which might have led to a different outcome, and only with great effort would he learn from Moses that such behaviour was an offence against God's invisibility, and that nobody who had been judged wrong in the face of right should shuffle off with a long face, for justice was both beautiful and dignified in its holy invisibility, whether it judged you right or wrong.

And so not only did Moses have to administer justice, he had to teach Law as well, and so he was greatly troubled indeed. He had studied Law himself at boarding school in Thebes, including the Egyptian law scrolls and the Codex of Hammurabi,* a king who had lived by the Euphrates. That helped him find verdicts in many of the cases he had to deal with; for instance, if an ox gored a man or woman to death, then the ox was to be stoned and its flesh was not to be eaten, but the owner of the ox was innocent, unless the ox had been wont to butt in times past and its owner knew of this but did not keep it properly enclosed, then the owner too must be put to death, unless he could redeem his life with thirty shekels of silver. Or if someone dug a pit and failed to cover it over properly, and an ox or ass fell into it, then the owner of the pit should make good the damage by giving money to the owner of the animal, but the dead beast became the pit owner's property. And then there were all the other cases that came before him: bodily assault, maltreatment of slaves, theft and burglary, damage to land and crops, arson and breach of trust. In all these and a hundred other cases Moses delivered judgement based on Hammurabi and determined what was right and wrong. But there were too many cases for one judge, flooding the site-by-the-spring; if the Master examined a single case in any appropriate detail, he would fall behind schedule and have to postpone others, and new cases never ceased to accumulate—in a word, he was the most troubled of men.

XIV

FOR that reason it was most fortunate that his brother-in-law from Midian, Jethro, paid him a visit in Kadesh and gave him a piece of good advice that Moses' conscientious nature would have prevented him from discovering by himself. Soon after his arrival at the oasis, Moses had sent to Midian and requested that his brother-in-law return his wife Zipporah and their two sons, whom he had asked Jethro to shelter in his tent during the Egyptian tribulations. However, Jethro was kind enough to come himself and to return his wife and sons to him personally, and to embrace Moses and look around, and to hear from him how everything had gone.

Jethro was a portly sheikh with a cheerful disposition and suave, even-tempered gestures, a man of the world, the prince of a civilized and socially adept people. Welcomed with great ceremony, he was invited to stay in Moses' tent and heard, not without astonishment, that one of his own gods—surprisingly the imageless one—had proved so exceptionally successful with Moses and his kin, and also how Moses had managed to rescue his people from the hands of the Egyptians.

'Who would have thought it!' he exclaimed. 'He is evidently greater than we assumed, and what you tell me makes me fear we have not accorded Him the attention He deserves. I shall make a point of seeing that our people show Him greater reverence.'

Public burnt offerings had been scheduled for the following day, something that Moses rarely arranged. He was not particularly taken with offerings; they were not essential to the Invisible One, he said, and other peoples practised them too, all over the world. Yahweh had said, 'Obey my voice above all, that is: the voice of my servant Moses, for then I will be your God, and ye my people.' But on this occasion there would be freshly slaughtered meat and burnt offerings to please

Yahweh's nose, and also to celebrate Jethro's arrival. And on the day after that, early in the morning, Moses took his brother-in-law along to the 'strife-water' so that he could attend a court session and watch how Moses sat in judgement over his people; they surrounded Moses from morning till evening, and there was no end to it.

'Now let me have a word with you, dear brother-in-law,' said the guest, as he and Moses left the tribunal. 'What in the world are you giving yourself so much trouble for! Sitting there all alone, and the people standing around you from morning till evening! Why are you doing that?'

'Because I have to,' answered Moses. 'The people come unto me and want me to judge between one and another and show them the statutes of God and His laws.'

'But my dear man, how can you be so inept!' replied Jethro. 'Is that how to govern, and is it right for a ruler to work himself to the bone doing everything himself? You're tiring yourself out and it's pitiful to watch; you can barely see straight, and you've lost your voice doing all that judging. And the people are no less tired. It isn't the right way to go about things—you can't settle all their affairs by yourself indefinitely. And nor is it necessary—now, just hear what I have to say! If you keep representing your people before God while making sure He gets to hear about all the really important things that affect everyone—that is quite enough! Take a look at this rabble of yours,' he said, gesturing towards them, entirely at his ease, 'and see if you can find some tolerably respectable, honest types among them, whom you can place over the others, to be rulers of thousands, rulers of hundreds, rulers of fifties and rulers of tens, to judge the people according to the statutes and laws you have provided. And let them come to you only when there is some great matter, but otherwise let them deal with the lesser matters themselves—you needn't even know about them. I wouldn't have my tum-tum and wouldn't have been free to visit you if I'd thought I needed to know everything and had to run around everywhere like you do.'

'But the judges will accept gifts,' answered Moses gloomily, 'and judge in favour of the godless ones. For gifts make the seeing blind, and pervert the course of justice.'

'I'm aware of that,' Jethro replied. 'Quite aware in fact. But to an extent you have to let that happen; wherever judgements are pronounced and order prevails, you tend to get gifts making things a bit more complicated, but it isn't really such a great problem. Look, the people who accept gifts are just ordinary folk, but then the people themselves are ordinary folk anyway, so ordinary things make sense to them and they'll be quite at home with that ordinariness in their community. What's more, if the course of someone's justice has been perverted by one of the judges who rule over ten, because the presiding judge has taken a gift from the godless, then let that someone follow legal process and take action pursuing the court of first instance by appealing to the judge who rules over fifty, then the one over a hundred and finally the one over a thousand—he is the judge who gets the most gifts and consequently has a clearer view of the situation, so our person is bound to get justice from him, if he hasn't got bored by then, that is.'

Thus spoke Jethro with suave gestures that made life easier for anyone who saw them, showing that he was the priest-king of a civilized desert people. Moses listened to him dolefully and nodded. He had the compliant soul of the lonely, spiritual man who nods pensively at worldly cleverness and accepts that it is likely right. Moreover, he actually did follow the advice of his dapper brother-in-law—it was unavoidable. He appointed lay judges who, in accordance with his teachings, kept jurisdiction flowing at the large spring as well as at the smaller ones, judging all the more commonplace cases (such as when a donkey fell into a pit), so that only the capital cases came to Moses, although the really significant ones were decided by the sacred lots.

Thus he was no longer excessively involved in run-of-the-mill affairs, but had his hands free for the work he intended to complete of shaping the formless body of the people, work for which Joshua, his youthful strategist, had successfully fought, providing him with an appropriate workshop: the oasis of Kadesh. Justice was undoubtedly an important example of the implications of God's invisibility, but it was only one example, and it would require wrath and patience to master the vast and lengthy task of reconstructing these unruly hordes not only as a people much like any other that feels at home with ordinariness, but as an extraordinary one, a people apart, a pure entity, raised to serve the Invisible One and consecrated to Him.

XV

THE tribes soon noticed what it meant to fall into the hands of a workman like Moses, who was both wrathful and patient and accountable to the Invisible One, and they realized that his unnatural demand that they refrain from all cries of joy following the drowning of their enemies had been only a beginning—the harbinger of something that lay far ahead of them in a realm of purity and holiness. It was a beginning that would require the fulfilment of certain prerequisites before the people could understand Moses' demands as anything but unnatural. What the uncouth multitude was really like, the extent to which it was naught but a raw material of flesh and blood, lacking even the basic notions of purity or holiness, and the extent to which Moses would have to begin at the beginning and teach them the very first steps—all this can be deduced from the elementary nature of the regulations he instated to accompany his early work on them, chivvying and chiselling and chipping away, which was not much to their liking, for the block of stone stands not on the mason's side but against him, and the first strike taken to give it a shape seems the least natural of all to the block.

With his wide-set eyes and flattened nose, Moses was always among them, sometimes here, sometimes there, sometimes in this encampment then in another, shaking his fists at the ends of his thick wrists, niggling, berating, carping, straightening out their lives, chiding, rectifying and purging, taking as his touchstone God's invisibility, Yahweh's, the same Yahweh who led them out of Egypt to have them as His own people, and who wanted them to be holy, like Himself. For the time being they were nothing but an uncouth horde, shown by the fact that they emptied their bowels in their encampments, just where they happened to be at the time. That was a disgrace and a pestilence. You should have a place outwith the camp whither you can go if you have to, do you hear what I'm saying? And you should have a little shovel to dig with before you squat, and when you have finished, you should cover it again, for the Lord, thy God, walketh in the midst of thy camp, therefore shall thy camp be holy, in other words clean, so that He doesn't need to hold his nose and turn away from you. For godliness begins with cleanliness, and purity in its coarsest form is the coarse beginning of all purity. Did you understand that, Ahiman, and you, Naemi? Next time I want to see each of you people out there with a shovel, or I'm telling you, the Destroyer shall smite thee!

You should be clean* and bathe yourself often in running water for the sake of your health, for without it there is no purity or holiness, and sickness is impure. But if you think coarse behaviour is healthier than clean customs, then you are a fool and shall be afflicted with jaundice, fig warts or Egyptian boils. If you do not practise cleanliness, then the horrible black pox will flare up in you and seeds of pestilence will go from blood to blood. Learn to tell purity from impurity, lest you be found wanting before the Invisible One, for then you are riff-raff. Therefore if a man or woman has a fretting leprosy and an evil issue from the flesh, or scabs or scabies, they shall be declared unclean and not tolerated in the camp, but shall be taken outside before the camp and set apart in uncleanliness, just as the Lord has set you apart so that you may become pure. And whatever such a person has touched, whatever lain upon, and the saddle ridden upon, all these shall be burnt. But if a person has become clean again in apartness, then shall he count seven days to be sure that he is really pure, and should wash thoroughly with water, then he may return.

Distinguish, I tell you, and be holy before God, otherwise you cannot be holy as I want you to be. Your food is a mixture of everything, a mess without discrimination or holiness; it is an abhorrence to me to watch you eat. But there are things you should eat and things you should leave aside, and you shall have pride in the one and disgust at the other. Whatever is cloven-footed and cheweth the cud, you may eat. But whatever cheweth the cud but divides not the hoof, like the camel, he is unclean unto you, and ye shall not eat of his flesh. But take note! The dependable camel is not unclean as a living creature in the face of God, but it is only unsuitable to eat, just as unsuitable as the swine, which you also should not eat, for although it divides the hoof, yet it cheweth not the cud. And therefore distinguish! Whatever has fins and scales in the waters, them shall you eat, but whatsoever slithers without fins, such as the race of newts and salamanders, these are also from God, but you should avoid them as a food. Among the birds, you should spurn the eagle, the goshawk, the osprey, the vulture after his kind. Also ravens after their kind, the ostrich, the night owl, the cuckoo, the tawny owl, the swan, the eagle owl, the bat, the bittern, the stork, the heron and jay and also the swallow. I forgot to mention the hoopoe, you should avoid them too. Who would want to eat a weasel, a mouse, a toad or a hedgehog? Who is such a brute they'd eat a lizard, a mole or a slow-worm, or anything that creeps upon the earth or that goeth upon the belly? Do it and you'll make of your soul an abomination! The next time I see someone eating a slow-worm, I'll make sure they'll never want to eat one again! It's true nobody dies of them, it isn't harmful, but it's shameful, and thou shalt find many things shameful! For that reason, you should not eat of the carcass, for that's harmful, too.

In this way he gave them statutes for eating, and restrictions in matters of food, but not only in these. He did so in matters of love and lust, too, for in this area there was much coarse carrying-on. Thou shalt not commit adultery, he told them, for marriage is a sacred boundary. But do you even know what it means not to commit adultery? It doesn't just mean thou shalt not covet thy neighbour's wife, because that's the least of it; it means a hundred other restraints too, out of deference to God's holiness. For though you live in the flesh, you are pledged to the Invisible One, and marriage is the quintessence of purity of the flesh in the sight of God. Therefore you shall not take a wife and her mother as well, to give only one example, for that is not seemly. And you should never, ever lie with your sister and witness her shame and she yours, for that is incest. You shouldn't even lie with your aunt, for that is worthy neither of you nor her, and you should shrink from it. If a woman have her sickness, you shall shun her and not approach the fountain of her blood. But if something shameful happen to a man in sleep, he shall be unclean until the next evening and painstakingly wash all his body in water.

Do I hear that you prostitute your daughter and take her whore's wages? Stop that, because if you persist I shall have you stoned. What do you think you are doing lying with a boy as you lie with a woman? That is an absurdity and in it the nations are defiled, and you shall both be put to death. But if a person, whether man or woman, does it with a beast, they shall be exterminated and strangled to death, together with the beast.

Imagine their dismay at all these restrictions! At first it felt like there would be practically nothing left of life as they had known it if they followed all these rules. He was chipping away at them with his chisel and there were chips flying everywhere. The punishments to be meted out on the worst transgressions were no laughing matter, and behind his prohibitions stood young Joshua and his destroying angels.

'I am the Lord thy God,' he proclaimed, taking the risk that they might believe he himself really was God, 'which brought thee out of the land of Egypt and have severed you from other people. Ye shall therefore put difference between clean and unclean and not go a-whoring after other peoples, but be holy unto me. For I, the Lord, am holy and have severed you from other people, that ye should be mine. The most unclean thing of all is to give your attention to some other god but me, for my name is Jealous. The most unclean thing is to make a graven image, whether it be like a man or woman, an ox or sparrowhawk, a fish or worm, for to do so is to turn from me, even if it intends to portray me, and whoever does so might just as easily lie with his sister or with a beast; there is not much space between them. Take heed! I am among you and I see everything. If one of you goes a-whoring after the Egyptian beast gods and gods of the dead, I shall wreak vengeance upon him. I shall hunt him in the desert and cast him out like scum. The same shall be for him who sacrifices to Moloch*—whom, as I well know, you retain in memory—by burning away his strength, for he is an abomination and I shall deal with him harshly. For that reason you should not make your son or your daughter pass through the fire according to the ways of stupid peoples, nor should you go by the flight or the cries of birds, nor murmur in secret with diviners, observers of times and enchanters, nor with necromancers, nor shall you use my name to practise magic. If there is any scoundrel who swears by my name falsely, it shall be exceedingly futile for him, and I shall devour him. And it is even magic and an abomination to the people to prick marks in the flesh, make the head bald above the eyes, or cut the face in mourning—I shall not tolerate it.'

How great was their dismay! Now they were not even allowed to cut their faces in mourning, or do a little tattooing. It became clear to them what having an Invisible God was all about. It meant grave restrictions if you were in covenant with Yahweh; but since the destroying angels stood behind Moses' prohibitions and they had no inclination to be driven out into the desert, the actions he had forbidden began to seem quite dreadful to them, albeit at first only in connection with the punishment, but soon it was the punishable action itself that carried the stamp of dreadfulness, so that in committing it one felt dreadful even without thinking of the punishment.

'Keep a tight rein on your heart,' he told them, 'and do not cast a covetous eye on another's possessions, for that could easily lead to your taking them from him, whether by sneaking thievery, which is an act of cowardice, or by killing him, which is an act of barbarism. Yahweh and I want you to be neither cowardly nor brutal; you should be halfway between the two, in other words: decent. Is any of this making sense to you? Theft is a creeping misery, but murder is a blazing atrocity, whether out of rage or greed, or greedy rage, or raging greed, and whosoever commits it, I shall set my face against him and he will not know where to hide. For he has shed blood, and blood commands dread for what is holy and a great secret, an offering at my altar and an atonement. You shall not eat blood, nor meat that is in blood, for the blood is mine. But if someone is daubed with human blood, his heart shall grow sick with cold terror, and I shall chase him so that he runs from himself to the ends of the earth. Say Amen to this!'

And they said Amen, holding on to the hope that murder only meant killing, which few of them felt inclined to do, or if so, then only occasionally. But it turned out that Yahweh gave the word just as wide a meaning as adultery, and that it applied to all manner of things, meaning that murder and manslaughter began with relatively mild transgressions, and blood was spilt through any kind of injury to any other person by means of deceit or fraud, transgressions almost all of them were drawn to. They were not to deal fraudulently with one another, not to testify against someone untruthfully, they were to have just measures and just weights, a just pound and a just bushel. It was all highly unnatural, and at first it was only their natural fear of punishment that lent a semblance of naturalness to these commands and prohibitions.

That they should honour their fathers and mothers, as Moses had demanded of them, also had wider implications than at first it seemed. Anyone who raised their hand against or cursed their begetter would be—well, yes—done away with. But such obeisance was meant to extend also to those who only *might* have been your father. Thou shalt rise before a hoary head, cross your arms and bow your own silly head, do you understand me? This is deemed seemly before God.—The sole consolation was that now that your neighbour wasn't allowed to kill you, there was a chance that you too might become old and grey, so that the others would have to stand up for you.

Eventually, however, it became apparent that old age was a metaphor for age in general, and applied to everything that was not of today or yesterday but came from far away: pious traditions, the customs of the fathers. 'These you shall hold in honour and awe. And to that end you shall hallow my holy days, the day on which I led you out of Egypt, the day of the unleavened bread, and always, the day on which I rested from all my works of creation. You shall not profane my day, the sabbath, with the sweat of your labour—I forbid it! For I have brought you forth out of the land of Egypt, out of the house of bondage, with a mighty hand and with an outstretched arm, where you were a bondman and a workhorse, and my day shall be the day of your freedom that you will keep holy. Six days shall you plough your field, or be a plough-wright or a potter or a copper-smith or a carpenter, but on my day you shall put on a clean garment and be nothing but a man or a woman, and raise your eyes to the Invisible One.

'You were an oppressed bondman in the land of the Egyptians—remember this in your conduct towards strangers under you—the children of Amalek for example, whom God delivered into your hands—and do not vex them! Look upon them as you might look upon yourselves and grant them equal rights, or I will intervene, for they stand under Yahweh's protection. What you should not do is make an ignorant and presumptuous distinction between yourself and the other, thinking you are the only true one, the one who matters, while the other is a mere shadow. You are in this life together, and it is only by chance that you are not he. Therefore do not love yourself alone, but love him in the same way, and do unto him as you would that he do unto you, if he were you! Be pleasant towards each other and kiss each other's fingertips in passing, and bow to each other with gentle manners and utter the greeting "Be hale and healthy!" For it is just as important that he is healthy as that you are. And even if it is only outward refinement that you behave in this way and kiss each other's fingertips, the gesture will leave something in your heart of the way you ought to behave towards your neighbour.—Say Amen to all this!'

And they said Amen.

XVI

THEIR Amen counted for little, however—they had repeated it solely because he was the man who by happy chance had led them out of Egypt, sunk Pharaoh's chariot and won the battle for Kadesh, but until such time as his teachings and impositions, with all their barriers, commands and prohibitions, had become sufficiently, or even seemingly, second nature to them, much time would pass, such was the daunting task he had taken upon himself to raise a holy people—a pure entity that would pass muster before the Invisible One—out of the unruly multitude. He worked at this by the sweat of his brow in Kadesh, his workshop, keeping his wide-set eyes on everything and everyone—chiselling, chipping, forming and levelling the unwilling block with stubborn patience, periodic lenience and frequent forgiveness, but also with blazing wrath and censorious implacability, often despairing when the flesh he worked upon proved wayward, forgetful and backsliding, or when people yet again failed to dig a hole with their small shovels, or ate slow-worms, or slept with their sister or their animals, when they tattooed themselves and sat with diviners, skulked about in order to steal, or killed each other. 'O you unruly tribe!' he would say to them then. 'Just wait! The Lord will suddenly come over you and destroy you.' But to God he would say, 'What shall I do with this flesh, and why do I not find favour in Your sight that You load this burden I cannot bear upon me? I'd rather muck out a stable that's seen no spade or water for seven years, or clear a jungle with my bare hands to grow fruit there than forge a pure entity for You out of this lot. Why must I bear this whole people at my bosom, as if it was me who begat it? I'm only half related to them, on my father's side. So please, just let me enjoy my life and forget the task, or You might as well strangle me instead!'

But God answered him from within his soul with a voice so clear he actually heard it with his ears and prostrated himself with his face to the ground:

'It is precisely because you, on the side of the man who was so hastily buried, are only half related to them, that you are the very man to work on them and raise them to be a holy people unto me. For if you were well and truly one of them, you wouldn't see them and couldn't act on them. And anyway, what you just said is all just affectation—complaining like that to me, wanting to be freed from the task in hand. You can see, can't you, that what you are doing to them is taking effect, and that already you have succeeded in giving them a conscience, so that they feel awful when doing something awful. So don't stand there in front of me pretending you have no appetite for your torment! It is my appetite you have, a godly appetite, and without it you would find your life disgusting, just as the people found manna disgusting after just a few days. So yes, only if I strangled you, could you go without it.'

The tormented man himself appreciated that, nodded with his face to the ground as Yahweh spoke, then rose again to his torment. But he was a tormented man not only in his capacity as a moulder of the people, but because torment and heartache also reached into his own family life; there was resentment, jealousy and bickering on his account, and no peace in his tent, and you could say it was his own fault, for his sensual appetite was the cause of the misery—aroused by his work he had become attached to an Ethiopian woman, the famous Ethiopian.

It is known that in addition to Zipporah, his first wife and mother of his sons, he was living with an Ethiopian woman at that time, a woman who had come from the land of Cush to Egypt as a child and lived among the Hebrew tribes in Goshen, where she had joined the exodus. Doubtless she had known many a man before Moses, but he nevertheless took her to his bed. She was a gorgeous female in her own way, with towering breasts, rolling eye-whites, voluptuous lips that must have made kissing a powerful experience, while her skin was balmy with spices. Moses adored her because she helped him relax, and he found it impossible to let her go despite having to bear the opposition of his entire household in the matter, not only that of his Midianite wife and his sons, but more especially the disapproval of his half-sister Miriam and Aaron. Zipporah, who had much of the suave worldliness of her brother Jethro, found she was able to come to a tolerable arrangement with her rival, in particular because the Ethiopian concealed her feminine triumph over Zipporah and was pointedly submissive in her presence; Zipporah treated her with mockery rather than with hatred, and with Moses, too, she tended to address the matter ironically rather than allowing free rein to her jealousy. Their sons, however, Gershom and Eliezer, who belonged to Joshua's armed regiment, were too disciplined to be openly indignant at their father, but it was nonetheless noticeable that they were annoyed and ashamed on his account.

Things were entirely different with Miriam, the prophetess, and with Aaron, the unctuous. Their hatred of the Ethiopian paramour was more venomous that that of the others because it acted as an outlet, so to speak, for a deeper and more general resentment that united them against Moses; for some time now they had begun to envy his intimate relationship with God, his spiritual mastery, and the fact that he personally had been chosen to execute the work, which they thought was mainly a delusion on Moses' part, for they considered themselves to be just as good, indeed better than him, and said to each other,

'Does the Lord speak only through Moses? Does He not also speak through us? Who is this man Moses who has set himself above us in this way?' This was the underlying cause of their objection to his relationship with the Ethiopian woman, and whenever they nagged their poor brother, upbraiding him for his nights of passion, it would serve as a starting point for further accusations, and soon they would accuse him of the injustice they had suffered as a result of his eminence.

One day, then, as the evening was drawing in, they were in Moses' tent tormenting him, as I have said, in the way they usually did: the Ethiopian woman here, the Ethiopian woman there, and that he couldn't get enough of her black breasts, and what a scandal it was, and what a humiliation for Zipporah, his first wife, and how compromising it was for someone who claimed to be a prince of God and Yahweh's sole spokesman on earth…

'Claimed?' he retorted. 'What God has appointed me to be, that I am. But how mean it is of you, how very mean, to deprecate my pleasure, my relaxation on the breasts of my Ethiopian. For it is no sin before God, and there is nothing against lying with an Ethiopian among all the prohibitions that He gave me. Not that I know of!'

He obviously selected prohibitions according to his taste, they replied, and no doubt he would soon be proclaiming that sleeping with Ethiopians was compulsory, for after all, he reckoned he was God's sole spokesman. They, on the other hand, Miriam and Aaron, were born of Amram and were grandchildren of Levi, true grandchildren while Moses was ultimately nothing but a foundling picked out of the flags, and so he ought to learn a little humility, because by insisting on keeping the Ethiopian woman in spite of the offence it was causing, he was simply proving what a proud and arrogant person he was.

'Can I help it if I am called?' he said. 'And is it my fault if I stumble upon a burning thorn-bush? Miriam, I have always treasured your prophetic gifts and never denied you have a talent for the timbrel—'

'Then why did you ban my hymn "Horse and Rider"?' she asked, 'and why did you forbid me to play the timbrel and lead the women in a round dance, just because God had apparently prohibited his flock from celebrating the demise of the Egyptians? That was horrid of you.'

'And you, Aaron,' continued the embattled Moses, 'I gave you the office of High Priest of the Tabernacle, and placed the ark, the ephod and the Brazen Serpent under your care. That is how much I trust you.'

'That was the least you could have done,' retorted Aaron, 'because you were so inarticulate that without my eloquence you would never have converted the people to Yahweh, nor would you have persuaded them to leave. But you call yourself the man who led us out of Egypt. If it is true that you cherish us, however, and are not smugly setting yourself above your more pure-bred siblings, then why don't you listen to our advice instead of stubbornly ignoring our warning that your black paramour is a danger to our entire tribe? It is certainly a potion as bitter as gall for Zipporah, your Midianite wife, and your behaviour is an insult to all Midian, which could even provoke your brother-in-law Jethro to declare war on us, all because of your black whim.'

'Jethro', countered Moses with great self-control, 'is a sophisticated gentleman who will understand very well that Zipporah—revered be her name!—can no longer give such a tormented and overworked man as me the relaxation he needs. The skin of my Ethiopian, however, is like cinnamon and clove oil to my nose, and all my senses yearn for her, and so I beg you, dear friends, please let me keep her!'

But they weren't having it. Yelling at him, they demanded that he not only separate from the Ethiopian and banish her from his bed but that he should also cast her out into the desert with no water.

At that the vein in Moses' forehead swelled in rage and he began to shake his fists violently by his thighs. But before he could open his mouth to answer, quite a different kind of shaking began—it was Yahweh intervening on His servant Moses' behalf, setting His face against those cold-hearted siblings so that they would never forget the experience. Something terrifying and unheard-of happened.

XVII

THE foundations quaked. The earth bucked, shivered and lurched beneath their feet so that they could barely stand up and all three of them were sent staggering about in the tent, whose support poles seemed gripped by giant shaking fists. The ground heaved, swaying not only to one side, but jerking with a wholly bewildering, vertiginous force in every direction at once. It filled them with terror, while at the same time they heard rumbling and clattering deep below them, and from above and the sides came a din as if from a very powerful drum, and other sounds, too—groaning, thundering, cracking. It is a strange feeling, and an oddly embarrassing one, when you are about to explode in anger and the Lord comes and takes the words out of your mouth and Himself explodes instead, and so much more powerfully than your own explosion would have been, shaking the whole world, when all you could have shaken were your fists.

Moses was the least terrified and the least pale, for he was always prepared for God. But he nonetheless tumbled out of the tent with the others, Aaron and Miriam, who were deathly pale, and what they saw was this: the earth had opened its maw and a large crevasse, evidently intended for Miriam and Aaron, gaped in front of the tent and had missed them only by a few cubits, or the earth would have swallowed them. They also saw the mountain in the morning beyond the desert, Horeb or Sinai—saw what was happening to Horeb, and what was going on at Sinai! There it stood, engulfed in flames and smoke, hurling burning hunks of rock into the sky accompanied by the roar of distant blasts, and streams of fire poured down its flanks. Its vapour, criss-crossed by lightning, obscured the stars above the desert, and a soft ash rain began to fall on the oasis of Kadesh.

Aaron and Miriam fell on their faces, for the crevasse intended for them terrified them, and the sign given by Yahweh on the mountain had instructed them that they had gone too far and spoken foolishly. Aaron cried out:

'O dear Master, this woman, my sister, has blethered most spitefully. Please accept my plea, do not let the sin of trespassing against the Lord's anointed one rest upon her!'

And Miriam also cried aloud to Moses:

'Master, one could not speak more foolishly than my brother Aaron has done. Please forgive him, and do not let this sin rest upon him lest God devour him for taunting you so rashly about your Ethiopian!'

Moses was not entirely sure whether Yahweh's manifestation had really been intended for his siblings and their hateful outbursts, or whether it had been a coincidence that He had summoned him at exactly that moment to come and talk to Him about the people and his work of educating them—for he had been anticipating such a sign from Yahweh from one hour to the next. But he left them believing their assumption, and answered:

'Now you see! But take heart, children of Amram, I shall put in a good word for you when I follow God's call to meet Him up on the mountain. And then you will see, and all the people shall see, whether your brother's fitness has been impaired by his black paramour or whether in fact God-given courage dwells in his heart as in no other. I shall ascend to the fiery mountain, quite alone, shall rise on high to God to hear His thoughts and commune on familiar terms and without fear with the Fearsome One, far from mankind, but in man's interest. For I have long known that He wishes to concentrate all I have taught the people to sanctify them before Him, the Holy One, into a compact form, something that will be to the point and everlasting, so that I can bring it back down to you from His mountain and it will belong to the people in the tabernacle, together with the ark, the ephod and the Brazen Serpent. Farewell! I may perish in God's turmoil and in the fires of the mountain—that could well happen, and I must be prepared for it. But if I return I shall bring you His word everlasting, the law of God.'

That really was his firm resolve; the decision to do so was for him a matter of life and death. For to bring this stiff-necked, constantly backsliding horde to accept God's moral code and fear his commandments, nothing could be more effective than for Moses, all on his own, to venture up into Yahweh's terrifying presence on the spewing mountain and to return from there with the edicts in his arms—then, he thought, they would obey the law. So when the people came running from all directions to his tent, their knees trembling, terrified by signs and omens and by the earth shaking and rupturing under their feet—which was repeated once and then twice more, albeit more weakly—Moses rebuked them for the undignified trembling of their knees and encouraged them to regain their composure: God had called upon him, he said, and it was for their sake, and now he was going to climb up to Yahweh at the top of the mountain and, God willing, bring something back for them. In the meantime, they should all go home and prepare to leave; they should sanctify themselves, wash their clothes and refrain from lying with their wives, for on the following day they would be leaving Kadesh and moving to the desert, to a place that was closer to the mountain, facing which they would pitch camp and wait for him to return from his frightful rendezvous and, perhaps, bring something back for them.

And that is what happened, or something like it. For Moses, as was his wont, had considered only that they should wash their clothes and not go near their womenfolk. Joshua ben Nun, on the other hand, the youthful strategist, put his mind to preparing everything else that would be needed for such an expedition, and he and his troop made sure that the travellers had all the right provisions, for example enough food and water for thousands of people in the desert, and they even organized a messaging service between Kadesh and the camp near the mountain. With those who did not want to leave Kadesh, or could not, he left Caleb, his lieutenant, and a detachment of police. But when the third day arrived and all preparations had been made, all the others left with their carts and cattle and headed towards the mountain, a day and a half's journey away. Here, at an appropriate distance from Yahweh's abode, Joshua constructed a compound for them, and warned them in strict terms and in Moses' name that nobody should presume to climb the mountain nor even go as far as to touch its foot, for the right to approach so close to God is reserved for the Master alone, and apart from all else it was life-threatening, and anyone who touched the mountain would be stoned or shot with an arrow. They did not find this difficult to accept, for such a base people has no desire to get close to God, and to a common man the mountain did not look in the least inviting, neither by day, when Yahweh stood upon it in a thick cloud flashing with lightning, and certainly not by night when the cloud glowed and the whole summit along with it.

Joshua was exceedingly proud of the God-given courage of his master, who, on the first day, and in front of the entire people, had set out for the mountain alone and on foot with his walking staff, equipped only with an earthen flask, one or two small loaves and several tools: pick, chisel, trowel, graver. Very proud the young man was, and very pleased too with the impression such holy audacity must have on the multitude. But he was also concerned for his revered master's well-being and had pressed him not to venture too close to Yahweh and to beware of the hot molten sludge that ran down the mountainsides. He also let him know that he would be paying him a visit now and then, just to make sure everything was in order up there, and that the Master did not lack the bare necessities in God's wilderness.

XVIII

Moses strode through the wilderness with his walking staff, his wide-set eyes fixed on God's mountain, which smoked like a furnace and intermittently spat fire. The mountain had a peculiar shape, encircled by depressions and ridges that seemed to divide it into storeys or looked like paths leading upwards, but which were in fact only natural terraces with yellow rock faces. On the third day the Chosen One crossed several foothills and, reaching the rocky foot of the mountain, began his ascent, the walking staff in his grip steadying his pace as he climbed over rough terrain and through scalded, burnt-black bushes, step by step and hour after hour, higher and higher and ever closer to God, or as far as was humanly possible, for the sulphurous vapour that filled the air and smelled of hot metals gradually made breathing difficult, and he began to cough. He nonetheless managed to reach the highest of the depressions, or terraces, a short distance below the summit, from where he had a wide view of the desolate, rugged mountain range on either side and of the desert as far as Kadesh. Closer to his observation point, he also saw the people's compound, a tiny shape far below.

Here, the coughing Moses found a mountain cave with a rocky overhang that afforded him protection against flying boulders and flowing sludge, a place to sojourn, where after settling in and catching his breath he would set about the work to which God had ordained him and which would keep him occupied under gruelling circumstances—for the metallic vapours lay heavy on his chest and even gave water a sulphurous taste—for no less than forty days and forty nights.

But why so long? A question that misses the point! The point was to fix in writing the everlasting compact, the binding compendium of the commandments, God's concise moral law, and to engrave it into the stone of His mountain for Moses to carry down to the fickle horde, to the bloodline of his hastily buried father, who were waiting in the compound below, so that it would stand inviolable among them from one generation to the next, engraved in their souls and carved into their flesh and blood, the quintessence of human decency. From Moses' heart came God's resounding command to hew two tablets from the stone of the mountain and to write on them what God would dictate, five words on the one and five words on the other, ten in all. It was no easy task to cut these tablets, to level them and turn them into tolerably dignified vehicles for the everlasting compact; for this solitary man, though he had drunk the milk of a stonemason's daughter and was blessed with thick wrists, it would be a piece of work susceptible to many obstacles and would occupy a whole quarter of the forty days. The work of inscription itself, however, was a problem whose solution might easily have increased the number of days Moses would spend on the mountain to even more than forty.

For how should he write? At his Theban boarding-school he had learned Egypt's decorative pictorial script as well as its common modifications, also the sacred jumble of wedge-shaped figures that made up the Euphrates script, by means of which the kings of the world exchanged thoughts on fragments of clay. He had also made the acquaintance among the Midianites of a third magic way of conjuring meaning through pictures of eyes, crosses, beetles, yokes and variously drawn snaking lines, a script used in Sinai and clumsily copied by the desert-dwellers from the picture script of the Egyptians, but whose characters did not denote whole words or single ideas symbolized by objects, but only parts of them, open syllables that had to be read together. None of these three methods of recording thoughts suited him, for the simple reason that each of them was tied to the spoken language that gave it meaning, and because Moses was quite certain that he could never under any circumstances inscribe in stone the ten dictated words in Babylonian, Egyptian or the jargon of Sinai Bedouins. They must be engraved in the language of his father's kin, in the dialect they spoke themselves and in which he was working on their morals—whether they could read it or not. But how were they going to read it, since it had never been written before, there being no magic script available with which to conjure its spoken meanings?

Moses ardently wished one existed, one that they would be able to read soon, very soon, indeed one that children, such as they actually were, could learn within very few days, and therefore one that might well—with God's help—also be invented within very few days. For this way of writing would need to be newly devised and thought out—because it did not exist.

What an urgent, intense task! He hadn't considered it in advance at all, had only thought 'write' without reflecting that writing might not be as uncomplicated as he imagined. His head glowed and smoked like a stove, or like Sinai's summit, fired by the ardour of his aspirations for his people. It felt as if his head were emitting rays, or as if horns* were protruding from his head, so great was the strain of his longing and so singular his inspiration. He could not find symbols for all the words his kin used, or for the syllables their words were made up of. For even if the vocabulary of the people down in the compound was limited, he would still have too many characters to invent for the days he had planned to remain on the mountain, and more importantly, for his people to be able to learn them quickly enough. And so he took a different approach, and the divine stroke of genius this entailed made the horns stick out of his forehead in pride. He made a group of those noisy speech elements of the language produced by the lips, tongue and palate and also the throat, and set these apart from the few more open sounds that lacked those elements but were enclosed by them, and which only formed words when they alternated with them. Nor were there all that many of the enclosing noise-making sounds either, in fact barely twenty, and by ascribing signs to these, and establishing by rule whether they should be breathed or hissed, mumbled or rumbled, plopped or smacked, and by leaving out the breezy, more open voice sounds that arose by themselves to accompany these noise-sounds, you could combine the signs to make words and pictures, in fact any words, any word that existed, and not only in the language of his father's kin, but in all languages—you could even use them to write Egyptian or Babylonian.

A divine stroke of genius. An idea with horns. An idea like its progenitor, the Invisible One and Spirit, to whom the world belonged and who, although he had chosen the blood-kin below as his people, was the Lord of all the earth. The idea was also fully commensurate with its most imminent and urgent purpose, for which and from which it was conceived: the text for the tables, the binding compact. It is true that this invention was initially meant for the people whom Moses had led out of Egypt, because both God and Moses delighted in them; however, just as the words of the languages of all peoples could be written, if need be, using this handful of characters, and just as Yahweh was the God of all the world, so too was the text Moses intended to write, this compendium of the law, of such a kind that it could serve as the fundamental, rocklike moral compass in matters of human decency for the peoples of the world—everywhere.

Thus Moses, his head steaming, experimented with his graving tool on the rock face, and loosely basing his work on the marks of the Sinai people, he cut signs for burbling, grumbling and murmuring sounds, fluttering and spitting, hissing and purring, and once his graven abbreviations were clearly differentiated and pleasingly assembled—lo and behold! you could write the whole world with them—everything that took up space, and everything that took up no space at all, everything that was made and everything that was made up, absolutely everything and anything.

And he wrote, that is to say, he gouged, chiselled and levelled the brittle stone of the tables, which he had hewn with so much effort, a task that had gone hand in hand with the invention of the characters. It is hardly surprising that all this took him forty days.

His young assistant Joshua came up on several occasions to bring him water and flatbread, without the people needing to know about it; they thought Moses was up there alone, living in God's presence and conversing with Him, and for strategic reasons Joshua did not want to disabuse them of that assumption, which was why his visits were short and took place at night.

Moses, meanwhile, sat and worked from the moment the daylight rose over Edom until the hour the sun sank beyond the desert. One has to imagine him sitting up there, stripped to the waist, his chest covered with hair, with powerful arms that were probably inherited from his ill-used father, with his wide-set eyes, flattened nose and parted, greying beard, chewing on a flatbread and coughing now and then from the metallic fumes of the mountain, and how he hewed the tables in the sweat of his brow, then chiselled and polished, and how finally, having propped them up against the rock face, he squatted before the tables and toiled over every detail, carefully engraving his crow's feet, those universally potent runes, on the polished surfaces, having first sketched them out with his graver.

On the first table he wrote:

I, Yahweh, am thy God; thou shalt have no other Gods before me.
Thou shalt not make unto thee any graven image.
Thou shalt not take my name in vain.
Remember my day, to keep it holy.
Honour thy father and thy mother.

And on the other table he wrote:

Thou shalt not murder.
Thou shalt not commit adultery.
Thou shalt not steal.
Thou shalt not do thy neighbour wrong by bearing false witness.
Thou shalt not cast a covetous eye upon thy neighbour's possessions.

This is what he wrote, leaving out those breezy sounds that arose as a matter of course. And all this time he felt as if rays like a pair of horns protruded from his forelocks.

When Joshua came up the mountain for the last time, he stayed a little longer, for two whole days, since Moses' work was not yet done, and they wanted to descend together. The young man sincerely admired what his master had achieved, and consoled him on account of one or two characters that, despite all the love and care he had given them, and much to Moses' chagrin, had splintered and become indecipherable. But Joshua assured him that the overall impression would not suffer as a result.

The last thing Moses did in Joshua's presence was to paint the letter incisions with his own blood to make them stand out better. There was no other pigment for the job at hand, and so he pricked his strong arm with his graver and carefully smeared his dripping blood into the letters to make a reddish gleam in the stone. When the blood was dry Moses took one table under each arm and handed his staff to his young man to carry, and thus they descended together from God's mountain and walked towards his people's compound in the desert opposite the mountain.

XIX

When they had reached a certain proximity to the camp, just within hearing distance, a muffled noise came to their ears, a squeaking too, and neither could account for it. Moses heard it first, but Joshua was the first to mention it.

'Can you hear that strange noise over there,' he asked, 'that hubbub, that din? Something's going on over there, in my opinion—a scuffle, a brawl if I'm not mistaken. It must be quite violent, and quite widespread for us to hear it from here. If it's what I think it is, then it's good we're heading there.'

'It's good we're heading there at all events,' replied Moses, 'but as far as I can distinguish, that is neither brawl nor scuffle, it's revelry, with some sort of singing and dancing. Can't you hear the hooting and clashing of the timbrels? Joshua, what has got into them? Come, let us hurry!'

With that, heaving the two tables higher under his armpits, his pace grew faster, while Jehoshua shook his head. 'Singing and dancing…

singing and dancing...' Moses repeated over and over, gloomily at first and finally terrified, for that this was no scrap with one person on top and the other underneath, but rather a collective celebration, was soon beyond doubt, and the only question left was what kind of celebration it was, with all that whooping and bawling.

But soon, even that was no longer the question, if it ever really had been one. For what awaited them was horrible, and as Moses and Joshua hurried under the cross-beam of the camp's tall wooden gate, it presented itself to them in all its shameless exposure. The people had gone wild. They had cast aside everything that Moses had imposed upon them in order to sanctify them, God's entire moral code. They were wallowing in shocking regression.

Directly behind the gate was an open space that was free of tents, the assembly area—and here they were fornicating, here they were writhing, here they were celebrating their miserable freedom. Before singing and dancing, they had eaten their fill, which was obvious at first glance, because everywhere in the assembly area were vestiges of slaughter and gluttony. Who, what, had been the beneficiary of their burnt offerings, their slaughter, their stuffed bellies? There it stood, on a stone in the very middle of this naked ignominy; on an altar pedestal it stood, a sorry piece of work, a malicious idol, a golden calf.

It wasn't a calf, it was a bull, the truly gross phallic bull of all the world's peoples. They only called it a calf because it was rather modest in size, actually quite small, and it was also poorly cast, too, and preposterously shaped, an inept disgrace, and yet it was only too recognizable as a bull. Around this lousy piece of workmanship circled numerous round dancers, about a dozen rings in all, men and women hand in hand to the chime of cymbals and beat of timbrels, their heads thrown back and eyes rolling, knees flung up to their chins, with squeals and roars and crude gestures of reverence. They circled in opposite directions, one disgraceful ring to the right, the other to the left; at the centre of this vortex, however, in front of the calf, Aaron, too, could be seen hopping about* in the long-sleeved robe he wore as custodian of the tabernacle, and which he had pulled up around his knees, the better to fling his long hairy legs about. And Miriam led the women, beating her timbrel.

This only accounts for the dance around the calf. But round about that many other things were going on. It is hard to fathom how low the people could sink. Some were eating slow-worms, others lying with their sisters, and this in public—all in honour of the calf. Others squatted and emptied their bowels without a thought for their shovels. Men were seen burning their strength over the bull. Somewhere a man slapped his mother in the face.

At the sight of all this dreadfulness, the vein in Moses' forehead swelled to bursting. His face was red with anger as he wrestled his way through the crowd, tearing the rings of the dance apart, whose perpetrators came staggering to a standstill and stared at him with embarrassed grins, recognizing their master, who had now cut straight through to the calf, the core, the source and epitome of wickedness. He then heaved one of the tables of the law above his head with his powerful arms and brought it down hard on the ludicrous beast, whose legs gave way, then repeated the action with such fury that while the table itself was smashed to bits, only a formless mass remained of the shoddy object; he then raised the second table and finished the job, crushing the atrocity utterly, and because the second table was still intact, he dashed it to pieces with a single blow against the stone pedestal. And there he stood with trembling fists, groaning from deep within his breast:

'You stiff-necked horde, you godforsaken riff-raff! There lies what I brought down for you from God and what He inscribed for you with His own finger to provide you with a talisman against the misery of ignorance! There it lies, a heap of fragments, next to the wreckage of your false god. What shall I tell the Lord to stop Him from devouring you?'

And then he saw Aaron, the jumping-jack, standing nearby with downcast eyes and his greasy locks hanging down at the back of his neck, tall and witless. Moses took hold of the front of his robe and shook him:

'Where did the golden Belial* come from, that filth, and what did the people do to you that you have brought so great a sin upon them while I was on the mountain, and there you were, gambolling about like a billy-goat yourself in front of that debauched ring-dance?'

But Aaron answered:

'Oh, let not the anger of my lord wax hot, not with me, nor with my sister; the truth is we had to give in. You know that this people is set on mischief. You were away for so long; you spent an eternity up on the mountain, so that we all thought you would never return. And they gathered against me, shouting, "Nobody knows what has become of that man Moses who led us out of Egypt. He won't come back. He has probably been swallowed by the maw from which the mountain spews. Get up, make us gods which shall go before us if Amalek comes! We are a people like any other, and we want to enjoy ourselves in front of gods that are like the gods other people have." That's what they said, Master, because, with due respect, they thought they were rid of you. But tell me, what should I have done, when they were turning against me? I ordered them to bring me all their golden earrings which were in their ears, and I burnt these in the fire and made a mould and cast the little calf so that they had their god.'

'It doesn't even look like a calf,' Moses interjected disdainfully.

'It had to be finished in a hurry,' Aaron replied, 'because they wanted to have their feast the next day, which is today, and they wanted it in honour of lustier gods, which is why I handed over what I had cast. But you can't deny the resemblance, actually, and they were happy and said, "Here be your gods, Israel, who led you out of Egypt." And so we built an altar in front of it, and they brought their burnt offerings and their thanksgiving sacrifices and ate before rising to play and dance a little.'

Moses left him standing there and made his way back through the scattered members of the round dances towards the gate, where he took up position with Jehoshua under its roughly hewn cross-beam, then roared with all his might:

'Listen to me, those who are on the Lord's side!'

And many came to him who were of sound heart and had had qualms about taking part, and Joshua's armed youth gathered around the pair.

'You ill-starred people,' Moses began, 'what have you done, and how shall I make an atonement for your sin before Yahweh that He does not cast you aside as an irredeemably stiff-necked people and consume you? Making yourself a golden Belial as soon as my back was turned! Shame on you and on me! Can you see the rubble over there—I don't mean the remains of the calf, may the pest descend on it, I mean the other fragments? That is the gift that I promised you and that I brought back down for you: the everlasting compact, the rock of decency. It consists of the ten words that I wrote for you in God's presence and in your own language, and I wrote them in my blood, in the blood of my father, in other words in your blood. But what I brought for you now lies in ruins.'

Then many who heard this wept, and there was much sobbing and sniffing in the assembly area.

'It may be possible to replace it,' said Moses. 'For the Lord is long-suffering, and of great mercy, and forgiving of iniquity and transgressions. And He also leaves nobody unpunished,' he suddenly thundered, the blood rising to his head and his vein yet again swelling and fit to burst on his forehead, 'but I shall visit their iniquity, saith He, unto the third and fourth generation, being the jealous God that I am. We shall have judgement here,' Moses cried, 'and decree a bloody cleansing, for in blood was it written. The ringleaders must be found out, those who were first to cry out for golden gods and who were insolent enough to claim that it was the calf who led you out of Egypt when it was I alone who did so—saith the Lord. They shall be handed over to the destroying angels, and there shall be no respect of persons. They shall be stoned to death and pierced with arrows, and be there three hundred* of them! The others, however, shall put off all their ornaments and shall mourn until my return—for I shall go up to God's mountain again to see if there is anything I can still do for you—you stiff-necked people!'

XX

Moses did not attend the executions he had ordered on account of the calf; that was the stalwart Jehoshua's business. He was already back up on the mountain in front of his cave below the rumbling summit, and, while the people mourned, stayed there again for forty days and forty nights by himself in the metallic fumes. But why for so long this time? The answer was not only that Yahweh had commanded him to remake the tablets and inscribe what He had dictated anew, for that could be done more quickly this time, since Moses was by now a practised hand and, more importantly, already possessed the script. It was also because he had to endure a long struggle with the Lord before He would allow the renewal, a battle in which wrath and mercy, exhaustion over the work and love of the project were pitted against one another, and in which Moses would have to deploy his powers of persuasion and bring shrewdness to his petition to prevent God from declaring the covenant broken and thereby not only severing His bond with his stiff-necked unruly people, but also smashing them to bits, just as he, Moses, had done with the tables of the law.

'I have no wish to go before them,' said God, 'to lead them into the land of their fathers, and so don't ask me to, because I cannot rely on my patience. I am a jealous God and lose my temper, and you shall see if I don't forget myself one day and devour them on the way.'

And He submitted to Moses that He would take the people, who had been as poorly cast as the golden calf and could no longer be repaired—in fact there was no point in trying to raise them into a holy people at all, and the only thing you could do with them was to smash them to bits—and He would annihilate Israel in its present form, eradicating it completely, and instead would make Moses himself into a great people, and would live in covenant with him. Which Moses, however, did not want, saying, 'No, no, forgive them their sin, and if not, blot me out of Your book which You have written, for I do not want to survive them and become a holy people myself in their stead.'

And he appealed to God's sense of honour and said, 'Imagine, O Holy One, the following: if You kill all this people as one man, then the heathens who have heard their screaming, will say, "Pah! The Lord was not able to bring this people into the land which He swore unto them, therefore He has slain them in the wilderness." Do You really want the people of the world to say that about You? Now therefore let the power of my Lord be great and pardon the iniquity of this people according unto Your mercy!'

It was with this argument in particular that he convinced God and influenced Him to forgive, albeit with one restriction, for He announced that of this generation none would see the land of their fathers, except for Joshua and Caleb. 'Your children,' proclaimed the Lord, 'them will I bring in, but those who are now over twenty, they shall not see the land, their carcasses shall fall in this wilderness.'

'It is well, Lord, and all shall be well,' answered Moses, 'let's leave it at that.' For since the ruling coincided with Joshua's and his own intentions, he had no wish to oppose it. 'Now, allow me to renew the tablets,' he said, 'so that I may deliver Your brief sayings to the people below. In the end it was just as well that I smashed the first ones in my anger. A few of the letters hadn't turned out so well anyway. I can confess to You that I was secretly thinking of that as I dashed them to pieces.'

And he sat down once again, surreptitiously kept in food and drink by Joshua, and chiselled, scraped and polished, sat and wrote, and occasionally wiped his brow with the back of his hand, graving and smoothing the inscriptions into the tablets—and they were actually better than the first lot. That done, he again smeared his blood over the letters and descended from the mountain with the laws under his arms.

And it was announced to Israel that they should end their mourning and put on their ornaments again—with the exception of the earrings, of course, for they had been squandered for an evil purpose. And all of the people came before Moses so that he could hand over to them what he had brought: Yahweh's message from the mountain, the tablets with the ten words.

'Take these, blood of my father,' he said, 'and keep them holy in God's tent, but what they tell you, that shall you keep holy in all that you do and do not do! For this is the binding compendium of the law, the lapidary compact, the rock of decency, and God wrote it in stone with my stylus and in few words, and it is the be-all and end-all of human conduct. He wrote it in your language, but using symbols in which, if need be, any language in the world can be written, for He is the Lord everywhere, and therefore the ABC is His, and His word, even if addressed to you, O Israel, is at the same time addressed to all.

'I engraved the ABC of human conduct into the stone of the mountain, but it shall also be carved into your flesh and blood, Israel, so that anyone who breaks one word of these ten commandments shall inwardly be frightened of himself and of God, and his heart shall grow cold because he has stepped outside the boundaries set by God. I know very well, and God knows it before all do, that His commandments will be broken, and that His words will be disobeyed always and everywhere. But whosoever breaks one of them will at least feel his heart grow cold, for they are also written in his flesh and blood, and he knows very well that these words are binding.

'But cursed be the man who stands up and says, "They are no longer binding." Cursed be he who instructs you, "Rise up, and be rid of them! Lie, murder and steal, whore, defile and deliver thy father and thy mother to the sword, for that is seemly for man, and you shall praise my name because I proclaimed freedom to you." Cursed be one who constructs a calf and says, "That is your god. Do this and that in his honour, and dance around this devil's work in wanton cavorting rings!" Such a person may be very strong and shall sit on a golden throne and be regarded as the wisest of men, because he knows: the heart of man is set on mischief, even from his youth. But that will be all he will know, and whoever only knows that, it would be good for him if he had never been born. For he knows nothing of the covenant between God and man, which nobody can break, neither man nor God, for it is inviolable. The rivers shall foam with blood because of his grievous stupidity, so much blood that the redness shall drain from the cheeks of mankind—but mankind cannot do otherwise, the scoundrel* must be felled. And I will raise my foot, saith the Lord, and stamp him into the dung—and into the depths of the earth I will trample this blasphemer, one hundred and twelve fathoms deep, and humankind and beast shall forgo the place where I stamped him down, and the birds of the air flying high above shall swerve to avoid flying over him. And whosoever shall speak his name, he shall vomit in all four directions and wipe his mouth and speak: "Perish the thought! Let the earth be the earth once more, a vale of deprivation, perhaps, but at least no cesspit of depravity." All of you, say Amen!'

And all the people said Amen.

THE BLACK SWAN

In the twenties of our century Frau Rosalie von Tümmler, widowed for more than a decade, lived with her daughter Anna and son Eduard in comfortable though not luxurious circumstances in Düsseldorf on the Rhine. Her husband, Lieutenant Colonel von Tümmler, had lost his life at the beginning of the war, not in battle, but instead rather needlessly in a motoring accident, although one might still say 'on the field of honour'—a severe blow that was borne with patriotic devotion by his wife, who, only forty at the time, saw herself henceforth deprived of a father for her children, and, for her own part, of a cheerful husband, whose frequent deviations from the precept of marital fidelity were but a badge of his excessive vigour.

A Rhinelander by ancestry as well as in speech, Rosalie had spent her married years, twenty in all, in the busy and bustling city of Duisburg, where von Tümmler had been garrisoned, but following the loss of her husband she had moved to Düsseldorf with her eighteen-year-old daughter and young son, who was twelve years younger than his sister, partly to enjoy the beautiful parks for which the town is renowned (for Frau von Tümmler was a great nature lover), partly because Anna, a serious girl, was drawn to painting and wished to attend Düsseldorf's famous Academy of Art. For the past decade, then, the little family had been living in a quiet, linden-bordered avenue of villas, named after Peter Cornelius,* in a smallish house, which—surrounded by a garden and fitted with the rather outdated but homely furniture that was fashionable during Rosalie's early married years—was frequently the hospitable scene of small gatherings of relatives and friends, including professors from the Academies of Art and Medicine as well as one or two couples from the world of industry, who would come together of an evening and take due pleasure in conviviality and, as was the local custom, indulge in vinous merriment.

Frau von Tümmler was sociable by nature. She loved to go out and, within her modest bounds, to keep an open house. Her unpretentious, sunny disposition and warm heart, which expressed itself in her love of nature, brought her general affection. Small in build, but with a well-preserved figure and full, wavy hair that was already quite grey, she had delicate, albeit slightly ageing hands, on the backs of which the passing years had left all-too-many, and all-too-large, freckle-like spots (a remedy for which has yet to be discovered), and made a youthful impression by dint of her brilliant, highly animated eyes, which, with a glossy, light-brown tint of husked chestnuts, shone out of the most endearingly agreeable, womanly face. Her nose had an almost negligible tendency to redden, a characteristic wont to manifest itself precisely when she was in company and good spirits, and which she attempted to redress with the help of a little powder—unnecessarily so, for the general opinion was that it was delightfully becoming.

Born in spring, a child of May, Rosalie had celebrated her fiftieth birthday in a tavern garden decorated with lampions on the outskirts of town, where, at a flower-strewn table and surrounded by her children and some ten to twelve family friends, both men and women, she had enjoyed the clink of glasses and affable, occasionally amusing toasts and had made merry with the merrymakers—not, however, without effort, for her well-being had been affected for some time now—and that evening had been no exception—by symptoms of an organic crisis experienced at her time of life, namely the lapsing of her physical womanhood, a gradual process which she mentally resisted. She experienced surges of anxiety, heart palpitations, headaches, day-long depressions and a proneness to irritability which, on the evening of her birthday celebration, made the whimsical speeches some of the gentlemen had held in her honour seem unbearably stupid. This made her exchange faintly exasperated glances with her daughter, who, as she knew, required no special predisposition to intolerance to find such punchbowl humour excruciating.

She was on especially affectionate and confiding terms with this child, who, so much older than her son, had become a friend with whom she showed no reticence in speaking even of her transient condition. Anna, who was now twenty-nine and would shortly be thirty, had remained unmarried, a state of affairs which, for purely egoistic reasons, was not unwelcome to Rosalie, who preferred to hold on to her daughter as a housemate and companion than to yield her to a man. Taller than her mother, Fräulein von Tummler had the same chestnut-coloured eyes—though not really the same, for Anna's lacked the naïve vivacity of her mother's, and their gaze was meditative and composed. Anna had been born with a club foot, which, after an operation during her childhood that had brought no improvement in the long term, had excluded her from participating in sport and dancing, indeed in all those activities typically associated with the life of young people. Her exceptional intelligence, an innate talent intensified by her disability, had to compensate for what had been denied her. She had passed her school-leaving exams with ease, on the basis of only two or three private lessons a day, but had not subsequently pursued any strictly academic university subject, turning her attention instead to the fine arts, at first to sculpture, thereafter to painting, where, even during her schooldays, she had set her sights on the highly intellectual; spurning mere imitation of Nature, she had transfigured sense impressions into the purely conceptual, that is, into abstract symbolism and often into the cubistically mathematical. Frau von Tümmler viewed her daughter's paintings—in which sophistication blended with the primitive, decorativeness with profundity, and a highly developed sense of colour with asceticism—with doleful esteem.

'Outstanding, definitely outstanding, my dear child,' she said. 'Professor Zumsteg will greatly appreciate it. It was he who encouraged you in this style of painting and he has the eye and the understanding for it. After all, one does need an eye and the understanding for it. What are you calling it?'

'Trees in the Evening Wind.'

'That certainly gives us a hint of your intentions. Are those cones and circles on the grey-yellow ground meant to represent the trees—and that peculiar line spiralling upwards, is that the evening wind? Interesting, Anna, interesting. But for heaven's sake, child, what are you people doing to our beloved Nature! If only you could paint something for the soul for once, something for the heart, a beautiful still life with flowers, a bouquet of fresh lilac blossom, something so vividly achieved that one can practically smell its lovely fragrance, and then a few delicate figures of Meissen porcelain beside the vase, and a gentleman blowing a kiss to a lady, and then the whole scene would have to be reflected in the highly polished, gleaming tabletop...'

'Wait, wait, Mama! You certainly do have an exuberant imagination. But one simply can't paint that sort of thing any more!'

'Anna, surely you are not trying to persuade me that, with all your talent, you couldn't paint something like that, something heart-warming?'

'You misunderstand me, Mama. It isn't a question of whether I would be able to do it or not. It is simply impossible. The state of our times and of art no longer permits it.'

'All the sadder for our times and art! No, I'm sorry, dearest child, I didn't really mean to say that. If it is life's progress that makes it impossible, then sad is not the right word. On the contrary, it would be sad to be left behind by it. I fully understand that. And I also understand that one needs genius to think up such a significant spiralling line as that one there. It means nothing to me, but I can see that it is clearly significant.'

Anna kissed her mother, while taking care to hold the wet brush and palette she was holding well away from her. And Rosalie kissed her back, happy in her heart that her daughter, through an activity that was practical and technically subtle, albeit, as it seemed to her, abstract and deadening, had in her artist's smock found compensation and solace for all she had been forced to forgo.

Having experienced early on how much a limping gait could wither the sensual appreciation of the opposite sex for a girl's appearance, Fräulein von Tümmler had henceforth steeled herself against such a possibility with the kind of pride which, should any young man, since such things evidently happened, be attracted to her in spite of her physical affliction, discouraged such an inclination in the face of her cold and dismissive incredulity, nipping it in the bud. Once, soon after their change of abode, she had loved—and had felt painfully ashamed of her passion, the object of which had been the physical beauty of a young man, a chemist by education, who had had a mind to convert his knowledge into money as soon as possible and who, therefore, after sitting his doctoral examination, had rapidly succeeded in finding respectable and remunerative employ in a Düsseldorf chemicals factory. His bronzed masculinity and amenable character, which also appealed to men, combined with his practical competence, made him the object of infatuation in their circle, the heart-throb of all the women and girls, and thus it was Anna's odious fate to languish in a flock of other languishers and find herself condemned by her senses to an undistinguished feeling for whose depth she had struggled in vain to find self-respect.

Meanwhile, Dr Brünner (for that was the name of this stellar beau), precisely because he fancied himself as a man of ambition and practical talents, entertained a certain curatorial inclination towards anything superior and distinctive and had sought Fräulein von Tümmler's company unashamedly, chatting with her in society on matters of literature and art, muttering mockingly pejorative remarks to her in his ingratiating voice about one or the other of his female admirers and giving the appearance of desiring a pact with her in defiance of these nonentities, who, for their part, unrefined by disability, were pestering him with their wanton advances. Of her own state of mind, and the torments of happiness he had aroused in her by his disparagement of other women, he appeared to lack the slightest notion and seemed only to be seeking, and hoping to find in her intelligent company, shelter from the tribulations of the amorous pursuit whose victim he was, while courting her esteem for his person on the simple grounds that he valued her esteem. Anna felt a powerful temptation to grant it to him, although she knew that in doing so she would merely be attempting to veil her weakness for his manly allure. To her sweet consternation, his solicitations had begun to resemble actual wooing, a real choice and proposal, and Anna found herself constantly admitting to herself that she would have been hopelessly incapable of resisting his overtures had he spoken the crucial words. But these were never uttered. His appetite for the exceptional had not been enough for him to disregard her bodily defect, which, moreover, would come with a modest dowry. It wasn't long before he had detached himself from her to marry the daughter of a wealthy factory owner from Bochum, to whose native city and paternal chemicals business he had then removed, much lamented by Düsseldorf's female society, and to Anna's relief.

Rosalie knew of her daughter's painful experience and she would have known of it even if Anna had not, one day, in an unbridled outpouring of sorrow, wept bitter tears on her mother's bosom over what she referred to as her humiliation. Although not especially clever in other respects, Frau von Tümmler, not out of malice but purely by virtue of personal sympathy, had an unusually sharp eye for everything that belonged to the life of women, whether physically or mentally, everything that Nature had inflicted on womankind, so that in her circle it was rare for any event or change in circumstance in this area to escape her gaze. From a purportedly vacant smile, a blushing cheek or a gleam of the eyes, she could tell which girl was smitten with which young man, and she would confide her observations to her daughter, who knew nothing of such matters and had hardly any interest at all in knowing of them. Instinctively, sometimes with pleasure and sometimes with regret, she knew whether a woman drew satisfaction from her marriage or lacked it. She could detect a pregnancy infallibly at its earliest stage, and because that was something she found joyfully natural she would fall into Rhineland dialect and say, '*Da is wat am Kommen*' ('There's something on the way'). She took pleasure in noting that Anna liked to help her younger brother, who was taking advanced classes at school, with his homework, for by way of a psychological cunning as naïve as it was unerring she had guessed that the jilted girl, whether consciously or unconsciously, felt a certain vindication in the superiority of her service to the male sex.

It cannot be said that she took a particularly close interest in her son, a gangly redhead, who in looks took after his dead father and, moreover, showed little talent for the humanities, but instead dreamed of bridge and road construction and wanted to become an engineer. All she could offer him was a cool and fleetingly considerate friendliness, mainly undertaken for form's sake. Her daughter, on the other hand, was her only real friend, and she clung to her. Anna's reticence might have induced one to describe this bond of trust between the two women as one-sided, had her mother not already been aware of everything regarding her inhibited child's emotional life, a witness to the proud and bitter resignation of her soul, and had she not derived from this knowledge the right and obligation to unlock her own heart to her daughter in an equally uncompromising manner.

When she did so, she would accept, without umbrage and with good humour, her daughterly friend's many affectionately indulgent smiles, which could sometimes be wistfully mocking or even cringing, and kind-hearted as Rosalie was, she was also happy to be treated kindly herself, and to laugh at her own simple-mindedness, which she nevertheless held to be blithe and fair, so that she laughed at herself as easily as at Anna when she pulled one of her faces. And that was often the case, especially when Rosalie gave free rein to her fervency for Nature, to which she continually tried to win over her intellectual girl. There are no words for how she loved the spring, *her* season, in which she had been born, and which, so she claimed, fed her with secret currents of health and lust for life. Hearing the mating calls of birds in the newly mild air made her face beam with delight. The first crocus and the first daffodil, the splendour of hyacinths and tulips sprouting in the beds around the house, all brought this good woman to tears of joy. The dear little violets along the country paths, the yellow blossom of broom and forsythia bushes, the white and pink mays, and of course the lilac, and the way the chestnuts put up their candelabra, white ones and red—the daughter was expected to join her mother in admiring all of this and to share her rapture. Rosalie would fetch her from the north-facing room that had been set up as her studio, dragging her away from her abstract handicraft, and Anna discarded her smock with a smile and was glad to accompany her mother for hours at a time, for she was a surprisingly good walker, and whenever she was in company and able to disguise her limp by avoiding too strenuous movement and could stump along as freely as she liked, then she had considerable stamina.

The time of blossoming trees, when the country roads transformed themselves into something poetic, the familiar countryside along the paths where they walked arraying itself in the white and rosy promise of exuberant fruitfulness—what an enchanting season! The fluffy pollen of blossoming catkins on the tall silver poplars that lined the canal, along which they often strolled, drifted like snow in the wind, falling on them and covering the ground, and Rosalie, who found this charming, too, knew enough botany to explain to her daughter that poplars are 'dioecious', meaning that one plant could be unisexually male, while another bore only female flowers. She also liked to speak of wind pollination, or rather, of Zephyr's labour of love in service of the children of the meadows, his obliging transport of pollen to the chastely expectant female stigma—a kind of fertilization she found particularly graceful.

The rose season was utter bliss for her. She trained the Queen of Flowers on sticks in her garden, protecting her carefully with the best remedies against devouring caterpillars, and for as long as her splendour lasted, there would be bouquets of unwithered roses on the small tables and étagères in her boudoir—budding, half-blown or the fully bloomed red roses (for white were not her favourites)—from her own stock or given to her by those attentive female visitors who knew of her passion. She could dip her face into such a bouquet with her eyes closed, and when, after some time, she raised her head, would vow that this was the perfume of the gods, and when Psyche,* her lamp in hand, bent over the sleeping Cupid, it must surely have been exactly this fragrance with which his breath, his locks and cheeks filled her little nose; it was a heavenly aroma, and there was no doubt in her mind that as blessed spirits on high, we would breathe the scent of roses for time everlasting.—If so, came Anna's sceptical comment, it would not be long before we became so used to the scent that we wouldn't notice it at all. But Frau von Tümmler scolded her for her presumptuousness. If all she wanted was to jibe, then her argument could apply to all that was blessed, but unconscious bliss was bliss nevertheless. And it was one of those occasions when Anna gave her mother a tender kiss of indulgence and reconciliation, and they both had to laugh.

Manufactured scents and perfumes were something Rosalie never used, with the exception of a dab of refreshing eau de cologne from 'J. M. Farina, opposite Jülich Square'. And yet all that Nature can muster to please our sense of smell—the delicate, the sweet, spicy bitterness and even whatever was heavy or heady, all this she loved beyond measure, imbibing it deeply and gratefully, and with the highest sensuous reverence. Along one of the paths where they walked there was a declivity, a long hollow in the landscape that became a shallow gorge, the bottom of which was densely overgrown with jasmine and buckthorn bushes, from which, on sultry June days with a hint of thunder in the air, great clouds of almost soporifically warm fragrance came billowing up the slope. Anna, whom the fumes affected with a light headache, nonetheless had to accompany her mother time and time again. Rosalie breathed in the heavy surge of vapour with rapturous delight, stopped, went on, again came to a halt, leant over the edge of the scarp and sighed: 'Child, child, how wonderful! This, truly, is the breath of Nature, her sweet exhalation of life, warmed by the sun and drenched with her moisture, wafting towards us blissfully from her lap. Let us relish and honour it, since we, too, are her beloved children.'

'Or at least you are, Mama,' replied Anna, taking her besotted mother's arm and pulling her along with her as she limped. 'She doesn't like me half as much, and causes all this pressure in my temples with that concoction of odours.'

'Yes, and that's because you've set your face against her,' answered Rosalie, 'and because you don't honour her with your talent, but use it to set yourself above her, turning her into a mere subject for the intellect, which you yourself then glory in, with your sense impressions transferred into I don't know what—into coldness. I do respect that, Anna, but if I were Nature I would be offended by what you young ones are doing.' And she suggested, quite seriously, that if Anna were so bent on abstraction, and if there had to be transference of some kind, then she should try expressing scents as colours for once.

The idea came to her towards the end of June when the lindens were in blossom, a time of year that for her, once again, was singular in its loveliness, a time when for just a few weeks the trees in the avenue outside filled the whole house through the open windows with the indescribably pure and balmy magic of their fragrant late bloom, and when Rosalie's enchanted smile never once left her lips. It was then she said: 'That is what you lot should paint—see what your art can do with that! After all, you don't want to banish Nature from art altogether, and anyway, she is your point of departure for your abstractions, and you need sensuality in the first place in order to intellectualize it. Now, fragrance, if I may say so, is both sensible and abstract at the same time; one can't see it, it speaks to us ethereally, and so you must surely find it tempting to try converting something invisibly pleasing into something for our sense of sight, upon which the art of painting ultimately rests. Come on! Where are your palettes, you painters? Mix this bliss and apply it to the canvas as a colourful delight, which you might then call "Fragrance of Linden", so that the beholder knows what you intended.'

'Dearest Mama, you are astonishing!' replied Fräulein von Tümmler. 'You come up with ways of looking at a problem that no professor of painting would think of! But you do realize, don't you, that you are an irredeemable romantic with your synaesthetic mixing of senses and mystical conversion of scents into colours?'

'I no doubt deserve your learned mockery.'

'No, you deserve no mockery,' said Anna devotedly.

But when they were out walking one afternoon in the heat of mid-August, something outlandish happened to them that did seem like mockery. Passing between meadowland and the edge of a wood they suddenly noticed a scent of musk which, barely detectable at first, soon grew stronger. Rosalie sniffed it first, voicing her perception with an 'Aha! Where's that coming from?' Her daughter had to agree: no doubt about it, yes, there was something, and it was like the scent of musk. Two steps were enough to bring its source into view, which was quite repugnant. At the edge of the road, simmering in the sun, blowflies covering it and flying all around it, was a small heap of refuse, which they preferred not to inspect too closely. The small space contained animal excrement, possibly also human faeces, mingled with rotting vegetation as well as what looked like the putrid carcass of some small woodland animal. In short, there could be nothing more obnoxious than this seething heap. However, its fetid exhalations, attracting flies in their hundreds, could no longer simply be called a stench, but in the very ambiguity of their transitoriness and suggestiveness most certainly had to be referred to as a musky scent.

'Let's go!' said both women simultaneously, and Anna, dragging her foot more than usual as she set off again, slipped her arm through her mother's. They were silent for a while, as if each needed to reflect on this bizarre impression. Then Rosalie said:

'And there you have it! I have never liked musk, nor muskrat, which I suppose is the same, and I don't understand how anyone could use it as a perfume. Civet, I believe, belongs in the same category. No flower or tree blossom smells like that, but I remember in Nature Studies classes we were told that some animals secrete it from certain glands—rats, cats, the civet cat and the musk deer. Do you remember? In Schiller's *Love and Intrigue** there's this manikin, a lackey of some sort, completely silly, who is described as rushing onstage with a screech and filling the parterre with the smell of muskrat. How I had to laugh about that passage!'

They cheered up. Rosalie still had that warm laugh of hers that came bubbling up from the heart, even during a period of her life when the difficulties of adapting to organic changes, the fitful withering of her womanhood, were making life hard for her, physically and psychologically. She had a friend at the time, a being given to her by Nature. Very close to her home in a corner of the Hofgarten Park, which was accessed via Malkastenstrasse, her friend was an ancient, solitary oak tree, gnarled and stunted, with partly exposed roots and a squat trunk, from which, at a low height, thick, knotty boughs protruded, which themselves divided into thinner branches. Here and there the tree was hollow; it had been sealed with cement (the park management having done the hundred-year-old fellow a favour). However, some of its branches were already dead and no longer produced any foliage, their bare, crooked arms clawing the sky, while still others, albeit only a few lone branches, had grown quite tall and still turned green in springtime; their lobed and pointy leaves had traditionally been held to be sacred, and were once used to craft the victor's wreath. Rosalie loved all of this, and at around the time of her birthday would follow the burgeoning and sprouting and unfurling of leaves on the branches and twigs that life still managed to reach, in day-to-day touch with developments.

Nearby, on a bench at the edge of the meadow where it stood, she sat down with Anna and said:

'Stalwart old fellow! Can you look at him standing there, firm, with his sap still flowing, and not be moved? Take a look at those roots, as thick as an arm, so woody, and how they clutch the earth around them, anchoring themselves in the nourishing element. He's been through a storm or two in his lifetime, and he'll survive a few more. He's not going to fall over. He's hollow, cemented, and no longer capable of a full show of leaves, but when his time comes, his sap still rises—not everywhere, but enough for a bit of green here and there, and people respect that and cherish his courage. Can you see that thin little offshoot with its leaf-buds up there, nodding in the wind? There isn't much doing round about it, but that little twig is saving the day.'

'You are right, Mama, it is truly commendable, just as you say,' Anna replied. 'But if it's all right with you, I'd rather go home now. I'm having pains.'

'Pains? Is it your—but of course, my dearest child, how could I forget! Now I blame myself for having brought you with me. Here I am, gazing at that old fellow and not noticing you lean forwards as we sit here. Sorry! Take my arm and we'll go.'

Fräulein von Tümmler had always suffered from strong abdominal pains when her period came on—it was of little consequence, she had long grown used to it, and even her doctor referred to it as a constitutional discomfort one simply had to put up with. Her mother therefore, on their short walk home, felt free to speak of it to the stricken young woman in a manner that was gently soothing, with well-meaning cheerfulness and, in fact, indeed above all else, with envy.

'Do you remember', she asked, 'how it was like that your very first time, too, when you were only a young thing and it suddenly happened to you and you were frightened, but then I came to you and explained that it was simply natural and necessary and good, and actually it was a kind of glory day, because it showed you had grown into a proper woman? You have stomach cramps beforehand, that is unpleasant, I know, but not always necessary; I never had any, but it does happen, and I know of two or three other cases besides you where women have pains, and I think: pains, *à la bonne heure*?*—for us women that's something different from pain elsewhere in Nature, or for men, who don't have them unless they are ill, and then they make an awfully big fuss about it, like Tümmler, your father, who also did, even although he was a soldier and died a hero's death. Our sex has a different way with it, we suffer pain more patiently, we endure it, you might say we are born to it. For most importantly, we know a natural and healthy pain, the divinely ordained, sacred pain of childbirth, which is something entirely female, and which is spared men, or denied them. Those silly men are appalled by our practically unconscious ravings, and they blame themselves and hold their heads in their hands, and yet in spite of our screams, it is we who are laughing at them. When I gave birth to you, Anna, it was fairly hard. From the first contraction it lasted thirty-six hours, and Tümmler spent the whole time running from room to room with his head in his hands, but it was a genuinely grand festival of life, and it wasn't me myself screaming, *it* was screaming—it was pain's sacred ecstasy. Later, with Eduard, it wasn't half as bad, but for a man it would still have been much too much—I'm quite sure their lordships would be sincerely grateful for a chance at it! You see, pain is usually the way Nature, always benign, gives us a warning signal that an illness is developing in the body—Watch out! it says, there's something the matter, do something to stop it, not just the pains, but stop whatever the pain is pointing to. For us it can be like that, too, and it can mean the same warning, of course. But as you know, your stomach pains, before your period, they don't have that meaning, and they aren't warning you of anything. They are a particular variety of women's pain and therefore honourable, and that's how you must take it, as an act of female life. As long as we are women, no longer a child and not yet an incapable old woman, there is always, again and again, a surging abundance of the blood of life in our motherly organ, by which kind Nature prepares it to receive the fertilized egg, and if one is there, which in my long life, after all, happened only twice with a long interval between each, then our period stays away, and we are with child. Heavens, how pleasantly startled I was when mine stayed away the first time thirty years ago! It was you I was blessed with, my darling child, and I remember confiding it to Tümmler, and how I blushed and leant my head against his and said, in almost a whisper: "Robert, it's happened, everything points to it, at last I can say, *da is wat am kommen*…"'

'Dearest Mama, please do me a favour—could you not speak Rhenish like that—I find it irritating at the moment.'

'Oh, do forgive me, my precious one, that is the very last thing I wanted, to irritate you now. It's just that, in all my bashful joy of the moment, that really is what I said to Tümmler, and then, we were talking about things that are natural, weren't we, well it seems to me that dialect and Nature go together, just as Nature and nation seem connected, too—if I'm speaking nonsense, please correct me, won't you! You are so much cleverer than I am. Yes, you are clever, and as an artist you don't have the best relationship with Nature, but insist on intellectualizing it, turning it into cubes and spirals, and since we are talking of things that go together, I would very much like to know if there isn't a connection between your proud, ingenious attitude towards Nature—and the fact that she has singled you out for such period pains.'

'But Mama,' said Anna, who had to laugh. 'You chide me for being brainy, while postulating such indefensibly ingenious theories yourself!'

'I would be happy with the most simplistic of theories if it succeeded in cheering you up, my child. But I was being serious when I spoke about the pains that are genuinely female, and I meant it to be comforting. Just be happy and proud with your thirty years that you can enjoy the prime bloom of your blood. Believe me, I would gladly put up with any sort of stomach-ache if I could still be like you. But unfortunately I won't be like you any more, am less and less so, and it has become meagre and more irregular, and for the last two months I haven't had anything at all. Alas, with me it has ceased to be after the manner of women, as the Bible says—of Sarah, I think, yes, it was Sarah,* in whom a miracle of fruitfulness came to pass, but I suppose that's no more than a pious story of things that don't happen these days. When it ceases to be after the manner of women with us, then we are no longer women but only the dried-up shell of a woman, worn-out, useless, discarded by Nature. My dear child, it is very bitter. For men, it seems, it does not have to end during their whole lifetime. I know a few who are eighty who won't leave a woman in peace, and Tümmler, your father, was also like that—even later, when he became a lieutenant colonel, I had to keep my eye on him all the time! And what, all in all, are fifty years for a man? If he has any temperament at all, fifty won't stop him playing the charmer, and many a man with grey temples will make a conquest even with a very young woman. But the limit for us and our women's lives and blood, for our lives as complete human beings, is more or less set at thirty-five, and when we are fifty we have served our time and forfeit our ability to bear children, and in Nature's eyes, we are nothing but old clutter.'

'Oh but what words, Mama,' exclaimed Anna, 'and what aspersions, and how you seem to spurn the dignity that an older woman deserves when she has lived her life, and when Nature, whom you love, after all, gives her a new and more gentle status in life, a state of honour and greater amiability, and a stage of her life in which she can still be and give so much to people, whether these be family or persons less close! You say men are enviable because the limits set on their sexual life are less strict than those for women. But I am not sure that is something that deserves our respect, or that it's something to envy, and in any case, all civilized peoples have always shown the greatest reverence towards the matron, indeed have gone as far as considering her sacred, and we have every intention of considering you sacred, too, in the endearing and adorable dignity of your old age.'

'My darling girl'—and Rosalie drew her daughter closer as they walked—'you speak so elegantly and cleverly and with such excellence in spite of your pains, which I had hoped to soothe, but now it's you who are consoling your misguided mother over her unbecoming troubles. But all this about leave-taking and dignity is indeed hard, my dear child, and it's quite difficult even for the body to find its place in this new stage of life, because that brings enough trouble of its own. And if the person in question doesn't have much of a mind for dignity or the honour of being a matron and refuses to accept the withering of the body—then we certainly are in a pickle. For the soul to adapt to the new state of the body, that is the most difficult thing.'

'Of course it is, Mama, I understand that. But look, body and soul are actually one; the mind is as much part of Nature as the body; Nature includes minds, and so you need not be anxious that your soul will remain in disharmony with the natural changes of your body for long. The way you should think of it is that the mental and spiritual are merely emanations of the physical body, and while your dear soul might believe it has been dealt an all-too-difficult task in having to adapt itself to the changed life of the body, it will soon learn that it doesn't have to do anything at all but to allow the body to get on with conditioning the mind. For it is the body that forms the soul in keeping with its own condition.'

It was clear to Fräulein von Tümmler what her reason for saying these things was, for around the time when her mother was confiding to her the matters laid out above, a new face was to be seen at home, an additional face, and potentially embarrassing developments were in the making that had not escaped Anna's calm and caring attention.

The new face—hardly a particularly remarkable one in Anna's view, or at least not one that betrayed much intelligence—belonged to a young man of about twenty-four years of age called Ken Keaton, an American brought over by the war who had been resident in the city for some time and gave English lessons in one household or another, or was engaged by the wives of rich industrialists, in exchange for an honorarium, simply to give them practice in English conversation. Eduard, since Easter in the final year of secondary school, had caught wind of this and implored his mother to arrange for him to take introductory lessons from Mr Keaton several times a week during the afternoons. For while his grammar school offered him a great deal of Greek and Latin and, happily, sufficient mathematics, it did not offer him English, which, however, seemed of considerable importance for the future that Eduard had in mind. As soon as he had succeeded, by whatever means, in getting those boring humanities behind him, he wished to attend the Polytechnic, and then, so he planned, to go to England to further his studies, and from there—if he hadn't already done so to begin with—to proceed to that very El Dorado of technology, the United States. He was therefore overjoyed and grateful when his mother, respecting the clarity and resoluteness with which he had expressed his intentions, willingly fulfilled his wish. Working with Keaton on Mondays, Wednesdays and Saturdays he found to be very pleasurable, firstly in view of its usefulness, but also because it was fun to learn a new language from its very foundations, rather as a school beginner might do, using a little primer. There were words with bizarre spellings and extremely odd pronunciation, which Ken, forming the 'l' even deeper in his throat than the Rhinelanders, and letting the 'r' pass across this palate unrolled, performed in a drawl so exaggerated that it sounded as if he were deliberately making fun of his own mother tongue. '*Scrr-ew the top on!*' he'd say, and '*I sllept like a top*,' or '*Alfred is a tennis play-err. His shoulders are thirty inches brr-oaoadd.*'* For the entire one and a half hours of the lesson, Eduard found himself laughing about Alfred, the broad-shouldered tennis player, of whom much was made involving maximal use of '*though*' and '*thought*' and '*taught*' and '*tough*', and yet he also made very good progress, precisely because Keaton was not a trained teacher and used a completely casual method, in other words, he made the best of every opportunity, launching into the lesson without ado, and by incorporating slangy gossip and nonsense, initiating his student, who could have wished for nothing better, into the urbane, amusing and easy-going workings of his language.

Frau von Tümmler, drawn to the cheerfulness that prevailed in Eduard's room, would occasionally join the young people there, and taking part in some of their productive amusement and laughing heartily with the others over *Alfred, the tennis play-err*, she noticed a certain similarity between Alfred and her son's young tutor, especially in as far as his shoulders were concerned, for Ken's, too, were superbly broad. Otherwise, Ken had thick blond hair, and while his face was not particularly handsome, it was not unpleasant either; it was a boy's face, friendly and innocuous, and thanks to a hint of Anglo-Saxon character, it avoided, at least in its present environment, looking too ordinary. For all his loose, rather baggy clothing it was apparent that Ken was superbly well built, and with his long legs and narrow hips he exuded youthful vitality. He had fine hands, too, with a not-too-ornate ring on the left. His straightforward and entirely unconstrained—although not at all rude—manner, his comical German, which his mouth made as indisputably English-sounding as it did the few scraps of French and Italian he knew (for he had visited several European countries)—all this Rosalie liked very much; his marvellous naturalness impressed her especially, and now and then, and soon almost regularly, she invited him to stay for dinner after the lesson, whether she had taken part in it or not. Part of her interest in him derived from having heard that he was very successful with women. With this in mind, she observed him, and concluded that what the rumour claimed was conceivable, although she could not deny that it disturbed her somewhat, whenever he had to burp a little while eating and talking, to see him raise his hand to his mouth and say '*Pardon me!*', which he intended as a well-mannered gesture, but which drew unnecessary attention to the incident.

Ken, as he recounted at table, had been born in a small town in one of the Eastern states, where his father had changed his line of business several times—he'd been a '*broker*', the manager of a filling station and had also made money in '*real estate*'. The son had attended '*high school*', a place—if what he said was credible—where you learned nothing at all ('by European standards', as he respectfully added), after which, without thinking much about it, simply hoping to learn something, he had enrolled in a college in Detroit, Michigan, where he had paid for his studies with the work of his own hands, as a dishwasher, cook, waiter and campus gardener. Frau von Tümmler asked him how, with all he had done, he had managed to keep such white, indeed one might even say patrician, hands, and he answered that when doing rough work he had always worn gloves—yes, he had rolled up his sleeves, even taken off his shirt, but always kept his gloves on. Many workers over there did that, in fact most of them, construction workers for example, so that they didn't get calloused proletarian hands and kept their hands like those of a lawyer's clerk, complete with a ring.

Rosalie applauded the custom, but Keaton begged to differ: custom? The word was too good for it; it was not a 'custom' in the sense of an old European folk custom (he tended to use the word '*Continental*' for 'European'). Not like an old German folk custom—for example, the 'rod of life', when the lads, at Christmas and Easter, would whip, or as they called it 'pepper' or 'lash', the girls with green birch or willow switches, and supposedly they did the same to cattle and trees, which was meant to awaken health and fertility—now, that sure was a custom, an ancient one, and it was much to his liking. The peppering or lashing in the springtime was called 'Easter smacking'.

The Tümmlers had never heard of Easter smacking and were astounded to find that Ken was so knowledgeable about folklore. Eduard laughed about the rod of life, Anna pulled a face, and only Rosalie, in full agreement with her guest, showed herself delighted by it. Ken said that this was certainly quite different from wearing gloves for work, and you would have to search for a long time to find anything like it in America, if only because there were no villages in America and because farmers there were not the same as farmers here; they were entrepreneurs like all the rest and had no customs at all. All in all, and although his whole manner and bearing betrayed him as unmistakably American, he did not appear to be very attached to his great homeland. He didn't '*care for America*', as he put it, indeed, with its relentless pursuit of the dollar, its churchiness, its bigoted devotion to success and colossal mediocrity, and particularly with its lack of historical atmosphere, he actually found it dreadful. Of course it had a history, but that was not '*History*', but merely a short, banal '*success story*'. Certainly, aside from its deserts, it had beautiful, sublime landscapes, but there was nothing behind them, whereas there was so much behind everything in Europe, especially behind the cities with their deep historical perspectives. American cities?—he didn't '*care for them*'. They'd been put up yesterday and could just as easily be taken away again tomorrow. The smaller ones were dull backwaters, one the same as the other, and the large ones were horrid puffed-up monstrosities whose museums were packed full of bought-up 'Continental' cultural assets. Buying was, of course, better than stealing, but not much better, for in certain places anything dating from AD 1400 or 1200 was as good as stolen anyway.

Ken's irreverent tirades excited much mirth, and also elicited some reproach, and yet he countered this with the remark that it was precisely reverence that had caused him to speak in that way, in other words his respect for perspective and atmosphere. The earliest historical narratives, from around AD 1100 or 700, were his passion and his '*hobby*', and at college he had always been best in history—history and '*athletics*'. In those days he had already been keen to come over to Europe, where early history was at home, and he would certainly, even without a war, have worked his passage over here, whether as a sailor or washing dishes, simply to breathe historical air. But the war had come along at exactly the right moment, and in 1917 he had immediately enlisted, and all through his '*training*' he had feared the war might come to an end before they brought him over. But then, in the nick of time, he had squashed into a troop transport and managed to get over to France, and had even seen action near Compiègne, and he had received a wound, too, quite a serious one in fact, so that he had spent weeks lying in a hospital bed. It was a kidney wound, and now only one of his kidneys worked, which was quite enough for him. All the same, he said laughing, he was now something of an invalid and received a small invalid's pension, which was worth more to him than his ruined kidney.

He had nothing at all of the invalid about him, Frau von Tümmler maintained, and he replied: 'No, thank God, *only a little cash*!'

As soon as he was discharged from hospital, he had quit the army, indeed he had been '*honourably discharged*' with a medal for bravery, and had stayed on in Europe for an indefinite period, which he found wonderful, and where he revelled in early history. The French cathedrals, the Italian campanili, palazzi and galleries, the Swiss villages, and a place like Stein am Rhein—now, that was '*most delightful indeed*'. And then wine everywhere, the '*bistros*' in France, the trattorias in Italy, the homely taverns in Switzerland and Germany—'at the sign of the Ox', the 'Moor's Arms', 'The Star'—where would you find anything like that back in America? There was no wine over there, only '*drinks*', whiskey and rum, and no cool pints of Alsace, or Tiroler or Johannisberger at an oak table in a historic taproom or honeysuckle bower. '*Good heavens!*' People in America simply didn't know how to live.

Germany! That was his favourite country, although he had not yet seen so very much of it, and he really only knew the towns and villages on Lake Constance, and also, in fact far better, the Rhineland. The Rhineland with its dear, jolly people, so '*amiable*', especially when they were a bit 'tight', with its venerable cities full of atmosphere, Trier, Aachen, Coblenz, the holy city of Cologne—try calling an American city 'holy'—'*Holy Kansas City*', haha! The famous Hoard of Gold,* guarded by the Maidens of the '*Missouri River*', hahaha—'*Pardon me!*'

He knew more about Düsseldorf and its long history since the Merovingians* than Rosalie and her children put together, and spoke of Mayor Pepin,* of Barbarossa,* who built the Imperial Palace of Rindhusen, and of the Salian Church at Kaiserswerth, where Henry IV* was crowned as a child, of Albert of Berg,* Jan Wellem of the Palatinate* and many others, like a professor.

Rosalie then said that he could teach history as well as English. There would not be enough demand for it, he replied. Oh, not at all, was her answer. She herself, who had become keenly aware through him of just how little she knew, would take lessons from him at the first opportunity. He might feel '*a bit faint-hearted*' about it, he admitted, and in return she described an observation that had left an emotional impression on her: it was such a strange thing in life, and to a certain extent painful, that relations between youth and age were to such a marked degree characterized by timidity. Youth was shy of age because it did not expect age's dignity to show much sympathy for its immature way of life, and age shied away from youth because, while its admiration for youth was true and profound, it believed it had a duty to its own dignity to hide this admiration behind mockery and false condescension.

Ken laughed gleefully and approvingly, Eduard thought his mother spoke like a book, and Anna studied her mother's face inquisitively. Her mother was altogether vivacious in Mr Keaton's presence, and sometimes, unfortunately, a little affected. Rosalie often invited Ken to stay and eat with them and regarded him, even when he held his hand in front of his mouth and said '*Pardon me!*', with an expression of motherly affection, which Anna—who deemed the young man unremarkable for all his infatuation with Europe, passion for early dates such as AD 700 and familiarity with every 'Altbier'-pub in Düsseldorf—found unconvincing in terms of its apparently maternal feeling, which made her feel uneasy. Too often, when Mr Keaton's arrival was imminent, Frau von Tümmler would anxiously ask Anna whether her nose was too red. It was—although Anna denied it reassuringly. And if it weren't so before, then it turned an unusually deep red as soon as she and the young man were together. But by then her mother seemed to have forgotten it.

Anna's observation had been correct: Rosalie had begun to abandon herself to her tender feelings for her son's young preceptor without showing any sign of inward resistance to this rapid budding of her fondness, or perhaps without noticing it herself, and, in any case, without attempting to conceal it. Symptoms that in any other woman would never have escaped her female observation—her cooing and the exaggerated hilarity of her laughter at Ken's chit-chat, her rapt gaze and then her attempt to veil her increasingly shiny eyes—she seemed to consider imperceptible in herself, unless she was showing her feelings deliberately and was too proud of them to make a pretence.

The situation became quite clear to the worried Anna on one very warm and summery September evening when Ken had stayed for dinner and Eduard, after the soup course, asked permission to take off his jacket because it was too hot. The young men may feel free to do as they like, came the answer, and so Ken followed the example of his pupil. It appeared not to concern him that, unlike Eduard, who wore a coloured, long-sleeved shirt with cuffs, he had simply donned his jacket over his white T-shirt, and that his bare arms were now exposed—and they were very good-looking arms, round, strong, young and white, making it perfectly credible that during his college days he had excelled as much at '*athletics*' as he had at history. Ken was certainly far from noticing the state of confusion those arms had induced in the lady of the house, and Eduard had no eye for it either. But Anna observed her mother's confusion with pain and compassion. Rosalie, laughing and speaking as if in a fever, looked in turns red enough to have been doused with blood or alarmingly pale, and after every escape her fugitive eyes, unrestrainably attracted, returned to Ken's arms, there to dwell for a few self-forgotten seconds, an expression of deep and sensual sadness on her face.

Anna, aggravated by Ken's naïve innocuousness, which she did not entirely trust, drew attention, as soon as it was reasonable to do so, to the coolness of the evening which was already entering from the garden through the open French window and recommended, warning against catching a chill, that the gentlemen return to wearing their jackets. But Frau von Tümmler brought the evening to a close almost immediately after they had eaten. Feigning a migraine, she took leave of her guest in a rather cursory manner and retired to her bedroom. Stretched out on her couch, her face covered by her hands and buried in a cushion, overwhelmed by shame, dismay and bliss, she confessed her passion to herself.

'Good God, I truly love him, love him more than I have ever loved—how can that be possible? After all, surely I have been sent into retirement, with Nature conveying me to the placid and dignified estate of matronhood. Isn't it a cause for ridicule that I can still harbour lust, as I do in my terrified, blissful thoughts when I look at him, when I see his divine arms, by which I so deliriously yearn to be embraced, his magnificent chest, the contours of which, in my woefulness and rapture, I saw outlined under his jersey? Am I a shameless old woman? No, not shameless, because I feel shame in his presence, shame because of his youth and because I don't know how to meet him, how to look into his eyes, those artless, friendly boy's eyes, so unprepared for the heat of my desire. But I have been smitten by the rod of life, and he, innocent of it all, has peppered and lashed me, given me an Easter smacking! Why did he need to mention that in his youthful enthusiasm for old folk customs? Now the thought of those rousing strokes of his rod inundates my inmost self, drowning me in shameful sweetness. I desire him—have I never desired before? Tümmler desired me when I was young and I accepted it for what it was and yielded to his wooing, took him in marriage in his imposing manliness, and so we gave ourselves to a lust that followed his desires. This time the desire is mine, it starts with me, and what I have done is to cast my eye on him as a man casts his eye upon the young woman of his choice—that is the effect of the years, the effect of my age and his youth. Youth is feminine and age's relationship with it is masculine, but age, because of its ecklessness, is not joyful and confident in its desire, but full of shame and misgiving before youth and before all of Nature. Oh, I have much suffering ahead of me, for how can I hope that he will accept my desire for what it is and, if he does, yield to my wooing, as I did to Tümmler's? Of course, he isn't a girl, with those strong arms of his; he's a young man who will have his own desires and, according to what one hears, is very successful with women. He will have women, as many as he likes, in this town. The thought of it makes my soul writhe and scream with jealousy. He gives English conversation lessons to Louise Pfingsten in Pempelforter Strasse and to Lützenkirchen, that's Amélie Lützenkirchen, whose husband, the saucepan manufacturer, is fat, short of breath and lazy. In stature, Louise is extremely tall and has a bad hairline, but is only thirty-eight and good at fluttering her eyes. Amélie is just a little older and pretty, yes, unfortunately she is pretty, and her fat husband lets her do whatever she wants. Is it possible they are lying in his arms, or at least one of them, probably Amélie, although it could equally be that beanpole Louise—in those arms whose embrace I crave with an ardour their stupid souls could never raise; is it possible they are enjoying his hot breath, his lips, his hands caressing the contours of their bodies? And I am gnashing my teeth, these very good teeth that have needed so little treatment—I am gnashing them because of what I am thinking. And my body is more shapely than theirs, more worthy than theirs of his caresses, and what tenderness I could give him, what unutterable surrender! But they are gushing fountains and I am a dried-up well, not worthy of jealousy. Jealousy—torturous, wearing, gnashing jealousy! Did I not once see with these very eyes of mine that see everything—this was at the Rollwagens' garden party, that is, the machine-manufacturer Rollwagen and his wife, to which he was also invited—did I not catch an exchange of fleeting glances and smiles between him and Amélie, an exchange that almost certainly pointed to something secret? Even back then I felt my heart clench with a crushing pain, but I didn't understand what it was and didn't think of jealousy because I didn't consider myself capable of it. But I am capable, and now I do understand, and I won't deny my feelings but instead will rejoice in this pain that is so wonderfully at odds with my changing body. The mental and spiritual are merely emanations of the body, said Anna, and the body forms the soul in keeping with its own condition? Anna knows a great deal, Anna knows nothing. No, I won't say she knows nothing. She has suffered, loved senselessly and suffered shamefully, and so she knows quite a bit. But there are things she doesn't know. She claims the soul is conveyed along with the body to the placid and dignified estate of matronhood, and she is wrong about that because she doesn't believe in miracles and doesn't know that Nature can make the soul miraculously blossom even when it is so late, even too late—blossom into love, desire and jealousy, such as I am experiencing now in my blissful torment. Aged Sarah, from behind the tent door, heard what she had coming to her, and she laughed. That made God angry with her, saying: wherefore did Sarah laugh? I—I do not want to be the one who laughed. I will believe in the miracle of my soul and senses and revere the natural wonder of this pain and shame-born spring of my soul, and my shame shall be only because of the blessedness of this late visitation…'

Thus Rosalie's conversation with herself that evening. After a night full of agitated restlessness followed by several hours of deep sleep in the morning, her first thought on waking was of the passion which had smitten and blessed her and which it did not occur to her to decline, or reject on moral grounds. The good woman was enthused by the survival of her soul's ability to blossom in sweet anguish. She was not particularly religious and left the Lord God out of the picture. Her piety was devoted to Nature, and that made her admire and cherish what Nature, as if in opposition to herself, had wrought in her. Yes, it was contrary to natural decency, this blossoming of her soul and senses; it was exhilarating, certainly, but it did not embolden her and had to be concealed and kept secret from the world, even from her trusted daughter, and especially from him, the one she loved, who suspected nothing and could not be permitted to suspect anything—for how could she dare to raise her eyes to meet his youth?

And thus something that was socially utterly absurd entered her behaviour towards Keaton, a certain kind of subservience and humility that Rosalie, despite all the pride she took in her feelings, was incapable of banishing, and which, on any knowing observer, in other words on Anna, had a more painful effect than all the vivacity and exaggerated hilarity she had manifested when this began. Eventually, even Eduard noticed it, and there were moments when brother and sister, leaning over their plates, bit their lips, while Ken, conscious of the embarrassed silence yet uncomprehending, looked from one person to the other. Hoping for advice and enlightenment, Eduard sought an opportunity to confront his sister on the matter.

'What's up with Mama?' he asked. 'Doesn't she like Keaton any more?' And when Anna said nothing, the young man continued with a sardonic expression around his mouth, 'Or does she like him too much?'

'How dare you!' was her scolding answer. 'These are not matters for boys. Have the decency to hold back your improper observations!' But she went on to suggest he might be respectful enough to bear in mind that his mother, as all women must, was presently suffering a period of discomfort detrimental to her well-being.

'Very new and informative to me!' said the final-year pupil ironically. But her explanation was too general for him. Their mother, he went on, was agonizing over something more specific, and she, too, his greatly adored sister, was evidently agonizing over something—not to mention that silly boy, her brother. But perhaps the silly boy could accomplish something useful by proposing the dismissal of his all-too-amiable tutor. He might inform his mother that he had already profited enough from his teaching, and it was time for Keaton, once again, to be '*honourably discharged*'.

'Do that, dear Eduard,' said Anna; and he did.

'Mama,' he said, 'I think it might be expedient to put a stop to my English lessons and the expenses you have so kindly taken upon yourself on my behalf. Thanks to your generosity I have laid a solid foundation with Mr Keaton's help, and by undertaking some private reading I shall see to it that the foundation is not squandered. In any case, nobody really learns a foreign language at home, outside the country where everyone speaks it and where one is entirely dependent on it. When I eventually do get to England or America, the preparation you have allowed me will ensure that I shall have no trouble picking up the rest. As you know, my school-leaving exams are gradually approaching, and nobody will be examining me in English. On the other hand, I must see to it that I don't fail in classical languages, and that will require all my attention. So it is probably the right moment, don't you think, to thank Keaton cordially for his endeavours and release him in the friendliest way possible from further engagement.'

'But Eduard,' countered Frau von Tümmler quickly and initially rather impetuously. 'What you say surprises me, and I cannot say I approve. Granted, it proves your delicacy of feeling in wishing to save me further expense for this purpose. But the purpose is a good one, important for the future life you are considering, and things are not so bad for us that we cannot bear the expense of your language lessons, just as we have been able to bear the costs of Anna's art studies at the Academy. I cannot understand why you want to stop halfway through, rather than meeting your intention to master English. It might be said, my dear boy, and please don't take offence, that in so doing, your gratitude has fallen short of what might be expected for my willingness to support your project. Of course, your final exams are a serious matter, and I quite understand that as far as the classical languages are concerned, which you don't much care for, you still have some strenuous swotting to do. But your English lessons, Eduard, just a couple of times a week—surely they would be nothing more than a form of recreation and welcome distraction to you, or are you seriously suggesting they would add to your strain? Aside from that—and now let me come to the personal, the human aspect—the terms of our household's relationship with Ken, as he is called, in other words with Mr Keaton, have long since been such that we can no longer simply say to him, "You are no longer needed", and give him his marching orders, in other words that we could simply declare: "The Moor has done his work. The Moor may go."* He has become a friend of the house, almost a member of the family, and he would rightly feel sore were we to dispatch him in that manner. We would all miss him, and Anna especially, I think, would be upset if he could no longer come and enliven our meals with his intimate knowledge of Düsseldorf's history and could no longer tell us about the War of the Jülich-Cleves Succession, or about Prince-Elector Jan Wellem, whose statue is in the market square. And you, too, would miss him, and even I would. In short, Eduard, your proposal is well meant, but its execution is neither necessary nor entirely feasible. It would be best to leave things as they are.'

'As you wish, Mama,' said Eduard, and reported his failure to his sister, who replied:

'I thought as much, my boy. In actual fact, Mama's assessment of the situation is correct, and I myself had misgivings similar to hers when you announced that you were going to approach her. At the very least she is right in one thing, namely that Keaton is pleasant company and that all of us would regret his absence. Just continue with him, then.'

As she spoke, Eduard looked her in the face, which remained expressionless, then shrugged his shoulders and left. Ken was waiting for him in his room, and they read a few pages of Emerson* or Macaulay,* then an American '*mystery story*', which provided enough material for them to gossip for the final half-hour, after which Ken stayed on for dinner, to which he no longer had to be specially invited. His staying on after lessons had become a regular arrangement, and on those days of illicit, fearful and shame-afflicted bliss, Rosalie discussed the menu with her housekeeper Babette, chose something good for the meal and saw to it that, for the hour when they would sit together in the living room after dinner, they had a full-bodied Pfälzer or Rüdesheimer wine, of which she would then partake more liberally than usual, so that she might gaze with greater courage on the one she so unreasonably loved. Often, however, the wine made her feel tired and hopeless as she battled with herself, in which case she would struggle with herself to varying effect, undecided as to whether she should stay and suffer under his eyes, or retire and weep over him in her loneliness.

With the onset of the social season in October, she also saw Keaton outside the confines of her house, at the Pfingstens' in the Pempelforter Strasse, at the Lützenkirchens', or among larger circles of guests at Senior Engineer Rollwagen's. She would look out for him, then avoid him, fleeing the group he had joined to stand in a different one, chatting mechanically and waiting for him to come over and pay her some attention, always knowing where he was, amid the hubbub listening for his voice then suffering torments when she imagined she had noticed signs of some secret understanding between him and Louise Pfingsten or Amélie Lützenkirchen. Although the young man had nothing much to offer beyond his athletic physique, consummate ingenuousness and the unpretentious nature of his intellect, he was admired and sought-after among the members of this set and cheerfully profited from their German weakness for all things foreign, as well as being perfectly aware that his pronunciation of German and the childlike expressions he employed went down well with his audience. People enjoyed conversing with him in English, too. He could wear whatever he pleased. He did not possess '*evening dress*', but social conventions had become more relaxed in recent years anyway, and black tie was no longer compulsory at soirées or in theatre boxes, and even at events at which the majority of gentlemen wore evening jackets, Keaton was welcome in his customary lounge suit, a loose and comfortable outfit comprising belted brown trousers, brown shoes and a grey woollen jacket.

Thus was Ken free and easy as he moved through the drawing rooms, ingratiating himself not only with the ladies to whom he already gave English lessons, but also with those by whom he hoped to be engaged for the same purpose, at table cutting his meat, according to the custom of his homeland, first of all into little pieces, then, after laying his knife diagonally across the edge of his plate and letting his left arm hang, eating the mouthfuls he had already prepared for himself, holding his fork in his right hand. He abided by this routine because he had noticed that the ladies and men sitting opposite were observing it with such great interest.

He liked to chat with Rosalie, also in a tête-à-tête away from the others, not only because she was one of his employers or '*bosses*', but because of a genuine attraction. For while her daughter's cool intelligence and intellectual demands unnerved him, he found the mother's sincere womanliness sympathetic, and, without interpreting her feelings correctly (for it didn't occur to him to do so), he basked in the warmth that radiated from her to himself, fully indulging in it and paying little attention to her accompanying symptoms of tension, anxiety and confusion, taking them to be expressions of European nervousness, which he therefore held in esteem. Furthermore, however much she suffered, everything about her suggested rejuvenation, and that she had begun to bloom again, and people complimented her on her looks. It was true her figure had always kept its youthful appearance, but what caught the eye now was the brightness of her lovely brown eyes, which, although possibly indicating something feverish, nonetheless added to her attractions; equally conspicuous were her face's heightened colour, which quickly returned after any occasional pallor, and then the mobility of her now somewhat fuller features during conversation, which was generally amusing and gave her an opportunity, through laughter, to correct any involuntary facial expression. The guests at these socializing events laughed a great deal and loudly, too, for all partook of copious quantities of wine and punch, and anything that might have seemed eccentric in Rosalie's manner was drowned in an unbuttoned hubbub that was not very prone to surprise. But how happy she was when, in Ken's presence, one of the women said to her: 'My dear, you truly are astonishing! How ravishing you look this evening! You outdo the twenty-year-olds. Tell all! What fountain of youth have you discovered?' And even happier when her beloved agreed: '*Right you are!* Frau von Tümmler is *perfectly delightful tonight*.' She laughed, and at the same time blushed deeply, which could be explained by her joy at the flattery she had received. She averted her eyes from him, yet thought about his arms, and yet again experienced that flooding of her inmost self, a sensation of drowning in infinite sweetness that had overtaken her so often recently, which the others, if they really did find her so young and attractive, must surely see with their own eyes.

It was on one such evening after the party guests had dispersed that she betrayed the resolution she had made to keep her heart's secret: that improper and distressing, yet entrancing miracle that, hidden deep within herself, had befallen her whole being and which she had not even revealed to Anna, her daughter and friend. An irresistible urge to confide compelled her to break the promise she had made to herself and open up to her clever daughter, not only because she yearned to receive loving, understanding compassion, but also out of a desire to appreciate and honour what Nature was bringing about in her as the remarkable human experience that it was.

The two ladies had returned home in a taxicab at around midnight through a fall of wet snow. Rosalie shivered. 'Let me stay up with you for half an hour in your cosy bedroom, dear child,' she said. 'I am freezing, but my head is glowing, and I fear there will be little point in my trying to get to sleep for a while. If you could make us some tea, it wouldn't be a bad way to end the evening, I think. That punch at the Rollwagens' hits one hard. Rollwagen brews it himself, but he isn't exactly a dab hand; he mixes this rather dubious orange schnapps with Mosel wine then tops it up with German Sekt. We're all going to have a proper headache tomorrow morning, a bad "*hang-over*". Well, you won't. You're sensible and don't drink much. But I get carried away chatting to people and not noticing when they keep on filling up my glass while I think it's just my first glass. Yes, make us some tea, that would be good. Tea is a stimulant, but it is also soothing, and a hot cup of tea, taken at the right moment, will protect you against a cold. The Rollwagens' place was overheated—at least it felt that way to me—and then that sleet outside. Perhaps spring is on its way? In fact, I thought I had a first whiff of it this afternoon at the Hofgarten. But your foolish mother always does that as soon as the shortest day is past and it starts getting lighter. A good idea, Anna, switching on the electric fire! The heating here is low at this hour. My darling child, you know just how to make it nice and comfy so we feel snug together during our little one-to-one before bedtime. You see, Anna, I have been wanting to talk to you for some time—and you are quite right to think you have never denied me the opportunity to do so. But there are things, dear child, which require particularly intimate circumstances in which to discuss or even mention them, a propitious moment to loosen the tongue…'

'What kind of things, Mama? I can't offer you milk. Would you like a few drops of lemon?'

'Things of the heart, my child, things of Nature—wonderful, mysterious, almighty Nature, which at times does strange things with us, contradictory, indeed incomprehensible things. You know about these things, too. Recently, dear Anna, I have often found myself—and please forgive me for touching on this—thinking of the affair you once had with Brünner, of the misery you complained to me of in an hour not unlike this one, and which, in your rancour against yourself, you even referred to as a humiliation, by which you meant the shameful conflict in which your reason, your power of judgement, was pitted against your heart, or if you prefer, against your senses.'

'You are quite right to correct yourself, Mama. "Heart" is sentimental humbug. We shouldn't say "heart" when we mean something entirely different. Our heart is truthful solely when it speaks with the approval of our judgement and reason.'

'You may well say that; you were always one for unity and always held that Nature herself establishes harmony between body and soul. But that you yourself at that time lived in a state of disharmony between your desires and your judgement—that you cannot deny. You were very young then, and your desire had no reason to be ashamed before Nature, only before your judgement, which called it demeaning. Your desire did not pass the test of your judgement, and that was your shame and your misery. For you are proud, Anna, very proud, and that there may be such a thing as a pride in feeling itself, a pride of feeling that denies the necessity of passing any test or being answerable to some other authority, whether it be judgement or reason or even Nature herself—that is something you won't accept, and in that we differ. Because for me the heart has the highest authority, and if Nature instils into it sensations that no longer befit it and which appear to create a contradiction between the heart and her—well, certainly that can be shameful and painful, but the shame is only for one's unworthiness and is actually a sweet wonderment, a reverence for Nature and for the life that it pleases her to engender in a being that is already decrepit.'

'First, my dear Mama,' answered Anna, 'allow me to decline the honour you bestow upon my pride and my reason. At that time, and if a merciful fate had not intervened, they would have been pitifully inferior to what you poetically call the heart, and when I consider where my own heart would have led me, I can only thank God that its desires were not fulfilled. I am the last who should cast a stone. But we are not talking about me, but of you, and I shall not decline the honour of your wishing to confide in me. For that is what you want to do, is it not? Your words suggest as much, though they are obscure in their generality. Please instruct me in how I should understand them and relate them to you!'

'What would you say, Anna, if your mother in her old age were to be smitten by intense feelings of the kind that only belong to vigorous youth, or only to maturity, and not to faded womanhood?'

'Why the conditional, Mama? Evidently, the feelings you are describing are your own. You're in love then?'

'The way you say that, my sweet child! How freely! How forthright and honest you are in speaking a word I could hardly dare to speak, a word I have kept locked away deep inside me for such a long time alongside everything it conveys of shameful bliss and anguish—I have concealed it from all the world, and have kept the secret from you, too, have kept it so closely that you will likely feel startlingly disabused—disabused of your belief in the dignified matronhood of your mother! For yes, I am in love, passionately so, with lust and bliss and wretchedness, just as you once loved in your youth. My feelings can withstand the scrutiny of reason as little as yours could, and although I feel proud of this blossoming of the soul with which Nature has so miraculously endowed me, I nonetheless suffer as you once did, and I've felt irresistibly driven to divulge all to you.'

'My dear, precious Mama! You really can tell me everything. And when the telling gets hard, my questions will help. Who is it?'

'It will certainly be a shattering surprise to you, my child. The young friend of our house. Your brother's tutor.'

'Ken Keaton?'

'Correct.'

'So it's him. Well, Mother, you needn't fear I'll burst out exclaiming "Unimaginable!", although that's what people will do. How cheap and stupid it is to chide a feeling as unimaginable because you can't imagine having it yourself. And yet much as I fear you may find it hurtful, please forgive my asking you this out of sympathy: you speak of being smitten by emotions you are not entitled to, accusing yourself of having feelings you are no longer worthy of. Have you ever asked yourself whether the young person in question is worthy of your feelings?'

'Ken, worthy? I barely understand what you mean. I am in love, Anna. He is the most splendid example of manhood I have ever clapped eyes on.'

'And that's why you love him. Perhaps we should try letting cause and effect swap places so we can see them in their correct order? Isn't it possible that he only appears so splendid to you because you… because you love him?'

'Oh, my child, you are separating things that are inseparable. Here in my heart my love and his splendour are one.'

'But you are suffering, dearest darling Mama, and I should so very much like to help you. Couldn't you try for a moment—only for a moment, because perhaps even that would be good for you—not to see him in the transfiguring light of your love, but by the light of day, as he truly is, as the nice, appealing—I agree with you there!—pleasing boy that he is, but who in himself isn't actually someone to be passionate about, to suffer over?'

'I know you mean well, Anna. I'm quite sure you want to help me. But that shouldn't happen at his expense, not by doing him wrong. And you are doing him wrong with your "light of day", which is such a false light, so utterly deceptive. You call him nice, say he is no more than pleasing, and what you are really saying is that he is just an average person with nothing special about him. But actually, he's a quite extraordinary human being and his life touches the heart. Think of his simple background, and how he worked his way through college by sheer strength of will, surpassing all his fellow students in history and athletics, how he hurried to respond to the call to arms and conducted himself so admirably as a soldier that he was "*honourably discharged*"…'

'I'm sorry, but all of them are, unless they have done something particularly dishonourable.'

'All of them. You keep on insinuating how average he is, and trying to dissuade me from him, not directly, but by implying he's a simpleton, just a naïve boy. But you forget that there can be something noble in simplicity, something that will triumph, and that the background of his simplicity is the great democratic spirit of his vast homeland...'

'But he doesn't like his homeland.'

'Which makes him a true son of his country, and moreover, it adds to his distinction and sets him apart from the majority of his countrymen that he loves Europe for its historical perspective and old folk customs. But he also gave his blood for his country. You say they are all "*honourably discharged*". But are they all awarded a medal for bravery, a "*Purple Heart*",* to show that the courage with which a soldier threw himself into battle with the enemy has earned him a wound, and possibly a severe wound?'

'Mama dear, in war, I think, one person gets it and the other doesn't; one soldier falls and another gets away, without it having had much to do with the bravery of either of them. If somebody's leg is blown off or their kidney gets shot, the medal is a consolation, a small compensation for his adversity, but in most cases it is probably not a badge of particular bravery.'

'At all events, he sacrificed one of his kidneys on the altar of his fatherland!'

'Yes, he did suffer that misfortune. And thank God one can get by, at a pinch, with one kidney. Although only at a pinch, and actually it's a flaw, a defect, and the thought of it diminishes the splendour of his youth somewhat, and looking at him in the light of day, as one should, his build, for all it looks good—or perhaps we should say normal—is nevertheless missing something, so that physically he's disabled, no longer a complete human being.'

'Good God! Ken no longer complete, Ken not a whole human being! But my poor child, it's his completeness that makes him so splendid, and he can easily go without a kidney—that isn't only his opinion but everyone thinks that, I mean all the woman who are after him, with whom he probably finds his pleasure! My dear, good, clever Anna, do you really not know my main reason for confiding in you and beginning this conversation? It's because I wanted to ask you, and I want your honest opinion, whether, after what you have seen yourself, you believe he is having an affair with Louise Pfingsten, or with Amélie Lützenkirchen, or possibly with both, for which I am sure he would be complete enough! These are the doubts that keep me tormented, and I have wanted so much for you to tell me the plain truth of these matters, because you are in a position to cast a cool eye on them, to see them in the light of day, as it were…'

'My poor Mama, how you torment yourself, how you suffer! It hurts me so much. But no, I don't think so—in fact I don't know much about his way of life and feel little call to research it—but I don't think so, and I have never heard say he has the sort of relationship with Frau Pfingsten or Frau Lützenkirchen you suspect. So please put your mind at ease on that account!'

'God grant, my dear child, that you are not saying such things merely to console me and, out of pity, to pour balm on my anguished soul! But look, pity—however much I might seek it from you—is not appropriate here at all, because I am blissfully happy in my torment and shame, and full of pride in this spring of pain in my soul, and so please bear that in mind, my girl, when I appear to beg for your pity!'

'I don't think you do beg. But in a case like this, surely the bliss and pride are closely entwined with the suffering, in fact are one and the same, and even if you were not to seek pity, it would nevertheless be due to you from those who loved you and who wished you could take pity on yourself and try to free yourself from this absurd spell you are under… Forgive my words! I am sure they are wrong, but I can't be concerned with words. It's for you, my dearest, that I am concerned, and not only since today, not only since your confession, for which I am grateful to you. You have kept your secret locked away inside you with great self-restraint, but the fact of the secret itself, and that you have been going through something peculiar and strange for months, cannot possibly have remained hidden from those who love you, and they have seen it with mixed feelings.'

'Whom do you mean with "they"?'

'I'm talking about me. You have changed quite noticeably of late, Mama… Well, not changed exactly, for of course you are still the same person, and so when I say "changed", what I mean is that a kind of rejuvenation has come over your whole being—but no, that isn't the right word for it either, for of course it can't actually be a real and demonstrable rejuvenation of your sweet person. But now and then, for a moment or two, to my eyes at least, in a certain phantasmagorical manner, it was as if the Mama of twenty years ago, as I knew her when I was a girl, had suddenly stepped out of your dear and matronly figure—and more than that: all at once I thought I was seeing you as I had never seen you, that is, as you must have looked when you yourself were a very young girl. And this trick of the senses, if it was a mere trick of the senses, for there was something real about it, ought to have made me happy—it should have made my heart leap for joy, shouldn't it? But it didn't, and instead it gave me a heavy heart, and it was precisely when you became suddenly younger in front of my eyes that I had this terrible feeling of pity for you. Because at the same time I could see that you were suffering, and that the phantasmagoria I spoke of was not just related to your suffering, but was the very expression of it, its outward appearance, a "spring of pain", as you put it. My dear Mama, however did you arrive at such an expression? It isn't at all like you. You have a simple disposition, and are so lovable; you only have eyes for Nature and worldly things, not for books, and you have never been much of a reader. You have never needed to use words in the way poets do, such heartsore, morbid words, and if you do so now, it has something—'

'Something what, Anna? When poets use such words, it's because they do need them, because emotions and experience drag those words out of them, and that is probably how it is with me, too, in whom you find them so incongruous. That's not right. Such words belong to whomever has need of them, someone who will be unabashed to use them because they are dragged out of him. But as for your trick of the senses, your phantasmagoria, or whatever it was that you thought you saw in me, let me explain it to you. That was the effect of *his* youth. It was my soul wrestling to keep pace with his youth, so that shame and disgrace wouldn't wither me in the face of it.'

Anna wept. They held each other close and their tears mingled.

'And that too,' said the lame young woman, struggling to speak, 'what you've just said, dear heart, is related to that strange expression you used earlier, and there is something equally devastating about it on your lips. This deplorable frame of mind is destroying you; I can see it with my own eyes, and I hear it in what you say. We have to stop it, put an end to it, rescue you from it, no matter what the cost. Out of sight, out of mind. It all depends on resolve, on a saving decision. The young man cannot be allowed to come here any more; we must give him his notice. Even that isn't enough, for you see him elsewhere in company, too. All right, we must see to it that he leaves town. I am confident I can make him do that. I shall have a friendly talk with him, show him how he is wasting his time and life hanging around here, that he has long exhausted Düsseldorf's possibilities and ought not to get stuck here forever, that Düsseldorf is not Germany, which he should be getting to know better and more of, with Munich, Hamburg and Berlin all still waiting to be explored, and that he should show some flexibility, staying in one place for a while and then the other, before fulfilling his natural duty and returning to his own country to take up a proper profession instead of playing the invalid language teacher in Europe. I'll give him something to think about all right. And if he declines and is set on staying in Düsseldorf, where, after all, he has his connections, well then, we ourselves shall leave. We shall give up our house here and move to Cologne or Frankfurt or a nice little place in the Taunus,* and you shall leave behind what was torturing you and going to destroy you and, with the help of "out of sight, out of mind", you will forget it. The important thing is to keep something out of sight, a remedy that never fails, for it simply isn't true that one cannot forget. Perhaps you will think it's a disgrace to forget, but one does—take my word for it! And you will enjoy your beloved Nature in the Taunus and be our dear old Mama again.'

Such were Anna's words, spoken with much urgency, and yet how much in vain!

'Stop, Anna, stop, no more of this—I can't listen to it! First you weep with me, and your concern is so affectionate, and then you say these things and make proposals that are impossible and terrible to my ears. Banish him? We, move away? Where has your care gone now? You speak of my beloved Nature, but strike her in the face with your insolent demands, and you want me to strike her in the face by stifling the spring of pain with which she has miraculously blessed my soul! What a sin that would be, what ingratitude too, what disloyalty towards her, towards Nature, and what denial of belief in her benevolent omnipotence! Do you remember Sarah, and how she sinned? She laughed behind the tent door and said: "After I am waxed old, shall I have pleasure, my lord being old also?" But the Lord God was annoyed and said: "Wherefore did Sarah laugh?" In my opinion she laughed less because she was old and withered than because Abraham, her lord, was such an old man, in fact ninety-nine. What woman would not laugh at the thought of "having pleasure" with a ninety-nine-year-old man, even if the love life of men is less strictly limited than that of women. But my own lord is young, very young, and how much easier and more enticing must the thought be to me that—— Oh, Anna, my darling child, I do have pleasure; I have shameful and grievous lust in my blood and in my desires, and I cannot give it up, cannot flee to the Taunus, and if you were to persuade Ken to go away from here—I think I would hate you until the day I die!'

It was with great anguish that Anna listened to these unbridled, besotted words.

'Dearest Mama,' she said in a strained voice, 'you are very upset. Quiet and sleep are what you need most now. Take twenty drops of valerian in water, or even twenty-five. It's a harmless remedy, but often quite helpful. And rest assured that I shall not take it into my own hands to do anything that would hurt your feelings. I hope this assurance will also help to set your mind at rest, which is what I want for you more than anything. If I have spoken disparagingly of Keaton, whom I respect as the object of your endearment, although I must also curse him as the cause of your suffering, then I hope you will understand that I was only trying to soothe you. I am eternally grateful for the trust you place in me and I hope, indeed I fully believe, that our conversation has put your heart at peace a little. Perhaps our talk was the prerequisite for your recovery—I mean, for soothing your heart. Your beloved, joyful heart that is so dear to all of us, will find its true place again. It suffers as it loves—don't you think that, one day perhaps, it might learn to love without suffering, in a more rational way? You see, love—' (while speaking, Anna carefully steered her mother into her bedroom, intending to pour the valerian drops into the glass herself) 'love takes so many forms; what different feelings the word covers, and yet in the end it is only that one thing! The love of a mother for her son, for instance—I know Eduard is not particularly close to you, but such love can be very profound, very passionate, subtly but decidedly different from love for a child of her own sex and yet never stray outside the bounds of motherly love. How would it be if you used the fact that Ken could be your son to turn the tenderness that you feel for him into something motherly and, for your own good, to settle that tenderness within the bounds of motherly love?'

Rosalie smiled through her tears.

'In order to establish a more appropriate harmony between body and soul. Is that it?' she mocked sadly. 'My dear child, how I exercise your intelligence, how I strain it and abuse it! It isn't right of me, because I am engaging it in vain. Motherliness—I suppose that is also something a bit like the Taunus... Am I making any sense? I am quite exhausted, you are right. Thank you, my darling, for your patience and sympathy. Thank you, too, for your respect for Ken because of what you call my endearment. And, at the same time, don't hate him, as I would have to hate you if you drove him away! He is Nature's means of performing her miracle in my soul.'

Anna left her. A week passed, in which Ken Keaton twice joined the Tümmlers for the evening meal. On the first occasion an elderly couple from Duisburg was present, relatives of Rosalie's, the woman being a cousin of hers. Anna was well aware that certain relationships and emotional tensions almost inevitably radiated an aura of abnormality that was especially conspicuous to anyone uninvolved, and so she scrutinized the guests closely. Once or twice she saw the cousin, a puzzled look on her face, glance back and forth between Keaton and their hostess, and once she even glimpsed a smile behind the man's moustache. During the evening she also noticed a change in Ken's behaviour towards her mother, a mischievous readjustment or adaptation of his reactions to her, and that he refused to accept her mother's pretence—difficult enough—of taking little notice of him, coercing her instead into turning her attention towards him. On the second occasion there was nobody else present. Frau von Tümmler therefore took it upon herself to stage a droll performance directed at her daughter and inspired by their recent conversation, lampooning certain pieces of advice Anna had offered her and turning the whole travesty to her own advantage. For it transpired that Ken had spent the previous night carousing with some companions, an art student and two sons of industrialists, and that he had traipsed from one 'Altbier'-pub to the next until the early hours, only to arrive at the Tümmlers with a throbbing head, a first-class *hangover*, as Eduard, who had divulged the unsurprising consequence, expressed it. Later, as they were saying goodnight to one another, Rosalie caught Anna's eye for a moment with an elated, mischievous look, continuing to hold her daughter's gaze as she pinched the young man's earlobe and said to him:

'And as for you, sonny, take heed of this strict telling-off from Mama Rosalie, and bear in mind that this house is open only to people with sound morals and not to night owls and beery defectives who are barely capable of speaking German or seeing straight! Do you understand, you good-for-nothing? Mend your ways! When the bad boys beckon, don't follow them, and from now on you must stop spoiling your health! Are you going to mend your ways, then, really mend your ways?' And through all this she kept pulling at his earlobe, while Ken gave way to her light tugs in an exaggerated manner, pretending the punishment was exceedingly painful, squirming and grimacing pitifully under her hand, revealing his nice shiny teeth in the process. His face was very close to hers, and addressing that close face she continued:

'Because if you do it again and don't mend your ways, you naughty boy, I shall banish you from this town, d'you hear me? I shall send you to a quiet little village in the Taunus where you'll find Nature to be very pretty but where there won't be any temptations, and then you can teach the farmers' children English. This time, I'll let you go and sleep off your hangover, you little villain!' And she let go his ear, took leave of the closeness of his face, gave Anna one more pale, mischievous look, and left.

A week later something extraordinary happened that astonished Anna von Tümmler to such an extent that she found it extremely affecting as well as confusing—confusing because, while she was happy for her mother, she was unsure whether to consider what had befallen her fortunate or unfortunate. At ten o'clock in the morning she received a message from the housemaid asking her to go to see Frau von Tümmler. Since the small family took their breakfast separately—first Eduard, then Anna, and the lady of the house last—Anna had not seen her mother that morning. She found Rosalie recumbent on the chaise longue in her bedroom under a light cashmere shawl, somewhat pale, but with her little red nose. Smiling in a rather affectedly languorous manner, she gave her daughter a nod as she came stumping into the room, but said nothing, so that Anna asked:

'What's wrong, Mama? You aren't ill, are you?'

'Oh no, my child, don't worry, it isn't an illness. I was tempted, instead of sending for you, to go and wish you good morning myself. But I am feeling rather needy, and it seems advisable to take it easy, as it does with us women from time to time.'

'Mama! How am I to understand you?'

Whereupon Rosalie sat up and threw her arms around her daughter's neck and, drawing her down beside her onto the edge of the chaise longue until they were cheek to cheek, whispered in her ear quickly, blissfully, in a single breath:

'A triumph, Anna, sheer triumph—it has come back, come back to me after such a long interruption, completely naturally and just as it should be for a mature and vital woman! My precious child, what a miracle! What a miracle great and benevolent Nature has performed in me and, in so doing, has blessed my faith! For I have believed, Anna, and did not laugh, and now beneficent Nature has rewarded me and taken back what she seemed to have done to my body, proving it to be an error and restoring harmony between soul and body, albeit not in the way favoured by you. Not with the soul willingly allowing the body to work on it and convey it to the dignified estate of matronhood, but vice versa, vice versa, my dear child, with the soul proving its mastery over the body. Congratulate me, my dearest, for I am very happy! I am a woman again, a whole human being, a capable female, and may once again feel worthy of the appeal of youthful manhood, and no longer need lower my eyes before it with a feeling of inadequacy. The rod of life with which it has smitten me has struck not only my soul but my body too, and has turned it back into a gushing well. Kiss me, my darling child, and call me blessed, as blessed as I am, and join me in praising the miraculous power of great and benevolent Nature!'

She sank back and closed her eyes, smiling and pleased with herself, her nose very red.

'Dear, sweet Mama,' said Anna, willing enough to celebrate with her mother, yet with an uneasy heart, 'that truly is a great and touching event and points to the splendour of your nature, which was already noticeable in the freshness of your feelings and which now has lent that freshness such power over the physical life of your body. So you see that I entirely share your opinion that what has happened to your body is the soul's doing, the product of your powerfully youthful emotion. Whatever I may have said of such things on various occasions, you mustn't think of me as being so philistine as to deny the mind any power over the body, and that I instead grant the latter the final say in relations between the two. That both are dependent on each other—that much I know about Nature and its unity. However much the mind may be subject to the conditions of the body, the way that it is able to bring the body into line often borders on the miraculous, and your own case is one of the most splendid examples of this. But allow me to say this nonetheless, that this lovely, cheering event of which you are so proud, and it is a fact that you are rightly proud of it, does not make as great an impression on me—made in the way that I am—as it does on you. I can't say I find it changes things much, my splendid Mama, or that it greatly increases my admiration for your nature—or for Nature in general. As an ageing spinster with a club foot, I probably have good reason not to lay great store by the physical. The freshness of your emotions, precisely because they contrast with the condition of your ageing body, seemed splendid enough, enough of a triumph—indeed almost seemed to me to be a purer victory of the soul than this turn of events in which the indestructability of your temperament has taken on an organic dimension.'

'It would be better to say no more, my poor child. What you call the freshness of my emotions, in which you claim you delighted, is what you have more or less bluntly made out to be a nonsense over which I was making a fool of myself, advising me instead to retire to matronly motherhood and give my feelings a more maternal focus. Well, for that it would really have been premature, don't you think so too now, my little Anna? Nature has spoken against it. She has made my feelings her concern and intimated quite unequivocally that my emotions need not be ashamed before her nor before the flower of youthful manhood that is their object. And you genuinely think that doesn't change much?'

'What I think, my wonderful, darling mother, is that I certainly did not disregard the utterance of Nature. And more especially, that it is not my intention to spoil the pleasure you feel at her decree. You won't believe this. When I said that what has happened didn't change much, I was referring to outward reality, to the practical side of things, so to speak. When I advised you, when I sincerely wished for your sake that you might do something that need not even be particularly troublesome for you, I mean settle your feelings for the young man—forgive me for speaking of him so coldly—I am of course speaking of our friend Keaton—within the bounds of motherly love, my hopes were pinned on the fact that he could easily be your son. That fact, I'm sure you will agree, has not changed and cannot fail to determine the relationship between you from both sides, from your side as well as his.'

'As well as his. You speak of both sides, but you only mean his. You don't think he could love me except, at best, as a son?'

'I wouldn't say that, my darling, dearest Mama.'

'How could you say it at all, Anna, my faithful child! Bear in mind that you do not have the right; you have no authority in matters of love. You have so little discrimination in this area because you gave up too early, my heart, and have given such concerns a wide berth. Intellectual pursuits offered you an alternative to

Nature, and that is good—and all the best to you, it's a fine thing. But what makes you think you can judge and condemn me to hopelessness? Your observation is restricted and you can't see what I see and don't perceive the signals that tell me his feelings are ready to respond to mine. Are you trying to say that he is merely toying with me at such moments? Would you rather see him as insolent and heartless than allow me the hope that his feelings may attune with mine? What would be so miraculous about that? For all your remoteness from the ways of love, it can hardly have escaped you that young men often prefer a mature woman to an inexperienced younger one of the silly gosling type. A longing for his mother may even play a role in that—just as, by the same token, maternal feelings may flow into the passion of an older woman for a young man. But why am I telling you this? I have a feeling you said something quite similar to me when we were talking recently.'

'Really? In any case you are right, Mama. I agree with you in everything you say.'

'Then you shouldn't say I am beyond all hope, especially not today, when Nature has endorsed my feelings. I won't allow it, despite my grey hair, which, it seems to me, you have been taking into account. Yes, unfortunately I am quite grey. It was a mistake that I did not begin dyeing my hair a while ago. I can't suddenly begin doing so now, even if Nature has authorized me to do so, so to speak. But I could do something for my face, not only through massage, but also by applying a little rouge. You children wouldn't take offence, would you?'

'Why should we, Mama! When you go about it at all discreetly, Eduard doesn't even notice. As for me… it's true I think artificiality of that kind doesn't go very well with your sense of Nature, but it is certainly no sin against Nature to offer it some commonplace assistance.'

'That's right, and we also have to prevent motherly affection playing a too important or, indeed, the predominant role in Ken's feelings. That would be against my hopes. Yes, my faithful, darling child, this heart—I know you don't like talking or hearing about the "heart"—but my heart is swollen with pride and gladness at the thought of how differently I can face his youth now, with what new self-confidence. Your mother's heart is swollen with hope of life and happiness!'

'How beautiful, dearest Mama! And how adorable of you to let me share in your delight! I do share it, share it from my heart, and you shall have no reason to doubt that, not even if I mention that a slight worry has entered that shared joy—that's just typical of me, isn't it?—a moment of apprehension, *practical* apprehension, to repeat the word I used earlier for want of a better one. You speak of your hope and of all that justifies your harbouring it—I think what justifies it is quite simply your amiable person. But you have not gone so far as to define this hope and to tell me what it aspires to, what, in real life, it has set its sights on. Do you intend to get married again? To make Ken Keaton our stepfather? To accompany him to the wedding altar? It may be cowardly of me, but as your age difference is equivalent to that between a mother and her son, I rather dread the consternation such a step would foment.'

Frau von Tümmler stared at her daughter.

'No,' she replied, 'the idea is new to me, and if it puts you at your ease, I may assure you that it is also strange to me. No, Anna, you silly thing, I do not intend to give you a twenty-four-year-old stepfather. How odd of you to speak so stiffly and piously of the "wedding altar".'

Anna said nothing, her eyes, with nodding eyelids, gazing past her mother into blankness.

'Hope,' said her mother, 'who can define it in the way you demand? Hope is hope, how can you expect it, as you do, to ask itself what its practical aim is? What Nature has made of me is so beautiful—I can only expect something beautiful will come of it, but I cannot tell you how I think that will come about, how it will be put into practice or where it will lead. That's hope for you. It doesn't think at all—least of all about wedding altars.'

Anna's lips were slightly pursed. Between them she uttered a few quiet words, as if involuntarily and reluctantly:

'That would be a relatively sensible thought.'

In dismay, Frau von Tümmler contemplated the disabled young woman—who was not looking back at her—and tried to read her face.

'Anna!' she cried out softly. 'What are you thinking, and what behaviour is this? I have to confess that I really don't recognize you at all! Tell me, which of us is the artist, I or you? I'd never have thought that you could have dropped so far behind your mother in broad-mindedness—and not only behind her, but behind our times and their more lenient manners! In your art you are so progressive and up to date, so that a simple-minded person like myself can barely follow you. But in morals you seem to be living God knows when, in the year dot, before the war. After all, these days we're citizens of a republic, we have freedom, our standards have changed considerably and have become more casual, more relaxed—you can see that everywhere, in small things too. Take young men these days, for instance—they think it's stylish to let their handkerchief, which you used only to see a corner of protruding from the breast pocket, hang down—they let half the handkerchief hang down like a flag, and you can see it's quite clearly a sign, or actually a deliberate declaration of republican permissiveness. Eduard, too, follows this fashion of letting his handkerchief hang down, and it gives me a certain pleasure to see it.'

'You're a keen observer. Mama. But in Eduard's case, I wouldn't take your handkerchief symbol too personally. You often say yourself that the young man—and that is what he almost is now—takes very much after our father, the Lieutenant Colonel. Perhaps it isn't very tactful of me to bring Papa into our conversation and our thoughts just now. And yet—'

'Anna, your father was a first-rate officer who fell on the field of honour, but he was also a happy-go-lucky sort and a Don Juan right to the end, indeed the best example of those indeterminate boundaries that govern a man's sexual life, and I constantly had to keep both eyes closed on his account. For that reason I do not consider it particularly tactless of you to bring him up.'

'All the better, Mama, if I may say so. But Papa was a nobleman and an officer and lived, for all his happy-go-luckiness, as you put it, within a certain code of honour that means very little to me, but some of which, I believe, Eduard has inherited. It is not only outwardly, in face and figure, that he resembles his father. Under certain circumstances I believe he would react involuntarily, like his father.'

'What kind of circumstances are you thinking of?'

'Dear Mama, let me be quite open, as we always have been with each other! It is certainly conceivable that a relationship of the kind you envisage with Ken Keaton might remain entirely secret and unknown to society. However, given your delightful impulsiveness and your endearing inability to play-act and disguise your heart's desires, I have my doubts whether that would really work. Some cheeky rascal only has to taunt our Eduard with facetious insinuations to the effect that his mother is—what's that expression again?—living a loose lifestyle, and he would hit him, he'd box the fellow's ears, and who knows what kind of unlawful and dangerously foolish misconduct might result from his gallant heroism.'

'For goodness' sake, Anna, the things you think up! You frighten me! I know you are doing so out of care, but it's cruel, this care of yours, as cruel as any child could be in judging her mother...'

Rosalie wept a little. Anna helped dry her tears, tenderly guiding the hand in which she held her handkerchief.

'Dearest, finest Mama, forgive me! How I hate to hurt you! But please—don't talk of a child's judgements! Do you think I don't look—no, not with tolerance, that sounds condescending—but with due deference and tender concern upon what you now deem to be your happiness? And Eduard—I barely know why I thought of him—only because of his republican handkerchief. This is not about ourselves, nor even about people in general. We are talking about you, Mama. Look, you called yourself broad-minded. But are you really? We spoke of Papa and of certain old-fashioned precepts by which he lived and which, to his way of thinking, were not violated by the philandering with which he hurt your feelings. That you forgave him again and again was because—you must understand this—in principle you agreed with him, sharing a way of thinking in which his behaviour had nothing licentious about it. He was not born for libertinage, and it was not part of his thinking. It's not part of yours either—if it's part of anyone's, then mine, because as an artist I'm different from the rest of you, although in a different sense I am unfit to take advantage of my emancipation and déclassé status.'

'My poor child,' Frau von Tümmler interrupted, 'don't speak so sadly of yourself!'

'As if I ever spoke about myself,' Anna retorted. 'I am talking about you, about you—it's you I care about so dearly. What for Papa, the rake, was merely dashing, contradicting neither his own principles nor those of society, could only be licentious in your own case. Harmony between body and soul is undoubtedly a fine and indispensable thing, and you are proud and happy because Nature, your own Nature, has almost miraculously endowed you with it. But harmony between one's way of life and innate moral convictions is ultimately even more essential, and where that harmony is torn asunder, the sole outcome can be mental and emotional turmoil, and that means unhappiness. Can't you feel that this is true? That you would be living in conflict with yourself if you were to turn your dreams into reality?

In the end you, too, are tied to certain precepts, just as Papa was, and the destruction of that bond would be tantamount to destroying your own self… I am telling you what—with trepidation—I feel. Why did that word come to my lips again—destruction? I know I uttered it once before, in fear, and that I have felt it more than once. Why do I always get the feeling that this entire visitation, of which you are the delighted victim, has something to do with destruction? I want to confess something to you. Recently, a few weeks ago when we had our little chat and drank tea late at night in my room and you became so agitated, I was tempted to go to Dr Oberloskamp, who treated Eduard when he had jaundice, and me too once, when I had an inflamed throat and couldn't swallow—you never have to go to the doctor—anyway, I was tempted to speak to him about you and about everything you confided to me, simply, and for your sake, to obtain some reassurance from him. But I stopped short of doing so, I stopped myself very soon, out of pride, Mama, which I'm sure you can understand, because I felt proud of you and also for you, and because it seemed degrading to turn your experience over to one of these medicine men who may, with God's help, have the wherewithal for jaundice or a sore throat, but hardly for deeper forms of human distress. In my opinion there are sicknesses that are too good for the doctor.'

'I am grateful to you for both, my dear child,' said Rosalie, 'for the care that prompted you to speak of me to Dr Oberloskamp, and for rejecting that impulse. For how do you propose to draw even the loosest of connections between what you call my visitation—this Easter of my womanhood and what my soul has done with my body—and the concept of illness? Is happiness—illness? It isn't light-headedness either, but only life, life in ecstasy and grief, and life is hope—the kind of hope for which I cannot offer any explanation that might satisfy your reason.'

'I do not ask for any, dearest Mama.'

'Go then, my child. Let me rest. As you know, a little peaceful retirement is advisable for us women on such consummate days.'

Anna kissed her mother and stumped out of the bedroom. Both women, once alone, continued to dwell on the conversation they had held. Anna had not declared, nor was she able to declare, everything she felt in her heart. How long, she asked herself, beset by doubts, would this touching resurrection her mother had vaunted as her

'Easter of womanhood' actually last? And Ken, when, as was highly likely, he yielded to her wooing, how long would that last, and her mother, come late to love, wouldn't every younger woman fill her with trepidation and—from the very first day—would she not tremble at the thought of losing his fidelity, or even his respect? It was fortunate, at least, that her mother did not think of happiness as joy and pleasure, but as life with its sorrows. For Anna anxiously foresaw that the dreams her mother harboured would be fraught with sorrow.

Frau Rosalie, for her part, was more deeply affected by her daughter's reproaches than she let on. Not so much by the thought that Eduard, under certain circumstances, might have to risk his young life for her honour—a romantic notion which, though she had wept over it, was more inclined to make her heart beat faster. But Anna's doubts concerning her mother's broad-mindedness, and what she had said about licentiousness and the essential harmony between life and moral convictions, these things were uppermost in the good soul's thoughts throughout her day of rest, and she could not help but admit that her daughter's doubts were justified and that her views contained a fair element of truth. It was equally true that she was unable to suppress her profoundest joy at the thought of seeing her young love again under these new circumstances. And yet she continued to brood over what her clever daughter had said about 'living in conflict' with oneself, and her soul laboured over the question of whether she might incorporate the idea of renunciation into that of happiness. For could not renunciation itself bring happiness if it did not involve some miserable obligation but be practised in freedom and in conscious equality? Rosalie concluded that it could.

Three days after Rosalie's great physiological consolation, Ken reappeared at the Tümmlers, read and spoke English with Eduard and stayed to dinner. Her delight in seeing his nice, boyish face, lovely teeth, broad shoulders and narrow hips, shone from her endearing eyes, whose spirited radiance justified, one might say, the heightening of her cheeks with a little rouge, for without it the pallor of her face would surely have proved inconsistent with her eyes' joyous fire. She had a certain way, on this occasion and on every occasion following, of greeting Keaton when he came for his weekly visits by taking his hand and pulling him close to her, whereupon she would look into his eyes with such an earnest, vibrant, momentous gaze that Anna had the impression that she intensely desired to inform the young man of the experience her nature had granted her—and that she was indeed on the point of acting on that desire. An absurd apprehension! Of course that didn't happen, and for the rest of the evening the attitude of the lady of the house towards her young guest was happily characterized by a serene and steadfast amicability that eschewed both the motherly play-acting with which she had once teased her daughter, and all the bashfulness and diffidence, the distressing humility, that had intermittently distorted her behaviour.

Keaton, who had been pleasingly aware for some time that he, such as he was, had made a conquest of this grey-haired but attractive European woman, could not make much sense of her change in character. His respect for her, understandably, had dwindled with the awareness of her weakness, which had nevertheless excited his manhood; his unpretentious character felt sympathetically attracted to her own and he considered that those marvellous, youthful-looking eyes probably made up for her fifty years and ageing hands. The idea of beginning an affair with her, such as he had sustained for a while—not actually with Amélie Lützenkirchen or Louise Pfingsten, but with a different woman in the same set, somebody Rosalie had not even thought of—was not unfamiliar to him and, as Anna had already observed, he had begun, at least now and then, to speak in a tone that was teasingly flirtatious when conversing with his pupil's mother.

But this, as the young fellow discovered, no longer seemed to have the desired effect. Despite the handshake at the beginning of their every meeting when she pulled him so close that their bodies almost touched, and despite her intimate, penetrating gaze into his eyes, his experimental attempts met with a friendly but resolute dignity that put him in his place and allowed no development of what he wanted to develop, reducing him to disillusioned and servile subordination. He struggled in vain to make sense of this repeated experience. 'Is she in love with me or not?' he wondered, and attributed her rebuffs and rebukes to the presence of her children, the disabled girl and the sixth-former. But he fared no better when he happened to be alone with her for a while in the corner of a drawing room, and nor was there any improvement when he altered the nature of his little advances, discarding his playfully teasing manner and giving them a more serious, urgent and, as it were, passionate character. On one occasion he tried deploying his unrolled, palatal 'r', which they all liked to hear, to call her 'Rosalie' in a more ardent tone, and at least as far as the actual form of his address was concerned, this did not to his American ears sound particularly daring. But although, for a moment, she had blushed bright red, she almost immediately got up and left, and for the rest of the evening deigned neither to look at him nor speak to him.

The winter, which had proved less harsh that year, with little frost or snow but bringing all the more rain instead, had also ended early. There were days in February when it was sunny and warm and the air was as fresh as spring. Tiny leaf-buds dared to come out here and there in the bushes. Rosalie, who had lovingly greeted the snowdrops in her garden, could take pleasure earlier than usual, almost prematurely, in the daffodils, and very soon afterwards in the short-stalked crocuses, which sprouted in the front gardens of the villas everywhere as well as in the Hofgarten, and in sight of which passers-by, stopping and pointing them out to one another, revelled in their multicoloured abundance.

'Isn't it odd', said Frau von Tümmler to her daughter, 'how they resemble the meadow saffron? It's virtually the same flower! The end and the beginning—they are so alike that mistaking the one for the other, one might think oneself back in the autumn at the sight of the crocus, or imagine oneself in spring when one sees those flowers that flower last of all.'

'Yes, a slight moment of confusion. Your old friend Mother Nature has an altogether entrancing predilection for ambiguity and mystification.'

'You are so quick to speak against her with your sharp tongue, you naughty child, and where I express my wonder, you offer mockery. Just leave my beloved Nature be, because you won't get rid of my tender feelings for her with your jibing, especially not now when she is summoning up my season—I call it mine because, of course, the season in which we are born has a special kind of relationship with us, and we with it. You are a child of Advent, so you can genuinely say you arrived under a lucky star—almost under that of dear Christmas itself. You probably feel a particular affinity between yourself and that season, which may be cold, yet in our thoughts is a period of warmth and joy. For in my experience we really do have sympathetic relations with the season that gives birth to us. Its return gives us the reassurance and encouragement we need in life, a sense of renewal, of the kind I feel in spring—not just because it is spring, or the vernal season, as poets have called it, a season everyone loves, but because I actually belong to it myself, and feel it smiling upon me personally.'

'I'm sure it does, dearest Mama,' answered Winter's child. 'And rest assured that I shall not say a sharp word against it!'

It should nevertheless be said that the vital uplift that Rosalie was accustomed—or believed she was accustomed—to receive from the approach and burgeoning of 'her' season, even as she spoke of it, was not exactly manifesting itself in practice. It was almost as if the moral resolve that her discussion with her daughter had quickened in her, and to which she had cleaved so faithfully, went against her nature, as if even with that resolve, or indeed because of it, she were 'living in conflict' with herself. This was certainly the impression Anna gained, and the disabled girl blamed herself for talking her mother into an abstinence which her own liberal world-view did not support, but which to her had seemed expedient in the interests of the dear woman's peace of mind. Furthermore, she suspected herself of unacknowledged base motives. She asked herself whether she, who once had so mournfully craved sensual pleasure but never known it, had not surreptitiously begrudged it to her mother, and to that end had pressured her into self-restraint with all sorts of fabricated arguments. No, she could not believe she would do such a thing, and yet what she saw distressed her and weighed upon her conscience.

She saw that Rosalie quickly tired during the walks she so loved, and that at times, under the pretext of attending to some domestic task, she would insist on returning home after half an hour, or even earlier. She often rested, and yet despite taking less exercise, lost weight, so that Anna observed the thinness of her mother's forearms with concern when they protruded from her sleeve. Nobody lately would have asked her what fountain of youth she had drunk from. There were unappealing, tired-looking bluish rings under her eyes, and the rouge she had applied to her cheeks to please the young man and honour the recovery of her full womanhood proved a thin disguise for the sallow pallor of her complexion. But because she replied to enquiries as to her state of health with a cheerfully dismissive 'What do you mean—I feel fine!', Fräulein von Tümmler discarded the idea of asking Dr Oberloskamp to concern himself with her mother's worsening health. It was not only feelings of guilt that contributed to this reluctance, but piety too, the same piety that had gone into her remark that 'some illnesses were too good for the doctor'.

It was for these reasons that Anna was made all the happier by the enterprising spirit and confidence in her powers that Rosalie displayed when, gathered together one evening over a glass of wine, she and her children and Ken Keaton, who happened to be present, came up with a little plan. Not a month had yet passed since Anna had been called to her mother's bedroom to hear her wondrous announcement. Rosalie that evening was as charming and vivacious as in the old days, and she had every right to be considered the instigator of the excursion they agreed upon—unless one wanted to give Keaton the credit for it, since it was his historical chit-chat that had led to the idea in the first place. He had been talking of all kinds of palaces and castles he had visited in the Bergisches Land, of the Burg Castle on the Wupper, of Bensberg, Ehreshoven, Gimhorn, Homburg and Krottorf, and from there had gone on to mention the Prince Elector Carl Theodor,* who had moved his court away from Düsseldorf in the eighteenth century, first to Schwetzingen, then to Munich—which did not prevent his Stadtholder, a certain Count Grottstein,* from initiating all manner of important gardens and architectural projects. It was under his patronage that the Electoral Academy was founded, that the Hofgarten was laid out and Castle Jägerhof was built—and, added Eduard, also during those years, as far as he knew, the slightly more remote Holterhof Palace* to the south of the city near the village of the same name. Yes, of course, the Holterhof Palace too, Keaton confirmed, although he was forced to admit that, to his own astonishment, he had never set eyes on this late rococo construction, nor, despite its being so famous, had he ever visited its park, which stretched down to the Rhine. Frau von Tümmler and Anna had gone for a walk there once or twice, but had never found the time to visit the interior of the delightfully situated palace, and nor for that matter had Eduard.

'*Wat et nit all jibt!*'* said the lady of the house, with joking disapproval. It was always a sign of light-heartedness and contentment when she spoke in dialect. She added that they were 'fine Düsseldorfers!', all four of them—for one of them had never been there at all, while the three others had never explored the rooms within this jewel of a palace, through which every tourist makes sure of a guided tour. 'Children,' she cried, 'it can't go on like this! We must put an end to it. So off to Holterhof we go, all four of us! We shall have an excursion within the next few days. The weather is so fine now, the season so delightful and the barometer says "Fair". The flowers will be coming out in the park, and in its spring apparel it will probably be pleasanter that it was in the sultry summer heat when Anna and I went walking there. Suddenly, I feel a positive longing for those black swans with their red beaks and webbed feet—you will remember them, Anna, the ones we saw gliding along in their haughty melancholy on the park moat. The way they disguised their appetite behind a façade of condescension as we fed them! We shall take some white bread along for them… Wait now, today is Friday—let's go on Sunday, agreed? It's the only day Eduard can go, and Mr Keaton, too, I think. There will be a lot of people around on Sunday, but that doesn't bother me; I like mixing with people in their Sunday best and enjoy revelling with the revellers. I'm happiest when I'm where the fun is—at the fairs out by Oberkassel, where it smells of fritters and the children are sucking on their sticks of rock and you see those fantastically coarse characters shouting and hooting and ringing bells in front of the circus booths. I think it's marvellous. Anna takes a different view. She finds it sad. Yes, Anna, you do, and you prefer the genteel sadness of the pair of black swans on the moat… That gives me an idea, children: let's go there by water! Travelling by land on the tram is boring anyway. Not a bit of forest and hardly any open country. It's more amusing on the water; Father Rhine shall bear us. Eduard, would you mind looking for the timetable of the steamship company? Or, one moment… if we feel like a little luxury, we could give ourselves a treat and hire a private motorboat to take us up the Rhine. Then we'll be entre nous, just like the black swans… The only question is whether we should set sail in the morning or afternoon.'

They were in favour of the morning. As far as Eduard knew, the palace was anyway open to visitors only for a few hours into the afternoon. On Sunday morning then. Under Rosalie's energetic prompting, they quickly made firm arrangements. Keaton was charged with chartering the motorboat. They were to meet at their point of departure, the Town Hall Quay, on the day after tomorrow at nine o'clock.

And that is exactly what they did. It was a sunny morning with something of a breeze. On the quay a jostling crowd with children and bicycles accumulated, waiting to board one of the white ferries of the Cologne–Düsseldorf Shipping Line. The chartered motorboat lay alongside the quay, ready for the Tümmlers and their companion. Its skipper, a man with rings in his earlobes, a shaved upper lip and a reddish sailor's beard under his chin, helped the ladies aboard. Barely had the passengers taken their seats on a curved bench under a canopy held up by poles when they set off. The vessel made good time against the current of the broad river, whose banks, incidentally, were fairly uninteresting. They soon left the old castle tower, the crooked spire of St Lambertus' Church and the town's harbour installations behind them. More of the same kind of thing appeared around the next bend in the river—warehouses, factory buildings. Little by little the countryside emerged behind the groynes that protruded from the riverbank. Rural communities, old fishing villages, whose names Eduard knew, as did Keaton, lay sheltered in the lee of the dykes before a flat landscape of meadows, fields, willow bushes and ponds. And so it would continue for about an hour and a half, however many windings the river made, all the way to their destination. But how right they had been to take a boat, cried Rosalie, instead of taking those frightful roads through the suburbs, even if that would have meant covering the distance in a fraction of the time. She seemed to be wholeheartedly enjoying the elemental attractions of the journey by water. With her eyes closed, she softly intoned some happy song into the wind, which at times grew almost stormy: 'O water-wind, I love you—do you love me too, you water-wind?' Her face, thinner now, looked sweet under her little felt hat with its feather, and the light, woollen, grey-red checked coat with a turn-down collar suited her very well. Anna and Eduard had also equipped themselves with coats for the journey, whereas Keaton, who sat between mother and daughter, made do with a grey wool sweater under his felt jacket. His handkerchief hung down from his breast pocket, and twisting round suddenly with her eyes wide open, Rosalie stuffed it deep into his pocket.

'Let's have some modesty, young man,' she said, reprimanding him with an imperious shake of her head.

'*Thank you*,' he smiled, and asked what the *song* was that they had just heard her singing.

'Song?' she asked, 'have I been singing then? That was only a sing-song, not a *song*.' And again, she closed her eyes and began to hum, her lips barely moving: 'You water-wind, how I love you!'

And soon she started chatting away through the noise of the motor and—while frequently forced to hang on to her hat which the wind threatened to tear from her still bountiful, wavy grey hair—holding forth on how it would be possible to continue their Rhine journey beyond Holterhof to Leverkusen and Cologne, and then on via Bonn to Godesberg and Bad Honnef at the foot of the Siebengebirge. It was pretty there, a spruce little spa town among vineyards and orchards by the Rhine, and it had an alkaline mineral spring that was very good for rheumatism. Anna looked at her. She knew that her mother now sometimes suffered from lower back pain and had occasionally proposed taking Anna with her to Godesberg or Honnef in the early summer to take the waters. Her somewhat short-winded chattering into the wind about the beneficial properties of the mineral spring had something involuntary about it, causing Anna to speculate that her mother, even now, was not free of the aching complaint.

After an hour had passed they breakfasted on ham rolls and port wine, which they drank from small travelling cups. It was half past ten when the boat docked at a flimsy landing stage, which, unsuitable for larger vessels, had been built into the river very close to the palace and its park. Rosalie paid the boatman, for they had decided for convenience's sake that they would travel back by land on the tram. The park did not extend quite as far as the river. They had to follow a footpath across a dew-soaked meadow before seigneurial Nature—well-tended, trimmed and pruned—condescended to receive them. From a raised circular flower-bed with benches set in yew-hedge alcoves, avenues of magnificent trees, almost all of them budding, though many with shoots that were still cloaked in shiny brown protective scales, led away in several directions along finely gravelled walks—often with overarching branches—between rows, and sometimes even fourfold rows, of beeches, yews, lindens, horse chestnuts and tall elms. Rarer trees, brought here from afar, were also to be seen—single trees on open patches of meadow, strange conifers, fern-leaved beeches, while Keaton recognized the Californian giant sequoia and the swamp cypress with their smooth, aerating roots.

Rosalie took no interest in these sights. Nature, she opined, had to be familiar or it could not speak to the soul, but the splendour of the park seemed not at all to appeal to her sense of Nature. With barely an upward glance now and then at the proud tree-trunks, she walked along in silence at Eduard's side behind his young language teacher and stumping Anna, who, however, thought up a ploy to alter this arrangement. She stopped in her tracks and called her brother over to help identify the name of the tree-lined pathway they were on, as well as that of the winding footpath that crossed it. For all these paths had established names, such as 'Avenue of Fans' and 'Trumpet Avenue' and so on. When they resumed their walk, Anna made Eduard proceed beside her, and left Ken behind with Rosalie. He carried her coat, which she had taken off because it was much warmer in the windless park than it had been on the water. The mild spring sun shone down between the high branches, dappling the paths and playing on their faces, making them squint their eyes.

In her prettily tailored brown skirt suit that closely embraced her slim, youthful figure, Frau von Tümmler walked beside Ken, occasionally casting a veiled smile at her coat hanging over his arm. 'There they are!' she cried as they strolled along a moat that was lined with silver poplars, and what she meant was the pair of black swans gliding at a measured pace towards the approaching visitors through the somewhat miry water. 'How beautiful they are! Anna, do you recognize them? How majestically they carry their necks! Where is their bread?' Keaton pulled it, wrapped in newspaper, out of his pocket and handed it to her. It held the warmth of his body, and she broke the bread and ate of it.

'*But it is old and hard!*' he exclaimed reaching out, but he was too late to stop her.

'I have good teeth,' she replied.

But one of the swans pushed right into the riverbank, spreading its dark wings and beating them in the air, stretching its neck up and hissing at them angrily. They laughed at its jealousy, but at the same time were rather shocked. The birds then received their due. Rosalie threw them the stale bread, chunk by chunk, and swimming back and forth without indecorous haste, they accepted them with good grace.

'Nevertheless,' Anna said as they moved on, 'I fear that angry bird will not easily forgive your robbing him of his food. He was continually reminding us that he had taken umbrage.'

'Not in the least,' Rosalie replied. 'It was just that he was momentarily afraid I would eat all his food. He must have enjoyed it all the more after seeing me enjoy it.'

They arrived at the palace and the shiny round pond in which it was mirrored and at one side of which was a small island with a single poplar. On the gravelled forecourt in front of the flight of stairs leading up to the delicately curving winged structure of the building, whose considerable dimensions seemed to dissolve in the daintiness of its aspect and whose pink façade was certainly crumbling, stood several people who, while waiting for the eleven o'clock guided tour, were passing the time by comparing the figures on the armorial pediment, and above it the time-forgotten clock supported by an angel, as well as the stone garlands above the tall white doors, with the information in their guidebooks. Our friends joined them and, like them, gazed at the charmingly decorated feudal architecture and up to the oval oeil-de-boeuf windows in the slate-coloured top floor. Figures, Pan and his nymphs, clad with mythological scantiness, stood on pedestals to the side of the tall windows, weathered, as were the four sandstone lions, which, with sullen mien and paws crossed, flanked the stairway and front.

Keaton was evidently thrilled by so much history. He found everything '*splendid*' and '*excitingly continental*'. And it was '*Oh dear*' as soon as he thought of his prosaic country across the big pond! There was no such crumbling aristocratic grace over there because there had been no electoral princes or landgraves who, in their sovereignty and to the honour both of themselves and culture, could indulge their lust for grandeur. At the same time he was brazen enough towards this culture that stood on its timeless dignity to seat himself, to the amusement of the waiting visitors, astride the hindquarters of one of the guardian lions, despite its being furnished with a sharp spike, rather like those toy horses from which the rider can be detached. He took hold of the spike in front of him with two hands and—shouting '*Hi!*' and '*On, old chap!*'—pretended to clap spurs to the beast, and could not have displayed a more pleasant picture of youthful high spirits. Anna and Eduard avoided looking at their mother.

Then bolts rattled, and Keaton hastened to get down from his mount, for the castellan, a man with an empty, rolled-up left sleeve and military trousers, to all appearances, then, a war-disabled petty officer who had been compensated with this quiet post, had opened the door of the central portal to allow entry. The man positioned himself in the tall doorway and waved the visitors through while distributing admittance tickets to each person from a small block and, in so doing, managing to tear each ticket halfway through with his single hand. While this was going on, he also began to talk, his hoarse, croaky voice speaking from a crooked mouth, reciting information he had learned off by heart and already repeated a hundred times: that the sculptural embellishments of the façade were by an artist whom the Elector had specially summoned from Rome, that the palace and park were the work of a French architect, that what they saw was the most important Rococo building on the Rhine, although it also exemplified a transitional shift to Louis XVI style, and furthermore, that the palace had fifty-five rooms and had cost eight hundred thousand taler to build, and so on and so forth.

The vestibule exuded frosty mustiness. Upon entering, the visitors, amid much giggling from the ladies, were required to step into the large felt slippers that awaited them like a row of boats. The purpose of these was to protect the precious parquets, which were almost the main attraction of these chambers that had once been given over to pleasure and through which the visitors, shuffling clumsily or sometimes gliding, were now asked to follow the one-armed guide as he rattled off his lecture. Offering different patterns from one room to the next, the intarsias at the centre of the floors displayed various kinds of stars and floral fantasies. The shiny surface of the parquet, like untroubled water, picked up the shadows of the visitors and curved flamboyant furniture, while between the gilded columns entwined with garlands and the tapestries of flowery silk framed in golden borders, tall mirrors constantly reflected in one another the images of crystal chandeliers, amatory ceiling paintings, the medallions and emblems of hunting and music above the door, and, despite their numerous blind spots, succeeded in conveying the illusion of an endless suite of rooms. Unfettered luxuriance, the absolute will to pleasure, these were what the swirls of ornate preciosity and gilded scrollwork spoke of, held as they were, indeed bound, solely by the unswerving taste and style of the period that had bodied them forth. In the round banquet hall, around which Apollo and the Muses stood in niches, the inlaid woodwork of the flooring yielded to marble, as did the wall panels. Rosy putti drew back a painted drapery from an aperture, letting daylight stream down from the cupola from whose gallery, as the palace custodian parroted, music had once tinkled down to the banqueters below.

Ken Keaton led Frau von Tümmler by the elbow. It is the manner in which every American gentleman accompanies his lady across the road. Walking among strangers, separated from Anna and Eduard, they kept behind the caretaker, who hoarsely reeled off his text in wooden formal German, keeping the visitors informed of what they were seeing. He told them they were not seeing everything. Of the fifty-five rooms in the palace, he recited—and without leaving his prepared script for a moment he momentarily fell into a sort of awkwardly salacious tone, whereby his face with its crooked mouth in no way reflected the jocularity of his words—not all are open to view, at least not without a little help. The lords and ladies in those days had a great appreciation of pranks, secrets and mysteries, of hiding places behind the scenes, out-of-the-way closets with opportune openings accessible by means of mechanical tricks such as, for example, this one—and he stopped next to a wall mirror, which, in response to his pressing on a spring, slid aside and surprised the visitors with a view of a narrow spiral staircase with finely wrought openwork banister. At its foot, on a pedestal immediately to the left, stood the armless three-quarter torso of a man, who, a wreath of grapes in his hair and scantily attired in an inauthentic garland of leaves, with his upper body leaning back a little, priapic and welcoming, smiled down over his goat's beard into empty space. There were oohs and aahs. 'And so on and so forth,' said the guide, as he always did, and let the trick mirror slip back into place. 'Or like this one,' he said, walking a bit further and causing a panel of silk wallpaper, which had not been conspicuous before, to open as a secret door, disclosing a corridor that led into the unknown and emitted a musty odour. 'They liked that sort of thing,' said the one-armed caretaker. 'Other times, other manners,' he added with tedious sententiousness, and continued the tour.

It was not easy to keep the felt boats on one's feet. Frau von Tümmler lost one of hers and it slid a short distance away on the smooth floor, and while Keaton, laughing and retrieving it and, kneeling before her, put it back on her foot, they were overtaken by the sightseeing party. Again he put his hand under her elbow, but with a faraway smile she remained where she was, gazing after the others as they disappeared into further rooms, and, still supported by his hand, turned back and hastily felt for the place on the wallpaper where it had opened.

'*You aren't doing it right*,' he whispered. '*Leave it to me. 't was here.*' He found the spring, the door obeyed and the musty smell of the secret passage enveloped them as they took a few steps forward. They were surrounded by darkness. With a sigh that came from the very depths of her soul Rosalie threw her arms around the young man's neck, and he, too, blissfully embraced her trembling figure. 'Ken,

Ken,' she stammered, her face against his neck, 'I love you, I love you, and you know it, don't you, I haven't fully been able to hide it, and you, and you, do you love me too, only a little, tell me, can you love me with your youth, just as Nature has entrusted me, with my grey hair, to love you? Yes? Yes? Your mouth, oh at last your young mouth I've suffered for, your sweet lips, now, now—Can I kiss? Tell me, can I, my sweet awakener? I can do everything, like you, Ken, for love is strong, a miracle, it comes along and performs wonders. Kiss me, darling! I have hungered for your lips, oh, how I have suffered, for you must understand that my poor head resorted to all kinds of sophistry, like telling myself that broad-mindedness and libertinage are not for me, and that destruction threatens should I allow a contradiction between my way of life and innate moral convictions. Oh Ken, it was all that sophistry that almost killed me, and my hunger for you... And this is you, it's you at last, this is your hair, and this is your mouth, this breath comes from your nose, and your arms, these arms I know embracing me now, this is the warmth of your body I savoured, and the swan was angry...'

It would not have taken much for her to sink to the ground in his arms. He held her up and drew her further into the passage, and their eyes grew accustomed to its light. Ahead of them, steps led downward to the round arch of an open door, behind which murky light from above fell into an alcove whose tapestries featured lovemaking pairs of doves. A kind of causeuse* stood there, beside which a carved blindfolded Cupid was holding something that looked like a torch. There they sat down in the stale gloom.

'Ugh, a stench of death,' Rosalie shuddered, leaning on his shoulder. 'How sad, Ken, my darling, that we have been forced to find each other among the dead. In good Nature's bosom, fanned by its fragrance amid the sweet haze of jasmine and buckthorn, I dreamed it would be there, it should have been there I kissed you for the first time, and not in this sepulchre! Go away, leave that, you bad boy, I do want to be yours, but not among this decay. I shall come to you tomorrow, come to your room tomorrow morning, or who knows, this very evening. I'll arrange it, I'll outwit that know-it-all Anna...' He made her give him her word. By now they felt they ought to join the others again, either by going back or going on. Keaton decided they would go on. They took a different door and left the dead pleasure chamber behind them, finding themselves in a different dark passage where they turned corners and climbed stairs until they reached a rusty gate that vibrated as it gave way under Ken's hefty pushing and shaking, the outside of which was so densely entangled with leathery creepers and climbers that it was barely possible to get through. A heavenly breeze blew gently in their faces. The rush and rustle of water came to their ears, cascading down behind sprawling beds planted with early spring flowers, yellow narcissi. It was the back garden of the palace. The group of visitors was just approaching them from the right, without their guide and with Anna and Eduard bringing up the rear. The pair mingled with those at the front who were beginning to disperse towards the water features or in the direction of the park and trees. The way to deal with this was to stand there looking about them, then walk over to the brother and sister. 'Where on earth did you get to?' they heard, and replied: 'That's exactly what we wanted to ask you.' Then: 'How could we have lost sight of one another like that?' Anna and Eduard had even turned back to search for the strays, but in vain. 'After all, you couldn't simply have disappeared from the face of the earth,' said Anna. 'No more than you could,' replied Rosalie. None of them looked at each other.

Walking between rhododendron bushes they skirted around the wing of the palace and returned to the pond at the front, which was quite close to the tram stop. If the upstream boat journey along the winding Rhine had taken its time, the return journey on the noisy electric tram that sped past factories and workers' houses was accordingly expeditious. Brother and sister exchanged a few words now and then, or talked to their mother, whose hand Anna held for a while, having noticed she was trembling. Arriving back in town, they took leave of one another near the Königsallee.

Frau von Tümmler did not go to Ken Keaton. That night, towards morning, she was beset by a serious ailment that alarmed the household. What, at its first return, had made her so proud and happy, what she had celebrated as a miracle of Nature and sublime effect of feeling, had now ominously recurred. She had summoned the strength to ring, but on hurrying to her aid, her daughter and the maid had found her lying unconscious in her blood.

The physician, Dr Oberloskamp, arrived quickly. Coming to under the doctor's hands, she was ostensibly surprised at his presence.

'What, Doctor, you here?' she said. 'Has Anna troubled you to come? But it is only after the manner of women with me.'

'On occasion, my dear Frau von Tümmler, these functions require a degree of surveillance,' replied the grey-headed doctor. Speaking to the daughter he resolutely explained that it was necessary to admit the patient, preferably by ambulance, to the gynaecological clinic. The case demanded rigorous medical investigation—which might well reveal its harmlessness, he added. It was possible that these metrorrhagias, both the first, which he had just been informed of, and the present alarming second occurrence, had been caused by a myoma, which could easily be surgically removed. In entrusting herself to the care of the director and chief surgeon of the hospital, Professor Muthesius, Anna's Frau Mama would find herself in the most reliable hands.

They followed the doctor's orders without resistance from Frau von Tümmler, to Anna's silent astonishment. While all this was happening, her mother, with very wide eyes, simply stared into the distance.

The bimanual examination, performed by Muthesius, indicated a uterus much too large for the patient's age, irregular tissue swelling of the fallopian tube and instead of an already very small ovary, an abnormal growth. The curettage revealed carcinoma cells, some of which were ovarian in character; others left no doubt that cancer cells were reaching full development in the uterus itself. All the malignancy showed signs of rapid growth.

The professor, a ruddy-faced man with a double chin, whose watery blue eyes were apt to fill with tears unrelated to any simultaneous affectual change, raised his head from the microscope.

'Extensive evidence, I'd say,' he said to his assistant, who was called Dr Knepperges. 'We shall operate nonetheless, Knepperges. Total extirpation down to the last connective tissue in the lesser pelvis and all lymphatic tissue could prolong life, at most.'

But the picture presenting itself to the doctors and nurses on opening the abdominal cavity in the white light of the arc lamps was too dreadful a sight to permit hope of even a temporary improvement. The time for that had long since passed. Not only were all the pelvic organs afflicted by decay, but the peritoneum also revealed, even to the naked eye, murderous colonies of cells, the cancerous enlargement of all the glands of the lymphatic system, and there could be no doubt either that there were cancer foci in the liver.

'Well, Knepperges, take a look at this mess, will you,' said Muthesius. 'It probably exceeds your expectations.' If it exceeded his own, he showed no sign of it. 'We practise a noble art,' he added with tears in his eyes that meant nothing, 'but this is expecting a little too much of it. We can't cut all of that out. If you think you have detected this stuff metastasizing into both ureters, then you are correct. Uraemia can't be far behind. You know, I don't deny in the least that the uterus itself is producing this gluttonous brood, and yet I advise you to follow my hunch that the thing began in the ovaries—with unneeded granular cells that sometimes stay on there from birth, and which, with the onset of menopause and as a result of God knows what process of irritation, become malignant. In which case the organism, *post festum*, so to speak, becomes awash, overflowing, in fact veritably inundated with oestrogen hormones, which in turn leads to a hormonal hyperplasia of the uterine lining with accompanying bleeding.'

Knepperges, a gaunt, ambitiously self-assertive man, made a brief, subtly ironic bow of thanks for the guidance.

'Come on, then, *ut aliquid fieri videatur*,'* said the Professor. 'We must leave her whatever is essential to life, however much the word is inundated with melancholy in this instance.'

Anna was waiting for her mother upstairs in her hospital room when Rosalie was brought up in a lift, carried in on a stretcher and put to bed by nurses. While this happened, she woke out of her post-anaesthetic sleep and spoke confusedly:

'Anna, my child, he hissed at me.'

'Who, dearest Mama?'

'The black swan.'

She was already asleep again. But she often recalled the swan in the few weeks that followed—its blood-red beak, the black beat of its wings. Her suffering was brief. She soon fell into a deep unconsciousness, a uraemic coma, and when a double pneumonia overtook her as well, her weary heart could only bear up against it for a few days.

Close to the end, however, just a few hours before, her mind cleared once again. She raised her eyes to her daughter, who was sitting by her bed and holding her hand.

'Anna,' she said, managing to move her upper body a little further towards the edge of the bed, closer to her confidante, 'can you hear me?'

'Most certainly, my dear, dear Mama, I can hear you.'

'Anna, don't speak of Nature's deceit, of her cruel mockery. Don't treat her with contempt, just as I don't. I don't want to go away—from you, from life with its springtime. But what would spring be without death? Indeed death is one of life's great resources, and if for me it took the shape of resurrection, of desire for love, well, that wasn't deception, but benevolence and grace.'

Again, a tiny shift, an edge closer to her daughter, a fading whisper:

'Nature—I have always loved her, and she—bestowed love on her child.'

Rosalie died a gentle death, mourned by all who knew her.

EXPLANATORY NOTES

DISORDER AND EARLY SORROW

4 *muzhiks*: Russian peasants.

movie diva: perhaps the silent-film star Asta Nielsen (1881–1972).

13 *A lord with golden hair!*: the nursery rhyme continues: 'What does he want, what does he want? | He wants to fetch Marie. | What's the matter with him? | She has stolen his heart.'

15 *Macaulay*: Thomas Babington Macaulay, later Lord Macaulay (1800–59), author of *The History of England from the Accession of James the Second* (1848–55).

William III: William of Orange (1650–1702), who with his wife Mary ascended the throne of Britain after the Glorious Revolution of 1688.

Philip II: (1527–98), King of Spain, who, as a major figure in Friedrich Schiller's play *Don Carlos* (1787), makes a deep impression on *Tonio Kröger* (see Mann, *Death in Venice and Other Stories*, trans. Nicola Luckhurst and Ritchie Robertson, Oxford World's Classics (Oxford: Oxford University Press, 2026), 35–89).

Counter-Reformation: the efforts by the Roman Catholic Church, supported by Philip II of Spain, to roll back the Protestant Reformation.

16 *Marées*: Hans von Marées (1837–87), German painter.

17 *Germania*: personification of Germany as a robust fair-haired woman, often in armour.

18 *Yes, we had no bananas*: allusion to the American song 'Yes, we have no bananas', which reached the peak of its popularity in 1923.

Wandervogel: the Wandervogel Society, founded in 1901, encouraged many thousands of young people to go hiking: among them are the members of the Winfried society in *Doctor Faustus*, chapter XIV.

22 *'Joli tambour'*: 'The Handsome Drummer', a French folk song.

'Sire, mon roi, donnez-moi votre fille—': (Fr.) 'Sire, my king, give me your daughter—'.

28 *Charlemagne*: Charlemagne or Charles the Great, who became Holy Roman Emperor in 800, is said to have had exceptionally big feet.

33 *'Lest she . . . through sorrowful nights, sit weeping upon her bed!'*: a quotation from Goethe's poem 'Wer nie sein Brot mit Tränen aß' included in the novel *Wilhelm Meisters Lehrjahre* (*Wilhelm Meister's Apprenticeship*, 1795–6): 'He who has never eaten his bread with tears, he who has never, through nights of anguish, sat weeping on his bed—such a man does not know you, you heavenly Powers' (David Luke's translation).

MARIO AND THE MAGICIAN

35 *Torre di Venere*: Tower of Venus.

Cipolla: 'onion', a not uncommon Italian surname.

horrific end: Mann's phrase, 'Ende mit Schrecken', repeated in the final paragraph, is part of the proverbial saying 'Lieber ein Ende mit Schrecken als ein Schrecken ohne Ende!' ('Better an end in horror than a horror without end!'), originally spoken by Major Ferdinand von Schill in May 1809 when inciting a mutiny against the French troops occupying Prussia.

capanne: bathing-cabins.

36 *cornetti al burro*: (It.) buttered croissants.

37 *pranzo*: (It.) lunch.

Pensione Eleonora: named after the internationally famous actress Eleonora Duse (1858–1924), who was the companion of the Fascist poet and war hero Gabriele D'Annunzio (1863–1938).

38 *Byzantine*: the court ceremonial of the medieval Byzantine Empire was notoriously elaborate and obsequious.

39 *'La Duse'*: Eleonora Duse; see note to p. 37.

40 *sun of Homer*: quoted from the last line of the philosophical poem 'Der Spaziergang' ('The Stroll') by Friedrich Schiller (1759–1805): 'Und die Sonne Homers, siehe, er leuchtet auch uns' ('And the sun of Homer, behold, it shines on us too').

Fuggièro: an unlikely name, perhaps a (deliberate?) confusion of *fuggire* 'to flee' with 'Ruggiero', a name with heroic associations (e.g. the warrior Ruggiero in Ariosto's *Orlando furioso*, 1532). I thank Emanuela Tandello for these suggestions.

41 *Rispondi al mèno*: (It.) Answer at least!

43 *municipio*: (It.) town hall.

44 *A poet*: the German Romantic poet and aphorist Friedrich von Hardenberg, alias Novalis (1772–1801).

45 *Cavaliere*: (It.) knight.

forzatore, *illusionista* and *prestidigitatore*: (It.) strong man, magician, and juggler.

46 *frutti di mare*: (It.) shellfish.

47 *'Pronti!'* ... *'Cominciamo!'*: (It.) 'Ready!' ... 'Let's get started!'

49 *'Buona sera!'*: (It.) 'Good evening!'

Paura, eh?: (It.) Scared, are you?

50 *'Ha sciolto lo scilinguágnolo'*: (It.) 'He's picked the one with a ready tongue.'

giovanotto: (It.) young man.

sistema americano, sa': (It.) the American system, you know.

51 *Corriere della Sera*: leading Italian newspaper which under Fascism supported the government.

Duce: (It.) Mussolini's title as leader. His brother was Arnaldo Mussolini (1885–1931) who edited the Fascist party paper *Il Popolo d'Italia*.

52 *donnaiuolo*: (It., correctly *donnaiolo*) ladies' man.

'Parla benissimo': (It.) 'He speaks very well.'

simpatico: (It.) pleasant, congenial.

54 *'Non so scrivere'*: (It.) 'I don't know how to write.'

55 *Nubian*: Nubia is the ancient name for the area now comprising southern Egypt and northern Sudan.

57 *'Il boit beaucoup'*: (Fr.) 'He drinks a lot.'

58 *close to a million*: a five-digit number cannot be close to a million; this is presumably a slip on Mann's part.

60 *'È servito'*: (It.) 'At your service.'

'Lavora bene!': (It.) 'He's doing good work!'

62 *'Pensez très fort!'*: (Fr.) 'Think very hard!'

65 *una cioccolata e biscotti*: (It.) a cup of hot chocolate and biscuits.

'Subito!': (It.) 'Right away!'

68 *'Accidente!'*: (It., correctly *Accidenti*) 'Damn it!'

69 *'step-dance'*: a then fashionable dance, imported from America.

70 *'Balla!'*: (It.) 'Dance!'

71 *Una ballatina*: (It.) a little dance.

Circe: sorceress in Homer's *Odyssey* who turns Odysseus' sailors into swine.

tarantella: southern Italian folk dance in six-eight time which gets faster as it goes on. In Ibsen's *A Doll's House* (1879), Nora dances a tarantella, expressing her unconscious wish to escape from her husband's control.

73 *ragazzo mio*: (It.) my boy.

An ancient name: that of Caius Marius (157–88 BCE), a successful general, associated with the democratic party in the civil wars that helped to end the Roman Republic.

Salve!: (Lat.) Hail!

Roman salute: the well-known gesture practised by the Fascists.

74 *cameriere*: (It.) waiter.

Ganymede: in classical mythology, a beautiful shepherd-boy who was carried up to Olympus by Zeus to be his lover and the gods' cup-bearer.

salvietta: (It.) napkin; also alluding to the Roman greeting 'Salve'.

75 *un tratto di malinconia*: (It.) a touch of melancholy.

'Nossignore!': (It.) 'No sir!'

THE TRANSPOSED HEADS

79 *Sita*: the name of Rama's wife in the Sanskrit epic poem Ramayana (perhaps seventh–fourth centuries BCE), lending dignity to the character who is unnamed in the story Mann found in Heinrich Zimmer's 'The Indian World Mother'. The epithet 'lovely-hipped' (*schönhüftig*) is applied in Zimmer's account to the supremely beautiful goddess Pramlocha, whom Indra sends to seduce the hermit Kandu (see note to p. 90) (Zimmer, *Maya: Der indische Mythos* (Stuttgart: Deutsche Verlags-Anstalt, 1936), 74).

Maya: in Indian philosophy, the world of appearances which conceals from us the divine unity of Brahma. Cf. 'the eyes of the uncultured individual are clouded, as the Indians say, by the veil of Maya. To him is revealed not the thing-in-itself, but only the phenomenon in time and space' (Arthur Schopenhauer, *The World as Will and Representation*, trans. E. F. J. Payne (New York: Dover, 1968), i. 352). *Maya* is the title of the panoramic novel of turn-of-the-century Munich society which Aschenbach has written in *Death in Venice* and which Mann planned but did not pursue.

World Nurse: the goddess Mahadevi (Great Goddess), who in her benevolent aspect appears as Parvati, the wife of Shiva, and in her grim aspect as Kali ('the Black One') or Durga ('the Unapproachable').

the twice-born: i.e. members of the three higher castes, which included priests (Brahmins), warriors (Kshatriyas), and merchants and herdsmen (Vaishyas). The lower castes, collectively referred to below as Shudras, were manual workers and peasants.

Kosala: the kingdom of Rama in the Ramayana.

Sarasvati: goddess of speech, arts and music, and wife of Brahma, the creator of the world.

80 *Etad vai tad*: explained in the text as a doctrine of identity: 'This is that.'

Vedas: ancient Sanskrit sacred texts, transmitted orally with the help of rigorous mnemonic techniques from the second millennium BCE. The earliest known manuscripts date from the eleventh century. Shridaman may have heard of the Vedas but is unlikely to have read them. See also note to p. 90.

Brahmin . . . Shudras: see note to p. 79.

knowledge of essences: the understanding of the true nature of things, concealed from most people by the veil of Maya.

karma: the principle whereby the actions of individuals in one life shape their destinies in future lives.

lucky calf-curl on his chest: a calf-curl of yellow hair, signifying particular devotion to the gods Vishnu or Krishna.

82 *Kuruksheta*: site of the enormous battle which occupies Books VI to XI of the epic poem Mahabharata. It is on the eve of this battle that the warrior

Arjuna and the god Krishna have the dialogue which has become famous as the Bhagavadgita.

Indraprastha: city said in ancient Indian literature to be the capital of the Kuru kingdom; it features in the Mahabharata as the chief city of the Pandavas, the five brothers whose war with the Kauravas the poem narrates.

Yamuna: the second largest tributary of the Ganges, also called Jumna, whence Mann's 'Djamna'.

Alta-red: Alta is a traditional red dye used in South Asia and symbolizes prosperity.

83 *cella*: Mann borrows the Latin term for a small chamber within a temple.

85 *Nirvana*: the ultimate extinction of existence, and hence escape from the cycle of life and suffering.

Samsara: the incessant cycle of life, death, and rebirth which one can only escape from by attaining Nirvana.

87 *Drævidian*: speakers of non-Indo-European languages including Tamil and Telugu, found especially in southern India, and supposedly descended from the dark-skinned peoples defeated by the Aryan invaders.

89 *Prakrit*: vernacular counterpart to the learned Sanskrit language.

90 *Pramlocha*: Zimmer, *Maya*, 73–9, tells how the goddess Pramlocha, sent by Indra, seduced the ascetic Kandu. The gods were afraid that the extraordinary sanctity Kandu had acquired through his privations might do them some damage. So Kandu and Pramlocha made love for nine hundred years, six months, and three days (Zimmer, *Maya*, 78), though Kandu thought only a day had passed.

Rig Veda: collection of hymns, a particularly important source for knowledge of ancient religion and culture. See also note to p. 80.

96 *Lingam and Yoni*: respectively masculine and feminine sexual symbols.

Shakti: explained by Zimmer, *Maya*, 112, as 'the immanent strength of the transcendent god'.

98 *sickness unto death*: the term denoting existential despair in Søren Kierkegaard's *The Sickness unto Death* (1849), which itself adapts Jesus' words 'This sickness is not unto death' (John 11:4).

108 *Himævant*: the Himalayas.

118 *Gandharva prince Citraratha*: see Zimmer, *Maya*, 229. Gandharvas are minor supernatural beings whose males sing and make music while the females dance. Zimmer, quoting Goethe's 'Legende', tells how Renuka, wife of the Brahman Jamadagni and mother of five sons, the youngest being Rama, goes to draw water and sees reflected in the well the heavenly beauty of the Gandharva prince Citraratha. When she returns home, her husband notices that her soul is troubled by this sight, and orders his sons to cut off her head; only Rama obeys. Goethe got this story from Pierre Sonnerat, *Reise nach Ostindien* (1783), but suppressed the execution of the mother by the son.

128 *Kamadamana*: Mann found this name in Zimmer, *Maya*, 37, where it is explained as 'Vanquisher of Desires'. Zimmer tells the story of the prince Kamadamana who, having seen through the deceits of Maya, resolved to become an ascetic. The privations that Mann's Kamadamana imposes on himself are those practised by the hermit Kandu in Zimmer, *Maya*, 73.

Dankaka: Zimmer (*Maya*, 253) gives the name correctly as Dandaka, the name of a still extensive forest in southern India. It features in the Ramayana as the place to which Rama is exiled for fourteen years.

144 *Samadhi, meaning 'bringing together'*: the name indicates that he embodies the virtues of both Shridaman and Nanda.

148 *kokil*: songbird whose sweet song is mentioned by Zimmer, *Maya*, 75.

149 *Andhaka*: 'blind one', though he is only short-sighted.

151 *Satis*: widows who committed *sati* or suttee, i.e. burned themselves alive.

THE LAW

155 *numen*: divine being.

158 *Ramessu*: Ramses II (1295–1219 BCE), ruler of Egypt.

Sargon: legendary founder of Babylon, said to have been hidden in a basket of reeds, and found and brought up by a foster-father. Freud points out in *Moses and Monotheism* that many (semi-)legendary heroes, apparently of humble birth, are revealed to have more exalted ancestry: he mentions also Romulus and Cyrus (and might, but for discretion, have added Jesus). He notes, however, that although Moses' supposed parents are humble, he receives from the outset the education appropriate to his royal descent.

Levi: second son of Jacob, ancestor of one of the Twelve Tribes of Israel.

159 *Mose... 'son'*: Freud notes the similarity to such Egyptian names as 'Amon-mose', following J. H. Breasted, *The Dawn of Conscience* (New York: Scribner, 1934).

163 *Joshua*: his description is based on Michelangelo's statue of David on the Piazza della Signoria in Florence.

171 *a merciless Vespers massacre night*: the 'Sicilian Vespers' was a massacre of the French occupiers carried out by the Sicilians in Palermo at the hour of evening prayer (Vespers) on Easter Monday 1282. Goethe in his notes to the *West-östlicher Divan* describes the slaughter of the firstborn as 'a Sicilian Vespers in reverse' because here 'the stranger murdered the inhabitant, the guest the host, and guided by a cruel policy, they slew only the firstborn' (*West-Eastern Divan*, trans. and ed. Eric Ormsby (London: Ginkgo, 2019), 448–9.

175 *Miriam... sang 'Sing ye to the Lord... into the sea'*: see Ex. 15:1–21, where the song is attributed to Moses.

178 *Kadesh*: see Num. 13:26; for the battle with the Amalekites, see Ex. 17:8–14.

183 *tabernacle*: see the lengthy description in Ex. 26–7.

ephod: the garment worn by the High Priest.

'Urim and Thummim': sacred objects placed on the High Priest's breastplate: see Ex. 28:30.

184 *Codex of Hammurabi*: the Babylonian law-code issued by King Hammurabi around 2000 BCE.

188 *You should be clean*: these minutely detailed hygiene rules are in Deut. 23:13–15. Enlightenment readers of the Bible often mocked the fussiness of these rules: see H. T. Mason, *Voltaire and Pierre Bayle* (Oxford: Oxford University Press, 1963), 31.

191 *Moloch*: a god worshipped in Canaan, to whom children were sacrificed (see Lev. 18:21).

202 *horns*: (Hebr.) *keren* can mean 'horn' or 'ray of light'; the Vulgate translates it as *cornuta*, 'horned', hence the tradition that Moses had horns, as Michelangelo depicts him.

206 *Aaron, too, could be seen hopping about*: probably suggested by Heine's poem 'The Golden Calf', of which the last stanza runs: 'Aaron joins the mad surrender, | Even he, the faith's defender, | And he dances, wildly wheeling | In his solemn priestly coat, | Like a goat— | Drumbeats rolling, laughter pealing!' *The Complete Poems of Heinrich Heine: A Modern English Version by Hal Draper* (Oxford: Oxford University Press, 1982), 586.

207 *Belial*: a wicked being (but not here the name of a devil, as in *Paradise Lost*, Book II).

209 *three hundred*: contrast Ex. 32:28, which has 'about three thousand men'. Three hundred is still 10 per cent of the fighting men at Moses' disposal.

212 *scoundrel*: Hitler.

THE BLACK SWAN

213 *Peter Cornelius*: painter (1783–1867), a member of the Nazarene school which aimed to revive medieval religious art.

219 *Psyche*: heroine of the story of Cupid (Amor) and Psyche in Apuleius' novel *The Golden Ass* (second century CE); see Introduction.

222 *Love and Intrigue*: *Kabale und Liebe*, a play (1784) by Friedrich Schiller; its cast includes a foppish courtier, Hofmarschall von Kalb.

223 *à la bonne heure* (Fr.): at the right time.

225 *Sarah*: see Gen. 17 and 18.

227 *'Scrr-ew the top on... thirty inches brr-oaoadd'*: words and phrases which appear in English in Mann's text, as here, are printed in the translation in italics within quotation marks.

231 *Hoard of Gold*: allusion to the Rhine Maidens who guard the treasure of the Rhine in Wagner's *Ring of the Nibelung*.

231 *Merovingians*: a Frankish dynasty established from the fifth century onwards in what is now France and western Germany.

Pepin: or Pippin (714–68), Mayor of the Palace and later King of the Franks.

Barbarossa: the German emperor Friedrich I (122–90), nicknamed Barbarossa from his red beard.

Henry IV: (1050–1106), German emperor of the Salian dynasty.

Albert of Berg: probably a mistake for Adolf I vom Berg (1078–1152), who founded the dynasty of Counts and Dukes of Berg.

Jan Wellem of the Palatinate: Elector Johann Wilhelm von der Pfalz, Duke of Jülich and Berg (1658–1716).

237 *"The Moor has done his work. The Moor may go"*: a well-known quotation from Schiller's play *Fiesco* (1783), Act III, scene 4.

238 *Emerson*: Ralph Waldo Emerson (1803–82), American philosopher.

Macaulay: see note to p. 15.

244 *"Purple Heart"*: medal for bravery, established by George Washington, awarded only three times before 1932, but frequently from the Second World War onwards.

247 *Taunus*: a range of hills north-west of Frankfurt am Main.

262 *Elector Carl Theodor*: (1724–99).

Grottstein: (correctly Goltstein) Count Johann Ludwig von Goltstein (1719–76) was appointed governor of Jülich and Berg in 1768.

Holterhof Palace: based on Benrath, a mansion built between 1755 and 1769 and designed by the architect Nicolas de Pigoge (1723–96).

'Wat et nit all jibt!': (Rhenish dialect) 'Well, who would believe it!'

270 *causeuse*: 'A small sofa designed to seat two people' (*OED*).

273 *ut aliquid fieri videatur*: (Lat.) so that something seems to be getting done.

MORE ABOUT **OXFORD WORLD'S CLASSICS**

American Literature

British and Irish Literature

Children's Literature

Classics and Ancient Literature

Colonial Literature

Eastern Literature

European Literature

Gothic Literature

History

Medieval Literature

Oxford English Drama

Philosophy

Poetry

Politics

Religion

The Oxford Shakespeare

A SELECTION OF **OXFORD WORLD'S CLASSICS**

JOHN BUCHAN	**Greenmantle** **Huntingtower** **The Thirty-Nine Steps**
JOSEPH CONRAD	**Chance** **Heart of Darkness and Other Tales** **Lord Jim** **Nostromo** **An Outcast of the Islands** **The Secret Agent** **Typhoon and Other Tales** **Under Western Eyes**
ARTHUR CONAN DOYLE	**The Adventures of Sherlock Holmes** **The Case-Book of Sherlock Holmes** **The Hound of the Baskervilles** **The Lost World** **The Memoirs of Sherlock Holmes** **Sherlock Holmes: Selected Stories** **A Study in Scarlet**
FORD MADOX FORD	**The Good Soldier**
JOHN GALSWORTHY	**The Forsyte Saga**
JEROME K. JEROME	**Three Men in a Boat**
JAMES JOYCE	**A Portrait of the Artist as a Young Man** **Dubliners** **Occasional, Critical, and Political Writing** **Ulysses**
RUDYARD KIPLING	**Captains Courageous** **The Complete Stalky & Co** **The Jungle Books** **Just So Stories** **Kim** **The Man Who Would Be King**

A SELECTION OF **OXFORD WORLD'S CLASSICS**

	Late Victorian Gothic Tales
	Literature and Science in the Nineteenth Century
JANE AUSTEN	Emma
	Mansfield Park
	Persuasion
	Pride and Prejudice
	Selected Letters
	Sense and Sensibility
MRS BEETON	Book of Household Management
MARY ELIZABETH BRADDON	Lady Audley's Secret
ANNE BRONTË	The Tenant of Wildfell Hall
CHARLOTTE BRONTË	Jane Eyre
	Shirley
	Villette
EMILY BRONTË	Wuthering Heights
ROBERT BROWNING	The Major Works
JOHN CLARE	The Major Works
SAMUEL TAYLOR COLERIDGE	The Major Works
WILKIE COLLINS	The Moonstone
	No Name
	The Woman in White
CHARLES DARWIN	The Origin of Species
THOMAS DE QUINCEY	The Confessions of an English Opium-Eater
	On Murder
CHARLES DICKENS	The Adventures of Oliver Twist
	Barnaby Rudge
	Bleak House
	David Copperfield
	Great Expectations
	Nicholas Nickleby

A SELECTION OF **OXFORD WORLD'S CLASSICS**

Charles Dickens	**The Old Curiosity Shop**
	Our Mutual Friend
	The Pickwick Papers
George du Maurier	**Trilby**
Maria Edgeworth	**Castle Rackrent**
George Eliot	**Daniel Deronda**
	The Lifted Veil and Brother Jacob
	Middlemarch
	The Mill on the Floss
	Silas Marner
Edward FitzGerald	**The Rubáiyát of Omar Khayyám**
Elizabeth Gaskell	**Cranford**
	The Life of Charlotte Brontë
	Mary Barton
	North and South
	Wives and Daughters
George Gissing	**New Grub Street**
	The Nether World
	The Odd Women
Edmund Gosse	**Father and Son**
Thomas Hardy	**Far from the Madding Crowd**
	Jude the Obscure
	The Mayor of Casterbridge
	The Return of the Native
	Tess of the d'Urbervilles
	The Woodlanders
James Hogg	**The Private Memoirs and Confessions of a Justified Sinner**
John Keats	**The Major Works**
	Selected Letters
Charles Maturin	**Melmoth the Wanderer**
Henry Mayhew	**London Labour and the London Poor**

A SELECTION OF **OXFORD WORLD'S CLASSICS**

WILLIAM MORRIS	**News from Nowhere**
JOHN RUSKIN	**Praeterita** **Selected Writings**
WALTER SCOTT	**Ivanhoe** **Rob Roy** **Waverley**
MARY SHELLEY	**Frankenstein** **The Last Man**
ROBERT LOUIS STEVENSON	**Strange Case of Dr Jekyll and Mr Hyde and Other Tales** **Treasure Island**
BRAM STOKER	**Dracula**
W. M. THACKERAY	**Vanity Fair**
FRANCES TROLLOPE	**Domestic Manners of the Americans**
OSCAR WILDE	**The Importance of Being Earnest and Other Plays** **The Major Works** **The Picture of Dorian Gray**
ELLEN WOOD	**East Lynne**
DOROTHY WORDSWORTH	**The Grasmere and Alfoxden Journals**
WILLIAM WORDSWORTH	**The Major Works**
WORDSWORTH and COLERIDGE	**Lyrical Ballads**

TROLLOPE IN **OXFORD WORLD'S CLASSICS**

ANTHONY TROLLOPE

The American Senator
An Autobiography
Barchester Towers
Can You Forgive Her?
Cousin Henry
Doctor Thorne
The Duke's Children
The Eustace Diamonds
Framley Parsonage
He Knew He Was Right
Lady Anna
The Last Chronicle of Barset
Orley Farm
Phineas Finn
Phineas Redux
The Prime Minister
Rachel Ray
The Small House at Allington
The Warden
The Way We Live Now

A SELECTION OF **OXFORD WORLD'S CLASSICS**

A SELECTION OF **OXFORD WORLD'S CLASSICS**

Hans Christian Andersen	**Fairy Tales**
J. M. Barrie	**Peter Pan in Kensington Gardens and Peter and Wendy**
L. Frank Baum	**The Wonderful Wizard of Oz**
Frances Hodgson Burnett	**The Secret Garden**
Lewis Carroll	**Alice's Adventures in Wonderland and Through the Looking-Glass**
Carlo Collodi	**The Adventures of Pinocchio**
Kenneth Grahame	**The Wind in the Willows**
Anthony Hope	**The Prisoner of Zenda**
Thomas Hughes	**Tom Brown's Schooldays**
Charles Perrault	**The Complete Fairy Tales**
Anna Sewell	**Black Beauty**
Robert Louis Stevenson	**Kidnapped** **Treasure Island**